*Advertising in the
Broadcast and
Cable Media*

Wadsworth Series in Mass Communication/*Rebecca Hayden, Senior Editor*

General

The New Communications by Frederick Williams

Mediamerica: Form, Content, and Consequence of Mass Communication, 2d, by Edward Jay Whetmore

The Interplay of Influence: Mass Media & Their Publics in News, Advertising, Politics by Kathleen Hall Jamieson and Karlyn Kohrs Campbell

Mass Communication and Everyday Life: A Perspective on Theory and Effects by Dennis K. Davis and Stanley J. Baran

Mass Media Research: An Introduction by Roger D. Wimmer and Joseph R. Dominick

The Internship Experience by Lynne Schafer Gross

Telecommunications

Stay Tuned: A Concise History of American Broadcasting by Christopher H. Sterling and John M. Kittross

Writing for Television and Radio, 4th, by Robert L. Hilliard

Broadcast Programming: Strategies for Winning Television and Radio Audiences by Susan Tyler Eastman, Sydney W. Head, and Lewis Klein

Advertising in the Broadcast and Cable Media, 2d, by Elizabeth J. Heighton and Don R. Cunningham

Strategies in Broadcast and Cable Promotion by Susan Tyler Eastman and Robert A. Klein

Modern Radio Station Practices, 2d, by Joseph S. Johnson and Kenneth K. Jones

The Magic Medium: An Introduction to Radio in America by Edward Jay Whetmore

Audio in Media by Stanley R. Alten

Television Production Handbook, 4th, by Herbert Zettl

Sight-Sound-Motion: Applied Media Aesthetics by Herbert Zettl

Journalism

Reporting Processes and Practices: Newswriting for Today's Readers by Everette E. Dennis and Arnold H. Ismach

Excellence in College Journalism by Wayne Overbeck and Thomas M. Pasqua

When Words Collide: A Journalist's Guide to Grammar & Style by Lauren Kessler and Duncan McDonald

News Editing in the '80s: Text and Exercises by William L. Rivers

Reporting Public Affairs: Problems and Solutions by Ronald P. Lovell

Newswriting for the Electronic Media: Principles, Examples, Applications by Daniel E. Garvey and William L. Rivers

Free-Lancer and Staff Writer: Newspaper Features and Magazine Articles, 3d, by William L. Rivers and Shelley Smolkin

Magazine Editing in the '80s: Text and Exercises by William L. Rivers

This Is PR: The Realities of Public Relations, 2d, by Doug Newsom and Alan Scott

Writing in Public Relations Practice: Form and Style by Doug Newsom and Tom Siegfried

Creative Strategy in Advertising by A. Jerome Jewler

Pictures on a Page: Photojournalism and Picture Editing by Harold Evans

second edition

Advertising in the Broadcast and Cable Media

Elizabeth J. Heighton
San Diego State University

Don R. Cunningham
Cunningham, Root & Craig, Inc., Los Angeles

Wadsworth Publishing Company
Belmont, California
A Division of Wadsworth, Inc.

Senior Editor: Rebecca Hayden
Production Editor: Sally Schuman
Designer: Cynthia Bassett
Copy Editor: William Waller
Technical Illustrator: Marilyn Krieger
Cover: Cynthia Bassett

Printed in the United States of America

 2 3 4 5 6 7 8 9 10——88 87 86 85 84

Library of Congress Cataloging in Publication Data
Heighton, Elizabeth J.
   Advertising in the broadcast and cable media.
   Bibliography: p.
   Includes index.
   Rev. ed. of: Advertising in the broadcast media. 1976.
   1. Broadcast advertising.   2. Cable television advertising.   I. Cunningham, Don R.
   II. Title.
HF6146.B74H44   1984   659.14   83-5805
ISBN 0-534-02914-0

To Bob and Dottie, again

Elizabeth J. Heighton is a professor of telecommunications and film at San Diego State University. Before entering the academic world, she was employed for several years in broadcasting and advertising. After graduating from the University of Washington, she worked at KIRO and KIRO-TV, in Seattle. Later, in San Francisco, she was employed by the J. Walter Thompson Company and then by Batten, Barton, Durstine & Osborn, where she worked in media. She completed a master of science degree at Syracuse University and was then appointed to the San Diego State University faculty. Professor Heighton has been active in both academic and professional groups for many years. She has served on the board of directors of the San Diego Advertising Club and as education chairperson of the American Advertising Federation, Western Region. In 1974, she was named Advertising Woman of the Year by the American Advertising Federation. A Broadcast Preceptor Award was presented to Professor Heighton and her coauthor, Don R. Cunningham, in 1977 at the Broadcast Industry Conference at San Francisco State University. Professor Heighton has filled several posts with Women in Communications and is a member of the Broadcast Education Association. At San Diego State University, she serves as executive director of the Advertising Resources Center.

Don R. Cunningham is chairman and chief executive officer of Cunningham, Root & Craig, a Los Angeles advertising agency. After graduation from Northwestern University's Medill School of Journalism, he joined the advertising department of the Procter & Gamble Company, working in brand management. He left the client side of the business to join a Cincinnati agency, Stockton-West-Burkhart. Five years later, he joined Earle Ludgin in Chicago. In 1956, Cunningham moved to Foote, Cone & Belding, also in Chicago. He spent the next 18 years at FCB. Cunningham opened that company's first office on the continent of Europe, in Frankfurt am Main. After four years in Germany, he returned to the United States, where he became General Manager of FCB's Los Angeles office and a member of the board of directors. In 1974, he started his own agency, which has become Cunningham, Root & Craig.

Cunningham has served as a board member of the American Advertising Federation, vice chairman of the Better Business Bureau of Southern California, governor of the Southern California Council of the American Association of Advertising Agencies, a member of the Advertising Council Western Region Committee, president of the Advertising Review Council of Southern California, and a board member of the Los Angeles Advertising Club.

preface

The evolving nature of the telecommunications industry has greatly affected traditional broadcast advertising in recent years. This revised edition updates and expands the coverage of a specialized, but major, segment of the advertising industry. Many books deal with basic principles of advertising, but this text is designed to focus on the electronic media in a comprehensive manner. The approach of the text is primarily from the view of the advertiser and advertising agency, which make the decisions on campaign strategies.

This book is divided into four parts. The first traces the history of broadcast advertising and the structure of the modern-day industry. The role of advertisers in the growth of radio, television, and cable TV is a fascinating one, and the changing complexion of this role over the years is examined to determine its effect on the industry and on the public. What has evolved is a complex group of interdependent businesses that provide programing to audiences and audiences to advertisers.

The second part of this book is concerned primarily with specific procedures for developing broadcast advertising campaigns. The determining of advertising objectives and the role of marketing research are detailed. With the advent of new technologies, media planning has become more complicated, and a discussion of cable has been added to the section on planning strategies. The creative process, often undisciplined but critically important, is analyzed in detail. Individual chapters are devoted to the selection of talent, the producing of commercials, and the subsequent evaluation process. A number of case studies are included as examples of the various aspects of campaign development.

Buying and selling time in radio, television, and cable are the focus of the third section of this book, which is prefaced by a thorough and updated analysis of audience research methodologies. Because buying procedures do vary, depending on marketing needs, sales are examined at the network, spot, and local level. Direct response advertising and videotex, important new dimensions in broadcast advertising, are the subject of a new chapter.

The controversies and criticism surrounding broadcast advertising led to the development of the final part of the text. The discussion of truth in advertising, an elusive subject, forms the foundation for examining the regulation of advertising by the Federal Trade Commission, the Federal Communications Commission, and the industry's own self-regulatory mechanisms.

Every chapter has been thoroughly updated. Important additions include an examination of advertisers' use of cable and other new technologies and a look at new federal regulations that affect the industry. Some of the more interesting controversies are examined: children's advertising, political advertising, the advertising of controversial products, advertisers' First Amendment rights, applications of the FCC's Fairness Doctrine to advertising, and organized consumer boycotts of advertisers' products.

This text is designed for all those who want to expand their knowledge of all components of the broadcast advertising industry. The book is informal in many respects, but it has been very carefully researched. The lengthy acknowledgments reflect that each of the chapters has been read by both professionals and academicians who specialize in particular areas.

Elizabeth J. Heighton
Don R. Cunningham

contents

acknowledgments

The authors wish to thank the following professionals for their generous and important contributions to this textbook.

James R. Allen, Vice President, Executive Producer, McCann-Erickson, Inc., San Francisco

Robert F. Anderson, Managing Director, Southern California Chevrolet Dealers Association, Los Angeles

Jesse Bedi, Supervisor, Advertising Research, Levi Strauss & Co., San Francisco

Spencer Boise, Vice President, Corporate Affairs, Mattel, Inc., Hawthorne, California

Clayton H. Brace, Vice President and General Manager, McGraw-Hill Broadcasting Company, Inc., San Diego

Warren Braren, Circulation Director, Times Mirror Magazines, New York

Sherm Brodey, Director, Promotion Services, Arbitron Ratings Company, Beltsville, Maryland

Andrew Butcher, President, International Communications Group, Inc., Los Angeles

David P. Castler, Executive Vice President, ASI Market Research, Inc., Los Angeles

Jean Craig, President, Cunningham, Root & Craig Advertising, Inc., Los Angeles

William P. Croasdale, Senior Vice President, BBDO International, New York

Ralph Daniels, Vice President, Broadcast Standards, National Broadcasting Company, New York

Stuart deLima, Advertising Sales Manager, Western Region, USA Network, Los Angeles

Susan A. Elliott, Assistant Director for Advertising Practices, Federal Trade Commission, Washington, D.C.

Robert F. Ferraro, Vice President, Manager, Blair Radio, San Francisco

Marie C. Fox, Manager of Print Production Services, McCann-Erickson, Inc., San Francisco

Laurence Frerk, Promotion Director, A. C. Nielsen Company, Northbrook, Illinois

Don O. Gabbert, Senior Vice President, McCann-Erickson, Inc., San Francisco

John Galbraith, Senior Vice President, Allen and Dorward Advertising, San Francisco

Freeman F. Gosden, Jr., Partner, Smith, Hemmings & Gosden Direct Response Advertising, Los Angeles

William F. Greene, Senior Vice President, Gallup & Robinson, Inc., Princeton, New Jersey

William H. Griffith, Director of Advertising, Kaiser Aluminum & Chemical Corporation, Oakland, California

Jerry Hamilton, Vice President, Botsford Ketchem, Inc., San Francisco

Richard L. Harmon, Manager, Product Press Relations, Hewlett-Packard Company, Palo Alto, California

John T. Hart, Research Director, Foote, Cone & Belding/Honig, San Francisco

Alice M. Henderson, Vice President, Program Practices, CBS Broadcast Group, New York

K. Patrick Hodges, Vice President, Manager, Katz Radio, San Francisco

Bob Hoffman, Vice President, Creative Director, Allen and Dorward Advertising, San Francisco

Elaine K. Hosozawa, Vice President, Tele Research, Inc., Los Angeles

John J. Houlahan, President, Houlahan/Parker Marketing Research, Whittier, California

Otis Hutchins, Media Director, Cunningham, Root & Craig Advertising, Inc., Los Angeles

Karl L. Koss, Manager, Corporate Advertising, General Electric Company, Fairfield, Connecticut

Jerome Lansner, Senior Vice President, National Association of Broadcasters, Washington, D.C.

Arthur Lawrence, Group Product Manager, Whitehall Laboratories, New York

Scott McCoy, Western Regional Manager, Advertising Sales, Warner Amex Satellite Entertainment Company, Universal City, California

William J. McKenna, President, AdTel Marketing Services, Chicago

Chandler R. Meloy, Communications Director, California Milk Advisory Board, Modesto, California

Valerie G. Schulte, Assistant Attorney General, National Association of Broadcasters, Washington, D.C.

Steve Sewell, Federal Communications Commission, Washington, D.C.

Ronald H. Smithies, Director, National Advertising Division, Council of Better Business Bureaus, Inc. New York

Frank Tuttle, President, Association of Independent Commercial Producers, Los Angeles

Michael F. von Gonten, Senior Vice President, Burke Marketing Research, Cincinnati

Clifford B. Wilton, President, Wilton, Coombs & Colnett, Inc., Advertising, San Francisco

David J. Yoder, Media Director, Chiat/Day, Inc., Advertising, San Francisco

The authors are deeply indebted to the scholars who read the manuscript and offered many helpful suggestions:

Joseph F. Butler, S. I. Newhouse School of Public Communications Syracuse University

Charles Guccione, Marketing Department, Pace University

Leonard J. Hooper, Department of Advertising and Public Relations, University of Florida

K. Charles Jameson, Telecommunications and Film Department, San Diego State University

Arthur L. Savage, Jr., School of Radio-Television, Ohio University

James R. Smith, Communication Department, State University of New York, College at New Paltz

John P. Witherspoon, Center for Communication, San Diego State University

Donald G. Wylie, Telecommunications and Film Department, San Diego State University

Introduction to
Broadcast Advertising

chapter one

Commercial Broadcasting —An Historical Overview

***It is inconceivable that we should allow
so great a possibility for service
to be drowned in advertising chatter.***
Herbert Hoover

Ever since the mid-1890s, when the youthful Guglielmo Marconi conducted experiments with Hertzian waves on his father's estate in Italy, the *wireless* has stirred fascination, ambition, and avarice. (This phenomenon of physics was not called *radio* for several years.) In the wake of Marconi, early experimenters in several countries built receivers and transmitters to pursue the grand obsession. In the United States, Dr. Lee De Forest led the way with a dedication that approached the evangelical. He invented a significant improvement in the vacuum tube, called the "audion," which he patented in 1906. Over the next few years, more radio inventions were patented. The struggle was on among those who wanted to monopolize the new medium.

"Patent wars" were still raging in the early 1920s when the earliest radio stations in the United States went on the air. American Marconi, Westinghouse, General Electric, American Telephone and Telegraph, and other corporations were anxious to seize the initiative and reap the profits that this new invention promised, although most of these firms were interested in point-to-point rather than broadcast communications. Manufacturing equipment for both sending and receiving signals loomed as a lucrative enterprise for these ambitious corporations. Young David Sarnoff, who worked for American Marconi, was confident of the profit potential, and he predicted that what he called "music boxes" would achieve significant sales. American Marconi eventually evolved into the Radio Corporation of America (RCA), with Sarnoff as chairman of the board. As it turned out, Sarnoff had underestimated the sale of radio receivers: the public response was tremendous. In 1922, 100,000 receivers were sold; in 1923, more than a half-million were sold; and in 1924, the figure climbed to one-and-a-half million.[1] At an average retail price of $75 each, there was potential gold in the ether.

In 1919, Westinghouse engineers established an experimental radio station in East Pittsburgh in the garage of their assistant chief engineer, Dr. Frank Conrad. After all the primitive gear was built and installed, occasional broadcasts began. Dr. Conrad, to his surprise, soon discovered that hundreds of amateur radio buffs were listening in. To test the equipment, he read from newspapers and played phonograph records. His listeners complained that they were tired of the same old records. Couldn't he play something new? America's first disc jockey, admonished by radio's first critics, was offered some new records if he would announce that they came from the Hamilton Music Store in Wilkinsburg.

By the end of 1920, 30 broadcasting stations were on the air, although they only broadcast music and talk for a few hours a day. Licenses for these stations were issued by the Secretary of Commerce under the Radio Act of 1912. By the end of 1922, more than 400 stations were in operation. They sprang up across the country, built and financed by newspapers, churches, universities, department stores, hotels, and the big radio receiver manufacturers. Difficult as it may be to believe, all these stations were assigned by the government to operate at 833.3 kilocycles, which was the only wave length allocated to "news, lectures, entertainment, etc." (Other frequencies were used by the military, ship-to-ship, ship-to-shore, and so on.) As the stations proliferated, so did the problems. Early gentlemen's agreements, whereby stations in the same general area took their turn on the assigned frequency, soon degenerated into bickering as stations randomly increased power and changed their hours of broadcast. The listener at home often heard only a jumble of radio signals. The chaos on the air finally forced the government to act and reassign stations to other wave lengths.

Who Will Pay the Bill?

During the early 1920s the Department of Commerce was responsible for licensing stations. That department, Congress, and the small but growing radio industry discussed the need for new regulatory legislation to replace the outmoded 1912 act. Several National Radio Congresses were held, called by Secretary of Commerce Herbert Hoover. "How will radio be financed?" was a question asked with greater and greater urgency. Even though the first stations had been little more than engineering experiments, they were dedicated to exploring all the potentialities of the new medium. As equipment and personnel costs began to rise, the question of financial support had to be answered.

Several possibilities for supporting the new industry were considered: soliciting donations from listeners, charitable foundations, or wealthy patrons; imposing a levy on the sale of radio equipment; or copying the British system and imposing an annual tax on each radio receiver. The concept of a radio service wholly supported by advertisers was barely considered. In 1922, at the first National Radio Congress,

---

[1]Curtis Mitchell, *Cavalcade of Broadcasting* (Chicago: Follett, 1970), p. 79.

Hoover dismissed such an idea when he declared, "It is inconceivable that we should allow so great a possibility for service to be drowned in advertising chatter."[2]

In the meantime, the 500-plus stations across the country were basking in an unprecedented popularity. Radio was a major topic of conversation, and audiences eagerly absorbed whatever was sent their way. Singers, actors, and musicians, prompted by stories of radio performances that had turned unknown Cinderellas into celebrities, were anxious to perform. No one was paid, and cross-town travel, makeshift studios, and unreliable equipment did not deter them. Still, for the radio station operators, the costs of equipment and regular personnel steadily increased. A way had to be found to pay the bill.

WEAF and Toll Broadcasting

In 1922, AT&T put a station on the air in New York City. WEAF, one of the most important and interesting of the early radio stations, soon announced that it would "rent" time at the rate of $100 for ten minutes. The station believed that *continuous* broadcasting could perform a service akin to toll long-distance telephone service. (Indeed, WEAF was run by the "long lines," or long-distance, arm of AT&T.) The station would be available to anyone who wanted to communicate something and had the money to pay the bill. The station's first *sponsored* program was broadcast on August 28, 1922. H. M. Blackwell, a real estate salesman, spoke for ten minutes on the glorious living awaiting new residents in the Queensboro apartments in Jackson Heights, New York. Time charges were $50.[3]

Early Advertisers Give Radio a Try

Although the WEAF broadcast generated interest, sponsors did not stampede to the station. Advertisers approached the new medium with uncertainty and some trepidation. Gillette sponsored a talk on fashions in beards and mustaches, and a toothpaste company and a greeting card company presented talks closely associated with their respective products. A department store sponsored a fashion talk show and later branched into home furnishings. The beautiful movie queen Marion Davies talked about "How I Make Up for the Movies." Her studio was afraid that her image would be sullied by a commercial radio appearance, but her sponsor — Mineralava, the manufacturer of a facial mudpack — was delighted. Her broadcast promise of an autographed picture brought in 15,000 requests.

Advertisers became increasingly curious about the potential of the new medium and began to buy more and more radio time. The most popular programs were *fully sponsored* (no one had thought of selling time on a spot announcement basis), and the program title, talent, and sponsor were tightly entwined (the A&P Gypsies, the Best Foods Boys, the Champion Sparkers, and the Ipana Troubadours).

---

[2]Herbert Hoover, *The Memoirs of Herbert Hoover: The Cabinet and the Presidency, 1920 – 1933* (New York: Macmillan, 1952), p. 140.

[3]Gleason L. Archer, *History of Radio: To 1926* (New York: American Historical Society, 1938), p. 397.

Audiences were becoming more discriminating. The days of amateur talent, newspapers read over the air, and repeated playings of phonograph records were passing by the late 1920s. Programs oı this nature had lasted a long time, but listeners came to expect professional entertainment. Stations in small and medium-sized cities soon exhausted their supplies of good talent and were hard pressed to provide new programs to their listeners. Big city stations were luckier. The ones in New York City were envied for their vast programing resources. At the same time, some early radio advertisers were realizing the vast potential of the medium. Many of them enjoyed national distribution of their products, and they hoped that the territory covered by their radio programs would be extended.

The Networks Are Launched

Local stations needed to find better programing, and advertisers wanted to reach national audiences. These goals were met when the National Broadcasting Company (NBC), a subsidiary of the rich and powerful RCA, was formed in 1926. NBC started with 26 stations (WEAF was the flagship), purchased from AT&T. A year later, a competitor was organized, the Columbia Phonograph Broadcasting System, with an interconnection of 16 stations. (*Phonograph* was later dropped from the name.)

Both NBC and CBS were headquartered in New York City. The number of their affiliates increased rapidly. NBC was so successful that it established a second network in 1927. Its "red" network operated out of WEAF, and the "blue" one, from WJZ, also in New York City. Years later, in 1943, under an order from the Federal Communications Commission supported by the Supreme Court, Sarnoff sold the "blue" network. The price tag was $8 million, and the network was renamed the American Broadcasting Company (ABC).

The networks, unsure of themselves and concerned with their public image, were at first reluctant to experiment with program material. Programs were ceremonial rather than creative, and announcers were selected for their perfect elocution. A rule at NBC required staff announcers to wear tuxedos after 6:00 P.M. Advertising was brief, sedate, and strictly controlled; many taboos had to be respected; advertisers keyed their messages to some rather stuffy classical and semiclassical music programs. Listeners could hear the *Maxwell House Hour,* the *Palmolive Hour,* and the *General Motors Family Party. The Stetson Parade* and *Wrigley Review* presented somewhat lighter entertainment.

Working independently, the networks found it difficult to fill every hour with quality programs. Advertising agencies could provide better programing in many cases, because they concentrated on just a few shows. So the agencies were relied on more and more to supply programs to the networks. As the networks prospered, advertisers pressed for even more control of the programs they sponsored and the commercial messages they presented. Gradually, the realities of a competitive marketplace changed the nature of radio commercials from well-mannered statements of program sponsorship to plugs for specific products. The trend was accelerated as the major advertising agencies got more and more involved in network program production. Clients were anxious to have their broadcast circulation match their product distribution. At the same time, they asserted what they considered to be their right in controlling program content. (See 1.1.)

Because clients were their livelihood, advertising agencies strove to meet their advertisers' marketing needs through top-notch programs. Soon, several large advertising agencies were producing the most popular network programs. They had gained financial and creative control over a major portion of network programing. Affiliates simply broadcast what was fed to them.

At the local level, stations without network affiliations functioned largely as promotion vehicles for their owners, who had other, more important business affairs. Radio was often a secondary interest to the licensees. But as some of the larger unaffiliated independent stations succeeded in selling time to advertisers, many other stations were prompted to copy the practice. Radio advertising and the new networks also got a big boost from major companies that used the new medium in their national advertising campaigns. Their success convinced the more conservative local adver-

1.1/The All-American Boy

Wheaties, the Breakfast of Champions, was synonymous with one of radio's most popular and successful heroes—Jack Armstrong, the All-American Boy. Beginning in 1933, this adventure series sponsored by General Mills kept both youngsters and adults in a perpetual state of suspense as Jack and his buddies encountered baffling mysteries and imminent danger and then executed nick-of-time escapes. They always caught the culprits.

During Jack's 18-year run on network radio, he aged only nine years, from 17 to 26. In his later years, he was a clever sleuth who worked for the "Scientific Bureau of Investigation," but his "growing up" didn't help the lagging program ratings. The sponsor, which owned Jack body and soul, quietly retired him from the airwaves in 1951.

No listener could forget Jack's loyalty to Hudson High and his favorite breakfast cereal. The program theme song went like this:

Wave the flag for Hudson High, boys,
Show them how we stand!
Ever shall our team be champion,
Known throughout the land!
Rah Rah Boola Boola Boola Boola
Boola Boola Boola Rah Rah Rah.
Have your tried *Wheaties*?
They're whole wheat with all of the bran.
Won't you try *Wheaties*?

Photograph courtesy of General Mills, Inc.

For wheat is the best food of man.
They're crispy, they're crunchy,
The whole year through.
Jack Armstrong never tires of them
And neither will you.
So just buy *Wheaties*
The best breakfast food in the land!

tisers to try radio. In many cities, local merchants juggled their advertising budgets so they could sponsor local radio programs.

Radio Advertising through the Great Depression

At the time the stock market crashed in 1929, CBS had 47 affiliates and NBC had 58. Most of the programs were variety and popular-music shows. Dramatic programs made their debut, and this "theater of the mind" added tremendous new excitement to the medium. *The Eveready Hour* and *True Story*, sponsored by Macfadden Publications, were only two of a slowly growing list of commercial dramatic productions in the early 1930s. Competition between the networks stiffened as they increased the number of affiliates and the size of their staffs. In 1931, CBS employed about 400 people, and NBC's two networks had a staff of about 1,900.[4]

The radio industry held its own through the first dreadful years of the Great Depression. The networks and many stations, in fact, were prospering. Welfare workers reported that destitute families were giving up cars, major appliances — anything — to their creditors, but not the radio. After the purchase of a receiver, radio was, unlike other entertainment, "free." It provided an escape, an hour of entertainment, a vicarious experience that lifted the listener above what seemed to be a hopeless economic bust. People still had to eat and clothe themselves, and more and more advertisers discovered radio's tremendous power to sell. The decorum that had originally surrounded the commercial message was quickly losing ground to shouting announcers.

Federal Regulatory Actions

The chaos on the air had finally been quieted with the passage of the *Radio Act of 1927*. Congress brought a semblance of order to a disorganized and poorly regulated industry. The legislation established the Federal Radio Commission (FRC), which was authorized to "maintain control of the United States over all channels." It permitted the licensing of stations "but not the Ownership thereof." The airwaves belonged to the public, but broadcasting was not relegated to common carrier status. The financing of radio would be left to the free enterprise system. Initially the regulations on advertising were scant. The 1927 law merely stated that programs must be "announced as paid for or furnished, as the case may be, by such person, firm, company, or corporation."

In the next few years the new FRC worked through the enormous task assigned it by Congress. By the early 1930s, the inadequacies of the 1927 act were clear to the industry, the new Roosevelt administration, and Congress. The administration wanted telephone regulation transferred from the Interstate Commerce Commission and combined with broadcasting in a new communications commission.

---

[4]Mitchell, *Cavalcade of Broadcasting,* p. 11.

With talk of a new broadcasting law, educators and other special interest groups mobilized. They had seen a tremendous potential outlet for public education slip through their fingers and into the hands of commercial broadcasters. In the early and grim depression years, many stations established by educational organizations either closed or were sold. Now, the special interest groups proposed to Congress a plan whereby all station licenses would be declared null and void after enactment of a new law. A new commission would then accept applications for station licenses and reserve 25 percent of the channels for educational, religious, agricultural, labor, cooperative, and similar nonprofit associations. The fight was on, as the broadcasters rallied to save their stations. A flood of propaganda was issued against the "self-seeking reformers" who were depicted as threatening radio with their "powerful lobby." Educators have rarely come out on top in a head-to-head confrontation with commercial interests, and this battle proved no exception.

Congress passed the *Communications Act of 1934* and instructed the new regulatory body to schedule hearings and consider proposals on educational broadcasting. Many of the provisions of the 1927 act were incorporated in the new law. Telephone jurisdiction was transferred to the new Federal Communications Commission (FCC), and the five seats on the commission were expanded to seven. The changes made little impact on the broadcaster. (The act was a victory for the status quo, and the approximately 600 commercial broadcasting stations could now once again return to their programing and profit concerns.)

Industry Growth

Although electrical transcriptions had been developed in 1929, until the mid-1930s most of the commercials heard on radio were delivered *live*. All network programing, in fact, was live. This meant that networks and stations had to maintain an expensive stable of actors and musicians for a wide variety of programs and commercials.

The advertising industry, however, was developing an interest in recording commercials on discs. The advantages were obvious. Commercials could have as many production elements as the advertiser wanted without the cost of maintaining talent for each broadcast. The quality could be strictly controlled; mistakes could be eliminated. The practice opened up vast new possibilities for advertising on a *spot* basis. An advertiser could now use the precious 20 seconds between popular network programs by purchasing time from affiliated stations. The national advertiser could also buy time on popular independent stations or tailor time purchases to fit product distribution or specific marketing needs. Advertisers soon learned that putting their commercials on "wax" was much cheaper and still efficient. (Audio tape was unknown in radio until the late 1940s.)

The practice of using discs was a shot in the arm to station sales and also to the new national firms that sprang up in major advertising centers to represent stations scattered across the country. The sales efforts of these *rep firms* brought new business to the broadcasters and made the business of buying time on local stations infinitely easier for the advertising agencies.

Companies set up to measure the size of the listening audience provided a much needed service to networks, stations, and advertisers. The days of inexpensive production were gone; advertisers needed to know if their investments were going to pay off. (See 1.2.)

A company established by Archibald M. Crossley was the first to provide estimates of audience size in terms of ratings. (In a general sense, the word *ratings* refers to estimating audience size for a given program as a percentage of the total *potential* audience.) Later, C. E. Hooper's "Hooperatings" dominated radio measurements from the mid-1930s until the end of the 1940s. Both companies used telephone interviewers, and respondents were asked to identify the program and stations they were listening to at the time of the call. Fan mail was also analyzed, and door-to-door interviewing techniques were used. A market research firm, the A. C. Nielsen Company, branched into audience measurements in the 1930s. With a mechanical device

1.2 / Just Send Your Name and Address and the Top from a Box of...

Sponsors constantly sought reassurance that people were listening and responding to their programs. They prodded the advertising agencies to "prove" the success of their sponsorships, and premiums turned out to be a perfect answer. A simple promise of a gift—in return for some proof that the listener had purchased a product—generated an impressive number of requests. If the premium was particularly attractive, the response was sometimes almost beyond belief.

When The Mutual Broadcasting System's homey characters *Lum and Abner* offered a "newspaper" from their mythical home town, Pine Ridge, Arkansas, more than 400,000 requests were received. Lever Bros. mailed out more than 800,000 sewing kits after listeners to its soap opera *Big Sister* were told that they could have one for ten cents and a Rinso box top.

Premiums were popular on children's programs, too. For a box top, a young listener could get a picture of Little Orphan Annie, a Tom Mix periscope ring, a Red Ryder lariat, a Sergeant Preston totem pole, a Jack Armstrong magnesium parachute ball, a Lone Ranger sheriff's badge, and a host of other childhood goodies that often ended up being nothing for something.

Kate Smith's sponsor offered a picture of this rotund and very popular singer and received 45,000 cigar bands. (She was chosen by the sponsor in the early 1930s because they

Photograph courtesy of the Broadcast Pioneers Library, Washington, D.C.

were sure she would attract a male audience and, at the same time, not make women listeners jealous.)

called an Audimeter, attached to a radio receiver, it measured the use and actual tuning of radios in sample homes.

Other businesses sprang up to serve both radio and advertising. With the increased use of disc transcriptions, independent producers and transcription services produced programs for advertisers and stations. The programs were often syndicated and constituted an attractive buy for advertisers whose product distribution did not coincide with network coverage. Recording companies serviced the producers by dubbing the programs on 16-inch discs. Talent agents prospered. There had been a stampede of performers to radio from the dying vaudeville circuits, and these talent agents represented their clients to the radio industry. Unions were few, but there was increasing interest in organizing various groups of radio employees. Trade associations were also formed. The major trade organization, the National Association of Broadcasters (NAB), functioned primarily as a representative of the radio industry in its battle with the American Society of Composers, Authors, and Publishers (ASCAP). This music licensing organization insisted that the radio industry pay its members. Their music would not be free to radio broadcasters; a price would have to be negotiated, and it finally was.

Radio Programing

By 1938, 40 million radios could be tuned in across America. More than 700 stations were on the air, and advertisers were investing $150 million annually in radio sponsorships.[5] Major network customers were frequently companies selling consumer packaged goods. Prime time, of course, was during the evening, when the family gathered in the living room around the beloved "piece of talking furniture" to listen to dramas, comedy, and music-variety shows.

The daytime hours contained children's programing, which was scheduled before and after school hours, and an abundance of serials. These continuing dramas filled the network hours with unending tales of family trauma. Housewives loved the programs, and so did advertisers. A relatively small cast was needed, and since the Hammond organ had usurped the position of network musicians, production costs were reasonably low. Because so many soap manufacturers found these 15-minute serials an excellent way to reach their customers, the programs were soon dubbed *soap operas*. Almost 40 sponsored serials filled the airwaves by the end of 1938. By 1940, the average network station was devoting five hours each weekday to soap operas.[6]

Sponsors at both the network and local level sought the "right" program for their selling messages. It was not an easy task. Developing an attractive show, negotiating a price and a time slot on the network or station, promoting the program to audiences, and building sponsor-program identification could not be accomplished overnight. The most popular network programs had crawled up the ratings ladder over a period

---

[5]*Broadcasting Yearbook 1939,* p. 11.

[6]Francis Chase, Jr., *Sound and Fury: An Informal History of Broadcasting* (New York: Harper & Bros., 1942), p. 178.

of years. Tough competition on the other networks in a particular time period could make the task of establishing a new program almost impossible. It was often a risky business.

As the years went by, commercials became a bit more sophisticated, but not much. Advertisers considered subtlety and selling incompatible. Although commercials included extravagant product claims, the government and the radio industry at this time were not concerned about whether or not these claims could be substantiated. There were more important things to worry about; the national attention was turning to events in Europe.

Radio Goes to War

As the German high command secretly plotted for war, the disturbing events in Europe were absorbing the attention of the American press. The networks had expanded their news organizations in Europe in order to gather the news firsthand. News broadcasts, which had never attracted many sponsors, now found eager advertisers waiting to buy these highly rated programs. After the outbreak of World War II, many station owners feared that the government would take over their stations. But instead, the stations were asked to abide by self-censorship, discontinue any ad lib programs or unrehearsed man-in-the-street interviews, abolish weather reports (because the data might be helpful to the enemy), and cooperate with the government in the dissemination of information and what amounted to domestic propaganda.

The boom was really on now. The public held radio in high esteem for its outstanding reporting of war news and for the quality and quantity of entertainment. In 1940, there were 50 million radios in use, and advertisers were spending more than $200 million for time on the nation's 800 stations. This represented a 21 percent increase from the previous year's investment.[7] At first, in a surge of enthusiasm, stations and networks constantly broke into sponsored programs with the latest war news. This practice was eventually tempered by the exasperation of advertisers and the necessity of granting huge rebates to preempted sponsors. Programing settled down as the country and the industry adjusted to the war.

Consumers had to live with rationing when many manufacturers turned from production of consumer goods to war matériel. Automobiles, appliances, tires, and some other goods were impossible to get; the military consumed them all. Major hard goods manufacturers, however, wanted to keep their names before the public. When the war was over, they did not want to start from scratch in rebuilding their consumer markets.

The War Ends: Radio Rides High

As the nation celebrated the end of the war, radio stood high in power, prestige, and profits. The medium absorbed much of the public's time and interest, and it had

---

[7]Orrin E. Dunlap, Jr., *Dunlap's Radio & Television Almanac* (New York: Harper & Bros., 1951), p. 134.

proved its importance as a public service during the difficult war years. Not everyone was favorably impressed with radio's accomplishments, however. A letter published in the *Chicago Tribune* from inventor Lee De Forest, considered by some to be "the father of radio," was directed to a convention of the National Association of Broadcasters.

What have you gentlemen done with my child? . . . You have sent him out in the streets in rags of ragtime, tatters of jive and boogie woogie, to collect money from all the sundry for hubba hubba and audio jitterbug. You have made of him a laughing stock to intelligence, surely a stench in the nostrils of the gods of the ionosphere; you have cut time into tiny segments called spots (more rightly stains) wherewith the occasional fine program is periodically smeared with impudent insistence to buy and try.[8]

His admonition went unheeded, for radio was riding high. In 1946, radios were in nine out of every ten homes — a total of 60 million. Gross advertising revenues for radio had doubled during the war years and had reached $512 million by 1946.[9] At the beginning of the war, one-third of the networks' program schedules had sponsors. At the close of the war, the figure was two-thirds. Radio was an unprecedented success story, and its importance to the public was almost impossible to estimate. Advertisers had gladly paid its bills; in turn, they had multiplied their own profits. (See 1.3.)

The nation celebrated the return of peace, but radio faced new problems that would lead to staggering difficulties in the postwar years. Waiting in the wings, eager to make a grand debut, was a formidable competitor — television.

Television: The Grand Debut

Television, like FM (frequency modulation) broadcasting, had been snatched from its public introduction at the outbreak of the war only to be put on a shelf to wait for the crisis to end. Now the materials were once again available to build the new industry. Many broadcasters were eager to get in on the ground floor, because the potential was obvious. If every American household were to invest in a television set, fortunes could clearly be made. RCA rushed into production to put sets on the market, and other equipment manufacturers followed. The small screens (8 to 10 inches), poor picture, and the relatively high cost of the sets ($300 to $500 at first) were not a deterrent to sales. The public snapped them up as fast as they could be delivered to retailers.

The television industry grew and flourished like a hothouse flower. The country was in a postwar boom economy, and the public was eager for consumer goods. These included television sets and also all the other goods and services that manufacturers wanted to advertise. Because it was built on the established structure of the radio industry, the television industry was made operational very quickly. TV networks were built by the enormous revenues of the radio networks, and hundreds of local radio stations filed for television construction permits at the FCC. With FCC authorization, station operators scrambled to get on the air and sign a contract as a network affiliate.

---

[8]*Chicago Tribune,* October 28, 1946.

[9]*Broadcasting Yearbook 1948,* p. 16.

Advertisers, too, wanted to board the bandwagon, and many of them moved their most popular radio sponsorships to the new medium. The relatively high costs for time and production (compared with those of radio) did not deter them, and they accumulated both prestige and profits from their investments.

The television networks, with NBC and CBS dominating, gradually increased the amount of programing fed to affiliates. ABC ran a poor third in both programing and sales, but it moved up dramatically when merged with Paramount Theatres in 1953. Because videotape was unknown before the late 1950s, most programs were pre-

1.3 / "America's First Lady of Food"

Many sponsors were convinced that the key to success lay in signing a popular talent for a splashy entertainment series. General Mills was an exception. The reason was a simple and most successful network radio program, *Time for Betty Crocker.*

For decades, American women had been accustomed to the benign countenance of Betty Crocker on magazine ads for General Mills products. She was a natural for a radio service program.

By 1954, *Time for Betty Crocker* was carried on 320 ABC Radio affiliates. This four-and-a-half minute program was aired three times a day on Monday, Wednesday, and Friday — nine programs per week. Adelaide Hawley, who played Betty Crocker, responded to questions and comments from sidekick Win Elliot. The series was fundamentally a recipe show, and commercials for

Gold Medal Flour, Betty Crocker Mixes, and Bisquick were integrated into their dialogue.

The Nielsen rating averaged 7.2 percent, and the network estimated that the program reached an average of 8,400,000 households per month.* (This rating figure means that 7.2 percent of all the radio households in America listened to the program. Not bad for a show with weekly time charges of only $14,000.)

Hawley also appeared on a number of TV shows in demonstration commercials for General Mills products. Later her TV role was confined to *voice overs;* in other words, she was heard and not seen. (The attempt to personify Betty Crocker and show a particular person to the viewer was not altogether successful. General Mills decided to allow each audience member to create her or his own illusion of "America's First Lady of Food.")
Sponsor Magazine, December 27, 1954, p. 34.

The First Betty Crocker

Photographs courtesy of General Mills, Inc.

Adelaide Hawley,
Television's First Betty Crocker

sented live, as were the commercials. Advertising agencies and their clients were struggling with the new medium, learning how to turn it into a selling medium. The earliest television commercials were only glorified radio ads, often confined to a standup pitchman who clutched the product, stared at the camera lens, and delivered the spiel. *Supers* (printing superimposed on the image) were added, which gave the dealer's name, address, and the like. The commercials were inexpensive to produce, and copy could be easily changed. Products requiring demonstration (notably appliances) adapted quickly and effectively to the new medium. Advertisers were now released from radio's limitations and from the "frozen" character of print advertising. The advertising industry was entranced with the potential of the new medium. In Washington, however, the problems surrounding television seemed larger than the potential.

The "TV Freeze"

The burgeoning growth of TV was suddenly interrupted when the FCC declared a "freeze" on new station applications. Already buried in applications, the FCC needed to develop an orderly national allocation plan for assigning licenses. The freeze, imposed in 1948, was supposed to last only six months but was kept in effect for three-and-a-half years. This period provided radio with a brief respite, because there were still only slightly more than 100 TV stations on the air. Radio was still the dominant entertainment medium. In every city where television had developed to any extent at all, however, radio suffered. Once a TV set had been installed in a living room, radio was banished to other rooms, and its use declined. The radio networks saw that their huge prime-time audiences were slipping away.

In April, 1952, the FCC issued its *Sixth Report and Order,* which ended the freeze, established VHF (very high frequency) and UHF (ultra-high frequency) channel allocations, and reserved several hundred channels for educational use. More than 700 applications for TV construction permits could now be processed, and the real boom could begin. Radio's total time sales in 1952 were $473 million; television's, only $283 million. In two years, television passed radio with total annual time sales of $538 million.[10]

Radio Buckles, Then Rallies

As television's fortunes skyrocketed, the bottom dropped out of network radio. Broadcast time sales revealed a bleak trend for network radio in the 1950s (see 1.4).

As audiences deserted the big-name, high-budget network radio programs, so did the advertisers. Prime-time shows folded one by one, but the inexpensive daytime fare, such as soap operas and quiz shows, lasted many more years. For a while, the radio networks maintained the same time charges. But because of diminishing audi-

---

[10]*Broadcasting Yearbook 1958,* p. B135.

ences, radio was plainly losing its efficiency. After a good deal of advertiser-network negotiation, rates were lowered in 1951.

Only the troubles of *network* radio are reflected in the chart. During these same years *total* radio revenues rose because of increases in spot and local advertising. It became clear that radio was not going to disappear, but it was going to change. If the networks were to survive, they had to change with the times.

In the ensuing years, the networks reduced their service to their radio affiliates and adopted what was called a magazine format. It consisted of news, sports, and various program features, rather than the traditionally structured shows that had typified network schedules for many years. Since advertisers could buy *participations,* or single commercials, in the new format, they did not need to invest major sums in sponsorships.

Local stations, faced with cutbacks in network programing, were forced to experiment. The logical course lay in music and news. Program costs for these services were very reasonable. Besides, radio had established itself as an important news medium, and television would not invade music programing in any major fashion.

In addition to new program formats, radio received boosts from other areas.

1.4 /Networks' Fortunes in the Early 1950s

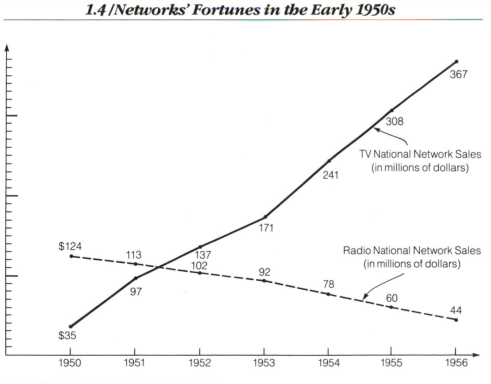

Sources: FCC figures and *Broadcasting Yearbook 1963,* p. 15.

Japan flooded American markets with transistor radios in the form of small cheap portables. Teenagers were now wired for sound, and the radio industry quickly learned that because radios could go anywhere a listener went, *mobility* was becoming one of the medium's primary assets. General Electric marketed a clock radio, an overnight success. Detroit installed more and more radios in automobiles, and the research showed that this "traveling companion" was tuned in a great deal.

FM broadcasting struggled through a difficult decade in the 1950s. The new transmitting system, the invention of Major Edwin Armstrong, had been designed but not developed before World War II. During the 1940s and 1950s most of the FM stations on the air were "satellites" that duplicated the programing of a commonly owned AM station. The few independent FM stations were in major markets and programed classical or innocuous background music. They lost money, and few advertisers would even consider buying time on stations that delivered such small audiences. Over the years, however, FM grew and expanded into a variety of music program formats. Sales of FM receivers increased, and audiences were pleased with the superior signal quality. As audiences grew, so did advertising revenues.

From TV Sponsorships to Participations

As television costs escalated, the old days of sponsor-produced and -controlled programing were on their way out. An increasing number of programs were *licensed* to the networks. In other words, a program series was contracted to the network, not to the sponsor as was previously the case. The network scheduled the program and sold either sponsorships or participations to interested advertisers. (See 1.5.) Since this new responsibility brought with it greater financial risks, the networks began to share the cost of *pilots* with the show's producers. If a pilot show was accepted for network scheduling, the network retained its financial interest in the series. When the time came to syndicate it domestically or internationally, further profits could be realized.

The changing trend from program sponsorships to participations satisfied most major advertisers. Costs had risen so dramatically that sponsorships were considered high risks. By purchasing a variety of participations, advertisers could distribute their budgets ascross the several networks in many programs on a constantly fluctuating schedule. Participations eliminated the problem of putting all the client's eggs in only a few baskets; thus, it also provided the opportunity to reach large audiences more frequently.

Color made its public debut on the home screen in 1954. NBC-TV, a subsidiary of the enormous set manufacturer RCA, produced a number of color "spectaculars" to whet the public's appetite. The new receivers, however, were several times more expensive than monochrome sets. Many viewers decided to wait until the price tags came down and the number of color program offerings went up. Advertisers, leery of the high costs of color production, played a waiting game before converting their commercials to color. Until a significant proportion of homes had color sets, the investment was not worth it. Ten years passed as the industry, the advertisers, and the public gradually converted to color television.

Videotape recording, introduced in 1957, was being improved constantly. In many cases, it eliminated the need for telecasting live programs. This new device was relatively inexpensive, and it allowed the elimination of on-air goofs with editing techniques. Some of TV's spontaneity was lost because of videotape, but the benefits were worth it, and advertisers became increasingly interested. What could be presented in live commercials was terribly limited, and the risks of a faux pas were ever-present.

During the 1960s, television networks expanded their empires. Approximately 320 new commercial stations went on the air. As reported by Nielsen, households tuned in their sets more and more each year. By 1972, the TV set was on in the average American household more than six hours every day.[11] The novelty of television had worn off, and TV watching had evolved into a national habit.

[11]*Nielsen Television '73*, p. 8.

1.5 / Hitching Sponsors to the Stars

Advertisers are often anxious to have their products displayed in close association with top radio and television personalities. S. C. Johnson & Son, Inc., began sponsoring the popular Red Skelton television show in 1954 and continued until the program went off the air in the early 1960s. In this 1954 picture, Skelton polishes an antique automobile with Instant J-Wax, a product that has since been discontinued.

Another popular entertainer, Bing Crosby, served as a commercial spokesperson for orange juice in a 15-minute spot radio program, Bing Crosby's *Minute Maid Show*. The program began in 1948 on half a dozen Eastern stations, and as product distribution expanded across the country, so did the program. Eventually 46 stations were carrying this daily show of song and chatter. Crosby continued advertising the orange juice until 1952. In 1968, he returned, this time doing television commercials for Minute Maid with his family.

Photograph courtesy of Johnson Wax.

Photograph courtesy of Coca-Cola Company Foods Division.

Television Since 1970

As television entered its maturity, advertisers invested a greater and greater proportion of their budget in the medium, partly because it was good business but also because of increasing time charges and production costs. Advertisers who needed national exposure felt the squeeze of escalating costs on the three major networks. In a horrendous race for prime-time ratings, ABC, CBS, and NBC spent millions on program development, all financed by advertising dollars. Major clients complained to no avail about capricious program scheduling, constant preemptions, and costs headed for the stratosphere. To add to their worries, special interest groups led by members of the new "religious Right" found a new focus for their attack on what they considered permissive TV programs. Because the networks had pretty well ignored complaints about violence, sex, and profanity, these groups threatened to organize consumer boycotts of advertisers that bought commercial time on "unacceptable" programs. (The debate on this issue is explored in Chapter 11.)

At the local level, more and more retailers allocated a portion of their advertising budget to television. They quickly learned that it was money well invested. In order to keep commercial costs low enough to attract new station business, ingenious producers and directors devised some cost-saving-techniques. Commercials tended to avoid "location" shots or elaborate settings. Closeups of the product and an announcer, stock film footage and sound effects, and many simple, inexpensive studio devices were used to create effective local advertising.

At the national level, clients demanded and got television advertising that was bright, personable, and very often distinctive. Commercials reflected the industry's awareness that its audiences were growing in sophistication. Research became increasingly important and expanded in both quantity and quality to help advertisers minimize marketing mistakes. "Positioning" of products and more intensive analyses of the target audience became common in developing advertising strategies. The idea that television is simply radio with pictures vanished.

The growing consumer movement of the 1970s prompted the Federal Trade Commission (FTC) to scrutinize advertising, particularly TV commercials. Many companies, uncertain of the degree of documentation that would be required by the FTC's requests to "substantiate your claims," made major modifications in their advertising practices.

One target of government action was cigarette advertising. The airwaves were filled with countless commercials that presented bright, attractive, youthful performers exhorting viewers to smoke one brand or another. The U.S. Surgeon General's report in 1964 on the dangers of cigarette smoking started a long chain of events that ended in 1971 when, by act of Congress, cigarette advertising was banned from the broadcast media. Disgruntled broadcasters had to look elsewhere for the $240 million in annual revenues that had previously been invested in cigarette commercials. The tobacco companies switched their expenditures to the print medium, billboards, sponsorship of sporting events, and other outlets.

Some new revenue came from a somewhat unexpected source. From the stunning example of a few successful office seekers, the nation's politicians learned how potent television could be in reaching voters and winning elections. There was concern about "selling" candidates the way soap was sold, but many politicians were convinced that winning elections could be accomplished by spot announcements on key TV stations. Expenditures by such candidates on local TV stations and on the major networks exceeded $117 million in the 1982 election year, according to the Television Bureau of Advertising.[12]

Advertising directed at children became a tremendously emotional issue in the 1970s and early 1980s. A number of consumer groups, led by Action for Children's Television, brought pressures on the FTC, the FCC, and Congress. Major reforms were sought, and so was a complete ban on *all* advertising on children's programs. The result was a compromise: a reduction in commercial time on children's programs and stepped-up self-monitoring of the content and persuasive techniques in commercials designed for children.

For the television industry, the advent of new technologies has proved to be the most exciting and perplexing development in recent years. Cable television, originally developed to improve the signal quality in areas of poor reception, has developed as a programing and advertising vehicle in its own right. With the government's deregulation of cable in the 1980s, millions of new homes will be added to cable systems. Experiments with two-way interactive cable promise the potential of direct marketing via a television screen. Other new technologies — direct broadcast satellites (beaming programs to a household's rooftop dish), multipoint distribution services (used primarily for pay TV channels), newly authorized low power TV stations, videotex, videodiscs, and other electronic wizardry — make it abundantly clear that the electronic media will change dramatically. Advertisers, along with broadcasters, will have to meet the challenge.

Radio Since 1970

As the 1970s dawned, the radio industry looked forward to an era of unprecedented growth. New stations sprang up everywhere. In only a dozen years more than 1,600 new stations went on the air, three-quarters of them on the FM band! Stereo had been introduced to FM in the 1960s and provided a tremendous boost to the growth of FM broadcasting in the 1970s and 1980s. As the years went by, FM evolved into the medium for various music formats, and many AM stations, not competing particularly well in that area, switched to news, talk, and information. Advertisers no longer cared if a station was AM or FM; their interest was in the numbers. What demographics could the station deliver and at what cost?

With so many stations on the air, all looking to advertisers for support, the scramble was on. The stations that prospered were the ones that polished their format in order to capture and build a loyal audience. Listeners tuned to a particular "sound" — a favorite program format — and with more and more stations on the air, predictable and consistent programing became important.

In an effort to achieve this consistency, stations turned to automation, recognizing

---

[12]*Broadcasting,* March 7, 1983, p. 84.

the merits of a tightly controlled, preprogramed service. Quality control was considered a major asset of automated systems. Many station managers, weary of personnel problems and discouraged by the loss of good staff members who always wanted to move on to bigger stations in bigger markets, switched from live to automated systems. A smaller staff could operate an automated station, and more time and effort could be spent selling time to local advertisers.

Demographics became the name of the game. Radio managers pored over the latest rating reports to see the quality of their stations' demographics, usually reported in terms of age and sex groupings. Women between 18 and 34 years old, who spend a high proportion of the consumer dollar, became a prime target. Advertisers placed their commercials on stations that delivered particular kinds of consumers in efficient numbers.

Radio revenues increased significantly, but it is important to note that the riches were not spread evenly across the industry. Many stations, in both large and small markets, still lose money today.

The increasing specialization of radio made the medium an excellent buy for small and large advertisers alike. Retailers on limited budgets might not be able to afford a top-rated station in a major market, but they could schedule a message on smaller stations delivering the right kind of audience for their marketing needs.

As stations sought their own place in a market's total programing menu, the networks adapted to changing listening patterns and to what affiliates wanted in program service. ABC had led the way in 1968 when it obtained permission from the FCC to originate four separate network services: the Entertainment Network, the Information Network, the Contemporary Network, and the FM Network. This scheme

"I miss the old days when I could walk in here and raise hell with the staff."

enabled affiliates to join the network that provided programing services (chiefly news) most compatible with the local programing carried on the station (chiefly music).

Since then, several new networks have been inaugurated—the RKO Radio Network, the National Black Network, and others, plus new networks originated by NBC, CBS, and Mutual. Satellites now promise a new era in networking because of reduced interconnection costs and increased flexibility. These hookups, including hundreds of stations, offer an attractive, relatively inexpensive, and easy-to-buy opportunity for national advertisers.

As direct competitors to the traditional radio networks, a number of *unwired,* or *rep, networks* were developed in the early 1970s by station reps. Several major firms organized the stations they represented into groups. In turn, time on these networks was sold to advertisers who wanted to use spot radio on an extensive basis. Agencies' time buyers no longer had to buy several hundred stations on an individual basis. By working through one or more station representative firms, they could buy spot networks on an almost tailor-made basis. Because the station reps handled much of the work, time buyers were grateful for less paperwork. Stations were also tremendously pleased, since they had a new source of spot business.

Conclusions

The American system of broadcasting is unique, and so is the role of the nation's advertisers in supporting this system. The early years of radio generated much debate over the source of financial support of the medium. Many schemes were proposed to develop radio as a noncommercial service. As these proposals fell by the wayside one by one, it became clear that the broadcasters would turn to advertisers to the benefit of both. The first 25 years of commercial radio were an exciting period that spanned an economic boom, a bust, and finally American involvement in a world war.

By the 1940s the best advertising on radio was nearing a popular art form. Commercials were enticing, personal, and very effective. Advertisers who knew how to use the medium were rewarded in the marketplace. They learned their lessons well. By the end of the war, the broadcast advertising industry, again with trepidation but also with fascination, looked forward to an exciting new medium called television.

The new industry was an immediate success for many reasons, primarily because America's television system was built on the established structure of a successful radio industry. The know-how, the capital, and public enthusiasm guaranteed a triumph. There was no question that the new TV stations and networks would be supported by advertising, and the nation's businesses were eager to invest. The public's use of television evolved into a national habit, and advertisers who learned how to use the visual medium made millions.

The total time that Americans spend each year with commercial radio and television is incalculable. It's all paid for by advertisers who produce thousands of commercials (both good and bad) annually. The criticisms directed at broadcast advertising would fill volumes. The accusations are familiar ones: Programing is constantly interrupted and cluttered with a cacophony of advertising messages. Commercials are too often obnoxious, tasteless, or tiresome. Unscrupulous advertisers have used public airwaves to mislead and deceive consumers. Children have been exploited by manipulative techniques, and some advertisers have dictated program content. Broadcasters have canceled quality programs because of low ratings and because of the lack of advertising support.

The accomplishments achieved by both broadcasters and advertisers should also be considered. For more than 50 years, advertisers large and small have financially supported a tremendous variety of programing. Most advertisers have attempted to use the media in positive and constructive ways. The information function of advertising has provided a service to consumers, for they have learned about many new products and services via the broadcast media. And, for the most part, broadcasters have jealously guarded their right to control the program content of their stations, free from interference from the government, advertisers, and special interst groups.

The public's use and reliance on both radio and television is enormous. The quantity of time Americans spend with broadcasting is a remarkable testimony to its power and influence. For advertisers, broadcasters, and the public, the broadcast media in the twentieth century have been an unparalleled success.

chapter two

Structure of the Broadcast Advertising Industry

The Game and Its Players

The most visible aspects of the broadcast advertising industry are the ubiquitous commercials and the sale on the cash register at the retail level. Less visible aspects encompass a wide variety of business enterprises that work together to their mutual benefit. In between the advertisers, which have goods or services to sell, and the broadcasters, including cable television, which deliver audiences to advertisers, are a variety of support companies: advertising agencies, station representatives, research companies, advertising suppliers, and many others. (See 2.1.)

For an overview of the broadcast advertising industry, it is appropriate to start at the beginning with the companies that are trying to reach the public with their commercial messages.

Advertisers

The broadcast advertiser may be a corporate giant with advertising expenditures of hundreds of millions of dollars a year. Such major spenders include Procter & Gamble (which always leads the list), Sears, Roebuck & Co., General Foods Corp., Phillip Morris Inc., K mart Corp., General Motors Corp., R.J. Reynolds Industries, Ford Motor Co., American Telephone and Telegraph Co., and Warner-Lambert Co. Advertisers may also be regional or local, and an increasing number of them are retailers. Regardless of a company's size, its advertising expenditures are considered business *investments*.

The larger corporations normally market their products throughout the United States as national advertisers. Their corporate structure can be complex, with tiers of departments and legions of people. Increasingly, the top management of major companies is becoming involved in basic advertising decisions. Because advertising portrays the company to its public, the chairman of the board or the company president wants to be sure the image is a positive one.

The marketing director usually reports directly to the company's top executive. He or she is part of senior management and is often responsible for both sales and advertising and, sometimes, for research. In many large companies, an advertising manager reports to the marketing director. Or, if there is no marketing director, the advertising manager reports directly to top management. Day-to-day supervision of the advertising department and contact with the company's advertising agency fall to the advertising manager.

In large companies producing a variety of products, brand managers are often employed to handle broad responsibilities for whatever brand is assigned to them. They usually act as marketing director for their own brand and handle product

2.1/Media Relationships in the Broadcast and Cable Advertising Industry

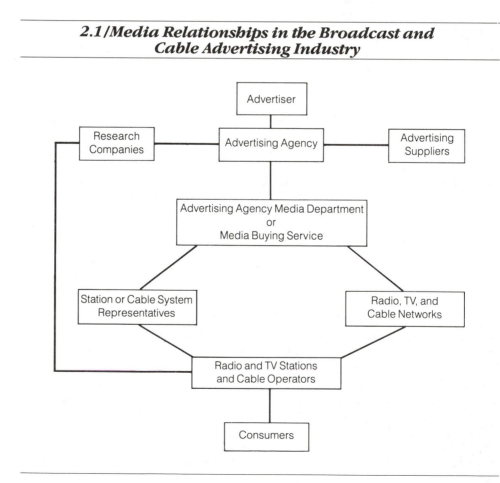

development, packaging, pricing, and promotions as well as advertising. A brand manager, sometimes considered the counterpart of an advertising agency's account executive, works closely with agency personnel to inform them of the product's market position, features, and special qualities (the bases for advertising claims). The brand manager communicates corporate policies and goals to the agency and is the first to screen a proposed campaign. He or she can normally reject a campaign but can seldom approve one independently. Experts in media, creative services, or research are often employed by a company to work with the brand manager. They generally set performance standards for the advertising agency and make sure the agency lives up to such standards.

The operations of local and regional advertisers are invariably simpler. Marketing problems, however, are just as serious to them as they are to the top management of a company like Procter & Gamble. Sometimes the company president or the store manager may serve as the advertising manager. If a full-time advertising or marketing director is employed, this person may use the services of an advertising agency or may hire a staff to handle the company's advertising "in house."

Advertising Agencies

Advertising agencies came into existence over 100 years ago as sales representatives for magazines and newspapers. The development of agencies was prompted by two things: (1) the companies' need to advertise in cities where their products were distributed and (2) the media's need to contact as many sources of advertising revenue as possible. Advertising agencies initially retained a commission on the sum paid to the media by the advertiser. Today, the well-known 15 percent commission is about all that remains of the original system.

Agencies generally derive their compensation from three sources: these media commissions, percentage charges on materials and services purchased for their clients, and special fee arrangements.

Media commissions, utilizing the standard 15 percent commission, mean that for every $1,000 the agency bills its clients, $850 goes to the media and $150 is kept as operating income. Thus, technically, the media today continue to pay the agencies.

Percentage charges on materials and services cover the wide variety of out-of-pocket costs that are included in the development of a campaign. Typically, these may include photography, illustrations, production, talent, film or tape dubs, printing, engraving, and freelance artwork. The usual agency markup on these costs is 17.65 percent of the net cost, which is equal to 15 percent of the gross. To better understand this, consider the following example: An agency spends $1,000 buying radio time for a client and earns a $150 commission. For the same client the agency also orders photography work billed at $850. The agency marks up 17.65 percent on the photography and bills its client $1,000. The markup is equal to 15 percent of the total photography bill. Thus, whether a client spends its money in media or in materials and services, the agency still earns its 15 percent.

Special fee arrangements are negotiated ahead of time between an agency and its client. Fees are normally used when commission income is not commensurate with the cost of the agency's efforts. The agency will earn more or less than the traditional 15 percent commission, depending on the circumstances. If, for example, an advertiser needs a large number of ads in relatively low-cost media (such as many trade journals), needs a great deal of "collateral" (nonmedia) work, or simply has a very modest budget, the agency will generally be compensated through a fee. Fees may be a flat monthly amount, or retainer, or they may be based on the agency's time spent. Fees are often used as minimum guarantees, with media commissions credited against the fee. There are also instances when the advertiser spends heavily in a medium (network TV, for example) in comparison to the amount of agency work required. In such a case, a fee may be agreed to that amounts to less than the 15 percent commission.

An agency's volume, or billings, is usually measured by the amount of advertising placed for its clients, but these figures are sometimes misleading to the unitiated. Although an agency with $100 million in billings sounds like an enormous enterprise, it really is only a $15 million business. The agency business as a whole does not reap huge profits, although larger agencies tend to enjoy a higher percentage of net profits than smaller agencies. The American Association of Advertising Agencies (AAAA) reported that its members' net profits as a percentage of gross income ranged from 3 percent to 5 percent from 1971 to 1980.[1]

Over the decades, agencies have grown in size and number, but the agency business is a relatively small one in terms of the number of people employed. The AAAA estimates that about 7,000 agencies employ about 85,000 people. The agencies ranged from the nation's largest, Young & Rubicam, with annual billings of approximately $2.5 billion and more than 50 offices worldwide, to one-person shops scattered in cities and towns across the 50 states.

Full-Service Agencies

Many of the nation's advertising agencies are called *full-service* agencies, for they offer their clients a wide range of advertising services. An agency is nothing more than the accumulated knowledge, experience, and creative genius of its staff. The following list outlines the basic elements of the classic full-service agency (see also 2.2):

1. *Management:* responsible in the broadest sense for the business operation of the agency. Running the business involves selecting and supervising key personnel, developing long-range plans, soliciting new business, and monitoring costs and budgets.

2. *Plans Group:* usually made up of department heads who can muster the agency's senior talent to aid their various clients. In the past, a plans group reviewed major recommendations before they were submitted to clients. Today, however, it increasingly helps to set direction and strategy at the outset, rather than sitting in judgment after most of the work has been accomplished.

3. *Account Management:* the marketing arm of the agency. It is responsible for primary client contact and for coordinating the agency's work for its clients.

---

[1] *Ten-Year Record of AAAA Advertising Agencies' Costs and Profits* (New York: American Association of Advertising Agencies, July 27, 1981).

4. *Creative:* composed of the "words and pictures people" — the writers, artists, and producers of both print and broadcast advertising. (Usually, the agency does not produce the finished work itself but uses outside specialists in support companies.)

5. *Media:* recommends where the advertising should appear and works closely with the creative staff in determining the media most effective for a given campaign. It buys time and space for clients, and its staff is primarily concerned with reaching the right audience an adequate number of times within the discipline of the budget. In performing a stewardship role, the media department conducts postcampaign analyses and checks to be sure the various media ran advertisements as ordered.

6. *Research:* provides the information the rest of the agency staff needs for its work. Much of the information must be gleaned from published (or syndicated) sources. When original information is needed, the research department negotiates with outside companies that specialize in providing tailor-made, proprietary research data.

7. *Radio/TV/Print Production and Traffic:* handles the actual production of a radio script, TV storyboard, or print layout into a finished advertisement. Personnel involved in this work are specialists and responsible for the ultimate production quality of commercials and print ads. They are familiar with various advertising suppliers and freelance talent so they can hire the right firm or person to handle a specific job. Traffic schedules agency work flow.

8. *Accounting:* handles all the advertising billing for the agency's clients. Included in the billing are charges for support services contracted by the agency, such as art, photography, film production, and talent. Billing also includes all media charges for time and space. It is customary for agencies to assume liability for paying media bills,

2.2 / Organization of a Typical Full-Service Advertising Agency

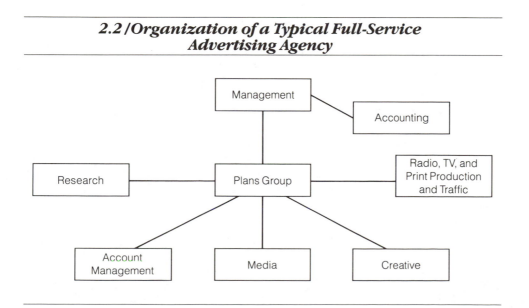

so they are required to scrutinize the credit rating of their clients. This works to the advantage of the media, because it is clearly easier for them to be informed about the payments and credit of several hundred agencies rather than thousands of advertisers. This agency responsibility is accompanied by a significant benefit: processing client payments to the media increases an agency's own cash flow and improves its own credit standing.

House Agencies

Some advertisers, large and small, have established their own agencies. Usually their only account is their company's product or service. House agencies were originally developed to save money. If an advertiser spent $1 million in advertising, it would expect to pay $150,000 to a full-service agency. But a house operation might be operated at a much lower sum. Sometimes savings are real, but sometimes they are illusory. Unless the advertiser can attract top talent and do so for less than the 15 percent saved in a regular agency commission, running a house agency may not be wise. (Top executives and key creative people in full-service agencies are usually supported by the operating income from more than one advertiser.)

There are advantages other than budget for the house agency, of course: in-depth knowledge of the client's product and management, shorter lines of communication and therefore faster responses, and greater control of the advertising program. Some advertisers use house agencies not as a money saver but in order to obtain what they consider better advertising. Such house agencies do not substitute for full-service agencies; rather, they serve as a coordinating vehicle for bringing together specialized independent advertising skills. Many of these skills come from small advertising companies operating in a particular area or from freelance practitioners.

Modular Agencies

In recent years an increasing number of modular agencies, which sell their various skills separately, have been established. Sometimes called *boutique agencies* or *a la carte services,* they sell whatever services a client needs. Work performed in a single area — whether in creative, in media planning and buying, in research, or in public relations — may be sold to an advertiser as a "module." These modules may either be contained within a single agency or be set up as separate businesses. Usually, a fee is negotiated between the agency and the client in this sort of arrangement, and the standard 15 percent media commission is generally not used.

Many small agencies offer modular arrangements to their clients but can also provide full service. A word is in order about agency size. Some people simply accept as an article of faith that there is an inherent disparity in the quality of work and service between a big agency and a small one. But big isn't necessarily good, and small isn't necessarily mediocre. In particular areas, such as research and media, it is difficult for a small "shop" to compete with the large staff and resources of bigger agencies. In large agencies, however, smaller clients often do not get the time and attention they think they deserve. Their advertising is usually handled by a small group of people and is sometimes relegated to less experienced staff members. Executive and creative talent at large agencies is naturally focused on the programs of its largest and most lucrative clients. Many small agencies are staffed by professionals who have worked for many years in large agencies for a wide variety of clients. Advertisers who elect to use a small agency are often a large fish in a small pond, and they are the focus of a great deal of time and attention from everyone on the agency staff.

Research Companies

The advertising industry cannot function without information — lots of it. The market for products and services is tremendously competitive, and so is the market for building and maintaining audiences. Specialized independent research companies and more and more sophisticated research tools have contributed inestimably to the success of both advertisers and broadcasters. Numerous companies devote themselves to providing information to the advertising industry, and it comes in the form of syndicated and proprietary research.

Syndicated research includes general market information, store audits on the movement of products through the marketplace, and a variety of other published materials, including reports on what various categories of advertisers have spent in various media. This latter category is helpful to clients who keep a watchful eye on their competitors. Audience research companies, notably Arbitron Ratings and A. C. Nielsen, syndicate audience estimates to broadcasters, advertisers, and agencies.

Proprietary research, in contrast, is often done in response to a particular advertiser's needs, and the data are held in strict confidence. This category includes product testing, consumer research, concept testing, and the evaluation of advertising programs. Larger advertisers who can afford the cost of specialized market and audience research are the main clients of research companies. The researchers have the know-how and the organization to take on projects that clients and their agencies would often find economically unfeasible. Their services, although not cheap, should save the client money in the long run, for they can help to avert marketing and advertising mistakes.

Various kinds of marketing data, methods of evaluation, and firms that measure ratings will be discussed in detail in later chapters.

Advertising Suppliers

The list of specialized businesses meeting the needs of advertising agencies and their clients is a long one. In the case of radio and television campaigns, a number of companies and freelance experts are employed to assist in developing commercials. If an agency does not have its own casting director, a freelance one is often hired to screen and select talent for commercials. Talent agents search their files and bring in their best prospects to audition for parts. Composers, music arrangers, and musicians are employed for radio commercials and for TV audio tracks. Production companies, usually on a competitive basis, bid for various commercial jobs sent to them by an advertising agency's production supervisor. (To limit overhead costs, agencies do not maintain studios or broadcast and film equipment. When commercials are produced, all these facilities must be hired.) Top television or film directors are available on a freelance basis, as are top camera people and other key production personnel. One editing house may handle film or tape editing exclusively; another company may specialize in release printing and duplication of the finished commercials.

Selecting the very best services from suppliers at the lowest possible price is one of the advertising agency's primary responsibilities. Coordinating these services and meeting deadlines are other ones. Thus, it is obvious that suppliers exist solely on the efficiency of their operations—their ability to do quality work on time.

Media Buying Services

By the mid-1960s, the increasing cost and complexity of buying television had prompted the development of media buying services. These services focused on one thing: buying media at the lowest possible cost. With the perishable nature of broadcast time, cost is always negotiable, and the negotiator with the greatest skill, the greatest budget, or both gets the best buys.

Media buying services staffed themselves with experienced buyers and offered their skills to advertisers and their agencies. Some of the early buying services suffered from questionable ethics, and others were badly mismanaged, resulting in a few spectacular financial failures. Many advertising agencies tended to regard the media buying services as an encroachment on their own turf, and thus the services got off to a somewhat shaky start.

Today, however, media buying services are generally recognized as offering a valued service. By pooling the budgets of many advertisers, their negotiators build up considerable clout. Most of the services specialize in broadcast advertising, but a few handle print and other somewhat specialized media such as outdoor and Yellow Pages advertising.

Some advertisers deal directly with buying services, and others have their ad agencies coordinate work with a service. Even very large agencies frequently use these services because of their experienced, competent negotiators. For medium-sized to small advertisers, the services are especially important in stretching limited budgets to deliver target audiences at the lowest possible cost.

Media buying services usually operate on a fee basis, or they may buy "on incentive," with remuneration dependent on the efficiency of the buy. This means the buying service succeeds in meeting particular goals by planning a schedule that reaches the right kind of audience in adequate numbers.

Station Representatives

Spot advertising activity tends to center in metropolitan areas. Yet no radio or television station, regardless of size, would consider it good business to maintain a sales office in each of these cities. Thus, practically every station in this country utilizes the services of a station representative firm to solicit spot business. These national sales organizations operate as an extension of the sales departments of the stations they represent. The *reps,* as they are called, provide an efficient communcation link between the advertising agency seeking to buy time for its clients and the broadcasting station eager to sell time to important national or regional accounts.

The value of the reps' service is obvious when the agency is located in New York and the station is located in California. A representative firm may handle the national sales of several dozen stations scattered across the country. Some reps handle sales for more than a hundred stations. In many cases, these large groups of stations are sold as an *unwired network,* tailor-made to the advertisers' needs. The time-buyer can select just the markets and stations desired, and the rep coordinates this package buy.

Inflationary times haven't escaped the station representative business. The costs of maintaining many sales offices became prohibitive. As a result, in the last decade several rep firms have merged or gone out of business. With approximately 8,000 commercial radio stations in this country, there aren't enough rep firms to go around. As a result, it is an increasingly common practice for a firm to represent more than one station in a market. Commonly owned AM and FM stations often share the same rep firm. In television, however, rep firms do not represent more than one station in a market.

Some firms represent just radio stations or just television stations or are split into two divisions to handle both. Some of the major station representative firms are Blair Television, Blair Radio, Katz Television, Katz Radio, Eastman Radio, Petry Television, McGavren-Guild, TeleRep, and Harrington, Righter & Parsons.

The station representative firm derives its income from commissions on spot sales. The percentage is not uniform but is negotiated with each client station. Commissions generally fall between 5 and 15 percent. The lower figure is more common for representatives of TV stations that sell many millions of dollars each year in spot. Radio stations grant higher commissions because the total dollar volume involved in a time sale is usually much less than in a TV buy.

As go-betweens for stations and agencies, reps are crucial to conducting spot business. The reps must be just as knowledgeable about the market and the station they represent as local station account executives. They should be able to provide basic data on the market and effectively "pitch" the station to a busy time buyer under pressure to select the right stations and times and to do so in a hurry. A rapport and mutual trust between time buyers and reps facilitates the process.

Mutual trust and good communications between the station and the rep is equally important. It's in the station's best interest to keep the rep constantly apprised of changes at the local level. These include the constantly changing *avails* (the commercial time periods available to advertisers), program schedules, changes in on-air talent, promotion and publicity plans, audience feedback, audience measurement surveys, and the constantly fluctuating competitive picture among stations in a particular market. (For a more comprehensive description of spot sales, see Chapter 12.)

Besides selling spot time for its client stations, the station representative firms also offer a variety of other services: general presentations on behalf of the market, counsel in programing decisions, advice on selecting a network affiliation and news services, analysis of audience research data, and guidance in preparing station promotion materials and in establishing station rates. Reps also run credit checks on advertisers for their stations and assist in the collection of delinquent accounts.

Television Networks

Television consumes more public time and attention than any other business enterprise. Every day tens of millions of Americans turn to their TV sets for entertainment, news, sports, information, and a variety of special interest programs. Over the decades, viewing options have widened as new stations go on the air and cable television expands its penetration. Most viewing, however, is focused on the three major networks. The strength of the networks lies in their almost universal availability to America's viewers and in the basic strength and appeal of their programing. Series programs and news and information have provided the backbone for program schedules that are designed to appeal to various viewing tastes and still attract mass audiences.

Various new technologies, including home video recorders, pay cable, and videodiscs, have resulted in modest erosions in this dominance, but the networks have not yet been seriously threatened with wholesale desertion by their audiences. The three parts of this "Great Triopoly," as it is sometimes called, are arms of extensive conglomerates.

The CBS Television Network is owned and operated by CBS, Inc., a huge corporation with interests in music, publishing, education, technology, crafts, toys, and a variety of other businesses. CBS, Inc.'s, broadcasting interests—which also include CBS News, CBS Radio, CBS Television Stations, and CBS Sports—have been tremendously profitable over the years. These divisions provided the capital that allowed the corporation to branch into other business enterprises.

The NBC Television Network is a part of the National Broadcasting Company, a wholly owned subsidiary of the Radio Corporation of America, which also owns and operates a number of radio and TV stations. This is one of the largest industrial conglomerates in the world, and like the smaller CBS, RCA has branched into many enterprises besides broadcasting. Its business interests are in publishing, education, communications equipment, and various home products and services, and it also has major government space and defense contracts.

The ABC Television Network belongs to a diversified entertainment complex, American Broadcasting-Paramount Theatres, Inc. Although this conglomerate is not as large as CBS or RCA, it is still a big company. The corporation is engaged in both record and motion picture production and distribution, theater management, publishing, amusement centers, retail stores, and commercial real estate. Broadcasting accounts for most of the corporation's revenues and profits, specifically from the TV network, its several radio networks, its owned and operated radio and television stations, ABC News, and ABC Television Spot Sales.

The three television networks engage in a tough, but still very profitable, competition. The high costs of programing, the expense of both land line and satellite program feeds, and payments of affiliates mean that advertising rates are very expensive. When one 30-second commercial in prime time can easily cost $120,000, it becomes obvious that this game is reserved for the big players. The large national advertisers are the only ones who can afford the high costs of network advertising time. And they pay the costs because the TV networks, by delivering huge national audiences, constitute their primary advertising vehicles.

Prime-time shows seem to attract most of the public's interest and certainly most of the television coverage in the nation's press. The three networks, however, find significant audiences and interested advertisers during other time periods. Daytime television delivers a large female audience, children watch the Saturday morning programs, and weekend or evening sports telecasts are particularly attractive to the male viewer. Other programs, either on a regularly scheduled or special basis, offer advertisers a variety of opportunities.

With the attention of the country focused on them, the three networks must function as if in the eye of a hurricane. They must maintain their economic viability and still please the public, the advertisers, and their affiliated stations. (The networks are usually unable to please, but can sometimes placate critics and the large number of interested government officials.)

The networks, of course, would not exist without their affiliates. Thus, they are concerned with building the strongest lineup possible at a price they can afford. Networks compensate affiliates for carrying their programing. The rate varies from market to market but always constitutes a small percentage of a station's gross revenues. It is in the networks' best interests to assist their stations in local audience promotion, and so the dialogue between affiliates and the networks is continuous. These communications can get particularly interesting and sometimes urgent in the areas of station payments, number of network minutes devoted to advertising, the length and frequency of "station breaks," reruns, and controversial programing. Some of the affiliations are strong and happy "marriages"; some are not. Yet, few TV stations would prefer to live alone.

Radio Networks

Tremendous changes in radio networking have occurred since television took over as the public's primary home entertainment medium. The radio networks have survived some difficult times; some have been absorbed into the major radio networks or have gone out of business. Network programing is not essential to a successful radio station operation, but many stations seek an affiliation in order to augment their own local schedules, particularly with network news, sports, and features. The future promises a profitable renaissance for network radio.

The term *network radio,* previously used to refer to ABC, CBS, NBC, and the Mutual Broadcasting System, has been an easy catchword for a variety of services. It now needs redefinition in order to reduce confusion.

1.   Traditional line, or wired, networks, numbering a dozen or so, are programing networks fed to affiliates by AT&T circuits or by satellite transponders. Most of these networks are national or regional in scope and offer advertisers exposure on several hundred radio stations. Wired networks are often organized to carry sports broadcasts or other special events to a regional group of stations.

2.   Syndicated radio programing networks are an outgrowth of the earlier syndicated services sold to stations that wanted a slick, professional, and consistent sound in "beautiful music," rock, country, or some other specialization. When these syndicators began selling time to national advertisers and inserting commercials in their programing service, they in effect became networks. Distribution was handled by the mails and is being converted to satellite delivery. Stations are compensated by the syndicator for the network commercials they carry, but a majority of the commercial positions is reserved for the local station to sell.

3.   Unwired, or rep, networks are really sales networks, put together by station representative firms, and they carry no common programing. The rep firm sells all or most of the stations it represents as a group in one package buy for a national advertiser. It's a flexible, inexpensive way to achieve national radio coverage. The commercials are the only common element aired by these stations.

Network radio's growing importance and profitability can be traced to a number of factors: improved research, which makes it easier to plan, buy, and evaluate advertising programs; the proliferation of networks, which makes it possible for an advertiser to zero in on a target audience; and the rising costs of competitive media.

Programing options for audiences and advertisers increase network radio's attractiveness. News is the staple of the traditional line networks. Fed to affiliates in short newscasts, it is designed to augment the station's own news coverage. Besides news, the networks provide sports, special features, commentary, and occasionally some experiments in other program services — drama and late night mystery shows, for example.

There is also a measure of prestige and excellence that network programing confers to the schedule of a local broadcaster.

For advertisers that use the syndicated radio programing networks, the advantage is a reasonably homogeneous audience listening to a favorite music format. These refined demographics are particularly attractive to advertisers seeking specific targets.

Because of the versatility of spot radio, which means that an advertiser buys on a market-by-market, station-by-station basis, many businesses do not advertise on the radio networks. If their product or service is not available nationally, they are obviously not prospects. They may, however, use the unwired, or rep, networks tailored for them by station representative firms.

The coming decade should see a proliferation of radio networks providing specialized services. The advantage to entrepreneurs is that with 8,000 commercial stations in this country, many of which are unaffiliated, there are plenty of opportunities to build a network without stealing affiliates from competitors. Some will be successful and others will fail, but network radio as a whole should prosper.

Television Stations

The approximately 800 U.S. commercial television stations are scattered across the country in more than 200 markets. The majority are VHF (very high frequency), Channels 2–13, but approximately 250 are UFH (ultra-high frequency), Channels 14–69. Owning a network-affiliated VHF station in a major market is a license to make money. Not all broadcasters are similarly blessed. Stations in small markets, and UHF operators in particular, scramble for advertising revenues and still often end the year in the red.

Federal Communications Commission rules state that no more than seven TV stations may be owned by the same licensee, and no more than five of the seven may be VHF stations. Since there is only one commercial TV station for every ten commercial radio stations, TV ownership patterns reflect greater concentrations of economic power than radio ownership patterns. Each of the networks owns five VHF stations in major markets, as do a number of other major group owners, such as the Westinghouse Broadcasting Company and Metromedia, Inc. The costs of building and equipping a station, or buying one, involve a capital investment in the millions. "Mom and Pop" outfits are simply not feasible in television broadcasting. A half-dozen or more commercial stations and one public station may be assigned to a major market. The commercial stations will prosper from enormous television advertising investments. in the same market, 30 or more radio stations may scramble for a far smaller share of advertising revenue.

New competition for the nation's commercial TV stations lies just around the corner. Thousands of applications are on file at the FCC for new low power TV stations that may cover, for example, a 15-mile radius. In a major urban area, such coverage is significant. Some of the applications are for pay TV services, but many are for advertiser-supported low power TV stations.

Any broadcasting licensee faces numerous responsibilities on a daily basis, and the first obligations must always be to the station's audience and the local community.

Every five years, at license renewal time, the FCC reviews the peformance of TV stations and their proposals for the upcoming five-year period. Rarely are licenses revoked, but they can be challenged by responsible individuals or groups. Safeguarding a valuable license is considered a station manager's primary responsibility.

Although television stations vary greatly in size and number of personnel, most stations share a common organizational pattern. Under the direction of a general manager, the work and staff are ordinarily assigned to one of several departments. (See 2.3.)

The *sales department* must bring in sufficient revenue to keep the entire operation functioning and making a profit. Since both spot and local accounts are vital to the station's financial success, many large stations employ both national and local sales managers. Spot business, traditionally the major profit maker, is now matched or exceeded by local advertising dollars in many markets. With the rising use of television by local retailers, stations will gain greater control of their economic destiny and not have to depend quite so heavily on their station representative firms. Local account executives are assigned a number of clients and spend most of their time servicing present advertisers and soliciting new ones.

The *production department* produces local programs and also tapes and films commercials. Since local advertisers and advertising agencies do not have their own studios, stations rent studios and provide the necessary crew. The fees from this service augment station income, and in some instances, TV production departments have been so successful that management has set up separate production subsidiaries offering both creative and production services.

The *accounting department* processes the paperwork of the station. A primary responsibility is billing the station's advertisers. If a station is an affiliate, detailed reports on programs and commercials must be prepared for the network. Payroll, general accounting, financial statements, and tax forms, among other responsibilities, mean that the accounting department's bookkeeping skills are essential.

The *program department* must keep pace with audience viewing patterns and preferences through the day. The rating reports show the percentage of Homes Using Television (HUT) in various time periods. In the early morning hours, the HUT level may be only 10 percent, but 12 hours later, it may increase to 60 percent. The program director tries to build a schedule that will serve and attract various audiences throughout the day and week. If the station has a network affiliation, then perhaps 12 hours of air time a day may come from network feeds. Selecting, purchasing, and scheduling appropriate nonnetwork programing is critical. Syndicated program series, motion picture packages, and locally originated programs all represent a sizable investment. Mistakes in programing judgment are costly for all stations. The program director of an independent station, however, has much more time to fill, often with less money. Public affairs and community service programs must also be included in a station schedule, although they can be expensive to produce and traditionally attract very small audiences. Nonetheless, such presentations are both necessary and desirable, and their cost is underwritten by the more popular commercial programs.

The *news department* requires a sizable budget and staff to cover the day's events. Television news, despite its many critics, enjoys higher public confidence than news from any other medium, according to various public opinion polls. News at the local

2.3 / Television Station Organization Chart

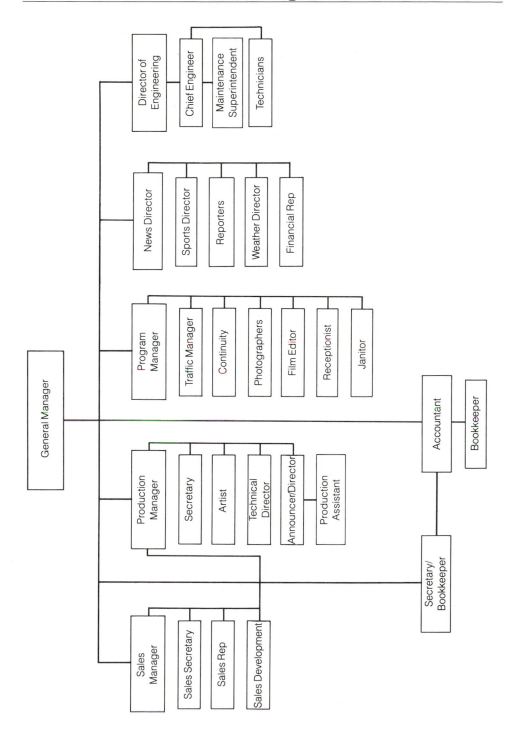

Adapted from *Television Station Organization Charts* with permission of the National Association of Broadcasters, Washington, D.C.

level has constantly improved over the years, and it constitutes the single most important factor in a station's public image. Equipment innovations have made the newsperson more mobile and better able to bring visual interest to reports. Advertisers have learned that TV news sponsorships have many pluses: they offer a "quality" environment, local identification, and audiences that are composed of large numbers of working adults.

The *engineering department* is responsible for keeping the station on the air and for delivering a good signal to its viewers. The chief engineer makes the key decisions about purchasing very expensive equipment. The engineering staff must maintain the equipment, meet the needs of the production department, and carefully abide by the FCC's many engineering regulations.

Radio Stations

No two of the nation's 8,000 commercial radio stations are exactly alike. Since the 1950s, when the major radio networks were forced to adjust to the public's enchantment with television, radio stations have had to rely less on network sources and more on their own ingenuity in developing programing. Most successful stations aim their programing at a particular target audience, which in turn attracts advertisers that are looking for certain demographics. Since radio is a local medium, like a newspaper, it is in an excellent position to establish close ties with the community. Success usually accrues to those stations that are truly local in flavor.

Competition is keen in radio. Signals in any one market may offer the listener a vast menu of programing, as in the Los Angeles area, where more than 80 signals can be heard. Further, the number of stations across the country has increased dramatically. In the decade between 1972 and 1982, FCC figures show, 275 new AM and more than 1,000 new FM stations went on the air.

Licenses must be renewed by the FCC every seven years, a term that was raised from three years by Congress in 1981 after lengthy lobbying by broadcasters. According to FCC rules, the number of stations any one licensee may operate is limited to seven AM and seven FM. There are a number of group owners, such as Westinghouse, Taft Broadcasting Company, the Cox Broadcasting Corporation, the Gannett Broadcasting Group, and others, but many stations are individually owned and managed by the licensees. Many stations in both small and large markets lose money each year, but for many other licensees, radio station ownership has been a lucrative endeavor. The industry as a whole has increased its total billings almost every year.

Specialized program formats designed to appeal to a particular segment of the total audience account for the great diversity in radio. A few stations in some markets have embraced an all-news format and may employ a staff of more than 100. Other stations are totally automated and hire only a sales staff in addition to the programing and engineering personnel who operate the system. Many small stations, though perhaps not very professional in sound, are highly integrated into community life. Most stations rely on some combination of music and news. They are typically headed by a general manager and usually organized into a number of departments. (See 2.4.)

Usually, the *programing department* selects music and on-air personalities and supervises and controls the station's "sound." Competitors are always ready to raid a station's audience, and so professional management is essential for success. It does not matter whether the sound is progressive music, middle-of-the-road (however defined), or all-news and talk; the amateurs are plowed to the bottom. In an attempt to increase both quality and profits, more and more stations are installing automated systems. They rely on sophisticated hardware to coordinate sources of programing, commercials and public service announcements, news, and other program elements.

If a *news department* exists at all, it may consist of one or two newspersons, who primarily "rip and read" from the wire services. Or in a major market, it may employ a sizable staff operating on a dead run to meet the requirements of an all-news programing format. News coverage — including weather, stock market quotations, and items of community interest — is tremendously important to audiences, and it lets a station build a local image of community involvement. Because news constitutes a "foreground" programing element, many advertisers are eager to sponsor newscasts.

The *sales department* of any station, large or small, is the only revenue-producing department. Under the direction of a sales manager (who is also often the general manager) the account executives are responsible both for sales and for servicing local advertisers. FCC figures show that approximately 75 percent of all radio revenues come from local advertisers; thus, the success of any station depends on an efficient and effective sales team.

Besides attracting local advertisers, all stations are eager to secure as much spot business as possible. National and regional advertisers buying radio time on a market-by-market and station-by-station basis almost always contract for spot an-

2.4 / Radio Station Organization Chart

Reprinted from *Radio Station Organization Charts* with permission of the National Association of Broadcasters, Washington, D.C.

nouncements, rather than program sponsorships. The commercials are recorded and sent to the station by the advertiser's ad agency. Stations depend on their representatives to solicit this spot business.

The *engineering department* of a radio station is obviously far less complicated than that of a TV station. Very often a chief engineer handles all the engineering duties. On-air performers sometimes handle engineering chores, and they must be licensed by the FCC in order to operate equipment.

The *business office* may consist of anything from a part-time bookkeeper to a staff of several people. Each month this department prepares the billing to advertisers, which includes an invoice and an affidavit of performance enumerating every commercial aired for that advertiser within the last month. In addition, the business office handles payroll, financial statements, various FCC reports, tax returns, and the like.

Cable Television

Cable television, originally called community antenna television, has emerged in recent years as a full-fledged advertising option. The cable systems, which date from 1948, were originally built to bring clear television reception to households in remote areas or where mountains, tall buildings, and the like interrupted the straight-line transmission of TV. The goal of the cable industry now is to "wire the nation," and this ambition has been given impetus by three circumstances. First, the FCC and the courts have substantially deregulated the cable industry. Second, major conglomerates with significant capital—Warner-Amex; Time, Inc.; Getty Oil, General Electric, and many others—are investing in cable, building new systems, and buying out smaller cable operations. Third, satellites have literally opened the skies to cable operators, and dozens of networks have been launched.

There are thousands of cable operators, ranging from giant MSOs (multisystem operators) such as American Television & Communications, Tele-Communications, Inc., Group W Cable, Storer, and Cox to small, independent systems that serve only a few thousand households. For all these systems the chief source of revenue is the basic monthly fee paid by subscribers. A second source of income is the "pay tiers"—pay cable channels that primarily provide movies, sporting events, and concerts. A third source, and a very modest one, is advertising. A majority of cable systems at present do not accept advertising, and the J. Walter Thompson Company, a major ad agency, estimates that most cable systems derive less than 5 percent of their gross income from advertising. Clearly, cable advertising has no place to go but up.

There are a number of growing pains that must be overcome. For example, many of the older cable systems have only a 12-channel capability, and they are in the process of converting to systems that will handle several dozen channels. Cable operators have to abide by the FCC's "must carry" rules, which mandate that all local broadcast television signals be carried on a cable system. In many markets that leaves few if any channels for pay tiers or advertiser-supported cable programing, at least until the system is expanded. In attracting advertisers, the cable industry presents a patchwork of systems that does not provide the same kind of blanket coverage available through conventional radio or TV. Audience measurement of the multitude of cable channels is difficult, and common sense tells advertisers that audiences are small and fragmented. These and other problems have prompted some advertisers and agencies to adopt a wait-and-see stance, yet many major advertisers have made significant investments in cable. Why?

Cable offers specialized programing that attracts specific audiences; costs are very reasonable, especially when compared with those of conventional television; there is flexibility in the length of commercials; exclusive sponsorships are available that closely tie the advertiser to the program; and cable has proved itself in very successful direct response advertising compaigns.

Advertisers who use cable find opportunities to buy time in national, regional, or local markets. For national coverage, satellite-fed networks distribute programs and commercials to cable systems across the country. For regional use, a number of cable systems can be interconnected through microwave linkups to cover certain areas. At the local level, advertisers may either use a locally programed channel or buy "breaks" in one of the satellite networks. The local cable operator simply inserts commercials at the correct time, using exactly the same procedure as radio and TV station affiliates.

Cable holds great promise, and it is undoubtedly the most attractive vehicle for advertisers in the "menu" of new technologies. The only things certain for the future are change and growth.

Conclusions

Commercials are a common part of American life. They are, in fact, inescapable unless one totally shuns the media. The success of these messages in motivating consumers has resulted in the development of a multi-billion dollar broadcast advertising industry. A complex set of organizations has developed, all designed to deliver a commercial message to a listener or viewer.

At the local level, broadcast advertising can be a fairly simple operation. The account executive of a local radio station, for example, may call on a local retailer directly, and together they will plan a schedule and develop some uncomplicated radio commercials that will be delivered live by a disc jockey.

In regional and national advertising, the process becomes much more complex. Stations are represented by station representatives; advertisers are represented by agencies; the services of research companies may be required; advertising suppliers are hired to produce commercials; and media buying services may be employed. The industry, therefore, tends to develop specialists rather than generalists. Advertising attracts creative, innovative people who enjoy the challenge of working in communications in a very competitive marketplace.

The networks, stations, and cable operators who provide the communications "channel" for the advertising industry also operate in a competitive marketplace. Billions of dollars are spent each year by advertisers who want to reach consumers through the broadcast media. In spite of the huge sums spent, many stations and cable systems lose money or barely break even. The challenge broadcasters face is in building program schedules that will attract audiences in sufficient numbers to constitute a salable commodity. Selling audiences to advertisers, however, must be tempered with broadcasters' public service responsibilities.

In the 1980s, the broadcast advertising industry will grapple with a host of new technologies, which include expanding cable systems, satellite services, videodiscs, low-power TV stations, and AM stereo, to name just a few. The introduction of new players to the game means that the industry will make adjustments. Increased competition for audiences is obvious. Some of these players may be technological successes but economic failures. No one has a crystal ball to predict the future structure of such a fluid industry.

The basic strategy in the broadcast advertising industry will not change, however. It has been, and will continue to be, designed to put advertisers in touch with consumers and to provide the nation's audiences with the best broadcasting service possible.

2.5 / Industry Trade Associations

Besides the various commercial enterprises discussed in this chapter, the industry also relies on its own trade associations. Operating on a nonprofit basis, these professional organizations represent various business entities.

In general their purpose is to help their members build profitable businesses, facilitate communication within the industry, conduct research, issue reports and other publications, and organize professional meetings.

Lobbying constitutes a major activity for many of these organizations. Intense concern over legislation at both the national and local level is often communicated to regulatory and legislative decision-makers. These issues can range from proposed local ordinances banning billboards to proposed major Congressional overhauls of the Federal Communications Commission and the Federal Trade Commission.

American Advertising Federation (AAF)

The American Advertising Federation is the only national association that brings together all the elements of advertising. The AAF's members are nearly 400 companies (advertisers, agencies, service firms, and media companies); approximately 200 local ad clubs and federations, with more than 25,000 members; 23 affiliated associations; and a group of over 100 college chapters.

The federation traces its origins to the 1967 merger of the Advertising Federation of America and the Advertising Association of the West, which were both founded early in the twentieth century. The most important activities of the new federation, which has its headquarters in Washington, D.C., involve legislative liaison with various governmental entities. It responds to proposed legislation at the national level, provides a continuous supply of information to local clubs and federations, and encourages its members to become involved in both national and state matters affecting the advertising industry. The annual convention brings together a wide variety of advertising professionals, leaders from Congress, and representatives of various regulatory agencies.

The AAF is also involved in a variety of education projects designed to improve the skills of its members, provide career information to students, and promote a better understanding of the advertising industry among the public. In recent years, it has played a leading role in establishing a program of advertising self-regulation through the National Advertising Division of the Council of Better Business Bureaus. (See Chapter 18.)

American Association of Advertising Agencies (AAAA)

The American Association of Advertising Agencies is the national organization of the advertising agency business. Formed in 1917, the AAAA serves as the representative of the country's leading advertising agencies. It is composed of 540 agencies, which maintain more than 1,000 offices in 237 U.S. cities and in 123 foreign cities. Close to 80 percent of all the advertising handled by agencies in the United States originates with AAAA members, and these agencies employ over half of the people working in American advertising agencies.

Headquartered in New York, with offices in Washington, D.C., and Beverly Hills, California, the AAAA operates with 35 national committees that cover nearly all the phases of advertising. Their work is directed toward three main objectives.

First, the association aims to foster, strengthen, and improve the advertising agency business. To this end, the AAAA has developed "Agency Service Standards," "Standards of Practice," and copyrighted contracts for space and time. In addition, the organization strives to maintain a continuing dialogue with governmental entities involved in advertising regulation.

Second, the AAAA seeks to advance the cause of advertising as a whole. Activities in this area include efforts to attract high caliber young people into advertising by explaining the business to students and vocational counselors. In recent years, the AAAA has cooperated with a number of other industry groups in organizing the National Advertising Division of the Council of Better Business Bureaus, an innovative approach to self-regulation. The AAAA is also involved in advertising research and in the recruitment of agencies that handle public service campaigns under the auspices of the Advertising Council.

Third, it tries to serve its members by doing things for them that they cannot do for themselves. This includes the exchange of information among members and extensive studies of agency operations and management systems.

Association of National Advertisers (ANA)

The Association of National Advertisers represents the buyers of advertising space, time, and services. Its more than 400 corporate members include the full spectrum of industrial, consumer goods, and service industries that include advertising as a major element in their marketing efforts. ANA members account for about three-fourths of the national advertising dollars spent by American companies.

Several internal groups help national advertisers use the broadcast media most effectively — the ANA Board of Directors, the Media Policy Committee, the Research Policy Committee, the Television Advertising Committee, the Radio Advertising Committee, and other committees.

In general, these committees work toward improving broadcast advertising effectiveness through one or more of the following means: providing representation in dealings with the media, agencies, governmental bodies and other groups that have a bearing on media usage; developing and disseminating information through workshops and research projects; and developing management skills by means of reports, seminars, and other instructional methods. General advertising and marketing information is gathered from members and disseminated to other interested members through the ANA Information Center.

In addition, the ANA plays an important role in negotiating union contracts with broadcast talent. Every three years, it and the AAAA negotiate new contracts with the American Federation of Television and Radio Artists and the Screen Actors Guild that cover the use of talent in radio and television commercials.

National Association of Broadcasters (NAB)

The National Association of Broadcasters, organized in 1922, is the national trade organization of the commercial broadcasting industry. Included in its membership are almost 5,000 radio and television stations, plus all the major broadcasting networks. These members elect from their ranks a board of directors that is composed of both a radio and television board, each with its own chairperson. The NAB is headquartered in Washington, D.C., where a full-time staff administers its affairs in the several areas.

Government Relations represents its members' viewpoint on public issues affecting the broadcasting industry to the federal government, particularly to members of Congress and to the FCC.

Public Relations is the communication outlet for important broadcasting industry news, spotlighting in particular the accomplishments of broadcasters.

Station Relations is devoted to providing NAB members with information on broadcasting matters, engineering and financial management reports, research data, and the like. These services are designed to help members administer day-to-day station operations.

The *Legal Department* advises station members and services the NAB staff, particularly the Government Relations Department.

National Cable Television Association (NCTA)

The National Cable Television Association, established in 1952, serves as the primary trade association for the burgeoning cable industry. Headquartered in Washington, D.C., where the major legislative battles are waged, the NCTA represents 2,300 cable system operators across the country. Some of these are enormous multisystem operators (MSOs), and others are small entrepreneurial companies providing cable service to outlying communities.

As a primary service to members, the NCTA staff lobbies for the cable industry at the FCC, before Congress, and in other pertinent areas of government. At the local level the association provides legal assistance to cable companies. Dealings with local telephone companies over pole attachment rates for stringing cable fall in this category of help. The NCTA publishes a variety of materials covering regulatory news, including FCC rules; the latest developments in technology; satellite services; advertising on cable; and local cable programing.

Various meetings and seminars are organized by the NCTA to keep its members up to date in the fast-changing world of cable TV. The annual convention, held in the spring, is the largest cable trade show in the world. This is a gathering of cable operators, government regulators, equipment manufacturers, TV pro-

gram syndicators, and others involved in various facets of cable.

Membership in the NCTA encompasses four categories: *active* (cable system operators); *associate* (companies that supply equipment or programing to cable systems); *affiliate* (businesses that provide a service to cable, such as law firms, consultants, publications, and educational groups); and *patron* (others with an active interest in cable television).

Radio Advertising Bureau (RAB)

The Radio Advertising Bureau is the national trade association of radio. Devoted to sales development activities across a broad spectrum, the RAB works with national advertisers and agencies to sell the merits of radio as an advertising medium. It calls personally on decision makers and uses research and examples of radio creativity to convince companies to buy radio time.

For its 3,500 member stations, as well as for station representatives and the networks, the RAB provides a variety of sales tools and backup sales development services. Today these services are built around sound; that is, audio cassettes containing sales ideas, examples of outstanding creativity, updated facts on radio, and a variety of sales training information are sent to members.

Every year, the RAB holds a series of meetings designed to contribute to both the sales and management skills of participating members. In other efforts to increase the profits of radio stations, the RAB has assisted retailers in making greater use of radio advertising. Through promotion and research activities, it has encouraged cooperative advertising programs in which national manufacturers share advertising costs with retailers.

With the ANA, the RAB holds a radio workshop each year that focuses on how to use radio as an effective marketing force for advertisers. Case histories are compiled and presented, along with examples of creativity.

Station Representatives Association (SRA)

The Station Representatives Association is the national trade association of radio and television station sales representative organizations. Its members, who account for approximately

$3 billion of spot sales annually, have contractual agreements with broadcasting stations to maintain sales offices in the principal advertising centers throughout the country. Such firms act as a station's exclusive sales force for nonnetwork advertising — that is, national and regional spot advertising.

The SRA cooperates with other industry trade associations — including the AAAA, the NAB, the Television Bureau of Advertising, the RAB, and others — to standardize industry procedures, to insure the vigor of the spot broadcasting industry, and to keep communication channels between the various elements of the industry open.

Much of the work of the SRA is done through standing committees such as Trade Practices, Research, Legal, Financial Management, and Personnel. As an example of what such committees can accomplish, the Trade Practices Committee, working with other groups, has generated a number of standard forms for processing the huge volume of paperwork generated in the broadcast advertising industry. These forms included a standard availability form, a confirmation/contract form, and a number of standardized billing forms. The research committees of the SRA work with various audience research organizations in order to advise them of the kinds of data needed by those who sell broadcast advertising time. The SRA also stays in close contact with the FCC in order to represent the interests of both the station representatives and their clients in any pending regulatory matters.

Television Bureau of Advertising (TvB)

The Television Bureau of Advertising considers itself the sales and marketing arm of the television industry. It was created in 1954 as a service organization to member TV stations, the three networks, station representative firms, and television producers and syndicators. Headquartered in New York, the TvB maintains offices in cities where significant television advertising activity occurs, such as Chicago, Detroit, Los Angeles, Dallas, and Atlanta.

Staff efforts are aimed at continually increasing the investments of television advertisers, and the TvB has established a goal of $21 billion annually in TV advertising by 1985. To achieve that goal, it works directly with advertisers and agencies. General as well as specially tailored presentations have been prepared for specific industries and prospective advertisers. In these presentations, the TvB reports on its research activities in order to document television's ability to solve marketing problems. TvB research projects have included measuring the public's attitudes toward the major media and the advertising they contain and analyzing with computers the efficiency of spot and network TV buys.

At the local level, the TvB conducts an annual Retail TV Commercials Workshop and various sales clinics. To assist local station account executives, it provides many sales aids, including case histories, reels of commercials in particular product or service categories, statistical reports on TV advertising trends, and a variety of special research data.

part two

Campaign Development

chapter three

Marketing Research

You Gotta Know the Territory

Developing intelligent advertising objectives is a complex business. "Blue sky" goals are folly; one way to avoid a disaster is to gather useful and plentiful marketing data. Knowledge is power, and knowledge about the marketplace cannot be attained without proper research. In its broadest terms, marketing research is scientific intelligence gathering, the analysis and evaluation of that data, and application of the data to marketing problems and opportunities. Advertising and marketing plans that are launched in a sea of uncertainty or ignorance run great risks. Although research will not eliminate the risk factor in marketing, adequate information can greatly reduce the chances of misjudging the market. Research information is a tool to be used by both the client and the advertising agency. It is not, however, a substitute for human judgment.

The responsibility for conducting marketing research varies. Many client companies maintain extensive research departments of their own that work in close cooperation with advertising agency personnel. All large agencies have research departments, and their activities are dictated by the nature and needs of the clients. Because of the growing sophistication of research techniques and the need for highly specialized information, research programs conducted wholly by the agency are becoming less and less common. An increasing number of independent research companies have prospered by providing either general market data on a syndicated (or subscription) basis or by conducting tailor-made, proprietary research programs to help clients find answers to specific questions (see Chapter 2). In most instances, major advertising agencies that service national brand manufacturers use three sources of data: (1)

internal research supplied by the client company, (2) general or specific data from independent research companies, and (3) the resource data within the agency.

Smaller agencies, advertisers, and broadcast stations that become involved in helping local clients do not have as much information available as the industry giants. Sometimes, the marketing patterns of smaller advertisers are relatively simple, such as when the distribution chain is direct, sales personnel are centralized, and the competition is pretty well understood. Even in such cases, however, the more data that can be gathered, the better the chances for developing an effective campaign. For example, a local chamber of commerce is often an excellent source of information relating to socioeconomic population patterns, housing trends, traffic patterns, economic forecasts, and the like.

Functions of Marketing Research

Regardless of the type or size of advertiser, marketing research is useful in a number of ways:

1. It reports on a company's status in the market and the status of competitive brands, and it provides a benchmark for future measurements.

2. It helps to identify problems, analyze competitive developments, and formulate a marketing plan.

3. As an outgrowth of that marketing plan, the advertising objectives can be determined realistically and thus will stand a better chance of success.

4. The availability of research data greatly enhances the creative work of the advertising agency. The copywriters and art directors who really do their homework will study the data, appreciate the objectives, and design a creative plan that will help fulfill the advertising objectives.

5. Armed with information regarding the marketing position of its client, the media department of an advertising agency can prepare a media strategy that will effectively and efficiently put the advertiser in touch with prospective customers.

6. Continuing marketing research provides constant feedback on trends, shifts, or unexpected competitive developments. This feedback allows the agency and client to modify the marketing plan and minimize unpleasant surprises.

7. Marketing research, conducted and maintained in a professional manner, greatly aids decision making. It is an important management tool in formulating future plans and in establishing budgets.

Categories of Marketing Research

Because marketing encompasses so many different activities — including product line, pricing, packaging, distribution, sales promotion, and advertising — it follows that marketing research reflects a wide diversity of information. The importance of certain kinds of data will vary with the advertiser and the problems encountered. Marketing researchers, as a result, devote their efforts to gathering and categorizing information most useful in resolving the most pressing problems of a client. Their research falls into a number of categories.

Research on the Market

Market information is concerned with a client's position in the marketplace, particularly as shown by sales analyses. Company records also reveal a wealth of data on product lines, distribution patterns, production levels, quotas missed or met, price changes, and past and present promotions and advertising campaigns. Sales records are usually broken down geographically, seasonally, and along product lines. These records are the most obvious starting point for a marketing research effort.

Syndicated market data can be obtained on a subscription basis from a number of independent research companies. Competitive data are very important and are reported by companies such as the A. C. Nielsen Company and Audits and Surveys, Inc. Both use a system of retail auditing of invoices, inventories, and sales records derived from a sample of retail outlets across the country. Subscribers can select the reports they want by product group. The sales volume of selected brands within each group keeps subscribers up to date on the market share of their brand in comparison with competitors. The movement of food products through warehouses is regularly audited by Selling Areas-Marketing, Inc., (SAMI) and reported to its subscribers. Major

---

3.1/A Horror Story

To illustrate the importance of marketing research, Paul C. Harper, chief executive officer of a major advertising agency, Needham, Harper & Steers, Inc., told the following anecdote to a meeting of business executives:

"A few years ago, a client of ours, a prominent meat packer, marketed a new product through us. The product was a meat pie in a pie-shaped container made entirely of steel. The marketer was in a rush to get the product to market. We tasted it, found it to be delicious, and prepared advertising which was tested and found to be effective. But because of their haste, this marketer did not home-test the product, feeling that the quality of what was in the can would speak for itself.

"Enough of these meat pies were produced to cover the states of Indiana, Kentucky and Tennessee. Trade relations were good and large orders were placed almost immediately. Within weeks they got good retail distribution promptly in the three state area. The

advertising began to run, and consumers bought large quantities.

"Three days after the advertising started to run, the reaction hit. The problem was terminal. There was no implement in the American kitchen capable of opening that all-metal pie-shaped tin. Unopened meat pies were returned by the thousands to the retail stores, and by the thousands of cases to the meat packer's regional headquarters. This headquarters happen to be located on the Ohio River. The regional manager went briefly mad trying to figure out what to do with 75,000 cases of unopenable meat pies. He finally arrived at a solution. The cases now rest at the bottom of the Ohio River.

"Every step in the marketing book had been followed, except the home testing of the package. The advertising worked, but the product didn't."

Reprinted courtesy of The Conference Board.

package goods companies train their sales representatives to be alert to and report changes in competitive activities.

Other market data are available through trade publications, trade organizations, and such publications as the *Annual Survey of Buying Power* published by *Sales Management* magazine. The government, particularly the U.S. Bureau of the Census, publishes a wealth of market data that may be particularly useful to certain kinds of advertisers. A more complete list of research materials is found at the end of this chapter (see 3.2, p. 60).

Product Research

Product information is particularly important in determining product appeals — or shortcomings. Most of it is available within the client company. The research technique may be no more complicated than a reading of company records and a long conversation with engineers or designers. For packaged products, data on the product — on color, packaging, convenience, shelf life, and special features — should be analyzed for relative strengths and weaknesses. (See 3.1.) Certainly, agency personnel assigned to an account use the client's product, if at all possible. Familiarity with a product, and with its competitors, increases knowledge that can be used in formulating plans.

Many advertising agencies have unearthed quite interesting differences in the way the client and the consumer perceive a product. Because the former is so close to the product, it often is easy to misjudge a consumer's rather casual response to that product. In some instances, what the manufacturer believes to be the product's most important quality is overlooked by the consumer, who is buying it for a totally different reason. Discovering those reasons is the purpose of what is popularly called *benefit segmentation* research. Customers are segmented into groups according to *why* they buy a brand — that is, according to their perceptions of the product's several attributes or benefits. Toothpaste, for example, seems to be a simple product designed for only one use. Depending on the brand, however, customers may buy the product because of one of the following benefits: (1) flavor and appearance, (2) whitening qualities, (3) decay prevention, and (4) price.[1]

With a thorough product analysis, particularly one revealing benefit segmentations, it is obviously easier to develop the brand's *positioning* (discussed in Chapter 4), and to provide direction to the creative people.

Consumer Research

Consumer research looks at the attitudes, behavior, and demographic characteristics of consumers. The aim of such research is not to enable the advertising industry to manipulate consumers like so many puppets. Its objective is simply to gather, report, and analyze segmentations, which involves identifying and describing groups of consumers in relation to various criteria. The data may be reported demographically

---

[1]Ronald D. Michman and Donald W. Jugenheimer, eds., *Strategic Advertising Decisions: Selected Readings* (Columbus, Ohio: Grid Publishing, 1976), p. 145.

in terms of age, sex, income, and location. Beyond these simple break-outs, researchers may classify consumers by consumption patterns or by social, cultural, or other factors.

In addition to customer "profiles," consumer research can also reveal differences in perceptions of brand image, levels of brand loyalty, and product consumption. For repeat-purchase products, identifying heavy product users is very important. Almost every household may have coffee in a kitchen cupboard, but if a coffee company discovers that more than half the instant coffee is guzzled by a relatively small proportion of the adult women, that's valuable information. Who are these women? Where do they live? Where do they shop? What brands do they presently buy? The answers to these and other questions, as well as the answer to the key question—What are their media habits?—can greatly increase the effectiveness of marketing and advertising programs.

In some instances, consumer research has led to the development of new products specifically designed to fit the needs of a particular market segment. Convenience foods, new features in automobiles, and new package designs have often been developed because consumer research revealed either a dissatisfaction with an existing product or a real desire for a new product.

Consumer research may entail anything from basic analysis of census data to elaborate survey projects. Some of the most commonly used techniques are summarized below.

Consumer Panels   Studying the purchase patterns of "panels" of consumers is a popular research technique. Some major advertising agencies have established their own continuing consumer panels. Others are maintained by independent research companies; the Market Research Corporation of America and National Family Opinion, Inc., are two well-known examples. Households in these panels are carefully selected, and the sample is designed to serve as a valid indicator of the total marketplace. Diaries are provided, and family members are asked to record their purchases in terms of brands, quantities, prices paid, store where purchased, and so on. The resulting data also include demographic information on the sample, correlated to the buying habits of participants. For their cooperation, families usually receive some modest remuneration or are awarded points toward premiums of their choice.

Focus Groups   In focus groups, a discussion leader prompts anywhere from five to a dozen consumers to engage in a free-wheeling exchange on a given subject. The topic may be no more exciting than laundry detergents, but these consumers, when properly directed, may have plenty to say. To suit an advertiser's need for information, members may come from special groups—women with preschool children, college seniors, businessmen who travel, or tennis players. These sessions, lasting about two hours, are usually recorded and subsequently analyzed. Several advantages are associated with focus groups: the responses are immediate, in contrast to those yielded by some survey research techniques; members of the group can interact and build on others' comments; and the insights revealed in such a session may represent "bargain" information for a client with a big problem and a rather small budget.

Before a client and its advertising agency get carried away with the results of one or more focus group sessions, a few caveats are in order. The group should either be representative of the larger market or be confined to *known* customer profiles. The discussion leader must be trained to pry out the wanted information, solicit the participation of everyone, and keep the lid on the one or two who like to dominate the discussion.

Research directors often agree that focus groups have been misused in marketing research. Such groups are useful for generating ideas, discussing product attributes or liabilities, revealing experiences with a product, and discovering how well an intended message is understood. "Focus groups are very useful for initial, exploratory fishing expeditions," said one research director. They should *not*, however, be used to evaluate advertisements. That is a job for professionals, not laymen.

Audience Analysis   Consumers are available only as members of an audience. The audience can be found in newspapers, magazines, outdoor media, direct mail, a variety of specialized media, and, of course, the broadcast media. Syndicated information analyzing these audiences is available from several independent research companies. For use in long-range planning, these reports may include a wealth of information: consumer demographics, product purchases in a variety of categories, seasonal buying patterns, time spent with various media, correlations between media habits and buying behavior, and even psychological profiles of various types of consumers. Some of the major companies syndicating these data are Yankelovich, Skelly & White; Simmons Market Research Bureau, Inc.; and SRI International's Values & Lifestyles Program (VALS).

Basic broadcast audience measurement, popularly known as "the ratings," is dominated by two industry giants, Arbitron Ratings and the A. C. Nielsen Company. Radio audience data from Arbitron are the most widely used, although a number of competitors have made some inroads. Arbitron uses individual diaries, and respondents are asked to keep track of their radio listening for a one-week period.

TV audiences are measured by both Arbitron and Nielsen, relying on one-week diaries sent to cooperating households. In certain markets, electronic meters are attached to television sets to measure at what time the set is switched on, the channel to which it is tuned, and at what time it is turned off.

Because audience estimates are so important in both programing and advertising decisions, Chapter 10 explores the methods used and data reported by these companies in much greater depth.

Motivational Research   The importance of motivational research to advertising was demonstrated in the 1950s by Dr. Ernest Dichter and his Institute for Motivational Research. The research, an outgrowth of clinical psychology, sought to explore people's deepest attitudes and beliefs regarding a product, its function, and its satisfactions. The new techniques caught the fancy of a number of researchers, because people responding to straightforward questions often do not tell the whole truth. Their reasons include possible embarrassment, a desire to increase their own status, or motives they may not even realize themselves. (The feedback from such respondents can be very misleading!) Motivational research is an attempt to circumvent these problems and dig out true attitudes and beliefs. Although a number of methods can be used, two are most common.[2] *Projective techniques* ask a respondent to provide word associations, complete a number of sentences, or respond to various visual materials. *Extended interviews* with individuals or small groups deal in a rather unstructured manner with feelings and experiences. These far-ranging conversations may last several hours and are usually recorded for later analysis.

Motivational research is somewhat out of fashion now, but it has not disappeared. It is a valid system for gathering consumer information, even though it is rather time-consuming and expensive.

Survey Research   Survey analyses of consumer attitudes can be very useful, but ideally they should be considered along with consumer behavior. The two are not the same. What people actually do in the marketplace is often quite different from what they say they will do. When interviewed, consumers may say that they do not like a product's packaging and therefore are not inclined to buy it. The truth may be that they consider the price too high but are reluctant to admit it. Or people may try a complimentary sample of a new product, express great interest and satisfaction, but never buy or use it again. Why? Unless the researchers pry out the real reasons, they may never know.

How can this information be obtained? Three methods are commonly used—the *personal interview, the mail survey, and the telephone survey*. The most flexible of the three is the personal interview, because questions can be more extensive. There is latitude for personal observations, and cooperation rates can be excellent. The disadvantage is obviously the relatively high cost.

A mail survey can either be sent to a wide cross section of respondents or focused on a narrow target audience. Interviewer bias is eliminated, and respondents can answer anonymously, allowing the use of questions that might pose a problem in a personal interview or telephone survey. The cost per respondent is fairly low, but so is the response rate. Some bias is at work when a low percentage of those surveyed bothers to complete the questionnaire. Are those respondents representative of the entire sample? Who knows?

A telephone survey is regarded as a fast and fairly economical way of obtaining a broad range of consumer information. In a given period of time, one interviewer can reach more people on the telephone than in personal interviews. Directories offer excellent opportunities either to draw a random sample or to focus on a special group listed in the Yellow Pages, such as auto dealers, chiropractors, or plumbers. Unlisted or new numbers cannot be included in the sample, and telephone surveys are not conducive to lengthy questioning. During the hours when interviewers phone (daytime and early evening), many people are simply not available.

Even with trained interviewers or a carefully constructed mail survey, the answers will only be as good as the questions. Questionnaires should be prepared by a professional researcher, who can ask the right questions, assure their clarity, eliminate ambiguities, and avoid any possibility of antagonizing or prejudicing the respondents. (Preliminary research with focus groups is often helpful in designing questions for

─────────────────────────────

[2]Kenneth E. Runyon, *Advertising and the Practice of Marketing* (Columbus, Ohio: Merrill, 1979), p. 115.

survey research.) In most cases, advertising agencies and clients contract for survey research with independent research companies. The questionnaire is developed by the agency and client, but the actual survey work is "farmed out."

Survey research, beyond selecting a method and carefully constructing the questionnaire, must provide for a representative sample of adequate size, acceptable margins of error, and professional analysis of survey results.

Concept Testing

Translating consumer research data into the actual development of advertisements can present problems. For example, not everyone is a "best" prospect for a given product, even though he or she may buy and use it. Consumer research may suggest that concentrating on heavy users is the best plan. Or it may suggest that since the heavy users have great brand allegiance, the better prospects for an advertising campaign are light users who may be induced to use a product more. Or perhaps the best prospects are people who know about a product but haven't tried it. A different approach in the advertising concept would be necessary for each group of prospects. To further complicate matters, there may be great differences within any group in consumer attitudes, brand experiences, and what consumers *expect* from a product. Therefore, it is essential that the creative team clearly understand the specific objectives of a given campaign. A product is always sold on the basis of *benefits*, and there may be many. Selecting the right benefit, or benefits, to advertise in the best way to the "right" group is an unsure business at best. Concept testing can sometimes reduce the numerous options and put the client and agency on the right track.

Of all the various kinds of research discussed in this chapter, concept testing is undoubtedly the most controversial. Creative people, especially, usually hold strong opinions (either pro or con) about the accuracy and usefulness of this research. There are many different ways to test. One of the most interesting (and also controversial) is the use of laboratory experiments in *autonomic* responses. With the assistance of some exotic machinery, the involuntary responses of subjects to commercials, print ads, or other kinds of stimuli are measured.

1. *Psychogalvanometer* measures emotional response with an electronic device that detects perspiration. By means of lightweight electrodes attached to the fingers, a physiological reaction is measured by recording the resistance of the skin to an unfelt electrical current. As the subject views an advertisement, various degrees of intensity are displayed on a physiograph in the form of peaks and valleys. These reactions may be correlated to a second-by-second analysis of a commercial.

2. *Pupillometer* measures the dilation of the pupil as a person views an ad. The conclusions of this research suggest that the more interested the subject is in the message presented, the greater the dilation factor. Conversely, the pupil will constrict when the person views disagreeable or unappealing stimuli.

3. *Eye camera* traces the movement of the eye as the subject views a TV or print advertisement. The camera can trace what portions of the ad attract attention and the length of time the person focuses on a particular portion of visual information.

4.   *Voice pitch analysis* uses a recording of the voice of a person responding to questions about an advertisement. A computer can analyze changes in voice pitch linked to the emotional response of the subject. True emotional commitment is separated from those remarks considered to be "lip service" or to reflect confusion.

5.   *Brain wave measurement* monitors a subject through small electrodes attached to the scalp. Responses on the brain's left side (reflecting the logical aspect of thought) and right side (the emotional aspect) are tracked on a computer as the person views an ad. The data are useful in determining what parts of the ad register best and what the effects of repeated exposure are. These laboratory experiments have been used to help an advertiser select the most effective spokesperson for an upcoming campaign.

What do advertising professionals think of these laboratory experiments? The responses vary from the enthusiastic to the skeptical. The objectivity of the data appeals to some people, and also the revelation of information that cannot be obtained by more conventional methods. Some researchers believe that these methods are most useful in testing advertising for products purchased on an emotional level — cosmetics, high-fashion clothing, perfume, and the like. Many respondents have difficulty verbalizing their buying motives in these categories.

The cost of these laboratory experiments confines their use to the fairly affluent advertiser, but the primary criticism is not focused on the cost or the data but on what the data *mean*. One agency research director said, "No one has nailed down what the results mean." And another said, simply, "I don't know what they're telling me." They are disturbed that the samples are small, the research is conducted in a very artificial setting, and the equipment tends to be obtrusive.

Less exotic methods expose subjects to advertising and then ask them to articulate their response or complete a questionnaire. The results are designed to measure such factors as attention and obtrusiveness, recall, persuasion, the clarity of the communication, the relevance to the consumer, and the intent to buy.

A variety of methods is used to obtain this information. In print advertising, it is a relatively simple matter to send an interviewer carrying a magazine or two on a door-to-door canvass. It would be difficult to use the same technique in the broadcast media, unless the interviewer carried a tape recorder to play commercials for consumers and then recorded their responses. Most audience researchers use other methods.

Two common techniques for testing commercials are telephone interviewing and theater, or group, testing. The former technique measures recall of TV commercials by telephoning a sample of homes 24 hours after broadcast. Theater testing of both programs and commercials has been used for many years. The results must be interpreted with the knowledge that audience members are captive, for all intents and purposes, and their attention is therefore highly focused.

Another service offers its subscribers both the benefits of information derived from a consumer panel and the ability to test commercials on a cable television system. Two panels of households cooperate by keeping purchase diaries of food, drugs, and similar items. The advertiser can carefully follow these records and, at the same time, test commercials by inserting one of them in a cable system directed to one panel and providing another to the second panel.

These three methods — telephone recall, theater testing, and commercial testing on cable systems — are explored in depth in Chapter 9.

Test Marketing

Test marketing involves an experimental method in which products and advertising are tested in selected markets. A long research and development process precedes the test, especially when the subject of the research is a new product. A large manufacturer turning out a multiplicity of products will be constantly researching new product ideas for feasibility and marketability. Only a fraction of these ideas will ever reach the prototype stage, and of those that are advanced to a test marketing situation, the fatality rate is terrific.

Test marketing is a complex business, but most of this research is directed toward measuring four key consumer responses: awareness of the product, attitudes toward the product, purchase, and repeat purchase. Understanding these aspects of consumer behavior is vital for devising successful marketing strategies. For large corporations contemplating marketing new products on a national basis, test marketing is an obvious way to reduce the risks. It can make it possible to identify a bust in a test market stage or to modify a product or plans so that a failure can be turned into a success.

For a new product, one or more markets may be selected for testing. A number of urban areas are regularly used for test marketing — Charlotte, N.C.; Columbus, Ohio; Denver, Colo.; Fort Wayne, Ind.; Houston, Tex.; Little Rock, Ark.; Milwaukee, Wis.;

"Before deciding to change it, bear in mind that this box has done a great job for over ten years."

Nashville, Tenn.; Phoenix, Ariz.; Salt Lake City, Utah; Seattle, Wash.; Tulsa, Okla.; and others. A McCann-Erickson executive has enumerated the reasons for using these markets:[3]

• *Populations are large enough to give reliable, projectable indications.*

• *They are small enough to cover with media at a comparatively reasonable cost. TV buying is especially efficient.*

• *The markets are fairly isolated from a media standpoint. What goes on in other areas is not frequently seen or heard, and thus does not intrude. Test-market advertising does not spill over into other areas.*

• *The population is representative of the rest of the country in demographic terms.*

• *The trade is supplied within the market. In other words, warehouses in other areas do not control distribution, so product shipping figures are not confused.*

In test marketing, it takes a tremendous amount of work to set up distribution, locally promote and advertise the product, and then measure results. Store audits are conducted to keep track of sales. A consumer panel may be enlisted to record household purchases. Interviews and focus groups may be used to solicit consumer responses to the new product. Repeat purchase patterns are studied, and consumer profiles are carefully charted to determine the product's greatest market potential. Test marketing is a costly and time-consuming proposition, however, the results of the research are worth the investment to an advertiser considering spending millions to launch a new product in the national marketplace.

Test marketing for an established product (with new features or packaging, for instance) sometimes involves the use of two matched markets. They may be cities or metropolitan areas, or even states or regions, that are extremely similar in terms of economic, social, and cultural characteristics. One of the areas serves as a control, and the new marketing campaign is launched in the other. Different advertising programs may be conducted in each market and their results compared. Advertising weights can be varied, different media used, and various concepts incorporated into the campaign. The efficiency and effectiveness of new marketing schemes are then measured and evaluated in an effort to find an optimum that can be applied in national campaigns.

Postcampaign Evaluation

Both the client and the advertising agency will profit from a thorough analysis of a marketing program and learn as much, or more, from the failures as from the successes. Was the marketing plan realistic? Did sales reach the hoped-for levels? What role did the advertising program play in this success? Should advertising levels and the budget be increased in the next year? How much did other factors, such as promotions or premiums, contribute to total sales? What was the level of competitive activity during this campaign? What went right? What went wrong? How can we improve in the future?

---

[3]J. Douglas Johnson, *Advertising Today* (Chicago: Science Research Associates, 1978), p. 276.

Answers to many of these questions can be obtained from company and agency records kept throughout the campaign. Evaluating the data, along with the objective judgments of the people most deeply involved in the campaign's formulation, can be invaluable in preparing future marketing and advertising plans.

What Research Can and Cannot Do

1.   Research is a management tool, not a decision maker. It provides new insights and answers questions. Interpretations of research can serve as guides in formulating plans, but research cannot and should not dictate the marketing plan.

2.   The quality of the data is a direct outgrowth of the integrity of the research. Surveys that have unclear objectives, inadequate samples, or poorly designed questionnaires or that attempt to cover too much ground can render the results of a major effort useless.

3.   The value of research is increased if the most appropriate sampling method is selected and carefully drawn up. However, unless the field staff is thoroughly trained and supervised, the care expended will be wasted.

4.   Marketing plans are made for the future. Research data are history. The marketplace may change drastically or not at all, but it is crucial to keep the possibility in mind.

5.   It is not necessary to reinvent the wheel every time a research project is undertaken. A continuing long-range research program, carefully planned and executed, can build an invaluable body of data over the years. Such a sophisticated program requires management's commitment to budget for it, as well as the expertise of true professionals to conduct the research.

6.   Research data do not roll out of a computer to be carved in stone. Some degree of error is inevitable. The conclusions of a major pilot study should not be resurrected repeatedly as the answer to all questions.

7.   Research data should be realistically interpreted. They should not be stretched beyond the project's intended scope. Inferences can and should be drawn, because marketing research is usually unable to make predictions. These inferences, however, should be confined to situations similar to the one studied. Wholesale translations of the results of one project, applied to another set of problems, are rarely accurate.

8.   The results of survey research designed to record consumer attitudes should never be used as indicators of consumer behavior. The two are not the same.

9.   Consumer panels, subjects in a laboratory setting, or people interviewed during the course of a survey can provide valuable data. They are not, however, engaging in normal behavior. The degree of error of such marketing research methods is impossible to measure. Scientists have devised a number of ways to mitigate the problems posed by unnatural settings, but they will always be present to some extent.

10.   Marketing research does not always recognize the impact of repetition in advertising. Measurements may be made on the basis of a test market situation or of

consumers who respond to a one-time exposure. In this latter instance, what consumers may consider an exaggerated product claim at first may eventually become acceptable after repeated exposure. This credence, built up over a period of time, tends to substantiate the theory that if consumers are told something often enough, they will eventually come to believe it.

Conclusions

The marketing system of the United States is the envy of the modern world. Americans are accustomed to being able to find what they want when they want it, and in great abundance. The movement of goods and services to meet the demand is an amazing enterprise, but it did not just grow like Topsy. Too much capital has been invested to

3.2 / Research Materials

The following publications are useful in conducting marketing research.

• **Library references:** *Ayer Directory of Publications; Bradford's Directory of Marketing Research Agencies and Management Consultants in the United States and the World; Broadcasting Yearbook; Business Information Sources; Business Periodicals Index; Concise Guide to International Markets; The Conference Board; Dun and Bradstreet Directories; Editor & Publisher Market Guide; Encyclopedia of Associations; Encyclopedia of Business Information Sources; Funk & Scott Index of Corporations and Industries; Harfax Directory of Industry Data Sources; The Marketing Information Guide; The Annotated Bibliography; Moody's Services; Predicasts F and S Index United States; Readers' Guide to Periodical Literature; Sales Management Survey of Buying Power; Simmons Market and Format Research; SRI International Values and Lifestyles program; Standard and Poor's Services; Standard Directory of Advertisers; Standard Directory of Advertising Agencies; The Standard Periodical Directory; Standard Rate and Data Service; Statistical Reference Index and Abstracts; Supermarket Institute Index; Television Factbook; Topicator, Classified Article Guide to the Advertising/Communications/Marketing Periodical Press; Trade Names Directory; Ulrich's International Periodicals Directory; Wall Street Journal Index*

• **Advertising and marketing periodicals:** *Advertising Age, Adweek, Broadcasting, Direct Marketing, Editor & Publisher, Journal of Advertising, Journal of Advertising Research, Journal of Consumer Affairs, Journal of Marketing, Journal of Marketing Research, Madison Avenue, Marketing & Media Decisions, Promotion, Sales Management, Television/Radio Age, Variety*

• **Materials and publications of the following organizations:** *Advertising Research Foundation, American Business Press, American Association of Advertising Agencies, American Marketing Association, Association of National Advertisers, Cabletelevision Advertising Bureau, International Advertising Association, Magazine Publishers Association, Marketing Research Association, Outdoor Advertising Association of America, Radio Advertising Bureau, Television Bureau of Advertising*

• **Government publications, mostly available through the U. S. Superintendent of Documents:** *materials from the U.S. Department of Agriculture, U.S. Department of Commerce (Survey of Current Business), Federal Trade Commission, U.S. Bureau of the Census (Statistical Abstract of the United States), U.S. Bureau of Labor Statistics, Federal Reserve Board Bulletin*

• **Trade publications related to marketing specific products or services**

leave marketing systems to chance. Risks are always present, but they can be reduced by gathering and interpreting marketing research information.

No one is scrutinized more intensely than the American consumer. Marketing research now analyzes geographic, consumption, demographic, and psychographic distribution patterns. Consumers are also studied in terms of their response to both products and advertising and as members of audiences of various media.

Marketing research is a complicated business, and millions of dollars are spent each year to obtain useful data. Marketing research has multiplied in both quantity and quality over the years because of the need for the information and because of constantly improving data-gathering techniques. The result has helped marketers to minimize risks. It has also benefited consumers, since efficient marketing systems are the ones that provide the goods and services they need.

chapter four

Objectives, Strategies, and Positioning

Just Tell Me What You Want

If we could first know where we are and whither we are tending, we could better judge what to do and how to do it.

President Lincoln's observation regarding nineteenth-century politics can be applied just as appropriately to twentieth-century marketing problems. The changing complexion of the marketplace, the unpredictability of the consumer, the costs of advertising, and the high risks of the business world mean that advertising programs today must be put together with reasoned strategy and great care. Before an effective program can be developed, specific objectives for it must be defined. The question is: Exactly what is to be accomplished?

Understanding the overall function of advertising helps us to answer that question. The purpose of advertising is *persuasion*. In order to persuade, advertising is usually directed to one or more of the following five broad aims: to *create awareness*, to *promote understanding*, to *shape attitudes*, to *enhance recall*, and to *motivate action*.

Developing reasonable objectives for an advertising program must always be related to *communication functions*. Ask anyone what he or she thinks advertising is supposed to do, and in most cases the answer will be to "increase sales." Yet increasing sales *is not* an advertising objective, because it is not a communication function! Certainly, almost all advertising programs contribute to making a sale, but the relationship between the two is seldom a direct one. There are too many other factors at work in the marketplace.

The tendency to expect advertising to accomplish goals that are really beyond the scope of the communications process is a basic problem in defining objectives. For example, increasing sales 10 percent, expanding distribution 15 percent, or achieving a 20 percent market share is *not* a legitimate advertising objective. Advertising can contribute to each, but these goals are marketing objectives, and advertising is only one part of marketing. A total marketing plan analyzes all the variables — marketing history, data on the product or service, pricing, packaging, volume, seasonality, distribution, sales channels, target audiences, consumer attitudes, competition, forecasts, and so on.

A long-term marketing plan is helpful for a thoughtful advertiser, but in today's volatile marketplace, plans are constantly being reviewed and updated in response to changing conditions. Advertising objectives, an outgrowth of the marketing plan, likewise must be reviewed and updated, sometimes on short notice.

Legitimate advertising objectives are, or should be, specific. They are "targeted" toward a specific outcome and normally include the following four essential parts:

1. a specific communications job

2. a target audience

3. an expected result

4. a given period of time

For example, a detergent manufacturer might want (1) to communicate information about a product improvement (2) to users of a competitive brand (3) so that 50 percent of this audience will know about the change in the product (4) within the next three months.

Defining objectives is not simply an academic exercise; it is a practical necessity. Advertising is communication of ideas, and as such, it is intangible. Clearly defined goals are extremely important when dealing with intangibles, especially since people work better when they have a clear idea of where they're going. Since a great many people may be involved in all of the aspects of an advertising campaign, a common direction is essential. Objectives not only minimize wasted time and effort but also make it possible to measure results.

Criteria for Defining Objectives

Although there are no pat formulas for how to define advertising objectives to cover all needs, some general principles can be used as guidelines:

1. Objectives should be expressed as clear, written statements of the *communications* part of the marketing job.

2. Expected results should be realistic and within the capabilities of advertising.

3. It must be possible to translate goals into a plan of action; they must not be resounding, but empty, ideals.

4. Written objectives should be agreed to and understood by all the people involved in creating and approving the advertising.

5.   Advertising objectives should be separate from, but related to, marketing objectives.

6.   Objectives must be based on a thorough understanding of the market, the product, and the consumer.

7.   Goals should be measurable, and the techniques used to measure results should be established at the outset of any advertising program.

Establishing Advertising Objectives

An advertising agency (or the advertising department in a business) serves as the caretaker of the advertising budget. The sum may be great or modest, but before a penny is spent, a great deal of information must be conscientiously gathered and analyzed. One of the most important functions an agency can fulfill is to provide the client company with an objective picture of its products or services in terms of the marketplace. For an agency with a new account, or for personnel newly assigned to an account, it means beginning at the beginning.

Learning as much about a client as possible is a first step in defining advertising objectives. What is the product? What are its benefits? How is it made? How many models? What colors? What special features? How is it distributed? Where? When is it bought? What times of the year? What days of the week? Who does the buying? How frequently? Why do they buy it? What brands are competitive? What are their special features? The questions could fill a dozen pages, but these few serve as examples of what the agency account team must know if it expects to participate intelligently in designing a client's advertising program. The answers to many of these questions are often relatively easy to come by, but not always. It is the function of marketing research, discussed in the last chapter, to seek out some of these answers. Then, the researchers can provide the latest figures that give both the client and agency an up-to-date perspective. The information that advertising planners need usually falls into two basic categories—*product* (or service) analysis and *consumer* analysis.

Product Analysis

One of the first considerations when formulating intelligent advertising objectives is the present status of the product in the market. The classic development of a national brand product might be described as consisting of four stages: *introduction, growth, maturity,* and *decline* (which may or may not be avoidable).

If the product is to be *introduced* to the market, or is still in the introductory stage, the advertising objectives may be relatively clear-cut. In order to introduce the product to prospective consumers, the "news" function of advertising will be exploited to its fullest. Television, particularly, has proved to be extremely valuable in this respect. An introductory campaign may have a number of secondary objectives as well. For example, it may also be designed to help develop new distribution channels or to arouse the enthusiasm of dealers.

Thousands of new products are introduced each year, and the failure rate is a marketing manager's nightmare. Most products that do secure a foothold in the market, moreover, are unlikely to be an overnight success. A manufacturer may spend millions on research and development, invest more in product promotion and distribution, inaugurate a major advertising campaign, and find that it will still take years before the brand begins to return a profit. Some products never "turn the corner" and are eventually dropped. (Edsel automobiles and Red Kettle Soups are two well-known examples of extravagant marketing disasters. Less familiar failures are legion.) The smashing successes—excellent products introduced at the right time and in the right way—were usually accompanied by a brilliant advertising campaign.

If a product is in the *growth* stage of its development, the advertising objectives may simply be introducing it to new areas and contributing to a marketing plan designed to enlarge the market share. Print ads and broadcast commercials may call attention to a "cents-off" coupon packed in the product, demonstrate the product in use, or announce a special sale. The growth stage may also expand the product to new consumer groups. Typewriters had been an office necessity for generations before the industry expanded its market to make them common in the home and to promote them as gifts to students. Another example of a campaign designed to broaden usage was developed for V-8 Cocktail Vegetable Juice. "Wow, I could have had a V-8" obviously encourages consumption and suggests it as a substitute for other drink products at times other than breakfast.

In the product's *maturity* stage, a wide variety of advertising objectives may be appropriate. The goal may simply be to remind consumers that the product does indeed exist! Other objectives may include prompting the public to use the product, perhaps as a replacement for other products; suggesting new uses; seeking new users; attempting to neutralize a negative impression revealed from consumer research; or seeking to reinforce a favorable attitude among present users. Special problems are sometimes encountered in marketing a mature product. The baby food market, for example, changes continuously. The buyers are mothers and the consumers are obviously babies, and in a short time they both move out of this market. Thus, the advertising function for a baby food is constantly to reach new mothers and familiarize them with an established product.

A product in the *declining* stage is guaranteed to bring gray hairs to both the brand manager and the agency; it presents special problems and challenges. Obviously, the first question to ask about a product decline is "why?" Competition, unfortunately, never stands still, and many product failures can be attributed to a competitor introducing a bigger and better mousetrap or simply outspending a client in a major advertising blitz. Digital watches and clocks have greatly reduced the demand for the traditional type, and food processors have usurped the function of several other common kitchen appliances.

The decline and ultimate demise of a product can be the result of many marketing factors. Changing life-styles affect consumers' preferences. In recent years, for example, sales of both coffee and candy have been in steady decline, and for some companies it may be futile to swim against the stream. Sometimes, an advertising program provides a handy scapegoat for a product's decline. Mediocre advertising, however, merely accelerates a downward trend. To arrest such a trend is a tremendous challenge, and good advertising can help. A brief case study on just such a problem is summarized in 4.1.

Any product associated with a fad, and particularly certain products oriented to teenagers, may swing through a life cycle in a matter of months or a couple of years. Soft drink bottlers that cater to youngsters must constantly update their advertising programs to keep their share in this important youth market. Some product declines may be traced to the inconvenience of the product or its packaging. The frozen foods section of a supermarket is evidence of efforts to offset the inconvenience of certain food preparations. A working wife may be very willing to spend a little more to buy a prepared frozen dish; she may no longer buy brands that require elaborate preparation. The marketing problems of a product in decline must be faced realistically by both the agency and the client. "New, Improved" package labels in advertising campaigns may reflect a product in deep trouble. The product change may be minor, or it may reflect a total overhaul. In any event, because of the number of factors involved, the managers of a declining product should not expect advertising to accomplish marketing miracles.

4.1/A Glut on the Market

The California Milk Advisory Board and its advertising agency, McCann-Erickson, San Francisco, faced a marketing dilemma. California cows were outdoing themselves. The state's dairy farmers were getting more milk per cow and doing so on fewer farm acres. Production was up—way up—and consumption was down. Marketing research, to no one's surprise, showed that children and teenagers are the primary milk guzzlers. At about age 20, however, consumption drops off dramatically. Apparently, attention is attracted to other, possibly more interesting, beverages. What to do?

An advertising strategy was devised and directed to teenagers and young adults, with a secondary target audience of adults 25 to 49 years of age. Celebrities are considered surefire attention getters, so the agency lined up a group of product endorsers, including Jimmy Walker, Hacksaw Reynolds, Heather Locklear, Matt Dillon, Bernadette Peters, and Valerie Perrine.

The client wanted young celebrities who were liked and admired and could serve as role models to the target audience. (Expensive superstars would have fit the strategy also, but they didn't fit the budget.) An additional criterion was that consumers "would be a little surprised" that these celebrities actually drank milk. The campaign relied on television

Jimmy Walker

Courtesy of the California Milk Advisory Board

primarily, and TV was considered an important part of a total marketing plan devised to raise consumers' awareness of and consumption of milk.

Consumer Analysis

Who buys the product? When, where, how, and why? If research can answer these fundamental questions, the resulting consumer data will be invaluable in formulating specific advertising objectives. Consumer analyses usually cover four areas: (1) geographic distribution, (2) consumption distribution, (3) demographic distribution, and (4) psychographic distribution.

Geographic Distribution   Where do the client's customers live? Few products enjoy a pattern of consumer distribution that spreads like frosting on a cake. The urban, suburban, and rural distribution of the consumers is critical, and agencies must take account of the patterns in their media planning. There must be sufficient customers, or prospective customers, in a given area to make an advertising program worth the expense. The media are well aware of this and also of the advertiser's need to use spot campaigns. Radio, TV, newspapers, and outdoor signs are all media that can be localized. Even magazines offer advertisers regional editions, and sometimes specific market editions. Such media options enable the advertisers to invest their dollars where they anticipate the most promising return.

Consumption Distribution   Just as customers for a given product are not evenly distributed geographically, neither are their consumption patterns. In fact, research on most products and services shows that a relatively few heavy users account for the greatest portion of the consumption. Examples include airline travel for business, car rentals, hair coloring, expensive liquors, liquid dietary products, and nonprescription medications. In some cases it's an "either-you-do-or-you-don't" proposition. Pet owners buy pet food. Other people don't.

It may be that 20 percent of a client's customers consume 80 percent of the brand. Naturally, the advertiser wants to identify and seek out that all-important 20 percent. This knowledge is useful not only in subsequent media planning but also in the development of a creative strategy. "Schaefer's is the one beer to have when you're having more than one." This famous jingle was obviously directed to prodigious beer drinkers. In addition, the advertiser wants to discover how strong the brand loyalties are in these consumption patterns. Some product categories, such as toothpaste, enjoy high brand loyalty. In other categories, consumers constantly switch brands, perceiving little difference between them. They buy the best bargain. An advertiser's dream would be a successful product that enjoyed both high brand loyalty and heavy usage by a clearly defined group of consumers.

Demographic Distribution   Who are the customers and potential customers? Age, sex, education, income, family status, and ethnic grouping are broken out in many demographic analyses. These are the most easily identifiable consumer characteristics that assist the advertiser in further refining advertising objectives. In some instances, demographic profiles will be rather narrow. (Customers for chewing tobacco and sable coats are two extreme examples.)

Demographics are not carved in stone but are, rather, in a state of flux. Because of their effect on consumer behavior, it is incumbent on the advertising industry ￫ anticipate these changes.

For example, the nation's distribution of population by age groups is changing rapidly. Because of a declining birth rate, the youth market has been shrinking, and the market of seniors is expanding because of extended life expectancy. The median age in the United States is expected to move from 30 in 1980 to 35.5 in 1990.[1] That's a significant change in one decade. Marketers are paying more attention to the "maturity market." Myths that the aged are shut-in mobile home park residents on a meager income who buy only life's necessities are being dispelled. Researchers have discovered that the nation's seniors don't plan to take it with them but spend it now; they are an excellent market for everything from college courses to hot tubs.

Another important demographic change is the entering of millions of women into the work force. The greater independence, income, and opportunities of women create a ripple effect in the marketplace. On the one hand, though women now have more money to spend, they increasingly turn over some shopping responsibilities to other family members. Supermarkets, which have historically advertised to women, are beginning to recognize that their aisles are crowded with men who account for a significant portion of their total business. On the other hand, banks, insurance companies, airlines, and other businesses that have primarily targeted men are modifying their ad campaigns to attract women.

Education levels and occupational profiles are also in constant flux, but the greatest changes have occurred in family status and in various ethnic groups. With the divorce rate up and with increasing acceptance of an unmarried life-style, the number of households headed by a single adult is at a record high and still growing. The traditional family of working Dad, housewife Mom, and two children is very much a minority segment of the total population. Working single adults, with or without children at home, have become a distinct marketing target for a variety of convenience products. Many food companies, for example, now market single servings. Nor has the growing size of ethnic markets in proportion to the total population escaped the notice of advertisers who know that their products are popular in the black or Hispanic market.

All these changes in demographics require constant monitoring so that advertising campaigns can anticipate evolving situations. This awareness should be most visible in creative approaches — fewer stereotypes, hopefully, and a more realistic mix of people portrayed in commonplace situations. Additionally, there are and will be significant changes in the media as they adjust to changing demographics. Daytime television is no longer the exclusive province of the homemaker, and business and financial magazines and newspapers are not for men only. Other, less obvious adjustments will have to be made.

Demographic analyses may reveal a wide market in which customers cut across many categories. The market for soaps, automobiles, and many food products can show diverse demographic breakouts. In such an event, the advertiser may ask the researchers to look beyond the more obvious demographic characteristics of the market and search for significant psychographic qualities.

---

[1]*U.S. News & World Report,* September 1, 1980, p. 51.

Psychographic Distribution   Two consumers may have identical demographic characteristics—same age, education, and income, for example. But their buying and consumption patterns may be as different as grape juice and champagne. Why? The answer may come from psychographic research, which is often employed when demographic data are simply not enough to identify the consumers. This research is one of the newer and more elusive factors in planning advertising. Essentially, it asks the question *"Why* does the consumer buy this product?" It searches out common characteristics among product purchasers and employs modern psychological testing to obtain the information. The consumer profile for a particular product may show vast differences in demographics but a fairly consistent pattern in such traits as aggression, compliance, dominance, autonomy, adaptability, and the like.

For example, Merrill Lynch, Pierce, Fenner & Smith, Inc., discovered that its well-known and impressive "Bullish on America" campaign was off the psychographic target. The early TV commercials showed a pack of bulls at a full gallop while an announcer intoned that Merrill Lynch was bullish on America. When this client switched to a new ad agency, Young & Rubicam (the nation's largest), the agency's research staff concluded that the old campaign was really appealing to the "belongers"[2]—conformists who are unlikely to take risks. Yet heavy investors were found to perceive of themselves as achievers—self-confident unique individuals. The advertising strategy evolved to a new slogan—"a breed apart"—showing a single bull moving through assorted environments, most of them designed to symbolize a financial maze.

In another example of the value of psychographic research, Sunkist came up with a very precise demographic definition of the heavy users of lemons. Yet there are

[2]*Advertising Age,* November 9, 1981, p. 82.

"The sponsor is not totally convinced that this agency has entered into the spirit of this campaign!"

thousands of people with identical demographics who are *not* heavy users of lemons. The psychographic research, however, found significant differences between demographically identical groups in such areas as life-style, attitudes about cooking, and venturesomeness in menu planning. The data gave Sunkist an enormous head start both in planning an efficient media strategy to reach these creative cooks and in creating advertising that would capture their imagination.

Obviously, demographic and psychographic research must work hand in hand, and the result is often referred to as *life-style* research. It was defined as follows by an executive at the Leo Burnett advertising agency:

Life style research is designed to answer questions about people in terms of their activities, interests, and opinions. It measures their activities in terms of how they spend their time in work and leisure; their interests in terms of what they place important in their immediate surroundings; their opinions in terms of their stance on social issues, institutions and themselves; and finally, basic facts such as their age, sex, income and where they live.[3]

Consumer Awareness and Acceptance

Besides knowing the distribution of consumers in terms of geography, consumption, demographics, and psychographics, it is also helpful to identify consumers in terms of their awareness and acceptance of certain products.

The effectiveness of an advertising campaign will obviously vary with each consumer and with his or her status along the slope shown in the chart in 4.2. Consumers are usually scattered, and the fall-off rate is terrific. For any one consumer, most of the brands he or she sees advertised are ones that will *not* be purchased. Fortunately for the advertiser, there are so many prospective purchasers that the market for a product survives in spite of the tremendous attrition rate. Advertising objectives should be designed with this sequence in mind, because each area represents support for the next. Some consumers, exposed to advertising that particularly appeals to them and that offers a product they *really* want, progress through this sequence in the wink of an eye. Others never make it.

The *unaware* may be made *aware* by a campaign specifically designed to introduce a new product or herald a change in an existing product. The objective is pretty straightforward, and the campaign may be considered a success if subsequent market testing shows a great increase in consumer recognition. Gaining the *attention* of those consumers is quite another matter. Advertising in the mass media is basically incidental to the consumer's use of the media. People learn to "tune in" and "tune out" messages at an early age. Thus, it is important to set objectives that define as clearly as possible the most likely prospects for this product. Forget the rest. (Consumer research can turn up interesting data, however. In certain lines of men's furnishings, a high volume is bought by wives, who not only decide to buy the product but also select the brand. They should not be forgotten.)

─────────────────────

[3]Joseph T. Plummer, "Life Style Patterns: A New Constraint for Mass Communications Research," *Journal of Broadcasting* 16, Vol. XVI, No. 1, p. 80.

Perception is complicated by the fact that every person decodes messages in his or her own peculiar way. Consumers are selective in paying attention and also in retaining information. They pick out what is relevant, seek reinforcement of preexisting attitudes, and reject what is negative or meaningless. It is in this stage and in the *credibility* stage that the emotional context of advertising plays an extremely important role. The primary objective of an advertising campaign may be to proclaim that the product exactly fills a consumer's needs. It may do so by building a "lack" in the consumer's mind and then by demonstrating how the product can come to the rescue. Whatever device is used, the purpose is to solidify the consumer's perception and positive acceptance of the product.

Motivation, the last step before product purchase, is the area where that last little nudge is needed. Many factors in the marketing mix may provide the motivation. A half-price sale, a friendly clerk, a point-of-purchase display, and a dozen other factors may influence the final sale. It is axiomatic that advertising is most important in the early stages of this consumer scale. It is also obvious that, as the consumer approaches the moment of sale, more and more complex factors are at work. The sequence can get fouled up very easily, and this is one reason for the high attrition rate. Product *satisfaction* is fairly well beyond the control of the advertising program. Clearly, there will be no consumer satisfaction if the product does not perform as promised. Untruthful or deceptive advertising, particularly for repeat-purchase products, is folly. When it occurs, consumers deeply resent the advertising, the product, and the manufacturer and will probably never buy the product again. *Repeat purchase* can be affected by advertising that encourages repeat use, contains reminders, and suggests new uses for the product.

4.2 / Consumer Acceptance Sequence

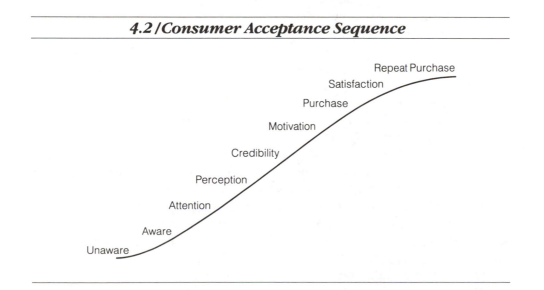

Examples of Advertising Objectives

Specific objectives for an advertising campaign, committed to writing, provide a common reference point for both the agency and the client. Here are some examples:

*   Introduce a new product.

*   Announce an improvement in an existing product, such as a change in formula.

*   Announce new features of an existing product, perhaps a new attachment for a household appliance.

*   Suggest new uses for a product.

*   Introduce new packaging and familiarize the market with it.

*   Demonstrate or dramatize a product feature.

*   Reinforce a favorable opinion among present users.

*   Suggest an increase in the frequency of product use.

*   Suggest an increase in the volume of consumption among present product users.

*   Extend the length of the product buying season. (Many food products are highly seasonal. A strong advertising effort may sustain the popularity of a product for longer periods of time. Turkeys and pumpkin pie are delicious on days other than Thanksgiving and Christmas, for example.)

*   Familiarize a new generation of buyers with the product, such as a toy.

*   Publicize a safety feature, such as with automobiles, tires, various home appliances, or shop and garden power tools.

*   Publicize a guarantee, warranty, or the superior service available with a product.

*   Persuade a prospect to visit a showroom, write for more information, telephone for a home demonstration, and so on. (This kind of advertising campaign is designed to move the prospect into contact with a salesperson, whose efficiency is enhanced by a list of "good leads.")

*   Familiarize the market with the many different products of a corporation. (The excellence of certain well-established brands can improve the image of lesser known brands.)

*   Bring new information to the marketplace as a public service. (Commercials for the oil companies and public utilities regarding the energy crisis are considered by some to be a public service.)

*   Advocate a position on a controversial public issue. Major corporations have launched campaigns to support particular ballot issues or to editorialize on what they consider to be excessive government regulation.

*   Educate the public about an entire industry and thus improve its image. (Independent insurance agents might conduct such an advertising program.)

*   Build company prestige and employee morale. (Institutional or corporate advertising often accomplishes this objective. Print ads or commercials may contain a "salute" to the outstanding performance of employees.)

*   Build a favorable image with retailers and dealers. (The purpose is to facilitate the

sales job of the manufacturer's representative, build preferred shelf space, and so on. Advertising for a home appliance manufacturer might stress not only product features but also the friendliness and service of its dealers.)

• Correct a wrong impression or misinformation or overcome bad publicity. (The Kraft Foods Company faced such a problem in 1974 with its macaroni and cheese dinners. The Food and Drug Administration and the manufacturer announced the recall of huge shipments of this product because of its salmonella content. To win back old customers in such a circumstance is an uphill fight.)

• Combat or neutralize a competitive claim. (Unfortunately, this objective too often degenerates into a "me too" campaign. There are better ways to do it.)

• Overcome an unexpected competitive development. (Such an objective is not an easy task when the competition has come up with a great product innovation and is in the process of announcing it to the world.)

• Demonstrate the superiority of a product by directly comparing it with a competitive product or products.

• Create a brand preference. (This objective might be possible in a product category where there is historically a great deal of brand switching.)

At the retail level, advertising objectives usually include one or more of the following:

• Promote specific merchandise.

• Generate store traffic.

• Tie in with a special event, such as Mother's Day, graduation exercises, and the like.

• Take advantage of a co-op advertising budget. (A retailer may promote the store and a specific product line and split time or space costs with the product manufacturer.)

Developing Objectives into Strategies

Once advertising objectives are defined, the advertising plan requires a *strategy statement*. A strategy is simply the *way* the agency plans to reach its objectives. It includes both creative and media planning, and the two must work hand in glove. The questions asked are "What shall we say?" "To whom should this message be directed?" and "In what medium or media?" It might seem fairly easy to answer such questions, but it isn't. For any single objective, there may be a dozen strategy avenues. That's part of what makes advertising and the decision-making process so fascinating. In designing an effective advertising program, all the alternate strategies must be sifted and weighed and the best one determined. The individual experience of the people working on this strategy and the collective experience of an agency or advertising department over many years are very valuable. ("Let's not do that! We tried that for Client X in 1979, and it bombed!")

Many advertising agencies have replaced the classic plans group of the past with a *strategy group*. This change represents more than a semantic dodge. An agency's strategy group is concerned with advertising directions at an early stage of development. (One criticism of the plans group was that it tended to act as a pseudo client, primarily concerned with an 11th-hour review of plans before they were presented to the client.)

The strategy group examines the facts on which advertising recommendations are to be based. It reviews the stated objectives. Then, it works with the account group in evaluating various ways to accomplish a given objective and in deciding on the best method.

"Positioning" the Product or Service

In the last decade, the marketing strategy of "positioning" has become a preoccupation of the industry. The term is often a "buzz word," bandied about and sometimes misunderstood. Positioning refers to a product or service's niche in the minds of consumers. Its crucial aspect is the perception of a product in relationship to competitive products or services.[4]

Classic examples of positioning in advertising include Burger King's "Have it your way" campaign. Hamburger aficionados were assured that they would get their favorite meal the way they wanted it and did not have to accept the standard fare of competing fast food restaurants.

Volkswagen's famous "Think small" campaign in the 1950s positioned the import against big, luxury American cars as small, inexpensive, and economical. The results are marketing history.

Johnson's Baby Shampoo was formerly oriented exclusively to an infant market. When the product was repositioned to include not only that market but also young women who wanted to wash their hair with a very gentle shampoo almost every day, the product's sales charts became a brand manager's dream. Later the product was positioned to be acceptable to the hairy-chested-male market.

No Nonsense panty hose, as a quality product reasonably priced and sold in supermarkets and other mass outlets, is positioned to stress function rather than fashion. The appeal is to women who want a good product at an inexpensive price for day-in, day-out use.

When Gillette introduced Right Guard as a man's deodorant, sales were moderately good. Later, however, the company repositioned this product as a *family* deodorant, because of its aerosol features. Sales went straight up. The product had not been changed, but the position of the product in the marketplace and in consumers' awareness made the difference.

Products in decline may be salvaged with repositioning based either on changing the character or personality of the brand or on promoting new uses for a familiar product. An example of the former tactic is the repositioning of Ivory Soap, the 100-year-old granddaddy of the soap brands, as a contemporary "natural" soap. Arm &

---

[4]Al Ries and Jack Trout, *Positioning: The Battle for Your Mind* (New York: McGraw-Hill, 1981). This excellent reference by two authorities explores the topic in depth.

Hammer, another brand in decline, was synonymous with baking soda and was usually used only for leavening. By suggesting new uses for this product, such as using an open box in the refrigerator, the company repositioned the brand as an alternative to high-priced, chemical-laden detergents and deodorizers.

The success or failure of a product can often be attributed to its positioning. Since there are usually many positions for any given product, sound judgment and expertise are essential in deciding which position to stress. In positioning a new product or repositioning an existing product, some of the following factors must be carefully weighed:

1.   A product's position cannot be developed as a figment of planners' imaginations. It cannot lack substance, and it must be a legitimate outgrowth of the product and its use. Consumers find positioning useful in comparing available choices, but the product must deliver what it promises, because positioning heightens consumers' expectations.

2.   A product's position cannot be too narrow in appeal. It must be perfectly matched with the demographics and psychographics of prospective customers and be relevant to the desires of that group. Research and testing can provide valuable data to determine if a position is on target.

3.   The product must be positioned *against* the competition. A "me too" strategy against a brand leader is marketing suicide. It is risky to enter the battlefield against the leading competitor. The high ground belongs to the leader for solid reasons. A wiser course is to move up the ladder by knocking off smaller game.

At present all we'll be allowed to say is that our tires are round — but they're running some tests on that, too.

Cartoon by Sidney Harris. Reprinted with permission.

4.   A new position usually requires a total overhaul in marketing strategy. This may include repackaging, new merchandising materials, and, obviously, a change in the advertising program. Repositioning an existing product implies a change from the old position, and that means an inevitable loss of some old customers. It is important to determine the believability of a new position. Millions of dollars have been wasted trying to change minds with advertising. If a new position cannot reasonably evolve from the old positioning, it should not be pursued.

5.   Positioning is more than the execution of a new creative strategy or the possible overhaul of an existing product. Proper positioning must be accompanied by a careful analysis of the current media strategy. If there's a shift in target audience, the media buys must also shift, or the repositioning effort is likely to be futile.

Establishing a Budget

Establishing an annual advertising budget is not easy. The client, who knows he must spend money in order to make money, must consider many factors in determining what he can and should spend on marketing. This total budget must support promotion and publicity programs, sales aids, point-of-purchase materials, advertising, packaging, distribution, and a host of other activities designed to move the product from the warehouse into the hands of the consumer.

The problems are more complex for large manufacturers of national brand products than for local retailers, but the latter have their share of headaches in deciding what they can afford to invest in advertising. It is not easy to measure the actual return on money spent in advertising, and those systems that have been designed constitute an inexact science. Very often, the response to the advertising investment may be delayed for weeks or months. An advertising budget must still be determined, however, and a number of approaches and "systems" are used to establish that annual figure. (See 4.3 for an amusing parable relating to advertising budgets.)

Task Method

The task system of budgeting is a favorite one, particularly with agency executives. When objectives have been established and the strategy determined, the job ahead is pretty clear-cut. For example, if it has been determined that demonstration TV commercials are necessary in order to accomplish a given objective, and if experience has indicated that 50 percent of the advertiser's prospects must be reached 10 times in order to achieve desired awareness levels, the price tag for all this can be calculated. The production experts can estimate the costs of producing such a commercial, and the media experts can estimate the costs of contacting the desired number of people (reach) the desired number of times (frequency).

The proposed budget that emerges from this exercise is often considered too expensive by a client. (Everyone wants the moon, but NASA knows the price of getting there.) Thus, it is necessary to cut or reorder the budget in ways that will still achieve a successful campaign. On the one hand, the advertiser may have to settle for reaching fewer prospects, if frequency is of primary importance. On the other hand, the client may have to be content with reaching the audience fewer times, if size of audience is paramount.

The task method provides an ideal intellectual start for budgeting, but it must invariably accommodate itself to what can be afforded.

Unit of Sale

Some manufacturers regularly budget a certain percentage of the product's purchase price for advertising purposes. A fixed percentage, or a dollar sum, is often assigned to the sale of automobiles or major durable goods such as home appliances. The percentages may vary drastically between product groups, depending on the competitive picture. The advantage of this budget system is that, if it is based on the previous year's sales figures, it's easy to determine the next year's advertising budget. It can, of course, be based on anticipated sales. The problem is that it is not a very flexible method.

Percentage of Sales

A common and quite popular formula for establishing an advertising budget is to allocate a percentage of total sales to advertising. It is usually based on the previous year's sales and may vary from 1 or 2 percent up to 12 or 15 percent or more. In highly competitive product categories such as cosmetics and over-the-counter drugs, a higher percentage of sales is usually assigned to advertising than in less competitive categories. The high markup on certain products reflects high risks and heavy investments in marketing costs.

The problem with this system is that the advertising budget is based on past performance, not future estimates. The method seems to suggest that sales precede

---

4.3 / The Man Who Sold Chewing Gum: An Ad Age Parable

It was common knowledge among his colleagues that William Wrigley, Jr., attributed the success of his chewing gum empire to constant and forceful advertising.

Once he was traveling to California on the famous Super Chief with a young accountant from his firm. As they were reviewing the figures for a quarterly statement, the young man said, "Sir, Wrigley's gum is known and sold all over the world. We have a larger share of the market than all of our competitors combined. Why don't you now save the millions you are spending on advertising and shift those dollars into the profit column for the next quarter?"

Wrigley thought for a moment and then asked, "Young man, how fast is this train going?"

"About sixty miles an hour," replied the young accountant.

And Wrigley asked, "Then why doesn't the railroad remove the engine and let the train travel on its own momentum?"

Reprinted courtesy of Advertising Age.

---

advertising, not the other way around. As a result, the percentage-of-sales system can be inflexible and often not very realistic. Sales will not necessarily increase uniformly when the advertising budget is increased. A short-term heavy advertising campaign may dramatically increase sales, or it may simply allow a product to hang on to its market share in the face of a major competitive promotion. In some cases, a cutback in an advertising budget for a well-established product may prove that the product can retain its market share with less advertising, at least for a while.

Other Systems

There are other ways to establish an advertising budget, and each business manager must determine what method will best suit the company's interests. Exact formulas may seem reasonable in theory but often break down in day-to-day practice. Instead of allocating a budget based on a percentage of sales or unit of sale, some managers prefer to establish a budget based on predicted sales, on last year's profits, or on estimated profits for the coming year. They consider it a more realistic approach than other systems, because rising sales do not necessarily mean rising profits. Too many other factors can affect the profit margin. For example, in a year of declining profits, the first budget to be cut may well be the advertising budget. But such a move may not make sense at all, because in a period of declining sales, the only effective tactic may be to increase advertising levels. Some companies watch their competitors closely and establish their advertising budget in accordance with what they know or think the competition is spending.

Most intelligently planned advertising allocations tend to be established by considering the advantages of all these systems. Advertisers must find the formula that works for them, and they may have to modify it each year. In addition to the systems briefly outlined above, they will consider general economic conditions, competitive factors, the relative importance of the retailer, the type of product, its newness and the public's familiarity with it, the recommendations of the advertising agency, evaluations of past advertising programs, and the sales expectations for the coming year.

Conclusions

There are probably few businesses that involve more decision making than the advertising business. Every client has a problem — or problems. The competition never stands still, and so the marketplace is constantly changing. Consumers can be fickle and very hard to please. It makes the crystal ball pretty murky.

Advertising programs cannot be put together willy-nilly. When a program that is poorly researched and ill-considered is a success, it can only be attributed to blind luck.

Objectives should always be formulated in terms of the communications function of advertising. The objectives must be specific, able to be translated into action, and within the proper realm of what can reasonably be expected with a given budget over a given period of time. A thorough analysis of a client's product or service — and also of customers in terms of geographic, consumption, demographic, and psychographic distributions patterns — is vital to intelligent planning.

Strategies, which grow out of advertising objectives, constitute the battle plan for achieving those objectives. There are usually a dozen strategies that could be used to achieve a particular set of objectives; experience and expertise are needed to select the best plan.

Positioning represents an attempt to fit a product or service into a potentially profitable niche in the total market. A sophisticated understanding of marketing techniques is required to assure that the positioning is appropriate. In many cases, sales are greatly increased when a product is repositioned as a result of extensive research and analysis.

Objectives, strategies, and positioning are the key supports in developing a viable advertising program. The decisions based on these three factors are ultimately tested in the marketplace. The right ones succeed.

chapter five

Media Planning

Demos and Psychos

No department in any advertising agency has witnessed more changes in recent decades than the media department. Its goal has always been to put clients in touch with prospective customers in the most effective and efficient manner. Years ago it really didn't seem that complicated to do so. Today, the media department's apprentices may wonder if they need a degree in higher mathematics to survive.

The advertising industry and the media in this country have undergone such tremendous changes that merely keeping track of them is an accomplishment. The agency media planner must not only understand the makeup of each advertising medium, but also be able to interpret it to others and prepare recommendations that sometimes involve millions of dollars. It's a huge responsibility, and mistakes are costly. Media planning and buying have become so complex primarily because of the abundance of new research and increasingly available computer facilities for rapid, in-depth analysis of research findings. Nothing can be left to guesswork, and so media plans are now formulated and analyzed in many different ways. The sheer volume of advertising means that the consumer is bombarded with messages. Yet every client wants his message to rise above the din. What can the media planner recommend?

Answers do not come easily, for the tremendous proliferation in media has greatly complicated decision making. There are numerous ways to put advertisers in touch with consumers. Which is best? All of the media can offer attractive options. As a result, the word of the media planner is largely devoted to evaluating the pros and cons of various possibilities in relation to the objectives and strategies of a given advertising campaign.

Television has significantly altered media planning because of its great impact on how the public spends its leisure time and because of its proved selling success. In spite of the high costs, TV, until recent years, was a relatively easy buy. Three major networks, their affiliates, plus a few hundred independent stations made up the television marketplace. Cable TV, spawning new satellite networks in addition to local origination, now presents some viable options to the media planner.

Radio, formerly quite simple for the national advertisers who used the handful of networks, is now also more complex. New and specialized networks are proliferating. Their constantly changing lineup of affiliates complicates the work of the media planner. There are about ten times as many radio stations on the air as there are television stations. Almost every station seeks to serve a somewhat specialized segment of the total audience, and so a media strategy involving radio requires extensive analysis in order to match consumer and listener profiles.

Other media have also undergone extensive changes. On the one hand, numerous newspapers have folded or have merged into larger business enterprises as a result of their economic problems. They have had to adjust to rising costs, declining circulation in proportion to population growth, and the public's new reliance on television as its primary news source. On the other hand, small neighborhood newspapers in urban and suburban areas have increased and now fill an important function in providing shopping information and very localized news. Many national mass consumer magazines have disappeared, to be replaced by more specialized magazines catering to specific interests and reader demographics and psychographics. Billboards have been banned in some communities. Direct mail costs have risen dramatically. The new technologies — including cable TV, satellite services, two-way interactive cable, videodiscs and cassettes, and AM stereo, to name just a few — have affected or may affect the public's use of the media. And because the public's use is affected, so are plans to reach that public with advertising messages.

Developing a Media Strategy

The media strategy of any advertising program must be as carefully analyzed and executed as the creative strategy. In creative planning (see Chapter 6), the process is rarely very orderly, but media planning can and should be disciplined and as exact as possible. Several options are usually prepared for review by the client and the agency's account management team. (Plans thrown together under a deadline obviously risk the client's money and should be avoided.) Even when one plan is selected, most media planners say, it is not written in stone. Plans are constantly revised and adjusted in response to marketplace changes.

Many questions must be answered before an efficient and workable media plan can be formulated. These questions, detailed below, fall into two categories — *marketing factors* and *communications factors*.

Marketing Factors

What Are the Objectives of the Campaign?
In most cases, objectives are determined by the client working closely with the agency's account management team. Advertising objectives are an outgrowth of larger

marketing objectives and must be related to them. When committed to paper, they can be reviewed by the media planner, who should be convinced that they can be carried out. Sometimes, the stated objectives present problems, however. For example, an objective to increase a product's market share by 5 percent may warm the client's heart but may have very little directional validity for the media planner. If, however, the objective is to demonstrate a product's superior performance to middle- and high-income men, ages 25 to 49, then the media planner can begin to zero in on the best of a number of media alternatives.

Advertising objectives should always be expressed in terms of what is to be communicated to whom. This is home base. With a clear understanding of these basic objectives, the media planner can move on to the finer points.

What Is the Geographic Distribution?

The client's distribution patterns may quickly eliminate certain media or strongly indicate the wisdom of using other media. For example, an advertiser whose product is distributed in only 20 percent of the United States is not a candidate for network radio. Regional or local media buys may be the answer, for they permit the agency to select only the important markets. One rental car company had always used network television, primarily because its competition did. Yet 80 percent of the car rentals for this client were confined to a handful of cities. This concentration of sales indicated that the TV networks, which have more than 200 affiliates each in as many markets, were an extravagant and wasteful buy.

Because a product's share of total sales will always vary from market to market, a media plan must ideally permit flexibility in adjusting advertising weights in each market. Advertising buys are an investment, and the various geographic markets must be analyzed in terms of their potential to return a profit on that investment.

What Is the Target Audience?

Stated in other words, the question is "Who and where are the best prospects?" The answer is usually based on the geographic distribution and on the demographic qualities of the target group. It is here that sufficient and accurate research data are critical. The advertiser should define as precisely as possible the target prospects for the media planner. The agency needs to know where the customers are; then, it needs to establish a consumer profile based on age, sex, income, education levels, and other demographics, plus psychographic profiles. Additional marketing research may be necessary to detail these profiles, and this information often includes customers' product and media usage. Media planners increasingly request detailed information from their clients on product users, particularly heavy users. If these profiles can be matched with the media habits of these present customers, planning is simplified. In some cases, however, the purpose of the campaign is to attract *new* product users, so an entirely different media plan may be required. It is not uncommon for a media plan to develop a primary and secondary target audience.

For certain kinds of advertisers, psychographic identifications of consumers are very important, for they attempt to qualify target audiences in terms of life-styles and various psychological qualities. It is not easy to translate them to media usage, however. Only a limited number of media have even scratched the surface in developing psychographic profiles of their readers, listeners, or viewers. When available, however, psychographic profiles help a media director in making subsequent subjective decisions between two media alternatives.

Since demographics and psychographics are not the same thing, they may relate only occasionally. On the one hand, a person may be venturesome at age 9 or 90, but consumer needs for products and services are vastly different for people in the two age categories. On the other hand, a 20-year-old woman and a 45-year-old one may both be excellent prospects for a particular cosmetic because they share a common trait—insecurity in social situations. They may both buy a product because they think it will make them attractive and therefore more confident. Yet these two women may or may not share similar media habits. This example suggests the complexities not only of identifying the market but also of reaching the market. Certainly, it would be helpful to know the marketplace in such microscopic detail that all media planning could be predicated on both demographic and psychographic data. Perhaps someday it will be possible.

What Are the Seasonal Factors and Shopping Habits?

Few products or services have consistent sales patterns 12 months of the year. The ups and downs of sales charts should be available to the media planner. For some products, sales may be concentrated in a short selling season. Iced tea mixes, children's toys, greeting cards, and swimming suits are a few obvious examples. Campaigns can be scheduled to break just before a high sales season.

The radio industry, in an attempt to attract new business, has been innovative in providing flexible schedules for seasonal advertisers. For example, an air conditioning company may order a schedule of commercials on either individual stations or a network to run when the temperature reaches a particular point. The same kind of options has worked in selling snow tires and antifreeze.

Seasonal factors may be further broken down to an analysis of sales by days of the week and even hours of the day. Most supermarkets schedule their advertising to coincide with heavy shopping days, Wednesday through Saturday. Shopping habits, broken down to hours of the day, may be significant for some advertisers. Late-night television always carries a few commercials for sleeping aids, because a certain number of the viewers are bound to be insomniacs. (This kind of fine tuning is most frequently performed when the actual buys are made.)

What's the Competitive Picture?

Competition, unfortunately, never stands still, and it is often maddeningly unpredictable. If the competition is aggressive, consistently outspends the agency's client, and dominates in one or more media, it is exceedingly difficult to devise an effective media strategy. One school of media-planning theory contends that it's better to use media in which the competition has little or no exposure than to meet on a battlefield where the competition dominates. This strategy has often worked very well, but it is simply not possible in all instances. If the target audience is available in one or two media in large enough numbers, it would be impractical to try reaching these same people through other less efficient, and perhaps more expensive, media.

Competitive information on media usage, advertising expenditures, and schedules is always useful. A number of independent organizations regularly syndicate such reports, but there is an inevitable time lag that agencies and advertisers must consider. Reports are based on past activity, perhaps 60 to 90 days earlier. Agency planning, however, is always for the future. Since the reports all use samples, expenditures can only be estimated. There is bound to be some error in the reports, and critics argue that expenditure levels are often inflated. Nonetheless, reports from independent researchers fill an important need in media planning. The most useful information reveals which media vehicles were employed, the markets in which the advertising appeared, the periods of the year, and the expenditures of the competitors.

Print media data are provided by LNA/PIB (Leading National Advertisers/Publishers Information Bureau) and Media Records. In the broadcast media, two independent companies, BAR and RER, syndicate reports on competitive activity.

Broadcast Advertisers Reports (BAR), established in 1953, monitors commercials on the ABC, CBS, and NBC radio and television networks, some of the cable TV networks, and 285 TV stations in the top 75 markets. (The Mutual Radio Network is not monitored.) Monitoring is accomplished with audio tape recordings. From these tapes, editors compile a syndicated report on markets, stations, programs, time and length of commercials, product class, brands, and estimated expenditures. Upwards of six million commercials are heard and identified annually to produce this service. Monitoring is conducted every day of the year, and reports are issued weekly and in quarterly summaries.

Radio Expenditure Reports, Inc., (RER), headquartered in Larchmont, New York, publishes a quarterly All Advertisers Report covering spot radio activity. The report estimates expenditures by category, company, and brand, compiled from questionnaires sent primarily to station representative firms and also to selected stations. The syndicated report is based on spot advertising activity on a sample of more than 2,000 stations in approximately 150 markets. National projections are made to adjust for markets not included in the survey and for nonresponding stations. RER, on request, also compiles individual market reports on any particular brand, category, or company.

What's the Budget?

Whatever the budget, the media planner always wishes it were a bit larger. Since many attractive options are available to any advertiser in selecting media, the problem is to choose the best one. The dollars must be stretched to their most efficient use. Adjustments always have to be made, because media costs may be disproportionately large in relation to the size of the audience delivered. Some media simply cost more than others. Further, certain markets may be more important to a client than others, and so the planner may have to allow for varying advertising weights. For example, a nationally distributed product having 60 percent of its sales in the top 20 markets might benefit by heavy campaigns in these markets and merely maintenance schedules in the balance of the country. In particularly important markets, the budget may have to be designed to combat an aggressive competitor. Certain demographic groups may be harder or more expensive to reach than others, and in this instance, media budgets will have to be modified.

Communications Factors

What Is the Message?

The advertising objectives of a campaign establish the basic message to be communicated to a target audience. The shape and form of this message are the work of the creative team, which is well aware of the special environment of each of the advertising media. Creative aspects, including the style and presentation of the message, may largely dictate media selection. Nothing can match the highly refined color reproduction of magazines, for instance, and the humor of an animated TV commercial is impossible to duplicate in other media.

The complexity of the message may eliminate certain media. If there are several important sales points, they may not fit into a standard 30-second TV commercial; print may be the answer. Outdoor is suitable for a simple communication and is often used in a media mix to reinforce a campaign run primarily in another medium. Even though radio is cost efficient, it may be discounted if the central message focuses on a demonstration of a product or if package identification is vital.

If a media mix is used, the central message, or *copy platform,* will be used in all media and should be adaptable to that mix. The challenge for the media planner is to develop a plan that will accommodate all the creative objectives and the media objectives in reaching the target audience effectively.

What Media Are Available?

In the practical business of devising a campaign strategy, all advertising media must be evaluated on two bases: (1) the suitability of the medium to deliver a particular kind of message and (2) the ability of the medium to deliver the right kind of audience for this particular advertiser and to do so efficiently.

All media have specialized and unique qualities, different coverage patterns and audiences, and different kinds of advertising environment. There is no "perfect" medium. Each has some assets and some liabilities. Thus, the experienced media planner must know what can be reasonably expected from television, radio, newspapers, magazines, outdoor, direct mail, and a variety of specialized media. Since this book is devoted to the broadcast media, the following sections discuss the advantages and disadvantages they present to the advertiser.

Advantages of Television If, as television's critics have said, the industry is not really in the business of delivering programing to audiences but rather delivering audiences to advertisers, then one must grant that it achieves this goal with huge success. The billions of dollars now annually invested in TV advertising by American and foreign business presents an impressive testimonial to the power of the medium in moving goods and services through the marketplace. What is it about television commercials that makes them so captivating and compelling? Why is TV such a persuasive selling tool? It may be helpful to analyze television from the advertiser's viewpoint, not the programer's or the viewer's, in order to understand the power and success of the medium.

The combination of sound and visuals, including both motion and color, offers the advertiser certain opportunities simply not available in other media. TV's unparalleled ability to *demonstrate* the product, to display it in the most favorable circumstances, and to familiarize the viewer with a package, sign, or trademark, is probably the medium's prime advantage over other media. Television is an exceptional vehicle for the introduction of new consumer products.

In addition, being able to presell the consumer is extremely important in this day of self-service shopping, for an indifferent check-out clerk is no replacement for an enthusiastic salesperson. Advertising is, in large part, a replacement for personal selling. Thus, TV's ability to reach consumers and influence their behavior is most attractive to the advertiser. TV's ability to persuade is increased by its ability to sell on an "eyeball to eyeball" basis. The effect of personal testimonials or of a compelling spokesperson on TV can elicit an emotional response in the viewer that is subsequently felt in the marketplace. Television need never worry about getting a foot in the front door, because it is usually firmly ensconced centerstage in America's living rooms. In theory, at least, the members of the family are relaxed, ready to be entertained, and receptive to the advertising messages. TV is an "up front" medium, which means that, when the commercial is on the air, the advertiser does not have to share the stage with anyone else. (In newspapers, an ad must compete for a reader's attention with everything else on the page.)

Americans are spending even more time with the medium. Nielsen reports that the average American television home now has its set (or sets) in use more than six-and-a-half hours each day. Although some social critics decry this trend, advertisers can only rejoice. From their viewpoint, television can be not only tremendously effective but efficient as well. Even though the costs may be high, the results are worth it. The TV networks constitute the only real national advertising medium in terms of mass coverage. Tens of millions of viewers may be simultaneously exposed to each commercial scheduled in prime time. If advertisers can match consumer profiles reasonably well to viewer profiles, efficiency is improved.

Prime-time television is not the only attractive buy for advertisers who want to reach mass audiences. Daytime, weekend, and early and late fringe time periods can deliver significant audiences with reasonably defined demographics at efficient prices. Television audiences are continuously studied in order to provide advertisers with as much data as possible about audience size and demographics at various times of the day. This information allows the advertiser who wants to reach 18- to 34-year-old women to identify the programs that deliver this important demographic group in large numbers. Because a television station's program schedule provides a rather extensive "menu" for each member of the viewing family, the option of reaching certain members is available to the advertiser. Daytime television catering to large numbers of women, weekend sports programs with broad appeal to men, and Saturday morning children's shows are just a few examples of the variety of times and audience compositions available to the advertiser; they also represent a variety of price ranges.

The television medium is also attractive to advertisers because of its relative flexibility. Time buys can be made on a last-minute basis, if necessary, and the advertiser can buy commercial schedules on either a network or spot basis. With one buy of network time, an advertiser has access to approximately 200 affiliate stations, and the purchase of that time can be a reasonably quick and easy negotiation. In spot buying, the advertiser can select just those markets and stations where it wishes to advertise. This market list may be matched with product distribution patterns and weighted up or down depending on the particular objectives of the advertising campaign. An advertiser with national distribution (and a hefty budget) may supplement a basic national network buy with "heavy-up" spot schedules in high-potential markets. Flexibility also allows schedules to be juggled and commercials rotated or moved from time period to time period, if necessary.

Spectacular scenery, fabulous colors, and glamorous talent can be captured in a blend of beautiful visual techniques and skillful audio execution. This advantage need not be belabored, for it has become cliché to note that the very best (and the very worst) material on television is the commercials. The constantly improving technology of TV offers advertisers a variety of creative options. Special effects, computer animation, and chroma-key techniques have all been used successfully to lend visual interest to commercials. A commercial extravaganza is not necessary for effective selling, however. Many advertisers are convinced by their own success that a simple "stand-up" television commercial with a convincing spokesperson can capture the interest of prospects and sell their products. Other advertisers prefer to use the intimacy and immediacy of TV to present commercials with "slice-of-life" techniques. If well executed, these commercials can generate a great deal of emotional involvement on the part of viewers.

Prestige is another benefit that television advertisers can reap. Participation in network sponsorships of specials—documentaries, important dramas, and live coverage of major current events—can identify the advertiser with quality, social concern, and corporate altruism to a degree not available in other media. This kind of sponsorship may effectively promote short-term sales, or it may improve a company's image through effective institutional commercials.

Cable TV promises advertisers exciting prospects in the coming years. The various satellite networks are programed for particular viewer interests—news, sports, cultural programing, and so on. These specialized audiences are very attractive to certain advertisers. Compared with the costs of conventional television, those of cable TV are low, even though in terms of cost per homes reached, cable is fairly expensive. Organized by rep firms, advertisers can now make regional cable buys. An important sporting event with high statewide interest, for example, can be presented through interconnected cable companies at a price far below that of conventional television.

Great scheduling flexibility can be negotiated in cable buys, particularly in message length. To find a competitive edge against conventional TV, many cable systems offer opportunities to place "infomercials"—messages that run several minutes or even longer. A full demonstration plus a longer sales pitch can be accommodated. Cable is also very successful in direct marketing. The commercials usually run one minute or longer and are followed with an address or a toll-free telephone number for immediate viewer response. (It's an easy matter to tabulate results from this kind of advertising.)

Cable TV also offers advertisers an opportunity to produce and sponsor their own special interest programs. Thus, a food company can use cable to present a cooking show, and an automobile manufacturer might sponsor a travel program. Placing such programing on local TV stations is becoming increasingly difficult, and it is virtually impossible on network TV. Many cable systems, hungry for revenues and catering to special viewer interests, welcome these programs.

Disadvantages of Television   The intelligent advertiser and an advertising agency's staff must recognize that television is not necessarily a magic solution destined to solve any and all marketing problems. Television's disadvantages as an advertising medium do not outweigh its advantages for most advertisers, but they should be considered. Time is perishable, and the commercial is a fleeting message. (The print advertising industry is gleeful to stress this point in underscoring the relative permanence of ink on paper.) A few commercials are sold in 10- and 60-second lengths, but most last 30 seconds. That simply isn't very long. This time limitation can produce considerable problems for the agency in designing effective and persuasive messages. The copy platform must be simple, and the selling concept clear. Commercials usually cannot deal with technical explanations, although sometimes TV can make the complex seem simple — as, for example, with animation. Nonetheless, the advertiser is severely restricted in the amount of detail and the sales points that can be presented.

The self-regulatory policies of the networks, in particular, and of many stations impose extensive restrictions on a variety of advertisers. Commercials for personal products, beer and wine, children's products, nonprescription medications, and quite a few others can run into serious "clearance" problems. As a result, many advertisers are frustrated that they cannot say and show what they want to in their commercials but must produce what they consider watered-down messages that will be accepted. Some advertisers — makers of contraceptive products and distillers of hard liquor, for example — find it virtually impossible to get on the air.

Some national advertisers have not used television because they consider it too expensive. They have determined that their budgets are more efficiently invested in other media. The production costs for a 30-second commercial may easily reach $100,000. In addition to time costs and production expenses, talent costs can skyrocket unless the situation is closely monitored. Depending on the number of actors and models hired for a commercial and whether the services of a high-priced celebrity have been used, an important cost factor is *residuals* — payment to talent for the reuse of a commercial. (Residuals will be discussed further in Chapter 7.)

Television advertising is generally confined to campaigns intended to sell mass consumer goods and services. Further, much TV programing is nonselective in terms of the audience it attracts, although certain kinds of program — sports, children's, and others — deliver narrower demographics. In general, selectivity is not at work in a network program that delivers 30 million viewers, and for some advertisers this is a disadvantage. They prefer to use other media. In using a television network with 200-plus affiliates, there will inevitably be some weak performers. If those markets happen to be especially important to an advertiser, extra dollars must be invested in spot buys in order to compensate for lower ratings on those affiliates.

Because the print media are usually paid for by the readers and thus selected and sought after, newspapers and magazines are often thought to enjoy much higher "loyalty" than broadcasting. TV audiences are fickle, and channel-hopping is common. The advertiser must realize that the viewers turn to TV for the program, not the commercial, which constitutes an interruption. Naturally, a string of commercials invites the viewers to divert their attention or leave the room. A number of studies over the years have attempted to measure viewer absenteeism during the "clutter" at station-break time. The results are sobering at best. The advertiser who concludes that his message is watched by the same number of viewers who watch the program is deluding himself. The actual figure of program viewers devoting full attention to the accompanying commercial message may be less than 50 percent.

This drop-off rate of viewers watching commercials represents another disadvantage of TV to the advertiser. It may be identified as some degree of viewer antagonism, but the exact degree is impossible to measure. Thus, to what extent criticism of the medium, both in specific and general ways, "rubs off" on the advertiser is not known, but it is certainly safe to conclude that television advertising itself has contributed generously to viewer antagonism!

Antagonism isn't just confined to commercials. TV programing has been the focus of a continuing debate over acceptable standards. In the 1980s, the religious Right, through a variety of organizations, has organized a campaign against what it considers excessive violence and sexuality on TV. Because these objections have been generally ignored by the networks, the special interest groups have gone to the parties who pay the bills—the advertisers. A monitoring program conducted by volunteers in these various groups has sought to identify the culprits—advertisers who sponsor such programs. The weapons have been the threat of boycotting these advertisers' products and the threat of sullying the corporate name by a massive publicity campaign. As a result, many clients have given their advertising agencies strict time-buying guidelines and a list of "don't buy" programs. This reduces the options for clients who must pay top dollar for commercial positions in "acceptable" programs. (See Chapter 11.)

Advantages of Radio   Mark Twain's comment "The reports of my death are greatly exaggerated" might well apply to radio. The industry rallied from a staggering blow dealt it by the new television industry during the 1950s. The recuperation was largely financed by advertisers, not out of dedication to a faltering medium, but because they considered dollars spent in radio a wise investment. Radio offered the advertiser certain advantages often unavailable in other media. Virtually every home in America has a radio; in fact, the average is over five sets per home. Listening in bedrooms, kitchens, family rooms, and almost every other room in the house means radio is a highly accessible and also very personal medium. Few cars are manufactured today without a radio, and the Radio Advertising Bureau (RAB) estimates that it is on more than 60 percent of the time the car is in use. This fact helps to explain why radio's prime times are the early-morning and late-afternoon commuting hours. Small transistor radios accompany listeners on a variety of outdoor activities. The result is that radio enjoys a mass coverage and accessibility unmatched by other advertising media. Its popularity has been apparent for many years. RAB studies report that the average adult listens to radio more than three-and-a-half hours a day.

The tremendous proliferation of stations in the past two decades has meant a proliferation of programing formats—such as all-news, contemporary music, country-western, and rock—each attracting a particular segment of the population. Because of the appeal to a limited group, many advertising agencies consider radio a "narrowcast" medium. (It is obvious that consumer profiles based on the advertiser's marketing research should be accurately matched with radio listener profiles, a task that is more easily talked about than accomplished.)

Radio is very competitive with other local media, and advertising time and production costs can be very modest yet still produce effective results. Although many large stations in major markets charge what seem to be high rates, they generally base them on audience delivered and frequently negotiate with the advertiser. The top stations charge rates commensurate with audience reach. Stations with less than spectacular ratings obviously offer lower rates, and they often constitute an attractive advertising buy. Most radio stations offer a variety of discounts to advertisers, depending on the number of commercials run each week, the number of weeks in the schedule, the total dollar expenditure, or some other basis. It is possible to run a high-frequency campaign on several stations on a relatively low budget. Although production costs for radio commercials can be considerable, they really do not have to be. Recorded music and sound effects and experienced talent can produce a low-cos but high-impact commercial that wins awards in advertising competitions and wins customers at the check-out stand.

The "theater of the mind" is an old cliché in radio, but it still applies. As a result of effective production, the radio listener can "see" the setting, the characters, and the product. If the advertiser wishes to place a commercial on a sandy South Sea beach, all that is needed for the listener to visualize the scene is proper sound suggestions. The warmth of the human voice, a catchy jingle, a "picture" painted with sound effects, or a popular disc jockey who can read copy with "friendly persuasion" offers attractive opportunities for the radio advertiser.

Because listeners use radio in very personal ways, and often in some degree of isolation, its function as a companion should not be overlooked. Many advertisers produce slice-of-life commercials that provide easy identification for the listener. Bright, topical, and humorous commercials may be tremendously effective in reaching the radio listener on an emotional level.

As with television, flexibility is another attractive asset. Radio stations can be selected in only those markets important to the advertiser. Schedules can be bought for only a few days or for an entire year. Commercials can be rotated and changed according to the advertiser's direction at no additional charge. Although local advertisers are the bread and butter of the industry, many national advertisers make significant investments in the radio networks. Program fare has changed with the times, and clients have found that network buys, usually newscasts, are extremely efficient. Costs are low, audience levels are impressive, and with one simple purchase the advertiser buys time on several hundred stations.

Disadvantages of Radio Advertisers who carefully construct their advertising objectives and critically evaluate what each of the media offers must also be aware of shortcomings. In the case of radio, one attribute is also a serious disadvantage. Although this aural medium can inspire the listener's imagination, it is still "blind." The product, its packaging, a store's interior, or its location cannot be shown as it can in television or the print media. In addition, radio is not particularly conducive to elaborate verbal detail on product attributes, colors, sizes, prices, store location, phone numbers, or mail order instructions. The fleeting, perishable nature of a commercial is a further limitation, as it is with television. In 30 or 60 seconds, it vanishes into the ether. For the station soliciting local advertising from businesses that have relied historically on newspaper advertising, this impermanence is a real handicap. Educating and reorienting retailers in relation to the advantages of the medium is a continuing task of local radio account executives.

The advertiser seeking some measure of market saturation must buy time rather extensively, because radio audiences are fragmented. Prime-time buys on a local television station or several full page ads in the local newspaper may reach an impressive audience. To duplicate this kind of coverage in radio, the advertiser must buy time on a number of stations over an extended period. The way audiences fragment by demographic groups is a constantly changing phenomenon in most major markets. Listeners' preferences may change, or stations may switch their programing format in a relatively short period of time. The astute radio advertiser must keep on top of such changes. Unfortunately, as in all media, buying for the future is usually predicated on past performance.

Listeners often tune in music programs, a staple of modern radio, only as an incidental background to their activities. Thus, the commercial must fight a wall of inattention, to whatever immeasurable degree that may exist, in order to communicate a message. An equally immeasurable response of listeners is to "button push," particularly in automobiles, deserting the commercial and finding another station. Listeners who change stations are often antagonized by advertising "clutter." Stations restrict the amount of advertising, and virtually all of them abide by a policy of carrying no more than 18 commercial minutes an hour. But that's still close to one-third of the schedule if a station is sold out.

Ever since the Lone Ranger last galloped down radio's memory lane, the medium has not been particularly suitable for reaching children. Modern programing formats are oriented to teenagers and adults, particularly young adults. Thus, other specialized audiences besides children may also be fairly elusive: men and working women may be available for only very short periods of time, and senior citizens and high-income listeners may also be very light radio users.

The advantages and disadvantages of both television and radio will affect each advertiser in different ways, and each must evaluate the media in terms of what success it can reasonably expect from them. Formulas don't work—only human judgment, and maybe a little luck.

How Should the Campaign Be Scheduled?

Beyond the obvious dictates of scheduling a campaign just preceding and during peak sales months, there are a number of other, more sophisticated, dimensions in media planning. Working within the budget framework, a media plan must be built by accommodating the variables of continuity, flights, gross rating points, reach and frequency, media dominance, media mix, cost efficiency formulas, and commercial length.

Continuity versus Flights   How long the campaign runs will be dictated primarily by budget size and the seasonality of sales. Planning can be pretty clear-cut for the highly seasonal advertiser, but what about the client whose product is purchased year-round? Many advertisers feel that it is important to sustain a fairly continuous advertising program in order to maintain a position or build a larger share in the marketplace. A local automobile dealer, for instance, must deal not only with seasonal patterns but also with the problem of constant customer turnover. Today's new car buyer can vanish from the car market for several years. This buyer must be replaced with new prospects.

Some advertisers, aiming at a broad market where products are bought frequently, may subscribe to the flight theory. This plan sacrifices continuity, since the advertising schedule is concentrated in shorter flights, perhaps spanning six or eight weeks or even less. Then, the advertiser withdraws from the media for a short time. The theory is that the effect of these short bursts of advertising will be sufficient to carry through a hiatus.

Sometimes, clients ask questions such as "What's better — to run 200 spots a week for four weeks or 100 spots a week for eight weeks?" There's no magic formula; each plan has its own merits depending on campaign objectives.

Gross Rating Points   Radio and television program ratings from Nielsen or Arbitron are used to determine gross rating points (GRPs). One rating point equals 1 percent of the "universe." The universe may be based on households or on a target audience. (If a TV program delivers a 20 rating, for example, that means that 20 percent of the households — or target audience — in a given market viewed the program.)

The media planner establishes a goal of a certain number of GRPs over a given period of time. The rating points for each commercial position are simply added together. For example, a TV schedule may call for three commercials a week on an early-prime-time game show that has a 15 rating. That totals 45 GRPs. Not everyone in the target audience was watching the show, of course, and of those who saw it, some saw the commercial once — twice — or all three times.

If a media planner has reach and frequency targets, it's an easy matter to calculate the GRPs that are needed to meet those goals:

$$\text{reach} \times \text{frequency} = \text{gross rating points}$$

Reach and Frequency   *Reach* indicates the number of people (usually expressed as a percentage of a target universe) who have been exposed to an advertisement at least once over a given period of time. The term is synonomous with cumulative, or unduplicated, audience.

Frequency is the *average* number of times this exposure takes place. Some people will be exposed many more times than this average figure, and some may be exposed only once.

Reach and frequency are closely linked variables. Because the total advertising weight consists of reach (expressed as a percentage of the target universe) multiplied by frequency, the improvement of one is always at the expense of the other within a given budget. The greater the reach, the less the frequency, and vice versa.

In the broadcast media a simple formula is used to compute frequency through the use of gross rating points:

$$\frac{\text{GRPs}}{\text{reach}} = \text{average frequency}$$

For example, a television schedule might attain 240 GRPs over a four-week period, reaching 60 percent of the target audience.

$$\frac{240 \text{ GRPs}}{60 \text{ reach}} = 4 \text{ average frequency}$$

All media deliver audiences in reach and frequency variables. For example, 200 GRPs in prime-time TV will achieve much higher reach figures than 200 points scheduled in daytime. In radio, 200 GRPs accumulated on three stations will have significantly lower reach levels than 200 GRPs spread across 10 stations. Special interest magazines build frequency, and so do radio stations with a specialized format. A single dominant newspaper in a particular market may provide excellent reach, with the number of advertising insertions building frequency. For advertisers spending a significant amount in one medium, frequency obviously builds once reach ceilings are achieved. Most advertisers, however, must decide where to put their emphasis (and their money) — in building reach or in building frequency.

For the majority of advertisers, reach has been the primary concern because of their desire to contact as many different customers or potential customers as possible. Because the logic is self-evident, it seems to make good sense, but it can be a mistake. If prospective customers are not exposed to an ad or a commercial frequently enough to capture their attention, then the advertising investment has been wasted.

Determining the correct frequency level is not an easy task. Every advertiser encounters unique problems, and media plans should be tailored to suit the situation.

"Baker, my father and his father, and father before him didn't care a whit about reach and frequency, and you can damn well bet that I don't either."

However, some general rules for determining low and high frequency can be applied in most cases.[1]

Lower Frequency	**Higher Frequency**
High brand loyalty	Low brand loyalty
Established brand	New brand introduction
Longer purchase cycles	Frequent purchase cycles
Light competitive activity	Heavy competitive activity
Simple advertising message	Complex advertising message
High attention to medium	Low attention to medium
Low-clutter environment	High-clutter environment
One or few messages	Multiple messages
Broad target audience	Narrow target audience
High product interest	Low product interest

Media Dominance versus Media Mix   Should the advertiser use a variety of media or dominate in one medium? The strategy for dominating a medium is based on the premise that the advertiser will achieve satisfactory reach goals and overshadow any concurrent competitive activity in that medium. In many cases, media planners know that a vast volume of their client's brand is consumed by a relatively small proportion of the total customers. If the media habits of these heavy users are concentrated, then it makes sense to develop a media dominance plan. Television, because of its impact, reach, and creative advantages, is used more than any other medium on an exclusive basis.

For a variety of reasons, however, most advertisers prefer to use a media mix. They have found that using several advertising media, all reinforcing one another, is not only more effective but also more efficient than using just one. For example, target audience reach can be greatly increased by using a combination of media. The *synergism principle* also applies to such a strategy. This theory suggests that the use of two media together reinforces and builds the effectiveness of each medium. In other words, one and one make three. Radio and outdoor are often used as supplemental media, not only because of reasonable costs but also because they are often considered reminder and reinforcing media. Radio, however, is very capable of delivering a full message.

Using the same message on TV and radio can be effective. Occasionally, audio tracks from TV commercials that can stand alone have served very well as radio commercials. It's an inexpensive way to widen the coverage of a campaign. The *imagery transfer* theory states that the TV commercial with a strong, memorable message will enjoy a kind of cerebral playback in the mind of radio listeners, provided they have had sufficient exposure to the TV commercial. The success of this transference is apparently greater with younger and better educated people, who have

---

[1]Joseph W. Ostrow, "What Level Frequency?" *Advertising Age,* November 9, 1981, p. S-4.

been able to quite accurately describe in laboratory experiments what they "saw" while listening to a radio commercial.

Imagery transfer and the reinforcement factor are partial reasons to use more than one medium, but the primary reason for using a media mix is to achieve an effective, efficient, and an increasingly broader reach of the target audience.

Cost Efficiency Formulas   Of all the variables considered in the development of a media plan, cost undoubtedly heads the list. Some media obviously cost more than others, but they need to be evaluated in terms of their ability to deliver the right audience. In spite of its high cost, TV may be very efficient in delivering a target audience and therefore represent an excellent buy. Media planners and buyers use a variety of simple formulas to bring costs and audience into a meaningful relationship. The most common are cost-per-thousand, cost-per-point, and persons reached per dollar spent.

Cost-per-thousand, or CPM, is the most commonly used formula. CPM really answers the question "What will it cost to reach 1,000 homes?" (Or women 18 to 49; or adult men; or preschool children; or whatever particular demographic group is important to that advertiser.) CPM provides the media planner with a comparison of different vehicles *within the same medium.* It's a simple formula. Simply divide estimates of the thousands of homes (or women, men, and so on) into the cost of time or space for the ad. The answer is the CPM.

$$\frac{\$350}{100 \text{ M homes}} = \$3.50 \text{ CPM}$$

In comparing different media, CPM figures vary tremendously. Prime-time television runs high, twice the CPM figures for radio. Newspapers, magazines, cable television, and outdoor all deliver a wide range of CPM figures based on the particular vehicle. A comparison of two media on the sole basis of CPM suggests that CPM is an indicator of value. This is not necessarily so, for if it were, only the media that delivered the cheapest CPMs would be used. It is also misleading to assume that CPMs in two media are necessarily a comparison of the same thing. In television, CPMs are usually based on the number of households or viewers at a particular time. Newspaper CPMs are usually based on total circulation, but they are not an indication of the actual number of readers exposed to an ad. In radio, CPMs are usually based on persons reached, not households. Thus, it's always important to ask the question "Cost-per-thousand *what?*" If the apples are kept separate from the oranges, false comparisons can be avoided. It's also important to know the basis for the cost figure used, because adjustments have to be made for the different lengths of commercials, ad sizes, color, and the like. CPMs for 30-second announcements should be evaluated separately from CPMs for 60-second announcements.

A high CPM is not necessarily a bad buy. In many instances, there are good reasons for paying a premium—Super Bowl buys, for example. Particular media may be preeminent in reaching the right prospects within an optimum editorial or programing environment. For example, a high household CPM is competitive if the buy has a minimum of *waste circulation;* in other words, if the target audience is a high percentage of the total audience, the cost can be recomputed in relation only to the target group. The final figures may be revealing, as shown below:

Station	Household CPM	Target Audience as a % of Total Audience	Target Audience CPM
A	$3.50	50%	$7.00
B	$5.00	80%	$6.25

Certain high-CPM media may be uniquely suitable for delivering a certain kind of message. Prime-time television or time buys for a major network sporting event usually have high CPMs, but the total circulation of these popular programs increases the advertiser's reach sufficiently to make the high CPM worth it.

Cost-per-point, or CPP, is simply a different way to evaluate the same data. CPMs are based on persons or households reached; CPPs are based on rating points. CPP answers the question "How much will each rating point cost for a given commercial position?"

In a given market, for example, a daytime TV program might deliver a 5 rating for a particular target audience, perhaps women 18 to 54. For a cost of $200, the computation is shown below.

$$\frac{\$200 \text{ cost for 30 seconds}}{5 \text{ rating}} = \$40 \text{ cost per point}$$

Persons (or households) reached per dollar spent is a third way to calculate efficiency. This calculation answers the question "How many persons will be reached for each dollar spent?"

For example, the audience tuned to a particular radio station is estimated at 16,000 persons at 8:00 A.M. on a particular day, and the cost of a commercial at that time is $20. The arithmetic looks like this:

$$\frac{16,000 \text{ persons}}{\$20} = \frac{800 \text{ persons reached}}{\text{per dollar spent}}$$

In order to make the most efficient use of every dollar spent, time buyers can quickly compute these figures in evaluating and comparing the options available on a number of stations.

Commercial Length and Ad Size The creative aspects of an advertising program and the budget will largely dictate the size of print ads and the length of radio and television commercials. The media planner, however, can provide comparisons on media costs for various ad sizes and commercial lengths. The options are far wider in print than in broadcast. Commercials, with few exceptions, run 10, 30, or 60 seconds. The standard length in radio is 60 seconds, whereas the TV standard is the 30-second commercial.

The media planner will remind the client who wants to use spot television (rather than network) that it is often very difficult to place 60-second commercials in prime time on network affiliates. (The availability of 60-second positions in prime time on independent stations constitutes one of their salient selling points.) Station breaks between network shows usually allow only enough time for a 30- and a 10-second commercial and a station identification. So the advertiser who wants to use prime-time spot television had better confine the commercials to 30 seconds.

In television, 60-second commercials usually cost twice the 30-second rate, and 10-second announcements are usually half the 30-second rate. In radio, 30-second commercials usually run about 70 to 85 percent of the minute rate. Therefore, many radio advertisers elect to go with minute commercials because they obviously save very little by using a 30-second format. All of these finer points of media planning and budgeting must be evaluated in relationship to overall objectives.

Conclusions

Media planning sounds as if it could be a science, but is not. It would be wonderful if all the questions involved in designing a media strategy could be fed into one end of a computer, and if all the right answers came out the other end. Unfortunately, it doesn't work that way. Even though mathematical formulas — and computers — can be invaluable in providing information, final decisions must come from people, not machines.

Fortunately, a media plan can be tremendously flexible. It can be altered by both marketing factors and communications factors. The former include campaign objectives, geography, target audience, seasonal factors, competitive considerations, and budget. Communications factors include all the intricacies of evaluating continuity, flights, gross rating points, reach and frequency, frequency distribution, media dominance, media mix, cost efficiency formulas, and commercial length. The job of the media planner is to weigh alternatives and then cut, fit, and rework the possibilities in order to devise an effective media strategy that will enable the client to achieve the advertising objectives.

chapter six

Creative Planning

An Original Idea, **Please**

Only a genius or a fool would presume to expound a perfect formula for creating persuasive and distinctive commercials. The creative process is essentially subjective, and no two agency copywriters or art directors will approach a problem or work through its solution in the same manner. Creativity is a highly individual process. Nonetheless, according to psychological research, very creative people tend to share such attributes as sensitivity and a restless intellect. They possess a compelling curiosity about life, people, and situations that prompts them to explore new ideas and seek out new experiences. Most are incurable eavesdroppers, and they constantly observe people coping with life's prosaic situations. For some creative people, writing a commercial is a slow, agonizing process; for others, it may come easily once the basic concept is developed. Some writers may suffer through an endless number of rewrites, but a few may be able to turn out a finished commercial in one draft. All members of the creative staff share one attribute, however—a tough hide. It's a vital characteristic, for everyone loves to be a critic. For better or worse, by the time the original commercial has been scrutinized by layers of staff at both the agency and client level, it may be unrecognized by its creator.

Writing Successful Commercials

First, a "don't." Don't ever write advertising based on dos and don'ts. A do for one product may be a don't for another, and a don't at one time may be a do at another.

Since rules are made to be broken, think each creative problem through on its own merits. A formula approach to advertising usually results in mediocre copy and often strays into the cliché. Stay with a few basic guidelines, such as those listed below, and then let your hard work, research, and imagination take over.

1. Be absolutely, positively, blindingly clear about the attributes of the product (or service). Get every scrap of information you can on the product — what it does, how it does it, why, and how it compares with the competition. Know the product's strengths and weaknesses, and if possible, use the product yourself.

2. Study the consumer. Who uses the product? What are the demographic and psychographic characteristics of your target audience? Do these people constitute a special group? What makes them special? How do they use the product — where, when and *why*? Form in your own mind a single profile of your audience, and write to that one person, not to an abstract statistic. Since advertising is a substitute for personal selling, how would you sell your product if you met the prospective customer face to face?

3. Watch and listen carefully and analytically to all the advertising that comes your way, especially the competition's. Examine the commercials you like and those you hate. Talk to people — advertising professionals and consumers. Ask them what they think of your product and what they think of various commercials.

4. Find out the legal and self-regulatory limits in which you must work. Broadcast media are particularly (and properly) tough about product claims. Don't ever lie or bend the truth; be able to document every single claim. Search the files for any problems that may have arisen in the past regarding advertising claims. If you don't do this homework, your agency or your client may be sued!

5. Keep the advertising objective foremost in your mind when you begin work. What does this advertiser want to accomplish? Stay on the track. Keep it simple (see 6.1).

6. Do plan to nail your audience to their collective seats in the first three to five seconds of the commercial. But don't overwhelm the audience with your cleverness. Commercial writing can and should be bright and witty, but the *product* must be the hero, not your deathless prose.

7. Respect your audience. Consumers are not morons, and they are more perceptive, better educated, and more sensitive than you may think. Don't write *down* — write up! Stretch your imagination, and invite your audience to accompany you.

8. Don't settle for "good enough." Get your efforts critiqued. Rewrite and improve what you've written. Try a number of approaches.

9. Don't get discouraged. Try, if you can, to detach your ego from your work. Write to please yourself first, and others will be pleased, too. Never settle for less than your very best.

The creative team in an advertising agency often consists of a copywriter and an art director working together on a common problem. In many small agencies, however, and with small local advertisers, creative work may fall to one person. Sales people (or account executives) from radio and television stations often find themselves writing "spec" commercials to use in soliciting new business. In radio especially, small retailers usually don't have the foggiest notion of how to construct a

6.1/Three Words to the Wise

Keep It Simple

Strike three.
Get your hand off my knee.
You're overdrawn.
Your horse won.
Yes.
No.
You have the account.
Walk.
Don't walk.
Mother's dead.
Basic events
require simple language.
Idiosyncratically euphuistic
eccentricities are the
promulgators of
triturable obfuscation.
What did you do last night?
Enter into a meaningful
romantic involvement
or
fall in love?
What did you have for
breakfast this morning?
The upper part of a hog's
hind leg with two oval
bodies encased in a shell
laid by a female bird
or
ham and eggs?
David Belasco, the great
American theatrical producer,
once said, "If you can't
write your idea on the
back of my calling
card,
you don't have a clear idea."

Reprinted courtesy of United Technologies.

commercial; the local station must double as an advertising agency. Methods of turning out creative work are as diverse as the people themselves, but analyzing the final product reveals that good commercials stand foursquare on the following factors: (1) advertising strategy, (2) commercial format, (3) emotional appeal, and (4) production techniques.

Understanding the Advertising Strategy

Chapter 4 explored the process of determining advertising objectives. A campaign may be dedicated to reinforcing brand loyalty, introducing a new product, demonstrating a product feature, or achieving some other specific goal. Based on this particular objective a campaign strategy is designed. Many strategies are possible for any given objective, but the challenge is to select the most effective one. The strategy essentially answers these questions: "What shall we say?" and "To whom should this message be directed?" In broadcast campaigns the message must fit into a very brief announcement, and it must be relevant to the selected target audience. The answers to these key questions—in other words, the strategy—guide members of the creative team as they begin their work.

Slogans, often considered synonymous with the term *copy platform,* have always been an important part of advertising. They are designed to summarize the central message the advertiser wants to leave with the consumer. A perfect match with the advertising strategy is essential. For the purpose of reinforcement, all the commercials in a campaign should use the same slogan. An effective slogan enunciates the most relevant aspect of the product or service to the target audience. For example, Federal Express: "When it absolutely, positively, has to be there overnight." Rolaids: "How do you spell relief?" Hertz: "There's only one car rental company big enough and good enough to be number one."

Additionally, a good slogan may carve out a distinct niche in positioning the advertiser against the competition. This can be especially effective in breaking away from the multitude of "me too" campaigns. For example, Avis: "Trying harder. It's still the best way to do business." "Get the Anacin difference." "Wouldn't you really rather have a Buick?"

In television it is valuable to study the elements used in campaigns that have been exceptionally successful in the marketplace. Harry Wayne McMahan identified seven key factors:[1] (1) *story*, a plot and characters that capture attention; (2) *demonstrations*, a convincing depiction of how people really use a product; (3) *stars and celebrities*, because Americans love their heroes, especially when they're a perfect match for a particular product or service; (4) a continuing central character (less expensive than a celebrity), usually owned as a "licensed character" by the advertiser. Examples include the Pillsbury Doughboy, Kellogg's Tony the Tiger, and Marlboro's cowboy; (5) *the look*, a distinctive presentation that over the years builds instant recognition with consumers; (6) *words*, carefully constructed into slogans, catch phrases, and summations ("Ring around the collar" may have been an aggravation to TV viewers, but it

---

[1] Harry Wayne McMahan, *Communication and Persuasion* (Spokane, Wash.: Stephens Press, 1981.)

made Wisk a top-selling detergent); (7) *jingles,* written with great care and expense, but worth every penny. (Ask a group of extroverted children to sing the commercials they remember, and they'll probably be occupied for at least an hour.)

Format of the Commercial

Just as the best radio and television shows are built around a well-organized format, so are the most effective broadcast commercials. The format provides the all-important structure on which hang the emotional appeal and the production excellence. The format permits the logical development of the selling idea. It should start somewhere, go somewhere, and take the audience along. The extraneous must be omitted. The message must grab audience interest in the opening few seconds. The penalty to the advertiser who neglects these basic points is an audience either mentally or physically absent during the commercial. Sadly, an hour spent with the broadcast media will yield ample evidence that many advertisers have never learned the most basic rules of persuasion.

Commercial formats provide many options to the creative team, yet experience has shown that certain ones are often classically harmonious with certain advertising objectives. A *demonstration* format, for example, is often used to prove that a product has a genuinely superior feature or to introduce a new product. A *problem-solution* format is obvious when the product can genuinely solve a problem. The most common formats for radio and television commercials are described below. Some can be used in both media, but others are unique to one or the other. Most demonstrations, for example, are virtually impossible in radio.

Dramatic Format

The five classic steps of the dramatic format are as useful to the modern advertising copywriter as they were to Shakespeare:

1. *Exposition.* This step sets the stage and often simply answers the question of who is trying to get what done.

2. *Conflict.* What's the problem? Who's the protagonist? Who or what is the antagonist? (The antagonist doesn't necessarily have to be a person. In the case of a commercial, it may be a headache, a dirty kitchen floor, or unexpected company.)

3. *Rising action.* The story builds, the conflict heightens the suspense, and the complications thicken.

4. *Climax.* The problem is solved, showing where and how the circumstances change. The product and the product user should be the heroes.

5. *Denouement, or resolution.* This step should wrap up the story, answer any unanswered questions, and clearly register the most important selling points and the product name.

As the story line developed in a 30- or 60-second TV minidrama unfolds, the picture should tell the story. (See 6.2.) It's an easy trap for copywriters to overwrite a

6.2 / Presenting a Computer in a Dramatic Context

Although this commercial focuses on a computer monitoring system used in hospitals, the intent is to build an image of dependability for Hewlett-Packard products. By presenting a dramatic situation, the message shows that quality computers can be counted on in critical situations. This 30-second commercial was created by Wilton, Coombs & Colnett Advertising, of San Francisco.

The HP Arrhythmia Monitor
When performance must be measured by results.

The patient in Room 7 doesn't know it, but he's very close to a heart attack.

A Hewlett-Packard computer system

has sensed the warning symptoms . . .

giving the nurses in the coronary care unit . . .

a few precious minutes . . .

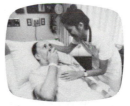

so they can help

head off the attack . . .

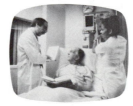

before it happens.

Hewlett-Packard.
When performance must be measured by results.

Watch our performance on network TV.

dramatic commercial and end up with what's essentially a radio commercial augmented with pictures. The viewer should be able to follow the story with the sound turned off. In radio, the copywriter can utilize the theater-of-the-mind concept.

It is tremendously important to cast likable and believable characters. They should be well defined and readily identifiable to the audience. The problem, obviously, is to avoid perpetuating stereotypes, such as precocious children, their frumpy housewife-mother, her befuddled husband, his exasperated boss, and so on.

Because most Americans have spent so many thousands of hours watching dramatic television programs and going to movies, the conventions of dramatic structure are familiar to them. This familiarity works to the advantage of the copywriter, who must squeeze both a story and a selling message into a very short time span. Quick cuts that jump both time and space can be accomplished almost instantaneously by a smooth dissolve in television or a music bridge in radio.

In commercials with a dramatic format, it's easy for copywriters to become so engrossed in developing the story and interesting characters that the product is given short shrift. It is absolutely necessary that the product provide the payoff at the commercial's climax.

Problem-Solution Format

The solving of a problem is perhaps the most common format used today in commercials. This format also sometimes results in obnoxious advertising. The plots, which often follow dramatic structure, are ridiculously simple: a problem is presented, and the product is introduced as a solution. The problem with the problem, however, is that it is rarely believable. It should be one that the product commonly solves. (No one believes a problem situation in which the British ambassador happens in for afternoon tea and wrinkles his nose at the finger smudges on the coffee table.)

The dilemma should take one of two routes: (1) a believable and logical development of a problem with which the audience can identify or (2) total hyperbole, with the complications so humorously exaggerated that the result is a farce. Anything in between will probably be resented as insulting or will simply be ignored.

Phony dialogue is undoubtedly the main fault of problem-solution commercials. The attributes of the product must be presented, and in the absence of an announcer, what device is left? The friendly neighbor who just happens to have a bottle of a new dish detergent in her apron pocket? Hopefully not. The product should be introduced as a logical outgrowth of the quest for a solution. Then, a demonstration and the enumeration of the product's attributes are in order. The characters in the commercial need not wax eloquent if the product can be just as effectively presented in a visual demonstration. Viewers are not idiots. They will get the message.

The usual closing sequence of a TV commercial in this format is a happy scene of activity that reinforces the idea that the problem has been solved. The product is always prominently displayed.

Demonstration Format

The sight, sound, motion, and color of television make it a perfect medium for demonstrating new consumer products. The mass coverage of television means that

6.3 / A Bright Idea

Commercial demonstrations need not be extravaganzas to be effective or to win Clio Awards. An everyday product, a light bulb, was demonstrated in an extraordinary way. An artist used it to light the subjects — an attractive mother and daughter.

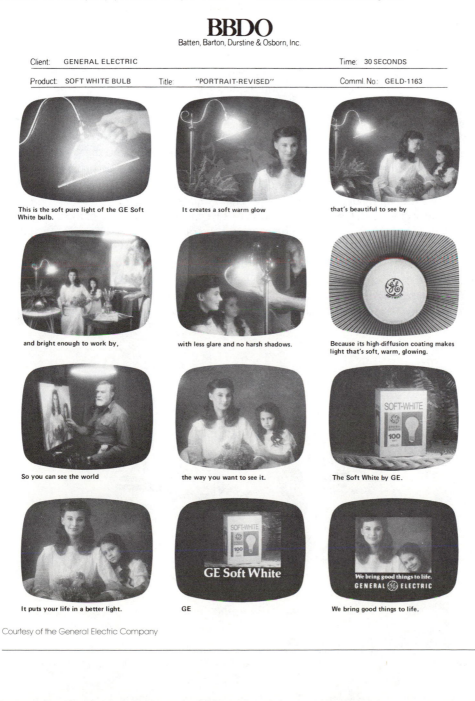

BBDO
Batten, Barton, Durstine & Osborn, Inc.

Client: GENERAL ELECTRIC		Time: 30 SECONDS
Product: SOFT WHITE BULB	Title: "PORTRAIT-REVISED"	Comml. No.: GELD-1163

This is the soft pure light of the GE Soft White bulb.

It creates a soft warm glow

that's beautiful to see by

and bright enough to work by,

with less glare and no harsh shadows.

Because its high-diffusion coating makes light that's soft, warm, glowing.

So you can see the world

the way you want to see it.

The Soft White by GE.

It puts your life in a better light.

GE

We bring good things to life.

Courtesy of the General Electric Company

this demonstration can be viewed simultaneously by millions of prospective customers. For these reasons, the demonstration format is one of the most popular commercial structures with advertisers. Demonstrations can be simple, using a voice-over announcer and a lot of closeup camera work, or they can be exotically staged in unusual locales with a lot of talent.

Demonstration commercials should strive to provoke curiosity and suspense and to provide sufficient visual evidence of a product's attributes. (See 6.3.)

Advertising people who produce demonstration commercials encounter numerous frustrations. One common problem is that a superb product may not show up very well on TV. The color, the texture, or any one of a number of other product qualities may not look right. Production personnel quickly learned how to "dress" a product to enhance the demonstration. Shortening has stood in for ice cream under hot lights, small pebbles for rice, and whipped cream for shampoo. These solutions may have been satisfactory to the production crew, but unless the advertiser and agency are willing to risk severe scrutiny by the Federal Trade Commission and the possibility of a formal complaint, the crew is well advised to "play it straight." Advertising agencies and their clients are now filing away demonstration evidence and affidavits by witnesses in case the legitimacy of their commercials is questioned.

Requests by the FTC for substantiation of advertising claims have made it clear that this regulatory body is concerned that TV demonstrations be relevant to "typical use" of the product. In other words the demonstration should prove what it sets out to prove and not stumble into a non sequitur. Torture tests are fun to watch, but if an automobile is dropped from a 20-foot cliff and a person climbs in and drives off, does it necessarily indicate the vehicle's ability to withstand five years of punishment on bumpy roads? Sometimes, in an attempt to build interest, demonstrations stray into

"His Timex is still running."

pure idiocy. (Efferdent, a denture cleanser, pronounced: "We simmered a string of pearls in a pot of cherry preserves.")

The considerable scrutiny by both the government and the networks' broadcast standards departments does not make it impossible to produce exciting, suspenseful, and interesting demonstration commercials. They can result in high product recognition and brand familiarity by consumers convinced of the credibility of television demonstrations.

Interview Format

The interview is suitable to commercials on both broadcast media, but it is particularly popular in radio. Production costs are quite reasonable, and the interview permits the advertiser to break away from the overused spokesperson format. The question-and-answer format provides great potential for comedy, characterizations, and a continuing story line for a series of commercials. Such commercials are fairly easy to write, and the creative team can approach them in a number of ways. A fully scripted commercial using professional actors may be the best way to control the message's direction and to maximize humor. (See 6.4.) Music, sound effects, and the acting can be thoroughly rehearsed to perfect the comedy timing.

As an alternative, the advertiser may elect to present spontaneous and unrehearsed commercials in a "man-on-the-street" format. An announcer, a tape recorder, time, budget, and patience are necessary. Perhaps several dozen people may have to be interviewed in order to get the kind of responses the advertiser wants. A lot of time must then be spent in editing to find those perfect responses and fit them into 30 or 60 seconds. The result of all this effort, however, should be a highly effective commercial that communicates that these are "real people in real situations" who are truly enthusiastic about the advertiser's product.

Testimonial Format

Advertising is a substitute for personal selling, and advertisers have learned over the years that nothing can be more persuasive than the testimony of a satisfied product user. Like the interview format, the testimonial format can be developed in several ways. The message can come from ordinary consumers, in which case the advertising agency must cope with unprofessional talent; but the results may be most effective and worth the trouble. Or the advertiser may elect to use professional talent. Regardless of the choice, a few guidelines should be followed. The setting of the TV commercial should be simple and compatible with product use. The message should focus very directly on the endorser and the product. The audience should be able to perceive the testifier as an actual product user, and the testimony should seem natural and truthful. (Professional actors, hired for the job, will drip sincerity.)

The testimonial can be delivered directly to a camera (or microphone in radio) or the talent can rhapsodize to an interviewer. More than any other format, the testimonial can achieve exceptional impact. Members of the audience may be greatly affected by advertising in which they perceive someone besides the advertiser talking about a product or service. The fact that almost all testimonials are bought and paid for can limit the believability of this commercial format. Because of this problem, the American Association of Advertising Agencies in its *Standards of Practice* (Section 1, b) states: "Specifically, we will not knowingly produce advertising which contains testimonials which do not reflect the real choice of a competent witness."

Self-regulatory groups have not been the only ones active in the area of testimonial advertising. In 1975, following a three-year investigation, the FTC issued guidelines covering certain aspects of testimonials and endorsements. In 1980, it issued additional guidelines. All were accompanied by lengthy statements, but they can be summarized as follows:

1. *General considerations.* Endorsements must reflect the honest views of the endorser. That person must be a bona fide user of the product at the time the endorsement is given and must make only claims that can be supported if made by the advertiser rather than the endorser. The endorsement may be paraphrased but not used out of context. The advertiser may use the endorsement only for as long as there is good reason to believe that the endorser, if a celebrity or expert (ordinary consumer endorsements are exempted), continues to subscribe to the presented opinion.

6.4 / A Carefully Scripted "Spontaneous" Interview

U.S. Radio

Coca-Cola

Soft Drinks
"Stanley"
McCann-Erickson, Atlanta

Anncr: Today we're talking to supermarket customers who have . . . oh, pardon me folks.
Man & Woman: Yes.
Anncr: I see you have the new two-liter bottle of Coca-Cola. How do you like the Big Mouth?
Woman: Well, he's terrific at ballgames.
Anncr: Who are you . . .?
Woman: Show 'em, Stanley.
Man: Throw the bum out!
Anncr: No, I meant, uh . . .
Woman: Or when he's calling the dog.
Man: Here, Trixi!
Woman: Or when he's calling a cab.
Man: Here, taxi!
Anncr: Uh, ma'am . . .
Woman: How about that for a big mouth?
Anncr: I was talking about the new easy-pour spout we call the Big Mouth on the new two-liter bottle of Coke.
Woman: Well, what about it?

Anncr: What do you think of the Big Mouth?
Woman: Well, he's great for getting the kid up in the morning. Hit it, Stanley!
Man: Get up, Harold!
Woman: Or putting him to bed at night . . .
Man: Go to bed, Harold!
Anncr: Ma'am . . .
Woman: Or do you know when a big mouth like this is really terrific?
Anncr: I'm not talking about . . .
Woman: When you're herding cattle.
Man: Get along, little Doagie.
Woman: Doggie, Stanley, doggie.
Man: Here, Trixi!
Woman: Hold it!
Man: Trixi!
Woman: Oh, we're going home!
Man: Here, taxi!
Anncr: Introducing the new two-liter bottle of Coca-Cola with the giant easy pour spout. And, unlike some big mouths, it has a resealable cap.
Woman: Yes. He's a big mouth . . . but he can be so tender and . . . I love you, Stanley!
Man: And I love you!
Woman: See what I mean . . .
Anncr: Uh-huh.

2. *Nonexpert consumer endorsements.* The advertiser must be able to prove that the average person can expect comparable performance. The ad must clearly and conspicuously disclose what performance can be expected or disclose that the endorsement has limited applicability. The endorsement of nonprescription drugs by consumers must be consistent with any determination about the product by the U.S. Food and Drug Administration.

3. *Expert endorsements.* Whenever an advertisement represents, directly or by implication, that the endorser is an *expert* with respect to the endorsement message, then the endorser's qualifications must in fact qualify him or her as a true expert. If the net impression in the advertisement is that the advertised product is superior to other products, then the expert must in fact have found such superiority.

4. *Endorsements by organizations.* Organizational endorsements, especially expert ones, are viewed as representing the judgment of a group whose collective experience exceeds that of any individual member, and whose judgments are generally free of the subjective opinions that vary among individuals. Therefore, the endorsement must be reached by a process sufficient to ensure that the statements fairly reflect the collective judgment of the organization. Such organizations might be comprised of engineers, scientists, or other specially trained experts.

5. *Disclosure of material connections.* When there is a connection between an advertiser and an endorser that might materially affect the weight or credibility of the endorsement, it must be fully disclosed. In the case of experts or celebrities, payment is not considered a material connection unless the advertising implies that the endorser is *not* being paid. Only compensation provided *in exchange* for endorsement need be disclosed. In addition, if an endorser owns stock or has some similar financial stake in the success of the advertiser, that connection must be disclosed.

Spokesperson Format

The spokesperson format is the traditional commercial technique in the broadcast media. Since the 1920s, announcers have delivered "straight sell" commercials for thousands of advertisers. This format was quickly adapted to television when that medium appeared, and it is still common today for many good reasons: The spokesperson approach can be very effective if the message is delivered by someone who has a strong, likable personality, who can establish an immediate rapport with an audience, and who relates to the product. Spokesperson commercials are usually quite inexpensive to produce in comparison with other formats. The selling is direct and ideally is compelling and convincing. Often, a maximum number of sales points can be woven into the commercial. Unfortunately, audiences accustomed to more elaborately produced commercials often find spokesperson commercials uninteresting. To increase audience attention, these commercials are often augmented with closeups of the product, short demonstrations, music, sound effects, and other devices.

Writing spokesperson commercials requires skill, because consumers will *hear* the copy and not read it. Long, involved sentences, unfamiliar words, and awkward phrasing should be avoided. The copy should sound natural, conversational, and as spontaneous as possible.

Spokesperson commercials run the gamut — from the DJ delivery of live copy on a small radio station to the compelling presence of a well-known Shakespearean actor. A fine line distinguishes spokesperson commercials from testimonials. A testimonial commercial is almost always phrased in the first person, and the talent relates personal feelings and experiences. ("I use Product X every day because . . .") In the spokesperson commercial, the talent, in the most convincing manner possible, declares: "You should use Product X every day because . . ." If one were to conduct a survey and ask consumers what commercials they remembered that had used celebrities, and if they were further asked to distinguish whether the talent had delivered testimonials or simply served as spokespersons, the chances are that most people would not discern the difference. Thus, in order to avoid the complications of FTC testimonial guidelines, many advertisers will simply use spokespersons to deliver their messages.

Symbolism Format

If an army platoon is not available to serve as talent in a television commercial, what alternatives are available to the imaginative copywriter? Perhaps with music, sound effects, and expert editing a dozen or more toy soldiers will serve just as well. The symbolism format is useful and flexible in presenting a wide variety of tangible products and intangible services to the marketplace. It is a more sophisticated advertising device than some of the other formats and offers the opportunity to design exceptionally interesting and engaging commercials. (Perhaps the ultimate attempt at symbolism cast Xerox as God opposite Brother Dominic.)

Since appeals to curiosity are commonly used to create a measure of suspense, the symbol should not be immediately compared with the product; instead, the comparison should be gradually revealed as the commercial progresses. The analogy must make sense and provide a logical parallel to the advertised product. Such advertising is attention-getting in form, but it should be augmented with narration that explains the comparison. It would be foolish to assume that an audience will necessarily or automatically deduce that the plays on a chess board represent expert financial planning by a local bank's trust department. A voice-over announcer must provide the explanation.

Just about everyone likes animals, and advertisers are increasingly turning to bird and beast to find a corporate symbol. Hartford Insurance uses a stag, Merrill Lynch parades a bull, and Qantas Airways is immediately associated with a cuddly koala. Charlie the Tuna is immediately recognizable, both as a symbol and as a presenter to several generations of Starkist consumers. Animals are also compelling in demonstrations. The American Tourister gorilla, representing a baggage handler, has been the star of a very funny television torture test.

Symbolic advertising is especially advantageous for advertisers confined to studio production because of a limited budget. A lighted match can symbolize fire; a cat with kittens can represent family responsibilites; and a toy boat on a small pond can double for an ocean cruise.

In radio, metaphors and verbal analogies can make an announcer's copy more colorful and create a vivid, though imaginary, picture in the listener's mind. Musical effects, especially on an electronic synthesizer, can produce tremendously effective sound suggestions.

In all symbolic advertising, the advertiser must be sure that the audience will understand the analogy and be convinced of its logical application to the product or service. If the device doesn't work, the audience will forget the entire message. If it backfires, the audience may remember the gimmick and forget the product!

Comparative Format

Most advertising is rife with comparisons, real or implied. A store that calls itself "the *best* in town" is implying that other merchants fall short. An analgesic that says it "won't upset your stomach" is implying that other products will. An ad that exhorts new-car buyers "to check the competition, then see us" is inviting comparisons. In what is called a dangling comparison, countless products claim to be bigger, better, stronger, or whatever. These ads are obviously alluding to competing products.[2]

For the sake of this discussion, however, *comparative advertising identifies competitors by brand name.* Until the 1970s this kind of advertising was almost unheard of in radio and television. A wave of consumerism prompted the FTC to challenge the networks in 1971 and urge them to accept comparative advertising. Both CBS and ABC had corporate policies that precluded the acceptance of commercials that named competing brands. (NBC had never adopted such a policy, but few if any advertisers produced commercials that would clear only one network.) The FTC argued that advertising that alluded only to "Brand X" was essentially uninformative and often confusing. True comparative advertising, it contended, would help consumers make informed choices between competing products. So, with some reluctance, broadcasters began accepting this new form of advertising.

Many product categories have experimented with comparative advertising, some successfully and some with disappointing or disastrous results. Automobiles, analgesics, appliances, beers, wines, soft drinks, and household products have led the pack.

Critics charge that comparative advertising invites unfair attacks on competitors and creates distrust and confusion in consumers' minds. For advertisers, one chilling aspect of comparative advertising is the risk that consumers will mix up brands when buying and confuse the "good guy" with the "bad guy." No one names a competitor with any good in mind. The truth seems precariously balanced, and too often irrelevant product features are compared. It is virtually impossible to present a fair comprehensive brand comparison in 30 seconds.

The networks turn down a great number of comparative ads and consider them a prime source of problems. (The procedures followed by NBC in handling complaints from competitors are included in comparative advertising guidelines in Chapter 18. See 18.1.)

---

[2]J. J. Boddewyn and Katherin Marton, *Comparison Advertising, A Worldwide Study* (New York: Hastings House, 1978). This study, sponsored by the International Advertising Association, explores the subject in depth and presents case studies from around the world.

The chairman of one ad agency, Ogilvy & Mather, Inc., roundly condemned comparative advertising, maintaining that "ferocious hostility erupts between corporations that used to be sensible, honorable competitors — all because of some stupidly provocative comparative advertising. It is not in our interest to reduce the advertising arena to the kind of mud-slinging that has hitherto been the special preserve of politics."[3]

The Alberto-Culver Company apparently agreed with those sentiments and filed a $7-million suit against the Gillette Company and its advertising agency, the J. Walter Thompson Company. The suit charged that a commercial for Gillette's Tame creme rinse conditioner disparaged its product, Alberto Balsam, and led to the destruction of the brand. After much litigation, the defendants agreed in 1979 to pay Alberto-Culver $4.25 million in an out-of-court settlement.[4]

Proponents of comparative advertising, however, maintain that, when properly executed, this kind of advertising is the industry's own brand of consumerism. They argue as follows: The problem is not with the theory of comparative advertising, but in its current practice. Comparisons heighten competition, because manufacturers seek to improve their brands' benefits. A "proper doubt" is introduced to consumers, who may have been buying a brand automatically with no real thought about it. Comparative advertising invites a trial, and thus, commercials must present comparisons that consumers can verify for themselves. Comparisons should be based on solid facts, not irrelevant brand differences. As a result, this kind of advertising should encourage more thoughtful shopping behavior, making consumers more aware of the responsibility to select products and brands with care. For present users of the advertised brand, comparative commercials reinforce brand loyalty.

Research studies and the opinions of experts are not always consistent, but a few basic guidelines have emerged in the relatively short life of comparative advertising in the broadcast media.[5]

1.   Comparative advertising should ideally be used when one brand is clearly superior and when that superiority can be dramatically demonstrated in the media.

2.   The brand attribute touted as superior must be verifiable by the consumer.

3.   Comparative advertising reinforces brand loyalty among present users and is effective in winning over the undecided consumer.

---

[3]Andrew G. Kershaw, "The Mischief of Comparative Advertising," *Papers from the 1976 Annual Meeting of the American Association of Advertising Agencies,* p. 17.

[4]*Broadcasting,* April 23, 1979, p. 60.

[5]Boddewyn and Marton, *loc. cit.*

Michael Etgar and Stephen A. Goodwin, "Planning for Comparative Advertising Requires Special Attention," *Journal of Advertising,* Vol. 8, No. 1, Winter 1979, p. 26.

Charles W. Lamb, William M. Pride, and Barbara A. Pletcher, "A Taxonomy for Comparative Advertising Research," *Journal of Advertising,* Vol. 7, No. 1, Winter 1978, p. 43.

Subhash C. Jain and Edwin C. Hackleman, "How Effective Is Comparison Advertising for Stimulating Brand Recall?" *Journal of Advertising,* Vol. 7, No. 3, Summer 1978, p. 20.

Nancy Giges, "Comparative Ads: Battles That Wrote Dos and Don'ts," *Advertising Age,* September 29, 1980, p. 59.

4.   Comparative advertising is most effective when presented in a demonstration or a testimonial. It is not conducive to fantasy, dramatization, or any other device that breaches reality.

5.   An advertiser who enjoys a dominant share of the market should avoid comparative advertising; it should be used in going after larger game, not smaller competitors.

6.   An advertiser should lean over backwards to present a fair comparison with a competitor. Otherwise, the commercial may never clear the self-regulatory screen of the broadcasters. In the worst scenario, the advertiser may have to "tell it to the judge."

Emotional Appeal

Novice copywriters often delude themselves into believing that a commercial that packs an emotional wallop will automatically sell products. This rationale couldn't be further from the truth. Sigmund Freud reminded his readers that "the voice of the intellect is a soft one, but it does not rest until it has gained a hearing." A housewife doesn't skip down a supermarket aisle like a fairy princess dropping advertisers' products willy-nilly into a shopping cart. If consumers were so emotionally suggestible that they bought everything they were told to buy, families would be bankrupt within a week. Emotional appeals have a hard time getting around budget limitations. A consumer's life-style is dictated by a variety of factors: education, family background, income, ethnic grouping, and social mobility. All of these identifying factors indicate a buying and consuming pattern that is reasonably predictable, if the advertiser is willing to pay for the research. The greater the quantity of valid demographic and psychographic data available, the easier the job is for the astute creative team assigned to design the message.

Armed with a clear profile of the target audience, the commercial writer needs to ask, "What is the customer *really* buying?" Insurance companies sell security, cosmetic companies sell glamour and self-esteem, and microwave oven manufacturers sell convenience. Understanding the consumer's problems and satisfactions provides the copywriter with a tremendous head start. The focus should be on the *result* of product use.

An objective analysis of much advertising, particularly print, provides ample evidence that exaggerated emotional appeals are usually confined to graphics and headlines. The same is generally true in the broadcast media. The opening few seconds should reach out to the listener or viewer on an emotional, not necessarily rational, basis. Emotion attracts interest, but rational and believable sales points are what sell the product. It should be noted that a few important product categories are exceptions. Such products are purchased and consumed on an almost exclusively emotional level: cosmetics, grooming products, perfumes, and so on. The consumer often subconsciously buys a new self-image along with the product. Most products, however, are not purchased on such an arbitrary basis, and so the copywriter must seek the optimum blend of emotional appeal and rational, factual promise. There is no magic formula.

A number of emotional appeals commonly used in commercial formats are listed below. The list is arbitrary at best, but it demonstrates that the advertising industry is aware of growing consumer sophistication.

Security Appeals

Survival and the attainment of a satisfactory level of security are two primary human motivations. These drives are manifested in the most mundane aspects of a consumer's life-style. If one peruses the marketplace to discover the products and services that cater to the need for security, the list soon becomes enormous. Needs for shelter, food, clothing, health, and safety encompass a vast marketplace. The advertiser that markets a product or service that helps consumers achieve the security they seek will do well to incorporate this appeal into the advertising messages.

Nonprescription medications use security appeals to promise relief to the sufferers of sniffles, sneezes, headaches, and hangnails. The emotional tone is sympathetic. Assurances are made. The product may or may not be effective, but the cold victim clutching a box of tissues with one hand and a throbbing head with the other probably isn't reasoning all that clearly.

Exaggerated promises, however, may run afoul of self-regulatory groups. Many years ago, the TV Code of the National Association of Broadcasters banned "man-in-the-white-coat" commercials. Actors dressed like physicians and standing in a laboratory set were not considered to be in the public's best interest. It is important that advertisers understand their obligations to the public (and to the FTC) and be absolutely truthful in their health and safety claims.

Personal products, often sold as nonprescription medications, present special problems in broadcast advertising. Radio and television enter the privacy of the home as invited guests; bad-mannered advertising is not welcome. The networks and most stations are extremely restrictive about what can be presented in commercials for feminine hygiene products, hemorrhoid treatments, and other personal products.

Sometimes, security appeals present a very threatening situation. Peace of mind is what the consumer seeks, and thus, many products and services stress safety as a basic emotional appeal. Insurance, lock systems, automobile tires, and traveler's checks are just a few examples. The commercial presents a threatening situation that is effective in stimulating conflict, or cognitive dissonance, in the receiver. *Cognitive dissonance* refers to people's desire to neutralize or resolve the degree to which their perceptions or beliefs are inconsistent. Threat appeals are most commonly used in the problem-solution format or in dramatized commercials. The plot is simple: a threat or fear is introduced (bad breath, vitamin shortage, insufficient insurance, an unsafe automobile), and the advertiser's product is presented as the solution to the dilemma. Although the plot is simple, consumers' response to the cognitive dissonance may be complex. They may ignore it, reject it, or feel that it is relevant to their circumstances and that possession of the product will eliminate the threat. In the latter case, the advertiser will have succeeded in his purpose.

Sex Appeals

Consumers invest billions of dollars in clothing, cosmetics, grooming aids, jewelry, accessories, automobiles, and myriad other products as they try to maintain their attractiveness to the opposite sex. If the product is, or can be, associated with sex appeals, the creative team must appreciate certain sensitive problems. Too often, advertisers have used these appeals in an irresponsible and exploitive manner. Overt sexuality in advertising may either offend consumers or eventually dull their senses. Slightly more subtle messages still leave plenty to the imagination. ("All my men wear English Leather, or they wear nothing at all.") If the product will make the user more attractive, comfortable, or confident, then the advertiser should certainly communicate that message. Advertising always contains a promise, and a promise extended in an emotional context can make the product highly desirable. However, the advertiser who incorporates sex themes that are not relevant to the product does a disservice to both the consumer and the advertising industry.

Broadcasters who are concerned about the public-interest aspects of their Federal Communications Commission license have helped to keep overt sexuality out of commercials. Advertisers have still been criticized for presenting women in commercials as sex objects and nothing more. Some women's groups have brought pressure on these advertisers, pointing out the destructive self-image these commercials present to women viewers and also to impressionable children, who can assimilate false ideas about sex roles at a very early age. Many advertisers have become more sensitive to how women are portrayed in commercials and have tried to avoid stereotyping. Other advertisers and their agencies who have been roundly criticized on this matter have made it clear by their comments, or their lack of comment, that they have no intention of altering their advertising strategies.

Good taste and a respect for the sensibilities of the audience should be overriding concerns of the creative team that incorporates sex appeals in broadcast commercials. Such sensitivity does not mean that these appeals cannot be presented in a bright and spontaneous way. Some of the most effective and delightful commercials utilize sex appeals with a touch of comedy to create an aura of light-heartedness. (Who seriously believes he'll be assaulted by a bevy of beauties if he changes brands of after-shave lotion?)

Love and Sentimental Appeals

Numerous products have been found to be eminently adaptable to advertising themes that stress love and sentimental appeals. Usually, the product is associated with a close and happy home life. Examples include baby products, camera equipment, pet supplies, and a wide group of food products often consumed in a social setting such as coffee, soft drinks, cereals, desserts, and snacks. The *result* of using the product or service is what is sold. AT&T doesn't preach about long distance equipment or rates; the consumer is encouraged to "reach out and touch someone." Greeting card manufacturers obviously rely on love and sentimental appeals in marketing their product, as do a number of proprietary medicine manufacturers, who stress concern for family members in providing relief for morning backache, iron-poor blood, and irregularity.

Almost any product associated with family life could probably attempt to use sentimental appeals in its advertising. Attempting it is one thing; succeeding is another. In broadcast commercials, the trick is to touch the viewers' hidden emotions yet avoid mawkish sentimentality. That's quite a trick in 30 seconds! With time so precious, the viewers must be projected immediately into the scene and be presented with a circumstance they can readily identify with. The classic film techniques of *cinema vérité* are often employed, and the viewers seem to enter the action through the "subjective camera." Some of the visual techniques include extreme closeups, quick cuts, reaction shots, the soft-focus lens, and colored filters. All these devices create a soft mood and increase the viewers' feelings of intimacy and involvement. Because of the sheer volume of advertising, some agencies have developed frankly sentimental campaigns designed to break down the wall of consumer apathy. An executive from Batten, Barton, Durstine & Osborn who creates commercials for Pepsi maintained that "telling isn't selling. Advertising does not have to use hard sell in order to sell hard."[6] Many experts agree that the difference between an ad that tells and one that sells is the style of the ad, not the researched strategy.

Most commercials with love and sentimental appeals incorporate a strong audio track. Music is most important in setting the mood and must be carefully selected. A soft-spoken announcer, invariably off camera in a voice-over role, delivers the soft sell. The excellence of the director, actors, and the tape or film editor is a prerequisite for creating and presenting the mood, but such excellence usually entails a considerable budget.

Humorous Appeals

More than any other emotional appeal, humor can be tremendously successful in getting consumers to like the commercial and thus the product. Humor in advertising is not always suitable to the product and to the objectives of a campaign. Undoubtedly,

[6]Larry Light, speech to the American Association of Advertising Agencies, Monterey, California, October 17, 1980.

"When you cry over commercials, Bernice, you're playing right into their hands."

however, many more advertisers could effectively use it than do. Why, then, are advertisers and agencies reluctant to pursue campaigns built on humorous appeals? There are many answers, all valid. The "funny" commercial, after a lot of work and expense, may simply not be funny; it may even be a disaster. The audience may remember and enjoy the comedy but screen out or forget the selling message. It is often difficult to make the humor germane to the selling points. The agency may slip into the trap of turning out humorous advertising that delights the client but does not evoke the same response from the audience. The creative team may have achieved a truly amusing script, but somewhere in the actual production the comedy may slip through the fingers of the producer, director, talent, film editor, or any one of a number of key people who translate an idea on paper into a piece of film or tape. Since comedy is usually defined as being "at the expense" of someone or something, some advertisers are reluctant to risk offense. (Nowadays, even the slightest touch of ethnic humor may be marketing suicide. We all love a joke, but usually not about ourselves.) Humor, so often topical, is thus often short-lived. Comedy usually does not stand up under heavy repetition. A final, but by no means minor, consideration is that clients and agencies are reluctant to risk embarrassment if the humorous commercials fail. No one will ridicule a straightforward advertising program, even if it's "dull as dishwater."

Despite the risks involved, there are a couple of excellent reasons for incorporating humorous appeals into an advertising campaign. First, the comedy attracts immediate attention. Second, if the commercial works, the audience will respond positively to both the advertising and the product. Humor may be subtle and sophisticated, burlesque and slapstick, or somewhere in between. (See 6.5.) Comedy deals in incongruities, the unexpected, and the nonroutine. It must walk a middle line between the serious and the absurd. A commercial that becomes totally absurd loses its humor, and the audience fails to identify with the characters and the situation. Reality, but not truth, is suspended in the comic situation—a most important point to the advertiser selling an actual product.

Writing humorous commercials is undoubtedly the most difficult of all copywriting challenges. When asked, "How do you do it?" one copywriter recalled E. B. White's admonition: "Humor can be dissected, as a frog can, but the thing dies in the process and the innards are discouraging to any but the pure scientific mind."

Convenience Appeals

Being able to use a product in a simple way may not seem to have a great deal of emotional appeal, but to the consumer it implies efficiency. Efficiency, in turn, suggests that two important things are conserved—time and effort. Busy people may respond emotionally and positively to a product that promises sought-for convenience. This is one reason why packaging today is so crucial in marketing products, particularly repeat-sale items. (The mousetrap may be no better than the competition's, but if it's more convenient, the consumer will buy.) If the convenience factor of a product constitutes its greatest strength and if the agency staff understands this, the resulting advertising may be straightforward, informational, and seemingly unemotional. But if it speaks to a consumer's real need, success is assured.

6.5 / A Moving Experience

KELLY ZAHRNDT & KELLY, INC.

ADVERTISING/PUBLIC RELATIONS

10805 SUNSET OFFICE DRIVE ST. LOUIS, MO 63127 (314) 821-6222

RADIO COPY

ANNOUNCER:	UNITED VAN LINES PRESENTS STILLER & MEARA.
STILLER:	THIS IS GONNA HURT YOU FAYE BUT I THINK WE SHOULD STOP SEEING EACH OTHER.
MEARA:	ARE YOU BREAKING OUR ENGAGEMENT RAY?
STILLER:	YES FAYE, I'M MARRYING MAE AND MOVING TO SAN JOSE.
MEARA:	CALL UNITED VAN LINES RAY.
STILLER:	BUT FAYE, AREN'T YOU UPSET I'M MOVING WITH MAE TO SAN JOSE.
MEARA:	UNITED VAN LINES TAKES THE UPSET OUT OF MOVING RAY.
STILLER:	UNITED VAN LINES CAN MOVE ME AND MAE TO SAN JOSE, FAYE?
MEARA:	UNITED VAN LINES KNOWS THE WAY RAY.
STILLER:	TO SAN JOSE?
MEARA:	YES RAY, UNITED HAS EFFICIENT SERVICE, PRE-PLANNED MOVING GUIDES, ALSO FREE RELOCATION INFORMATION FOR ANYWHERE IN THE STATES, AND OVER A HUNDRED COUNTRIES ABROAD.
STILLER:	DON'T YOU EVEN CARE ABOUT ME AND MAE, FAYE?
MEARA:	UNITED VAN LINES CARES RAY, THEY'RE THE QUALITY MOVERS. UNITED CAN MOVE ANYTHING FROM CHUBBY MAE'S REDUCING MACHINE TO COMPUTERS.
STILLER:	OK FAYE, I'M CALLING UNITED VAN LINES TODAY.
MEARA:	SO LONG RAY, GIVE MY BEST TO MAE.
STILLER:	GEE FAYE, I THOUGHT YOU'D CRY.
MEARA:	WHY SHOULD I CRY, I FOUND A GREAT GUY NAMED SY.
STILLER:	AND YOU'RE MOVING TO CHI?
MEARA:	JERSEY.
ANNOUNCER:	FOR THE NAME OF YOUR UNITED VAN LINES AGENT SEE THE YELLOW PAGES.

Courtesy of United Van Lines, Inc., and Kelly, Zahrndt & Kelly, Inc.

Curiosity Appeals

An emotional appeal that reaches the consumer's desire to explore the unusual, the novel, and the strange in order to find out what makes it tick can create tremendously effective advertising. The structure most commonly used is the demonstration commercial, and the device is often an unconventional approach that generates a high degree of suspense. Torture tests of cars, watches, tires, and appliances will generally hold the viewer to the end. What will happen?

The protagonist will win, of course, but *how* the winning is achieved may be unraveled in an intricate or unusual story-line. Special film techniques (such as microscopic photography) can build curiosity by revealing, bit by bit, the message to the viewer. Animation can take the viewer on flights of fancy that explore the phenomenon. Curiosity appeals are often ideal vehicles for introducing new products or services. Even familiar products may achieve a new level of awareness if the agency can produce a commercial that provokes inquisitiveness, perhaps by introducing a new package design or a new use or simply by withholding the name of the product until the commercial's climax. (The risks of the latter technique are obvious.)

Testing viewers, in what is really a game, generated a lot of curiosity in commercials for the American Express credit card. Well-known, but not particularly recognizable people were presented, asking, "Do you know me?" To learn their identity, the viewer had to wait until the end of the sales pitch.

Curiosity appeals are difficult to employ and should be thoroughly tested. The viewer or listener must be provided with sufficient stimuli throughout the commercial to sustain interest, and the payoff must satisfactorily resolve the suspense.

Ego Appeals

The advertiser with some understanding of the complexities of the psyche has abundant opportunities to promise gratification through commercials utilizing ego appeals. The enormous quantity of material goods produced by a capitalistic society requires high personal consumption rates to keep the system moving. The American consumer has obviously responded positively. (A quick look in any family's garage or basement will provide cluttered testimony to this fact.)

For better or worse, possessions provide tangible evidence of status in life. Comfort, luxury, and status symbols (however defined) are all related to emotional security. Pride of ownership may gratify the ego by providing eloquent testimony to the owner's good taste, desire for quality, and personal accomplishments. In an unabashed effort at snob appeal, a credit card company adopted this slogan as a position against its competition: "Some people travel with credit cards. Some people have Carte Blanche."

Ego appeals may be particularly important to the advertiser who markets a product or service that is purchased by discretionary income — in other words, by money not earmarked for essentials. Furs, designer jeans, and swimming pools are certainly nonessentials. However, many essential products also use ego appeals to sell high-priced models. Automobiles, appliances, stereo systems, TV sets, and home furnishings are typical examples. The advertiser should be careful to research the market and be sure that (1) an ego appeal is truly the most appropriate and effective emotional base for the advertising, and (2) the ego appeal is exactly "on target" for a particular segment of the market. If the second rule is violated, the advertising may backfire. Poorly constructed ego appeals can degenerate into frivolous "snob appeals," and consumers may go out of their way to disassociate themselves from that image — and the product. The growing sophistication of the public implies a need for subtlety, good taste, and soft sell in ego appeals.

Hero Worship Appeals

Everyone loves a winner, and to emulate a hero or heroine may be the secret desire of many people. This harmless fantasizing may be touched emotionally in hero worship advertising. In broadcast commercials, a sports figure is most commonly cast as the hero, for here is true Americana: the strong, youthful Lancelot who vanquishes the enemy. If Lancelot is handsome, personable, and poised on camera or microphone, so much the better. Often, stars from the entertainment world are employed in hero worship commercials. Such "beautiful people" may lend an image to a product it never before enjoyed. Testimonial formats are obviously the most common commercial structure for this kind of emotional appeal.

Believability should be the key concept in hero worship commercials. If the consumer does not accept the spokesperson as a true advocate of the product, this lack of credibility hurts both the talent and the product. The copywriter should spend some time, if possible, with the talent in order to write copy that fits his or her style and speech patterns. No one, least of all nonprofessional talent, is at ease with sentences and vocabulary foreign to his or her own style. Although professional entertainers are obviously highly trained and therefore more adaptable than sports figures, the copywriter must remember that celebrities are theoretically not playing a role in hero worship commercials but instead being themselves.

A common pitfall is placing the talent in the limelight rather than the product. Further, the agency creative team should avoid constructing a situation that results in the viewer or listener's not *liking* the talent. Ralph Waldo Emerson once observed that "every hero becomes a bore at last." If the listener responds negatively, talent ceases to play the role of hero, and the product suffers. Modesty should be a part of the presentation, and good humor, too.

Sensory Appeals

There are innumerable advertisers whose products minister to the creature comforts, and their advertising agencies face an enormous challenge in communicating a product's qualities in the media. We have five senses, yet television provides only sight and sound, and radio only sound. How can touch, taste, and smell be effectively communicated in the media? If these properties are crucial to the product, some substitute suggestions will have to be found. Video and both verbal and nonverbal audio can effectively communicate these appeals.

How does coffee smell? Perhaps it can be equated with sounds in a suburban neighborhood early in the morning. How does a soft drink taste? Perhaps as refreshing and exciting as a swim in the ocean surf. How soft will a hand lotion make the skin? As smooth as a rose petal? If these kinds of analogy are used, they must make sense and avoid clichés, or the viewer or listener will reject them as meaningless.

For the advertiser whose products can be demonstrated by sight and sound, or just sound, analogies are not necessary. The advertiser simply capitalizes on the impact the broadcast media can provide. In radio especially, good descriptive copy can do wonders. The listener's imagination should be expanded through verbal suggestions. In TV, of course, seeing is believing. A good director will make sure the cameras fully explore whatever sensory appeals are inherent in the product.

Production Techniques

The creative people seemingly control the direction of a commercial. With a thorough understanding of the campaign strategy, they develop the commercial's format and emotional appeal. But since a commercial doesn't exist until it is actually produced, the important ingredient of *style* rests with the production team. (Its work is explored in detail in Chapter 8.)

Style, executed in production techniques, makes the difference between an adequate communication and a truly delightful and memorable bit of persuasion. Advertising agencies, competent in the concepts of presentation, will be sure that (1) the best production house available is assigned a particular job, and (2) an experienced agency broadcast supervisor is on the set, understands the client's goals, and is responsible for the finished product.

What are those specific factors that make up production style? They include the proper selection of sets, lighting, stage props, color, music, sound effects, and that special chemistry of professional talent carefully cast in believable situations and characterizations. The perfect blend of makeup, hairdressing, facial expressions, costuming, gestures, and staging subtly contribute to the overall excellence of production. Attention to minute detail reflects a professionalism that makes the whole greater than its parts. Showmanship is the key concept, and presentation should be of the highest standard possible within the production budget.

Conclusions

The creative process is rarely orderly, and no one really expects specific formulas to apply. In advertising, however, the results of creative labors are expected to be both original and to carry out the advertiser's campaign strategy. Anyone working in the creative area of advertising, whether developing TV comercials for a multimillion-dollar account or writing radio copy for a small local retailer, faces similar challenges. Sometimes the perfect commercial comes to a writer "out of the blue," but that is unusual. In most cases, the work is arduous, demanding attention to the smallest detail.

What is the advertising strategy? What are the objectives of this campaign? What do we want to communicate? These are the basic questions the creative person must ask before developing a commercial. With a clear understanding of the answers, many writers, through a process of trial and error, finally end up with a commercial that will fulfill the campaign goals.

Advertising is communication, and in the broadcast media, commercials constitute a quick and perishable message. A commercial must be developed into some sort of format (such as dramatic, demonstration, testimonial, interview, and so on) and augmented with a suitable and attention-getting emotional appeal. With time limited to 30 or 60 seconds, everything extraneous must be eliminated; effective commercials are "tight." With a commercial in script or storyboard form and cut and polished to achieve the advertiser's goal, the groundwork is laid for the final creative touches that come when the commercial is actually produced.

chapter seven

Talent

Lights, Camera —You Have 30 Seconds!

We'll need two actresses for this commercial, plus a teenage boy to play the son of one of them. This is a national commercial, and all the talent is on camera. For the women we want talent age 35 to 40, housewife-looking types. Neatly groomed, but no fashion plates. Maybe a little on the plump side. For the boy, we need a kid about 16 —a big, husky, all-American type. No long-hairs. This commercial's for a laundry bleach, and this kid comes in a kitchen set from football practice all covered with dirt. We'll start auditions on Friday, so send me up about eight women for the housewife parts, and maybe six boys. Check their clearances, will you? We want union members, of course. Oh yeah, this client only pays scale. I think this commercial will probably run for one 13-week cycle.

The speaker is a casting director. At the other end of the line, a talent agent is taking notes. Calls like this one are common, because thousands of commercials, both national and local, are produced each year. They all need talent.

When the creative plans of an advertising agency have been approved by the client and commercials are ready to go into production, the first order of business is often casting. The importance of casting the right performers in the right roles cannot be overemphasized. It is so obvious it need not be belabored. Procedures for conducting auditions and casting will vary with the circumstances. In a local market situation, where commercials are being produced for a local retailer, auditions for talent may be simple and straightforward and be completed in a few hours. The pool of available talent is usually pretty limited for any given part, and the better performers are already familiar to local advertisers and agencies. Auditions may even be skipped when clients know exactly whom they want to hire.

At the national level, casting for elaborate commercials with big budgets is a lot more involved. Some large advertising agencies that turn out a multitude of commercials every year employ a full-time casting director. When commercials are approved and ready for production, this person contacts several talent agencies with a summary of talent requirements. Because most advertising agencies cannot justify the expense of a full-time casting director, they use the services of a freelance one. These people (and there are relatively few of them) are well known in the business and have extensive contacts with talent agents and the advertising community. Sometimes, casting responsibilities are turned over to the company that will be producing the commercials. The larger production houses may have a casting director on the staff, or they may hire a freelancer. Casting directors are usually used on high-cost, national commercials. For local and regional commercials and for commercials produced on a limited budget, casting responsibilities usually fall to the producer from the advertising agency or the director at the production house.

The performers used in commercials fall into five categories: professionals, celebrities and personalities, nonprofessionals, extras, and musicians.

Professionals are experienced actresses and actors. They usually earn no more than scale, the minimum established by their unions—the Screen Actors Guild and the American Federation of Television and Radio Artists. *Celebrities and personalities* almost invariably earn over-scale. *Nonprofessionals,* who do not belong to any performers' unions, and who play the role of a "principal," cannot be paid less than scale. They are usually real consumers who give product endorsements or employees who are shown on the job. *Extras*, who may be members of a union, are used in backgrounds or crowd scenes. *Musicians* are used in radio and in television, where they may be either on or off camera.

The Talent Agent

There are hundreds of talent agents in cities across the country. They represent clients who appear on stage and screen and in other media. Some of these clients are involved only in the performing arts, but a great many are eager and available to appear in advertising, whether print or broadcast. A few giant talent agencies employ several hundred people and operate branch offices across the country. Most talent agencies, however, are relatively small, sometimes a one-person shop. In any event, a talent agent may represent several hundred performers. Keeping track of all of them isn't easy. To help a prospective employer select talent, *head sheets* are prepared by the talent agent. These contain a head portrait and a minimum of very basic information. More elaborate composites are also available containing information on both sides of one sheet of paper, including several photographs (one a full head portrait), information on what the performer can do, special skills, and the kinds of market this talent fits. Credits are sometimes listed; union affiliations are always given. It is an increasingly common practice for talent agents to have videotapes of their clients available to show casting directors.

When talent agents are contacted by casting directors or by whoever is handling these responsibilities, they need to know what kind of talent is wanted, including a physical description (obviously not overly limiting) and also an indication of the kind of characterization needed. In addition, they need to know whether the commercial is intended for local, regional, or national use and approximately how long it will run. (A test commercial, for example, may be used for only a few weeks, but some commercials have run on the air for years. While a commercial is running, the talent used may not appear in commercials for competing products and services.)

A good talent agent, called with the specifications for an upcoming commercial, will typically send down four or five of the most likely prospects to audition for the part. The number sent depends on the casting director's request. A child's part will require that many kids audition for it, because a truly professional child actor is pretty rare. In contrast, auditions for a male announcer for radio copy may be confined to just a handful of pros.

Talent agents, who earn 10 percent of the gross of their clients' earnings, are always anxious to have one of their people land the part. Several talent agents are usually called, so the competition is stiff. For talent selected to appear in national advertising, a substantial fee and residual payments are the prize. If the performer has lines and must move around a set, the agents are very careful about what kinds of talent they select for the audition. Only a professional can win that kind of part. A neophyte may be sent, however, for a small part with no lines. Since the agent wants to find opportunities for less experienced talent, a bit part in a commercial may be ideal — it means some money and a chance to learn. It's the agent's job to be sure the performer's union memberships are in good standing and that he or she is "cleared" — that is, has not appeared for at least one year in a competitor's commercial. Good agents will always try to obtain over-scale payments for their clients. *Scale* is the minimum payment for union performers. Over-scale payments may be negotiated between an agent and a casting director at one-and-a-half, double, or triple scale or even more. Exclusive contracts with top stars can become very complicated.

Celebrity Talent

Celebrities have been doing commercials for decades. There was a time, however, when many would not consider doing anything so tawdry. Times have changed (see 7.1).

Eleanor Roosevelt was one of the first really famous people to do commercials who did not come from the world of show business. When an advertising agency approached the former first lady and asked if she would be willing to do a TV commercial for a margarine, Mrs. Roosevelt agonized over the possible damage to her public image. The $35,000 fee would purchase a tremendous number of CARE packages, reasoned Mrs. Roosevelt, and so she consented.[1]

Celebrity talent used in commercials since Mrs. Roosevelt's time comes from the entertainment world or professional sports. Their names would fill pages. Years ago, many celebrities did only voice-overs, so they could be cloaked in anonymity. In the 1960s, after a few top names were persuaded to endorse products in TV commercials,

---

[1] Joseph P. Lash, *Eleanor: The Years Alone* (New York: Norton, 1972), p. 304.

the stampede was on. (One casting director remarked, "I don't want to sound crass, but for enough money, you can get just about anyone.")

Top stars may command a guarantee that runs into hundreds of thousands of dollars. Multimillion-dollar deals are not unheard of; James Garner's $3-million contract with the Polaroid Corporation was announced in trade publications. In most cases, however, celebrities prefer to keep the financial arrangements out of the press. All performers collect residuals as the commercial runs, and in the case of celebrities, the residuals apply to the total negotiated fee. For these handsome fees, a top star may spend a day or less in production and easily fit it in with other commitments. The number of takes may be less than with other talent, because these celebrities are

7.1/Polaroid's Star Presenters

Mariette Hartley and James Garner have been star presenters for Polaroid.

Courtesy of the Polaroid Corporation.

experienced professionals. Sports figures need much direction, and the final result may lead the viewer to believe that whatever coaching they were given was not enough. Crews and directors, accustomed to working with celebrities, say the secret to success is completely thorough preparation. Because stand-ins are used while the lights are being adjusted, the star need only step in at the last moment. Most of them are cooperative and hard working; the word on prima donnas travels quickly through the grapevine, and such types are rarely used.

Testimonials by celebrities are increasingly criticized by consumer groups. (The Federal Trade Commission's guidelines on such advertising are included in the previous chapter.) Most advertisers, in order to avoid any possible legal problems, ask performers who deliver a testimonial to sign an affidavit. In it they swear to what they said (the commercial may be edited for time, but not content), and they testify that they have, in fact, used the product. These simple requirements are no great obstacle.

Critics have complained that these bought-and-paid-for endorsements are inherently misleading. The public has a right to know whether the spokesperson has any real knowledge of the product. The pronoun *we* is bandied about in a rather careless manner. "We at the Great and Wonderful Company" implies that the celebrity is closely associated with the sponsor and intimately knowledgeable about its corporate affairs.

These criticisms fall on deaf ears in most of the advertising industry. Celebrities are used—and overused—because of the public's fascination with stars. Celebrities make a hard sell easier, contend some experts, who believe that a star who is relevant to a particular product increases the sponsor's credibility.

This matter of relevance, accepted in the industry as an article of faith, has been challenged. Some of the most successful commercials violate this rule. Where's the relevance of Joe DiMaggio for Mr. Coffee and Frank Gifford for Planter's? "Celebrities

"... Sorry, Nolan, but I couldn't get you a panty-hose commercial..."

register. Relevance has relatively little to do with it," said a creative supervisor at the J. Walter Thompson Company advertising agency.[2] He contended that "non-relevant" stars are still successful "for some of the usual reasons commercials work, which is to say good scripts, good demos, good production values and good all-around execution. More to the particular point, they work because a star is a star is a star."

Because national commercials, in particular, often go through intensive pretesting, which is usually confined to measurements of recall and recognition, celebrities improve the scores on these tests. (See Chapter 9.) It's no wonder that advertising agencies recommend the use of celebrities to their clients. Numbers on a score sheet seem more reassuring than agency hunches.

Personalities are not celebrities in their own right, but they may be paid just as well. Some eventually become true celebrities. Ask a typical viewer if he or she knows Dick Wilson, Jan Miner, or Jack Eagle. A blank stare is the likely response. Ask the same person about Mr. Whipple, Madge the Manicurist, or Brother Dominic. The answer will be yes, accompanied by brand associations. Originally, many of these personalities were professional actors, but they were not well known to the public. They were in the right place at the right time, landed a part in a commercial, and gave such an outstanding performance that the advertiser built an entire campaign and brand identification around them. Many are now under exclusive contracts.

Auditions

The timetable in auditions is quite strict. Talent agents are rarely given more than a few days to round up their best prospects. They say it's never enough time. A talent agency may represent 50 performers who *might* be likely candidates for a given role. Agents will select only those performers who they know can do a particular job. Performers who have a record of being late or temperamental are often passed over.

The job of conducting auditions and casting talent sounds glamorous and enjoyable. In truth, however, it's a tough and exhausting business. The people who sit in on auditions will vary with the client, the agency, and the circumstances. The casting director is obviously there, and also the director of the commercial. The latter person should conduct the casting sessions, with the others "sitting in." (Directors are hired to direct, and that includes this important part of preproduction.) Agency personnel may include the producer, the copywriter, the art director, and an account executive. Sometimes a client representative is present. They must all be in general agreement on the objectives of the commercial, the general mood to be conveyed, and the basic talent requirements. Specifications should not be too limiting, however, because a performer may turn up in an audition who does not fit exactly what was visualized but who adds a unique dimension to the commercial.

Auditions are often conducted in an emotionally charged atmosphere. At stake are fees and residuals that may easily reach $15,000 or $20,000 for one day of shooting. The competition is horrendous. All performers want jobs, but only a few will land

[2]Gerry Scorse, "'Nonrelevant' Stars Hurt Creative Pride," *Advertising Age,* July 30, 1979, p. S-11.

parts. A limited, and probably insufficient, amount of time can be devoted to each person. No matter how objective the decision makers try to be, personal prejudices are always at work. The trend nowadays is to videotape auditions so particular performers can be reviewed at a later time. The poor ones are eliminated, and the best ones can be assembled for final decision making. A tape audition also reveals how the talent relate to a camera. Without tape, this quality is sometimes difficult to evaluate.

"Cattle calls," wherein dozens of people try for each role, should be avoided. Mass confusion is not necessary and just complicates the casting business. Performers and agents sometimes complain that freelance casting directors are most guilty of holding extensive auditions. Since they are paid by the day, they are accused of prolonging the job. (On the West Coast, the complaints are directed to casting directors who come from the East and stretch out the auditions in order to "justify and enjoy a trip to the Coast.") Performers aren't paid anything for an audition, and they aren't paid for the first call-back if the decision makers need another audition session. If performers are kept waiting more than one hour, they are supposed to be paid a small fee.

Decisions are usually made quite promptly; rarely do they take more than a day or so. However, if an advertiser is searching for a major TV spokesperson who will do a long series of commercials under exclusive contract, auditions may go on for weeks. Once performers are hired, they are notified where and when to report and the kind of clothes to wear. Professional performers maintain a wardrobe that provides something suitable for most commercials. A wardrobe is provided only in special circumstances.

Nonprofessional Talent

Some advertisers, seeking maximum believability, have used their own employees or actual consumers in commercials. These people must be paid the same fees and residuals as union talent. (Nonunion talent, through a provision in the Taft-Hartley Act, cannot be precluded from appearing in commercials. After doing a commercial, they have 30 days in which to join one of the talent unions if they want to do more commercials.) People who appear as themselves must be in a "natural setting" (the employee is shown on the job, for instance), and their remarks are supposedly original, not scripted.

Any agency will carefully consider using actual consumers in a commercial before recommending this idea to a client. The cost factor is difficult to estimate, because it may take days of interviewing and filming to happen on the right consumer spokesperson. Some agency producers have nicknamed nonprofessionals "the uglies." Although anyone can be spontaneous, not everyone looks or sounds convincing to an audience, and even fewer can really *sell* the product. When nonprofessional people are used, talent agents and the talent unions naturally grumble about it, because it eliminates an employment opportunity for one of their performers.

In recent years, the advertising industry has been the target of performers' strikes at contract renegotiation time. Commercial production with professionals grinds to a halt. If an advertiser needs to produce a commercial, the only remaining option is nonprofessional talent. The results are mixed, and usually the costs are higher, because professionals don't need as much time and direction. Amateurs can, however, bring a fresh spontaneity and innocence that may work very well. They need reassurance to assuage their fears, and a supportive production crew.

Special Problems (and Opportunities) in Casting Talent

What do casting directors and other decision makers look for in auditions? It obviously depends on the requirements of a particular commercial. Most performers find themselves typecast, even the most versatile ones. An experienced actress who has assumed a dozen different roles in stage plays may find herself confined to housewife roles in commercials. Casting directors seek performers who not only meet the type they are casting but also appear natural, real, and personable.

In the early days of TV, commercials usually presented only "beautiful people." Advertisers quickly came to realize that for many products, less glamorous — but sometimes more interesting — performers successfully established characters who seemed real, and therefore believable, to an audience. Realism in commercials is greatly enhanced with proper casting, but that's only part of the formula. Natural dialogue, good directing, and superior editing are the other major ingredients.

It isn't always easy even for a professional performer to "feel" the part he or she may have landed in a commercial. Pity the actress playing a housewife who must deliver a 30-second spiel on some floor wax to her "neighbor." Nobody really talks like that — and yet this phony baloney is produced in commercials year after year. Sometimes talent can persuade a director to change a line here and there to make the dialogue more natural. The suggestions are usually good ones, but agency personnel have to be very careful that changes do not affect the acceptability of product claims. Most national commercials have been reviewed by lawyers and the broadcast standards departments of the various networks before they are produced. Changing one word could mean that a commercial already cleared would no longer be acceptable.

Casting children presents special problems, and auditions may be more time consuming. In the search for the right child, looks aren't everything. Casting directors look for an engaging smile, a touch of mischief, a charming giggle, or some special spark. Shy children simply aren't hired. Inexperienced child actors may be put at ease with gentle questions about their interests. Older children may show their personalities if they're asked an offbeat question: "Are you married?" If at all possible, children should be asked to do in an audition what they will have to do in the commercial. A child hired for a chop suey commercial had better like the stuff. As a matter of fact, it is often necessary to hire a few extra children in case the first choices do not do well on the day of the shoot.

Parents all think their children are adorable, as cute or cuter than the rest of the kids they see on TV. When some small-fry spokesperson turns into an overnight star, talent agents are sometimes stampeded by ambitious parents who want the same success for their offspring. If they do land parts, after some coaching and pampering, many children lose their marvelous spontaneous quality. They smile, giggle, pose on cue — and lose all believability.

Directors who deal frequently with children always handle them with special care. The kids must be disciplined enough to get the job done but still enthusiastic and free enough to be natural on camera. The director's biggest enemy is fatigue, and so the hardest scene—one requiring dialogue, for instance—is usually shot first. In New York City and Los Angeles, the law requires that a social worker be on the set when children are working in commercials. The kids can work an eight-hour day only if they have 20 minutes on and 20 minutes off. Depending on the social worker, these rest periods may be strictly observed or not. For children who must miss school, special arrangements must be made to provide tutoring, and often the social worker serves as a teacher.

If a commercial has any unusual requirements, casting can turn into a first-class headache. If an animal, tame or wild, is needed, it may not be easy to find a human performer who can work well with it. In some commercials, someone special may be needed—a water skier, a magician, an acrobat, or a hay fever sufferer. The list of possible requirements is endless, but the list of talent may not be. If an advertiser wants to include members of minority groups in a commercial, and additionally needs unusual skills, the search process may be expensive and time consuming.

Performers must be able to adapt to a host of circumstances and personalities. The location may be a comfortable studio or a broiling desert at high noon. In addition, they must follow the instructions of a director and be able to perform with other actors and actresses. "Goofs" kill time, and time can kill a budget. Performers must also be able to adapt to either film or videotape. Some prefer to work with videotape, because of the instant playback. With their director they can immediately review a take and evaluate it. The performers can see what they have done, and the director can point out small details for improvement. Actors and actresses who rely on their

"It's not a good commercial, but we worked the sponsor's kid into it."

appearance, however, usually prefer film over tape. Film can have a soft, flattering quality, whereas tape is harsher. Besides, the TV camera always adds some unflattering pounds to the performer anyway.

A performer's life is not a succession of ego trips and checks in the mail. Complaints run the gamut. Auditions are often agonizing, especially if they're cattle calls. Some casting directors are not very considerate, and they can be abrupt and tactless in dismissing actors or actresses. Top performers sometimes complain that, even if they don't get a certain part, their ideas for that part are "borrowed." Later, when they view the finished commercial they auditioned for and see their interpretation of that role being used by another actor, they feel exploited. Performers are always under a great deal of pressure. There's no opportunity to build the role. The actor or actress in a 30- or 60-second commercial must be immediately "in character" when the director calls, "Action." When the director is inexperienced, professional performers may complain that they are asked to do take after take when it really isn't necessary. A director who doesn't have control of the situation presents real problems. Some advertising agency personnel, client representatives, and assorted hangers-on all envision themselves as the greatest dramatic coaches since Stanislavsky. The poor performer is told to do a part six different ways by six different people. A top director *directs* and never allows that sort of thing to happen.

As for talent payments, performers complain that they are never paid on time. They or their agents often have to bird dog the payment of fees and residuals. If the checks are not correct, it means more delays. Holding fees, which are due performers by advertisers who may wish to use a commercial again at a later date, are often "overlooked" unless the talent agent keeps careful records. The talent unions sometimes get involved in disputes over payments. Checks are made out to the performers but are mailed to the agents, who have power of attorney and can thus deposit them. The agents then pay their clients, deducting the 10 percent commission. ("Otherwise, we'd never be paid," said one agent.)

The "care and feeding" of performers by their agents is a subject unto itself. Talent may be egotistical, demanding, and unreliable and may take up a tremendous amount of the agent's time. On top of that, they may deeply resent paying the agent's commission. (For the agent, the commission sometimes doesn't seem worth the hand holding necessary.) Many performers, however, are gracious, cooperative, and strictly professional. They appreciate the high cost of production and report to the set on time and ready to go. Top performers can bring a great deal to a part and add a dimension to the commercial that was never envisioned in the storyboard stage. They latch onto a part almost immediately, and only a few takes may be needed. Often, the first take is the best. The performers are just as important as the creative team or the director. A look, a gesture, the posture, and the voice of a really gifted performer can turn an ordinary commercial into an absolutely delightful one.

Talent Unions

Several unions are involved in the talent side of radio and television commercials. The business of dealing with various unions in a situation where jurisdiction is not always clear cut can be confusing. Two elements of the complications involve the question of whether a TV commercial is shot on film or videotape and the extremely detailed contract provisions that cover the employment of performers.

American Federation of Television and Radio Artists

AFTRA was started in 1936 and represented radio artists in New York, Chicago, and Los Angeles. Today, AFTRA has more than 60,000 members in 50 states. The union is headquartered in New York, and its jurisdiction includes commercial radio transcriptions, phonograph records, slide-film recordings and other recordings not broadcast, local live television commercials, and videotape commercial recordings. The last category runs into some overlap, and some problems, with the Screen Actors Guild (SAG) — see below.

Most AFTRA members are actors, announcers, singers, dancers, and specialty acts, and many are employees of broadcasting stations and networks. A relatively small number can earn a living doing commercials exclusively, and that work usually constitutes moonlighting and augments an income from the programing side of broadcasting or from an entirely different line of work. Virtually all AFTRA members involved in commercial work are also members of SAG.

Screen Actors Guild

SAG, a few years older than AFTRA, was organized in 1933 by a group of actors disgruntled with the poor pay and difficult working conditions at the motion picture studios. Today, its membership is almost 52,000. Unlike AFTRA members, so many of whom have full-time jobs, SAG members must find acting jobs wherever they can. The television-commercials industry is tremendously important to these performers.

SAG jurisdiction covers filmed motion picture features; filmed television entertainment programs; industrial, educational, and religious films; and all filmed TV commercials. SAG shares jurisdiction with AFTRA over taped TV commercials. The determining factor in this last category is where the commercial is shot. If it is shot in a studio that is normally used for film and that is a SAG signatory, it falls under SAG jurisdiction. Members of both unions, paying two sets of dues, have started a grass-roots movement urging an AFTRA-SAG merger. Such a consolidation is increasingly discussed, and it appears to be inevitable though not imminent.

Extras

Commercials that require crowds or people in the background use extras, who may come from one of several unions or no union at all. Most major advertising agencies, advertisers, and production houses are signatories to contracts with the various talent unions. They agree to abide by those contracts no matter where they shoot commercials.

The *New York Extras Players,* which is part of the Screen Actors Guild, has jurisdiction in the New York area. Its contract covers the employment of all extras within 300 miles of the center of Columbus Circle in New York City.

The *Screen Extras Guild* has jurisdiction in more than two dozen cities across the country. Depending on a classification system for each city, advertisers may be obliged to give hiring preference to SEG members. In some of the smaller cities, there is no obligation to hire SEG members, but anyone hired as an extra must be paid union rates. Like the New York Extras Players, there is some likelihood that SEG will eventually merge with SAG.

AFTRA's contract covering principals also covers extras. Thus, if a TV commercial is taped under AFTRA rules, any extras hired will be AFTRA members.

Small local or regional advertisers, not situated in cities where unions hold jurisdiction, are not bound by contracts applying to talent. Extras are hired at whatever rate can be negotiated below prevailing union scale. This may be important to an advertiser on a limited budget or to one desiring a mob scene shot in a stadium, for example.

American Federation of Musicians

The American Federation of Musicians (AFM) represents more than 300,000 professional musicians in the United States and Canada. Like AFTRA and SAG, this union negotiates with national advertisers for contracts that cover the employment of musicians in producing radio and TV commercials. This income source is of growing importance to musicians as the volume of advertising increases and as more and more clients want to use music as an important part of their sales message.

Fees and Residuals

Performers hired as principals in commercials are paid the same whether they are represented by AFTRA or SAG. The reason is that the two unions join forces every three years when they meet with the American Association of Advertising Agencies and the Association of National Advertisers to negotiate new contracts. Together, the four make up a *Joint Policy Committee on Broadcast Talent Union Relations*. The contract they hammer out covers such matters as fees, repayment compensation, holding fees, length of sessions, exclusivity of talent, auditions, interviews, travel, meal periods, overtime, late penalties, foreign use of commercials, and so on.

Compensation gets the most attention in these negotiations and constitutes the most complicated issue. Session fees are simple and easy to understand. If performers spend the day acting before a camera or microphone, they should be paid for their services. In a commercial, however, the performance will be recorded and played to an audience many, many times. These performers, like stage actors, want to be paid for the number of times this performance is presented. (If they performed the same commercial live on TV every night, they would be paid accordingly.) It's the advertiser, not the performers, who elects to record the commercial, but the performers still expect to be paid. This expectation has resulted in the economic philosophy behind repayments, or residuals, in radio, TV, and cable commercials. Many other variables come into play as well. No one would expect an advertiser to pay a performer the same sum for a commercial played on CBS-TV as for a spot scheduled on a TV station in Fargo. The size of the potential audience is just one of the many factors considered in establishing payments.

In radio, AFTRA has exclusive jurisdiction, and performers may be categorized as actors, announcers, solos, duo singers, or group singers. They are all paid session fees and collect residuals during the air life of the commercial. The basis for computing these additional payments depends on the use of the commercial.

Wild spot radio commercials, which are very common, are placed on a number of stations in various cities on a spot basis. The advertiser may contract for an 8- or 13-week cycle (which may be renewed), and the session fees are credited to the payment due the performers in the first cycle. The sum paid to performers depends on the number of units the advertiser uses in scheduling a commercial. Units are accumulated according to the number of cities in which the commercial is used. Smaller cities may be assigned a value of one or two units, larger cities more. Thus, in wild spot, radio performers are paid on the basis of the total number of units and the number of cycles during the life of a commercial. If an announcer is used in both a 30-second and a 60-second version of a radio commercial, residuals accumulate separately for each commercial. The actual number of times a given commercial is aired is not a factor in computing wild spot compensation.

Other categories of radio payments include *network program commercials*, for use on the various radio networks during specified cycles — 1, 4, 8, or 13 weeks; and *dealer commercials*, in which a manufacturer provides commercials to local dealers, who then buy time on local stations. The complex contracts also cover payments for regional networks and foreign use and for recording commercials as demos (demonstrations) or for testing off the air.

Television residuals are similar to those for radio but a bit more complicated because of group singers, group dancers, helicopter and airplane pilots, hand models, and so on. Payments vary for on- and off-camera talent. The three primary commercial categories are wild spot, program, and dealer commercials.

Wild spot cycles in TV all run 13 weeks, and the commercial may be used as often as desired during this period. Payments due performers are computed on the basis of accumulated units, using a system similar to the one used in radio. If an advertiser wants to use a commercial beyond a 13-week period, a separate *holding fee* is due performers.

Program commercials are divided into A, B, and C classes, based on the number of cities in which the commercial is telecast. (C means 1 to 5 cities; B, 6 to 20 cities; and A, over 20). These classes indicate payment rates for advertisers whose commercials fall *within* a program. Network commercials obviously are in Class A. For performers who appear in a commercial that is used in both the wild spot and program commercial categories, the rewards are handsome.

Dealer commercials for television are similar to those in radio, but they are complicated by the addition of various categories. Other payment schedules are spelled out in the contract to cover such things as commercial billboards (program openings and closings), seasonal commercials (to be aired during the Christmas holidays, for example), foreign use, and the nonbroadcast use of commercials — in testing, for example, or at an industrial or trade show.

Cable television talent payments were added to the contracts in the 1980s. A special rate was established for commercials designed exclusively for cable use. The rate is slightly below regular television rates, based on the expectation of smaller viewing audiences. An advertiser may elect to use a cable commercial on a 4-week, 13-week, or 52-week cycle, and payments are adjusted on a sliding scale, based on both wild spot use and program commercials. Special contract provisions cover the use of the same commercial in both conventional television and cable.

Extras in TV commercials, as we have seen, are covered by contracts with the Screen Extras Guild and the New York Extras Players, except for videotape recordings made under AFTRA jurisdiction. The contracts state that the extras may be recognized in the commercial, as long as they are not part of the central action. In many cases, all the viewer sees is a hand, back of the head, and the like. Payments are usually on a *buy-out* basis: the extras receive a single payment, the advertiser is entitled to unlimited use, and residuals are avoided.

Musicians are usually paid on a flat fee basis for the use of a commercial during a 13-week cycle. If an advertiser wants to use a musical commercial after this period of time, a reuse fee is due each performer. Musicians are typically hired for three-hour sessions. The AFM contract specifies that no more than 15 minutes of "performing music" may be taken from such a session. (This obviously presents no problems for advertisers; completing two or three musical commercials in three hours would be considered a good day's work.) Overdubbing is a common technique in recording music. When musicians are hired to play in such a recording situation and are asked to play several instruments, additional fees are paid for performance on each instrument. Fees and working conditions are spelled out in the AFM contract, but it should be noted that singers are covered by the AFTRA contract.

Conclusion

The "face" of a company is presented to the public in its advertising. In the broadcast media, this image is personified in the talent used in commercials. The consumer's perceptions of and attitudes toward the company and its products are often indistinguishable from the consumer's perceptions of and attitudes toward the talent used in the company's advertising. As a result, casting talent has to be a careful, deliberate process dictated by expertise and experience. The best hunches of the decision makers are also at work, and so is the ingredient of luck. Talent represents a considerable expense to the nation's advertisers, especially those using performers who must be paid above scale. The livelihood of many people is dependent on the role of talent in broadcast advertising, so employment terms are spelled out in elaborate contractual detail. Much of the talent business is an outgrowth of this process, including all the complicated machinery of agents, unions, contracts, commissions, fees, and residuals. What really counts in this "people business" is putting the right performer in the right advertising spot.

chapter eight

Producing Commercials

Cue the Gorilla — and Hope for the Best

Every day, hundreds of commercials are produced for American advertisers. Thousands of people are involved in the business of making these commercials, and billions of sales dollars are generated by the results of their work. Commercial production may seem like an exciting and glamorous occupation, but in truth it's a lot of hard work under heavy pressure. There's nothing exciting about waiting around a studio for a couple of hours while lights are set or squinting into a Moviola editing machine far into the night. "Dubbing down" 24-track radio commercials for a couple of days isn't very glamorous either.

Producing commercials is a tough, competitive business, and the production team is tremendously important to the final result. Good commercials are grounded in the advertising objective, the commercial format, and a valid emotional appeal — decisions made by the client, the account group, and the creative staff. The final dimension of *production execution,* however, can only be added by the members of the production group. Their job is to make an idea come alive. When given a really original idea, they try to develop and polish it into a classic piece of art and salesmanship.

Producing Radio Commercials

Radio is primarily a local medium, supported by local advertisers, and so producing commercials is usually a "hometown affair." The $100,000-a-year creative types are not involved — and rarely are a lot of account executives, production experts, Hollywood hotshots, and high-priced talent. At the retail level, the radio station salesperson who lands the order soon finds that he or she must double as a copywriter and producer-director, since the local auto dealer who bought the schedule does not know how to write a commercial. Hopefully, the salesperson has some talent in formulating a solid idea, presenting it to a client, and producing it at the station's studios.

When advertising on "personality" stations with top-name disc jockeys, advertisers often prefer to give the station fact sheets instead of formal scripts. These sheets list the basic product information that the advertiser wants publicized. Using this information, an experienced DJ can develop an ad lib commercial in his or her own style, and it's often better than one that has been previously scripted. With this kind of freedom, good performers can be salespeople par excellence.

Live copy has been around as long as radio has. Unless there is top talent available, however, its effectiveness in selling products is debatable. Live copy is certainly the most flexible way to present radio messages, for copy can be constantly changed. In addition, there are rarely any talent fees—only the regular time charges. As for the quality of on-air presentations, that depends on the ability of the announcer. Some have a knack for weaving live commercials into their format, so listeners are not turned off but are as interested in the ads as in the program. Unfortunately, announcers may deliver live copy without inflection, phrasing, pacing, or even decent diction and pronunciation. And if the DJ salesperson is not enthusiastic, why should a listener be? How can this drawback of live copy be overcome? Pre-record the commercials, and maintain quality control.

All stations can produce and record simple radio commercials, and quite a number are equipped to do some very elaborate audio work. Their facilities may be used by local advertisers and agencies that want to embellish a straight spokesperson announcement with some music, sound effects, or perhaps a couple of voices. Production costs for such embellishments are very modest. Music and sound effects libraries are readily available to provide such things as a music bridge or the sound of a train whistle, and announcers are usually happy to pick up the few extra dollars (and a little prestige) for performing in freelance commercials.

For large advertisers and agencies, the production of radio commercials gets a bit more involved. Although they may use very simple spots, they often employ the services of a top talent. For national and major regional clients whose advertising is handled by an agency, radio commercials are usually produced by either an agency producer or by an independent production house. It depends on the client, the resources and talent of the agency, and the particular kind of radio commercials wanted.

If an agency really has expertise in radio, it prefers to handle the job with an agency producer-director. Because radio commercial production is a freelance business, an experienced hand will know just where to go for actors and announcers, for a composer-arranger, for musicians, and for the best studio facilities for any particular job. Producer-directors also need to know costs, because they must first have a fairly good idea of how the final product should sound before they can round up the assorted talent needed. They must know how they can achieve a certain sound and still stay within the budget. They will prepare a cost estimate for client approval, and it will contain items such as the following:

- talent — actors, announcers, musicians, and singers (The estimate for this category includes projected costs for scale and over-scale performers, length of recording session, agents' fees, and estimated residuals.)

- composer-arranger-musical director

- sound effects

- director (if not undertaken by the agency producer-director)

- recording studio rental, including engineer

- rental of any special equipment (certain uncommon musical instruments, for example)

- tape stock

- time and facilities for mixing

- number of tape dubs needed

- travel and expenses for producer or talent

Sometimes, the budget is fixed — perhaps $10,000 to produce a series of commercials. In such cases, the producer-director will simply have to live within that amount. There are always lots of places to cut costs in radio production. Talent is the major expense, and so this category is a logical starting point. The number of performers can be cut, or the agency can avoid using top-priced over-scale talent. Music is another category in which costs can be trimmed, such as by limiting the number of musicians.

Agencies usually ask performers or their agents to provide *demo* (demonstration) tapes for the purpose of voice selection. Often, a routine audition tape is sufficient, but a tailor-made demo may be desirable for a special part. In this instance, the talent is usually provided with copy, and the resulting tape can be evaluated with others in the final selection process.

In selecting voices, there has been a long-standing trend away from the didactic announcer. Actors are preferred, and all good announcers are pretty versatile thespians. Agency producers themselves are often talented performers. Although they may not work commercially, a strong dramatic background is a substantial help to them in producing commercials. First and foremost, such a background makes a producer very aware of what a good actor can do — and that's just about anything. Real radio buffs love to work with the medium, because they know anything is possible. But they also know it takes time, a lot of experience, and sometimes a touch of genius. Their enthusiasm for radio can be contagious, and clients often come to realize the tremendous creativity possible in an aural medium. Some small advertisers on a limited budget are often intimidated by their competitors' advertising, especially if it's in the form of a major television blitz. It's tough to meet that kind of competition on their own ground. In radio, however, an advertiser with a small budget and a big imagination can often outshine the competition — and create a lot of impact and excitement in the marketplace at the same time.

Sometimes, a production house, rather than an agency producer-director, is hired to do a series of radio commercials. Most such companies are in large markets, where they stay in constant contact with the local agencies. When they land a contract, they are responsible for the creative work. They are given a copy platform, or possibly a script, but they are in charge of creating the final copy, subject to agency and client approval. Radio production companies are usually small operations staffed by a variety of imaginative, very creative, and often slightly crazy people. The talents of the staff are usually complementary. One may be a fine composer, another the "house wit," another the production genius, and so forth. Their brainstorming sessions can yield some very exciting commercial ideas. Although the demos they produce are seldom completely approved and sometimes are totally rejected, the decisions are usually a matter of selection and revision. Some agencies, dealing with certain kinds of clients, would never consider farming out this kind of work. Not only are they reluctant to lose creative control, but they also say that it's too difficult for the staff of a production house to really know the client and the product in the short time usually available. Further, it's too easy for a long list of taboos to be violated in relation to certain

---

8.1/A Visit to a Jingle Factory

The control room, with its carpeted walls, low lights, and abundant plants, was the setting for a zany conversation that went something like this:

Producer: I'm glad you're here — but I have to tell you I think I blew that jingle: It's the wrong beat. We did it: "Do de dum, ching ching, de dum."

Executive Producer: No, no — it's supposed to be: "Ching, ching, do de dum, ching ching, do de dum."

The engineer pushed a few buttons on a space age console, and the enormous speakers came to life and filled the room with a pulsing beat. Punctuated by snapping fingers and toe taps, the unintelligible conversation sounded like a reunion of bop musicians.

Producer: I can fix it — I'll take it apart, maybe lose only two tracks. Don't panic, it'll be all right.

Executive Producer: I never panic.

Tuesday Productions, located in a northern suburb of San Diego, is hardly on the beaten track, yet clients from all over the country seek outs its services. Its primary product is commercial jingles, produced at the rate of 30 a month for every imaginable kind of client. This is a highly specialized production house that has proved its mastery of both music and advertising. Framed Clio Awards from the prestigious international advertising competition fill one wall. ("We print 'em in the back room," said the executive producer.)

Sales representatives in major markets phone in orders to Tuesday Productions, and a typical jingle commercial is written, produced, and ready for the client in three weeks. With some bare-bones information on what the client wants, the job is turned over to a lyricist-melody writer, who writes a simple set of lyrics and develops an accompanying melody line. At this point an arranger takes over, filling out the musical score (called "charts") for whatever musical instruments seem most suitable. After plenty of brainstorming by the small staff of 20 people, the jingle is ready for the producer, who calls in musicians and singers.

Because of the volume of work, production is scheduled every other week, with perhaps 18 commercials in production in one week. The musicians are superb — able to sight-read, work out any wrinkles in one or two brief run-throughs, and then "lay down the tracks" of one jingle after another. A typical production-day timetable looks like this: rhythm, 9:00–11:00 A.M.; brass, 11:00 A.M.–noon; strings, 1:00–2:00 P.M.; vocalists, 2:00–4:00 P.M.

A 24-track machine is used, and over-dubbing is the technique. Because of the versatility of the equipment, the engineer can isolate a track with a particular instrument or

products with a lot of restrictions, such as over-the-counter drugs, personal products, automobiles, and food products with health claims.

Improvisational groups have been used experimentally to produce radio commercials. A handful of actors and actresses, used to working with one another and full of wit and repartee, can sometimes latch onto an idea and turn out a brilliant commercial. The poor agency copywriter slaving over a typewriter might never think of anything so memorable — or outrageous. Usually, however, it isn't as easy as putting talent in front of microphones and locking the studio door! Many improvisational actors, usually accustomed only to stage work, depend on an audience for approval and encouragement, and they rely on their gestures and facial expressions to convey meaning and emotions. Radio is obviously not for them. In other cases, improvisational groups will turn out a long series of disjointed takes. The editing job is then horrendous, and the producer and engineer may still end up with

group of instruments. It is then possible to adjust levels, highlight certain instruments, soften others, add echoes, equalize the frequency responses, and generally cut, polish, and perfect the timing until the commercials are on a final master reel and ready for client approval. The finished product will usually contain both a 60-second and a 30-second version, segments with melody and lyrics, a musical bed (suitable as background to an announcer), and a 5-second tag (using singers and ending with a flourish). With careful editing, moving various segments around, many options are then available to the client. The announcer's copy over the bed can be easily changed. Multiple versions of the same musical jingle are often produced. (Tuesday Productions has finished more than 50 variations of the theme "This Bud's for you.") Other major clients include Levi Strauss, Suzuki Motorcycles, Michelob Light, Sanyo, Buster Brown Shoes, and Glass-Plus.

Convinced by experience and his company's success, the executive producer, Jim Jerauld, preaches what he calls *the seven elements of a jingle:*

1. *Concept* — an idea or gimmick that can be exploited musically. It is the selling proposition and is sometimes based on the advertiser's slogan. The concept must accurately reflect the product. Simple, direct statements are best.

2. *Lyric* — the concept crystalized. It should establish the selling proposition immediately, with no more than two thoughts in a 30-second jingle. Clichés are quite all right, especially if there's a twist.

3. *Melody* — the "heart" of the jingle, just as the lyric is the brains. Melody is the magical component that makes people *like* the jingle. The melody must be symmetrical and honor the natural inflection that would be used if the lyrics were said aloud.

4. *Arrangement* — the perfect selection of instruments to complement the concept. The arrangement must have the right tempo and still fit the allotted time.

5. *Hook* — a melodic device that is the part of the jingle that people remember. "Reach out and touch someone." "You deserve a break today."

6. *Talent* — musicians with perfect pitch who provide a perfect blend. They must be versatile in adapting to many different kinds of jingle. Singers should be the loudest part.

7. *Engineering* — the best equipment and an experienced person to run it. Mixing and "sweetening" are an art and add greatly to the finished product.

nothing. With luck, there might be a dozen commercial possibilities that will be presented to the agency and client. From this group, perhaps only half or a third will be used, and the client pays only for the ones that will air.

A primary advantage of radio production is that it can be a reasonably fast operation. The medium accommodates itself to deadlines, and commercials can be produced, dubbed down, and ready for distribution in a few days (see 8.1). High-speed dubbing machines turn out as many copies as are needed. Commercials are ordinarily mailed to stations on 5-inch reels at 7½ IPS (inches per second). Good radio commercials should be seen and not just heard. The medium is still a theater of the mind, and its primary tools are voices, music, sound effects, and, now, electronic synthesis. Together, they can create some bright, creative advertising that is a refreshing breeze in the broadcast day. Why then, when the costs are low and the options so plentiful, is there so much *bad* radio advertising? Part of the problem can be traced to the fact that most radio advertising is local, and there simply isn't enough time, talent, and money available to invest in it. In addition, with regard to national radio advertising, some people feel that TV and print capture the top creative people and that radio is often delegated to the young, inexperienced copywriter who doesn't really understand the medium or its potential. Perhaps part of the fault for bad radio commercials lies with advertisers who don't know good advertising from the mediocre and approve the latter if they can save a few dollars. Radio stations also share the blame. They not only air the commercials but often write and produce them as well. Landing the order is the priority, and after that, too little attention is given to production or on-air presentations.

The faults of radio advertising are no more nor less than those of any other medium. There has been, and will continue to be, a growing interest and dedication to producing more creative, amusing, and edifying commercials.

Producing Television Commercials

The time is 11 A.M. on the day of the shoot. Two dozen people are standing around a large videotape studio—camera operators, floor people, technicians, a scene designer, set dresser, gaffer, boom operator, four agency representatives, two client representatives, two or three staff members from the production company, a cook, social worker, and a number of hangers-on. Where is the director—the general who will lead these troops through the day? He's sitting cross-legged on the floor of the set, deeply engrossed in a conversation with the talent and flirting outrageously. She's blonde and beautiful, but smiles wanly. Her name is Susan, and in a week she will celebrate her third birthday. Right now she wants to go home.

It's a simple 30-second commercial, using a group of children who sing the jingle of the sponsor—a fast-food chain specializing in hamburgers. The day before the shoot, 25 children were auditioned, and 7 were selected. Earlier this morning, the director tried the 7 out as a group sitting together on a living room floor, devouring hamburgers, french fries, and soft drinks. That didn't work. Some sang, others gazed off the set in the direction of their mothers, and one picked his nose. They were regrouped in twos and threes. A fight ensued between two precocious "professionals" trying to upstage each other. Their innocence was gone. Finally the director picked Susan, the youngest, and coached her to sit alone and sing the jingle. She was darling—but so intimidated that she stopped singing halfway through the song. On the 11th take—finally, the tears. It's going to be a long day.

Preproduction Sequence

Developing Storyboards   All the problems, little and big, that arise on the day of production rarely show up on a storyboard. Very few commercials emerge from production looking exactly like the original. No one expects they will, because a storyboard is really just a board of *intent*. It provides a tangible proposal to the client, but it must always be augmented with written or verbal descriptions. The storyboard should be read with imagination—like the Sunday comics. There are too many contingencies that arise in actual production to operate in any other manner. (The Susans of this world see to that.)

The creative team in an advertising agency, often consisting of an art director and a copywriter, may develop many commercial ideas in storyboard form. The best ones are selected and usually revised several times before everyone concerned is satisfied. Some storyboards are elaborately prepared—done in color and mounted on big boards. In most instances, however, the client is presented with simple pen or pencil sketches. The form of the storyboard depends on the client, the abilities of the artist, agency policy, and client wishes.

Winning client approval is rarely a rubber-stamp operation. The creative team may have spent many weeks developing a series of commercials, but such a campaign will never make it to the airwaves without client approval. It's a temptation to the agency staff to sell, and sell hard. If the client is enthusiastically carried away, however, it may be very difficult or impossible for the agency to deliver the commercial this client envisioned.

An experienced advertising manager representing the client needs to be satisfied that the recommended storyboards will fulfill the advertising objectives, fit the budget, correctly position the brand against the competition, and capture viewer interest. A commercial idea that doesn't meet those criteria, no matter how unusual or clever, should not be approved.

Selecting a Production House   When the storyboards receive client approval, the agency producer goes to work. The producer carefully reviews the commercials in the series with the creative and account executives and then numbers and codes them with a nickname for easy recall. Next, he or she writes an accompanying *spec* sheet of production notes. The specs enumerate the requirements of this commercial in terms of sets, props, graphics, talent, crew, and myriad other necessities. (See 8.2.)

There are more than a thousand production houses in the United States. They range from the studios of a local TV station to major houses in New York or Los Angeles. How does an advertiser or agency select one? For local advertisers in medium or small markets, the process is not difficult: the local station is used. For more elaborate commercials and for those designed for regional or national use, the agency producer usually selects three production houses on the basis of their direc-

---

8.2 /A Spec Sheet

This ad agency is seeking bids from production houses for a new commercial.

McCANN-ERICKSON
McCANN-ERICKSON INC 201 CALIFORNIA STREET SAN FRANCISCO CA 94111 415-981 2262

PRODUCTION SPECIFICATIONS

CLIENT: DEL MONTE CORPORATION   PRODUCT: DEL MONTE MEXICAN FOODS

COMMERCIAL: RMMX-2369 "Something Big"

The accompanying storyboard represents an introductory commercial for a new line of Del Monte Mexican Foods. Production companies making bids should include all costs through screening of 35mm dailies. Music scoring and editorial completion will be contracted separately by McCann-Erickson.

A firm bid, broken out on an AICP form, must be received by May 24. Production contract will be awarded week of May 31. Photography must be completed before July 30.

Casting must begin immediately upon awarding job so that selected performer can be used in still photography for print advertising to break concurrent with August 30 air date.

Bids should include four days of initial casting, plus two days of call-backs. We are seeking a strongly masculine actor whose appearance and manner will match and enhance the mysterious, highly dramatic, low light mood of this commercial, someone fresh and not overused. Exclusivity includes all food products. Call-backs must be video taped for later review with Client.

Wardrobe, including serape and cowboy hat, must be authentic and worn-looking, without being soiled or in any way unappealing. The uniform of the guard outside the fiesta is that of a private patrolman.

Cans of the product will be supplied but production company will be responsible for color-correction of labels. The packs on the donkey train must be authentic; labels for the packs can be done on leather or canvas. Bids should include a home economist to prepare food shown in last scene.

It has been determined that the high mountain location can be found in the vicinity of Mammoth, California. Production company must Polaroid recommended locations, including deserted street locales for the early morning scenes against the Hollywood sign and the Bonaventure Hotel in downtown Los Angeles. The fiesta entrance can be constructed, but drawings must be approved beforehand.

Bids should include names and credits of the recommended director, cinemaphotographer, and production manager. Bids should cover costs for the director and production manager to attend a one-day pre-production meeting with Client and Agency in San Francisco. At this meeting we will present the director's shot board, casting tapes and recommendations, as well as Polaroids of locations, props, wardrobe, animals, etc.

Questions and bids should be directed to Anna Ludowieg, Broadcast Department, McCann-Erickson, Inc, 201 California St., San Francisco.

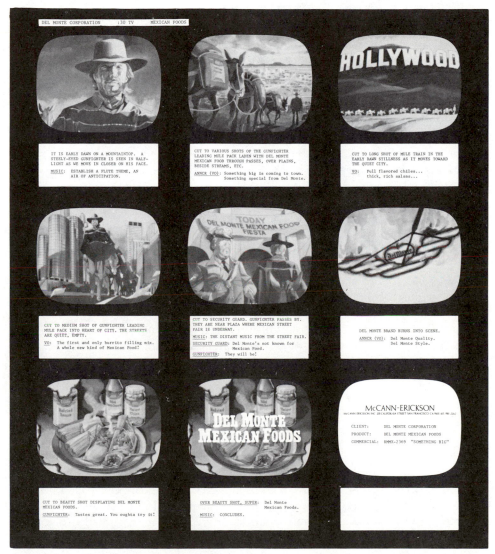

Courtesy of the Del Monte Corporation and McCann-Erickson, Inc.

tors and equipment, the quality of their previous work, and their reputation. Many of them, located mainly in New York and Los Angeles, tend to specialize in certain areas, such as food demonstrations ("table top shoots") or location shooting. The key factor, however, is what director is available.

Production houses, which constantly "pitch" agency producers, present reels of their directors' commercial accomplishments. An agency producer will screen these and evaluate such things as directing techniques, camera work, lighting, and the quality of the casting. Production houses may have one or perhaps half a dozen directors on the staff. Agency producers seek out top directors who specialize in particular kinds of commercials—working with children, animals, humor, food or beverages, and so forth.[1] Besides lining up the right director, an agency producer will also want to know who will serve as the production manager, the person responsible for attending to countless production details and keeping the commercial "on budget."

At the production house, the counterpart of the agency producer will break down the storyboard and the specs and will estimate expenses. That person must know costs, time, and staff and crew requirements as well as production. A sharp pencil is required, because the bid must be competitive in order to get the business but still return a profit to the production house. A markup of 35 percent is traditionally added for profit and overhead. All production houses add an OSIF sum for contingency ("Oh shucks, I forgot"), usually 10 percent of the total bid. Some agencies and clients specify that contingency monies are not to be touched without their approval; otherwise, it's too easy to raid this fund for items that should really have been covered in the original cost estimate.

If storyboards and specs are carefully prepared for the production house estimator, the agency will usually save some money in the long run. The production house should have sufficient time to prepare a bid carefully. If asked to bid in a frantic rush, houses will always bid higher, because they are compelled to protect themselves. The agency and client, which have carefully scheduled a production timetable, should allow enough time to review the bids thoroughly and engage in a little negotiating. A last-minute rush precludes such negotiations. All along the production line, adequate time to do the job right will save money. Overtime wreaks havoc on staff nerves, agency-client relationships, and production budgets.

Within a few days the agency will have the bids back from the three selected production houses. These bids are often submitted on a standard five-page form (for either videotape or film) developed by the Association of Independent Commercial Producers. (A cost summary sheet of this form is shown in 8.3.) Standardized bid forms permit easy comparisons on an item-by-item basis. One production house may estimate two days of shooting, another three days. There may be differences in estimates of everything from the amount of raw film stock needed to wardrobe requirements. With this information, the agency can determine what costs seem realistic and what charges may be out of line. The agency can then pursue some price negotiations. Usually, however, bids are within 10 percent of one another. If not, the

[1]David Elkind, "How They Choose Directors," *Millimeter,* September, 1980, p. 112.

8.3 / Standardized Form for Production Bids

Association of Independent Commercial Producers, Inc.

FILM PRODUCTION COST SUMMARY

		Bid Date	Actualization Date
Production Co.:		Agency:	Agency job #
Address:		Client:	Product:
Telephone No.:	Job #		
Production Contact:		Agency prod:	Tel:
Director:		Agency art dir:	Tel:
Cameraman:		Agency writer:	Tel:
Set Designer:		Agency Bus. Mgr.:	Tel:
Editor:		Commercial title:	No.: Length:
No. pre-prod. days	pre-light/rehearse	1.	
No. build/strike days	Hours:	2.	
No. Studio shoot days	Hours:	3.	
No. Location days	Hours:	4.	
Location sites:		5.	
		6.	

SUMMARY OF ESTIMATED PRODUCTION COSTS		ESTIMATED	ACTUAL		
1. Pre-production and wrap costs	Totals A & C				
2. Shooting crew labor	Total B				
3. Location and travel expenses	Total D				
4. Props, wardrobe, animals	Total E				
5. Studio & Set Construction Costs	Totals F, G, and H				
6. Equipment costs	Total I				
7. Film stock develop and print: No. feet mm	Total J				
8. Miscellaneous	Total K				
9.	Sub-Total: A to K				
10. Director/creative fees (Not Included In Direct Cost)	Total L				
11. Insurance					
12.	Sub-Total: Direct Costs				
13. Production Fee					
14. Talent costs and expenses	Totals M and N				
15. Editorial and finishing per:					
16.					
17.	Grand Total (Including Director's Fee)				
18. Contingency					

Comments:

AICP 1980

Courtesy of the Association of Independent Commercial Producers.

agency producer will want to find out why—there may be a misunderstanding somewhere. The agency account executive is given the bids, along with the recommendation and comments of the agency producer. Since only companies that are qualified to do the work are invited to bid in the first place, the house with the lowest bid is usually selected. Occasionally, however, one of the other houses is selected for some specific reason.

Although most commercials are handled on a competitive bid system, some advertisers prefer to negotiate a cost-plus or a cost-plus/fixed-fee contract with a production house. In the cost-plus system, the studio enumerates all the anticipated charges at cost, and a percentage of this is added as markup. If costs exceed this estimate, the advertiser is obliged to pay them. (In the bid system, the studio takes the risk for overages.) In the cost-plus/fixed-fee system, the charges are estimated at cost, and then a fixed sum—not a percentage of the costs—is added for overhead and profit. If costs exceed the estimate, the advertiser must pay them, but the fixed fee remains just that, fixed. Many clients, believing cost-plus systems are too open-ended, reject them because they dislike unpleasant surprises when production bills are submitted.

Cost Controls All advertising costs have risen dramatically in the past few decades, but in the production of TV commercials, it's been a case of runaway inflation. Production costs have doubled—in some cases tripled—in recent years. Clients and senior agency personnel have had to ask why, and what can be done about it.

Many of the reasons for the escalation are totally beyond the control of the client. Cost factors that are within client control, however, are increasingly scrutinized at the storyboard stage. There are many other expenses, but the following are the major targets in a cost-control program: locations and sets; the number of shooting days; travel expenses; fees for a director, camera operator, composer-arranger, or other high-priced personnel; the cost of talent fees and residuals; and editing costs.

Personnel are often paid flat fees, and this cost is not very negotiable. The question for the client and the agency is whether the services of a $5,000-a-day director are worth it. If they are, then the client must pay the bill and look around for other ways to save money. On the one hand, location shooting that involves travel, lodging, meals, and other expenses for talent and crew can run up bills that rival the national debt. One reason so many commercials are shot in Southern California is the proximity of many different locales. On the other hand, it's obviously cheaper to rent someone's home for a day at a cost of several hundred dollars than to try to build an authentic kitchen from scratch in a studio. And the resulting commercial often has a more authentic look than one shot in a studio.

In many cases, a studio shoot is the only option. The expense of a first-rate scene designer who designs and builds a studio set may be more than offset by the money saved in avoiding a location shoot. The end result is often as good or better than an outdoor setting—and no one worries about the weather. Stock footage, rear-screen projectors, chroma-key, and other devices are sometimes used in the studio to avoid a costly location shoot. Penny pinching may be counterproductive, especially for corporations that have achieved a prestigious image built over a long period. Consumers do not equate a high-quality product with a low-quality commercial. In addition, when the competition is spending heavily on lavish commercials, a client may feel forced to increase production budgets.

Set design and set dressing are obvious areas for exercising cost controls. Sets should be kept few and small, and they need not be furnished with authentic antiques or custom velvet draperies. Good designers know the business so well that they can build and furnish the appropriate set, provide the director with adequate shooting options, and still keep the costs within reason. Set designers must always put together much more than is ever seen in the camera viewfinder. The client may grumble that only 20 percent of the set will be seen, but the safety valve is there if the director needs to shoot the commercial another way.

Using lots of performers or star talent constitutes an enormous expenditure. The "borrowed interest" such talent provides to the product and the ad should be carefully analyzed. The session fee for a celebrity is one thing; residuals are quite another. There are many ways to cut talent costs. Avoiding the use of star talent and using fewer performers are the obvious ones. Many commercials close with a voice-over corporate tag. If the performer already appearing in a commercial is suitable for delivering this line, the costs of an announcer can be avoided. If the actor's face is not seen—in a demonstration involving only the hands, for instance—the fees are smaller.

Too often, commercials are produced in a hurry. Insufficient preparation leads to overtime payments. Also, if commercials are shot one at a time, rather than in a series, costs can multiply. It is extremely important to shoot several commercials at once, even if some of them won't be used for some time. If there's an abundance of footage available, it may be possible to simply re-edit and create new commercials without significant cost.

The costs of producing a television commercial can easily run up to $100,000 and more, even before one minute of air time has been bought! If the client wants to spend this kind of money, the agency is happy to oblige. Because some advertisers demand exceptional, extraordinary advertising and have been willing to pay the price, hotshot directors, star talent, and large casts are employed. Stock music is discarded in favor of specially composed or arranged background music. Elaborate sets are built and dressed by top personnel. Creative and production personnel experiment with intricate animation, fisheye lenses, complex optical effects, helicopter shots, and dozens of other ideas and devices that can send costs skyward.

Most advertisers are unable or unwilling to underwrite such commercial extravaganzas, insisting instead on cost-control programs early in the preproduction sequence. Ideally, this cost control begins with the creation of the commercial by the writer and art director.

Production Sequence

After a bid is accepted by the client, it cannot be changed without client approval. Six weeks is usually considered the minimum schedule from storyboard approval to finished commercial. It can be done in much less time, if necessary; production of other, high-budget commercials may go on for months.

The first step in the production sequence is a series of meetings between the agency production team and key personnel from the production house. This group is responsible for location search, set design, talent auditions, wardrobe and props, crew selection, and myriad other production requirements. Depending on the size of the budget and the needs of a commercial, a top director may be brought in. The director may earn $5,000 per production day or more, but the fee includes his or her talents in preproduction planning. In this kind of commercial, it would be a mistake to structure the creative aspects too tightly; otherwise, any director could be hired to shoot from a detailed storyboard. A particularly talented director can contribute ideas and suggest alternatives. Since the director is really hired to make an idea *work*, he or she must have a strong voice in talent selection.

Auditions are usually videotaped so the decision makers can review the final choices. This procedure may run up costs a bit, but it's worth it when 20 women, say, are auditioning for a mother role. Without a videotape, who can remember actress number 12 at the end of the day? Final casting of talent usually takes place shortly before the day of the shoot.

In most instances, a final meeting is held a few days before the scheduled shoot day, attended by all the people responsible for the finished commercial. This includes the director; the production manager from the production house; the agency's account supervisor, writer, art director and producer; and a client representative. The purpose of the meeting is to show the recommended cast (using the rough videotape made at the casting session), and to pass around photographs of other production details—locations, wardrobe, props, and the like. The group must reach agreement on all aspects of production and obtain the approval of the client representative.

"A bit part! What good is a bit part? The whole commercial lasts only 30 seconds!"

Depending on the commercials, other parties may be present: a home economist who prepares food, a stylist if a special wardrobe is required, hairdressers, or other specialists. Representing the client is the advertising manager, or perhaps some other person thoroughly familiar with the product advertised. This is important if the commercial demonstrates a complicated product or if there is some other technical aspect of the product or package that must be correctly displayed.[2]

It is difficult for a director to know the precise way the commercial will be shot, but he or she must have a fairly clear concept of how to make the commercial work. Thus, at this final meeting, the director will sometimes present a "shot board" of rough sketches that detail, second-by-second, the appearance of the finished commercial.

On the day of the shoot, when the crew reports and the performers check in for wardrobe and makeup, the agency producer may as well find a quiet corner and a cup of coffee, because now the director takes over. The director is boss on the set, but he or she always consults with the agency producer about major changes.

It is the responsibility of the production house to be sure that everything (sets, props, equipment, raw stock, costumes, permits, meal service, and so on) and everyone (talent, director, crew, and any specialists) are ready. Planning is critical to stay within the budget. On-set conferences, with high-priced talent and crew cooling their heels, are costly; and 11th-hour changes are extravagant and reflect poor planning.

Based on where a commercial is shot, the technical crew may come from the following unions: the International Alliance of Theatrical and Stage Employees, the National Association of Broadcast Employees and Technicians, and the International Brotherhood of Electrical Workers. If equipment trucks are needed, as they often are, or if generators or other heavy equipment must be hauled, a fourth union is involved — the Teamsters. The rules of these unions vary to some degree, and the agency producer must be conversant with them in order to estimate costs accurately. The most important regulations cover such items as overtime, breaks, travel expenses, and job responsibilities. It is on difficult shoots that union rules are most likely to be bent in the exigencies of production. (Union members who protest too much are unlikely to be invited back.)

The scenes in commercials are rarely shot in the sequence in which they eventually appear on the home screen. Directors usually shoot the most demanding scenes first — those involving dialogue among several actors, those using child performers, complicated demonstrations, and the like. When those portions of a commercial that require sound-on-film have been shot, the director can dismiss the audio crew. As the day winds down, the director is left with the easy shots — short reaction shots of performers, for example, or closeups of the product. These short takes may not be indicated on a storyboard. They are, however, relatively easy to shoot, and they provide the editor with creative options in assembling the final commercial.

Everyone stays on the set until the producer is satisfied that what the client wants

---

[2]Hooper White, *How to Produce an Effective TV Commercial* (Chicago: Crain Books, 1981). This useful reference is a step-by-step analysis of commercial production.

is on tape or "in the can." A commercial is usually shot with a number of options; there usually isn't just *one* way to do it. For this reason, good directors will often use about 3,000 feet of 35mm film in one day, even though a final 30-second commercial will contain only 45 feet. This ratio means that a lot of film will never be used, but all the extra footage provides tremendous creative latitude for the film or tape editor. Unused footage may be resurrected later to make new commercials. Compared with the cost of staff and time, film stock is cheap.

Postproduction Sequence

When the preproduction planning and the shoot are finished, still more work lies ahead. The postproduction sequence is certainly one of the most arduous and critical aspects of producing commercials. With videotape, of course, the process is much less complicated than with film, because of the immediate playback capability. Tapes must still be edited, however, and this is done electronically. Editing processes have improved dramatically in recent years. Computers now permit the editor to call up any scene instantly, move it backward or forward, and edit one frame at a time. Because of the versatility of tape, many commercials shot on film are transferred to tape for editing. Using a special electronic console, the editor is able to call up any portion of the various takes stored in the computer's memory. Fades, wipes, dissolves, and a vast variety of special effects can be added. (See 8.4.) Portions of a commercial may be slowed, held in freeze frame, or speeded up. For commercials that run a bit long — dialogue commercials, for example — speeding up the commercial not only resolves the timing problem but may increase its effectiveness.[3]

[3]Priscilla LaBarbera and James MacLachlan, "Time Compressed Speech in Radio Advertising," *Journal of Marketing,* January, 1979, p. 30. (The results of these researchers at New York University indicated that, if a commercial was speeded up 25 percent, the audience was not aware of it, and recall of the commercial was actually improved.)

"I'm sorry, but I just can't do another 'Gotcha' take today."

Checklist for Producing Good TV Commercials while Cutting Costs

With sky-high production costs, budget controls are immensely important to both the client and the agency. Excessive penny-pinching can ruin a potentially effective commercial, but spend-thrift agencies do a disservice to their clients. Conscious attention by an agency to important questions can keep advertising campaigns at a reasonable and cost-effective level. Some of these questions constitute a recapitulation of points mentioned in this book. The purpose of the following is to codify questions related to production and cost controls into a simple checklist.

1. In the creative planning stage, can simple storyboards be used, rather than expensive, detailed, "finished" frame-by-frame presentations? Polaroid photographs,

8.4/Special Effects

Advertisers learned long ago that animation and special effects helped to combat audience inattention. The price for such effects is high, but the results are worth it. Much of this work is performed either at the production house or the optical house, which specializes in the addition of special effects. The use of computers in developing animation and other effects has opened enormous possibilities. The costs vary greatly, but the end result can carve out a unique position for the client who wants to look as up to date as possible.

Cereals go snap, crackle, pop; antacids dissolve gas bubbles; and Raid kills bugs dead, because most people would rather look at clever animated ones than at the real thing. For the creative team with a big imagination, and for a client with a budget to match, animation and special effects present endless options.

Live action can be combined with animation, and the result may be a housewife chasing a bottle of dish detergent that thinks it's a hand lotion.

A complex subject—like the human digestive system—can be made simple by using animated diagrams. The end result may be the invisible made visible, as viewers watch aspirin rush to a headache.

Through object animation, packages can magically unfold themselves to reveal the product. The animators shoot a frame at a

time, and between shots, they carefully pull away the wrapping with tweezers. The same single-frame exposure technique can assemble or disassemble an automobile in a few seconds.

Multiple images can be combined to lend excitement and to convey emotional impact. Soft drink commercials oriented to young people often use this device.

Slow motion will reveal a torture test of automobile tires.

Time-lapse photography can show a pastry rising in a hot oven.

Reverse moves have shown a variety of talented cats doing a cha cha cha because of some pet food.

Colored filters can change the mood of a message. For example, a filter used with a perfume commercial can create a soft, glowing, romantic mood.

The freeze frame can stop action at the most graphic moment to arrest viewer attention and direct it to what is important. A freeze and a zoom-in on a pickpocket lifting a wallet focus the attention of the viewer, who would probably miss the action otherwise.

Corporate symbols and brand names can turn, spin, zoom in and out, and change shape, size, and, maybe, viewer attitudes.

These are just a few of the many special effects that, if expertly used, enable television advertising to approach an art form.

line drawings, and other simple artistic devices can be substituted. (Some agencies avoid presenting storyboards to their clients. They prefer to use a script and/or an oral presentation of the *idea,* for they consider storyboards too restrictive and inflexible.)

2.   Do the agency and client completely agree about the concept of this commercial? Is the commercial cut and polished before storyboards and specs are sent out for bids? Has any "dead weight" been eliminated? Does every element contribute to the central message?

3.   Are the production houses given adequate detail on requirements and sufficient time to prepare their bids? Are they asked to itemize all costs on the AICP form?

4.   Are the production houses that have been selected to bid the best choices for this job? Is the agency willing to try a new company in an effort to save money, or is it simply too easy to continue doing business with the same people?

5.   Are the bids carefully and objectively evaluated? If the house with the lowest bid is not selected, is there a solid reason for this decision? Is every projected expense necessary and realistic? Can anything be eliminated?

6.   Can nearby locations be used for outdoor shoots? Are studio sets reasonable in cost? Can they be used in several commercials?

7.   Are all the performers slated for this commercial necessary? Is over-scale talent necessary?

8.   Can any low-cost production devices be employed? (Examples are closeups, stills and drawings, stock footage, stock music, canned sound effects, and chroma-key.)

9.   Will this shoot produce several commercials, or just one? Are too many commercials being produced? Will six do instead of eight? Can 10-second commercials be "lifted" from 30-second commercials?

10.   Are editing costs in line? Will the production house handle the editing itself or send it to an editing house? If the latter is selected, have several houses been asked to bid?

11.   Are the special optical effects used reasonable and necessary?

12.   Can expenses be pared if one company is selected to handle all release printing (meaning the production of multiple copies) for the agency's clients, rather than having each production company handle this job?

13.   Can this commercial be run for a long period and still not "wear out" in terms of its message and presentation?

Editing on videotape is a growing practice. The creative options for tape rival or exceed those for film, and the editing chore may be accomplished in a few hours or a day. Film editing is a time-consuming proposition.

In film, the "dailies," or "rushes," which are copies of the camera original made in order to protect the original, will usually be ready the day following the shoot. After the footage has been screened, the editing process begins. In some cases, the production house provides editing services, but in many cases the job is farmed out to an editing house. (Because editing constitutes a major expense, some agencies also ask for bids from several editing houses.) One director noted that on the day of production he was king, but in the editing room he was just another peon. It's true, of course, because a commercial is the expression of the client. The agency and production house, as well as the director, are hired hands making sure a commercial reflects what the advertiser wants to say. There may be many heads peering over the shoulder of the film editor. When a *rough cut* of the work print is ready, it will be screened for approval by the agency and client. Changes invariably have to be made. The rough cut may be changed several times until a *fine cut* is approved and ready for the next step.

When the editing of the work print is nearly finished, the sound track is mixed. The mix may involve an announcer voice-over, singers, specially arranged or stock music, and a variety of sound effects. When it is finished, the sound track will be on either 16mm or 35mm magnetic film and synchronized with the finished work print. It's then ready to be sent to the optical house for completion. Special effects and animation may be added at the optical house to embellish the commercial.

The original film is cut to conform exactly with the work print, and the sound track is interlocked. The work is exacting, time consuming, and expensive. There may still be a few minor technical changes (such as correcting a missynchronization of audio and video) before a final corrected print is ready.

8.5/Film or Videotape?

Procedures differ throughout the production sequence, depending on whether the commercial is to be shot on film or tape. Creative and production considerations—not cost factors—usually dictate the choice. The old film-versus-videotape arguments in relation to cost controls are now largley invalidated. Tape may be cheaper than film, but the cost depends on the job. The differences between the two have been closing fast for several years. Below is an abbreviated summary of some of the advantages of each medium. In deciding between film and tape, those producing the commercial must evaluate each storyboard in terms of its own unique requirements.

Advantages of Videotape

• The director can immediately view playbacks.

• Editing can begin immediately after production.

• The medium is excellent for a low-cost, simple production shot in "real time" (a stand-up spokesperson pitch, for example).

• The lighting task is easier.

• A "live," here-and-now look results.

• It is easier to achieve special effects, such as speeding up, slowing down, and reversing the action and to add zooms, wipes, and computer animation through an analog computer.

Advantages of Film

• The medium is excellent for closeups of foods, faces, and other details.

• Equipment is more mobile for location shoots.

• Soft, "cinematic" qualities can be achieved that can be especially effective in commercials with strong emotional appeals.

• It is easier to make stop-motion or animated commercials that are shot one frame at a time.

• The medium is better for complex editing jobs that use montages and complicated dissolves.

• The director can often substitute 16mm for 35mm equipment without a significant loss in visual quality.

Commercials, whether filmed or taped (see 8.5) are dubbed to 2-inch tape and sent to stations and networks, where they are generally dubbed to ¾-inch cartridges for easy handling. It is expected that the industry will gradually change during the 1980s to a 1-inch videotape standard.

Traffic

For an agency with many clients active in both the print and broadcast media, processing the work that is in various stages of completion presents an awesome, if unglamorous task. Someone has to keep track of it all. Estimates, work orders, bids, contracts, and so on must be expedited, or deadlines will be missed. This task falls to the advertising agency's traffic department. One of its major responsibilities in the broadcast area is to ship commercials to stations and networks. The media department, which is responsible for buying time on broadcast stations across the country, must cooperate very closely with traffic. The traffic staff must know the commercial lengths bought on each station, the volume of the buy, and the starting and ending dates. Commercials are coded for easy identification and sent to stations with instructions that spell out exact rotation schedules. It's often a race against time to get the commercials to the stations in time for the starting date.

The traffic and production departments must handle additional duties — the details that are sometimes simply filed away but still terribly important. Music clearances must be taken care of through the American Society of Composers, Authors and Publishers (ASCAP) or through BMI, Inc. For the use of copyright music, fees must be negotiated and paid to the publishers and composers. Broadcast releases, contracts, and similar legal documents, including substantiation for advertising claims and proof of the authenticity of the commercial, must be obtained and properly filed.

Residual payments to talent constitute one of the most complex aspects of broadcast advertising bookwork. Such payments are often the responsibility of the traffic department. Because it handles the shipment and scheduling of commercials, it is the logical one to keep track of which commercial is running where and for how long. Some agencies prefer to turn the work over to an outside company that really acts as paymaster to thousands of performers and musicians. Talent & Residuals, a division of the Chicago firm of IDC Services, Inc., is one of the largest and best-known companies in this field.

Conclusions

A radio or television commercial begins with an objective, expands into a strategy, and is then developed both in terms of format and emotional appeal. The last dimension in this process is the actual production of a commercial. A commercial may require only recording an announcer reading a radio spot, or it may involve an extravaganza with star talent and an enormous production crew.

It's the job of the production team to take both the written and spoken ideas of the creative team and turn them into a finished tape or film — and that can be a complicated process. Many expert people may be needed, including casting directors, agents, performers, directors, producers, scene designers, camera crews, musicians, composers, postproduction editors, and many more. These people can contribute in both small and large ways to the commercial's success. Their contributions, plus the all-controlling reality of a budget, determine the final result. Along the way, many decisions must be made about the selection of a production house, talent, location, sets, and so forth. Some of the most important decisions are made in the editing room.

The entire process of producing commercials is really one of evaluation and selection. Unfortunately, too many people in the business turn out commercials that at best can be labeled mediocre. Nevertheless, there are many truly gifted and conscientious professionals whose touch of genius sets a standard for what *can* be done in broadcast advertising.

chapter nine

Evaluating Commercials

Will It Sell in Peoria?

By the time a commercial is produced, the investment may run into the tens of thousands of dollars. Is it a good commercial? How will an audience respond? Will it sell? Clients and agencies, seeking assurance, or "proof" if possible, often test commercials before investing any significant sums in time buys.

The subject of testing is itself a controversial one. Some professionals swear by it and say that the information they obtain enables them to confirm the winners and eliminate the losers. (In some cases, the results of such testing may indicate that only a small segment of a commercial needs to be changed. In order to make such corrections, commercials are often tested in storyboard or rough-cut form.) Other professionals won't have a thing to do with commercial testing. They believe that sample audiences are not representative and that a commercial exposed on a one-shot basis is not a valid indication of its possible long-range impact. Many agencies and clients would like to test commercials but simply do not have the money to do so. Because of the expense involved, most commercial testing is confined to relatively large advertisers who spend substantial sums in the broadcast media and who want to be sure their messages will achieve their campaign goals.

For those who are "believers," a number of independent research companies serve the needs of the advertising industry. Their philosophies and methodologies are diverse, and the advertiser and the agency can "go shopping for their services." These companies evaluate commercials in terms of awareness, recall, attitude change, image, subconscious reactions, and so forth. The methodologies of seven of the best-known ones are described in this chapter.

AdTel Marketing Services

Acting on requests from a number of major advertisers, the Advertising Research Foundation proposed in 1967 a brand new marketing research methodology. The plan was to measure the effect of advertising on actual sales through the use of two matched panels of households, which would be wired to a dual-cable TV system. AdTel Marketing Services is an outgrowth of that proposal, and today, this subsidiary of Burke Marketing Services, Inc., operates in a half-dozen markets scattered across the country. The identity of these cities, nicknamed AdTel East, AdTel Midwest, and so forth, is supposedly a secret, but all meet some basic requirements: they are demographically representative of the United States, have local TV service that brings in each of the three major networks, and have sufficient population to provide large, replenishable panels ranging from 2,100 to 3,500 households.

A dual-cable system establishes A and B panels, which are matched on the basis of demographics, media use, brand selection, and buying characteristics. The dual system provides alternate geographic groups of 80 to 90 households that are connected to one of the two cables. The result is a checkerboard TV distribution that permits AdTel to use one panel as a control and the other to test TV commercials.

The cable system, on instructions from AdTel, will substitute a cut-in test commercial in a commercial position that has already been paid for by the same corporate advertiser. The cut-ins are controlled through a console for each of the local station signals. An engineer, by pushing a button, can insert a test commercial on Cable A or B. (See 9.1.) In order to preserve the "real world" TV environment, AdTel requires that test commercials look the same as finished ones. Clients are entitled to an unlimited number of cut-ins without additional charges.

In order to measure the response (or lack of it) from viewers to the test commercials, AdTel uses weekly purchase diaries kept by cooperating households. Each purchase diary panel consists of approximately 1,000 households at a given time. Panel turnover is about 20 percent annually and is accounted for by moves, deaths, and those who just get tired of keeping a diary. Participating families are personally recruited and trained, and they are required to record purchases in a number of categories—for example, food, laundry-supplies, paper, personal-care, and health products. Panel households are compensated for their efforts by a monthly incentive plan.

In some of AdTel's new markets, the purchase diary has been replaced with the use of scanners in supermarket checkout stands. Each panel consists of approximately 1,250 households, matched demographically. An identification card is provided for each household to present at the checkout stand. This card triggers the universal product code scanner to recognize and record each item purchased by that shopping household. As an incentive to use the ID card, each panelist receives a discount on purchases.

The data generated by this record of actual shopping behavior are immense. AdTel sends its clients four-week reports reflecting household purchases by product category, units purchased, dollar volume, trial and repeat sales, brand switching, exclusive buying behavior, coupon redemption, purchasers' demographics, and so forth. The research is helpful in testing shelf placement, packaging, new products, new sizes, and a variety of other attributes of both the product and the store environment.

In testing television advertising, this methodology allows the advertiser to test and adjust the weight of the TV schedule and determine what results follow. The timing of the schedule, the dayparts used in the commercial schedule, the creative approach, the selection of talent, and so on can all be tested before a national campaign is launched.

Most of AdTel's clients are major advertisers who spend millions of dollars in television each year. Nevertheless, the cost of the service is significant, because of the complexity of the company's services. AdTel assumes responsibility for cut-in coordination at the cable company, the recruitment and training of cooperating households, processing of the data from purchase diaries or supermarket scanners, and the

9.1/How AdTel Tests Commercials

The AdTel cut-in system consists of a console for each of the three network stations. The top of the photograph shows the off-the-air signal from each of the stations. The second layer of screens represents

Cable A and Cable B. Test commercials can be cut in to either cable on any one of the three stations. The lower group of screens provides a preview of the videotaped test commercials.

warehousing and distribution of test products to cooperating supermarkets. What is particularly important in this methodology is that the client and AdTel can balance all the variables in Panels A and B except the one being tested.

ASI Market Research, Inc.

ASI Market Research, Inc., organized in 1962, is one of the largest and best known of the research companies. It has offices in New York, Chicago, and Los Angeles. About 350 people work at ASI's Los Angeles headquarters, which are located in Preview House, a comfortable theater on Sunset Boulevard. The theater is used to test feature films, TV programs, and commercials.

Audience members are recruited by telephone and by soliciting in areas of high foot traffic, such as shopping centers. For TV tests, the group sought is really a quota sample, based on equal representations of men and women and of those over and under age 35. These people are invited to Preview House for a "private screening" of new TV materials and told that they will be asked to give their opinions. The invitation is followed up with a telephone reminder and a fancy engraved invitation that the participants must bring with them.

As people file into the theater, they are asked to fill out a form that asks their sex, age, education, income, employment category, and time spent with TV. They are also asked some questions about product usage for commercials that will be tested that evening. Everyone is given a folder, and inside are more forms to be completed. One is a questionnaire for door prizes, and it asks respondents to check their choices of prizes by brand in a number of product categories. (It doesn't take much effort to figure out that commercials to be tested in any particular evening come from this list.) A master of ceremonies warms up the audience and explains the procedures for the evening's entertainment.

Of the 410 seats, 200 are equipped with a little electronic device that yields what is called an Instantaneous Response Profile. A dial permits the users to indicate by degree their response from "very good" to "very dull." A normal, or neutral, point is halfway between the two extremes. The signal from each recorder is automatically transmitted to the control room, where an operator watches the cumulative response track—a moving line on graph paper (see 9.2). Because of the demographic data secured on each member of the audience, and because this information is associated with each seat number, specific breakouts are possible. A cumulative response for just the men in the audience, for a particular product user group, or for an age group can be tracked separately, for example. After a short orientation session on how to use the Instantaneous Response Profile device, the show begins.

As a control, a McGoo cartoon is shown first, and ASI staff members report that it is remarkable how similarly it is tracked on the graph paper night after night. On a typical evening, following the cartoon, a half-hour TV pilot never previously shown on the air is played without interruption. After evaluation forms are completed on it, the emcee prepares the audience for the five commercials to be shown. The first commercial, like the cartoon, is also a control device, and after that four noncompetitive test commercials are shown. Evaluation forms are filled out, and respondents are asked to check the adjectives that come closest to describing each commercial—amateurish, dull, informative, silly, interesting, and so on.

After the commercials are shown, preselected panels of about a dozen people are escorted from the theater and into small conference rooms. Under the guidance of an ASI staff member, they discuss in depth their reactions to the commercials. Panel members know the session is being recorded on audio tape. They are unaware of the

9.2/Instantaneous Response Profile Curves

At the ASI Market Research theater in Los Angeles, 200 members of the audience manipulate the dials that produce the Instantaneous Response Profile. On a 0 to 1,000 scale, 500 marks the neutral position, and as viewers watch a commercial, their dial manipulations are recorded on a graph. If the curve goes up as a commercial is shown, it means the majority of respondents is dialing "very good." If the curve drops below 500, a majority is somewhere on the "very dull" side.

The graphs shown here are the result of a test commercial for a diet soft drink and were part of the total package of research analyses prepared by the ASI staff. By using these graphs, the client and agency were then able to analyze the test commercial on a second-by-second basis to see where various segments of the audience were most interested or least interested in the message.

An ASI staff member watches the development of the Instantaneous Response Profile curve as a commercial is shown to a test audience.

closed-circuit television camera that lets clients and staff members monitor the session in progress.

(Advertisers who wish to test radio commercials at ASI use an almost identical procedure. The emcee, however, asks the audience to rate the message, not in comparison to TV commercials, but against other radio commercials. Houselights are dimmed to encourage concentration.)

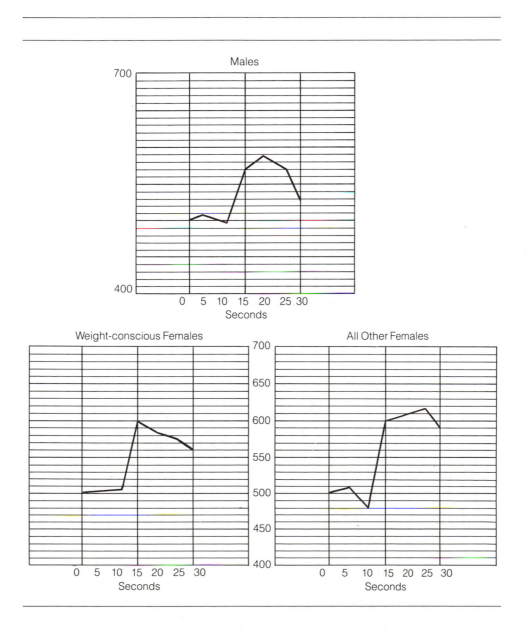

Approximately 30 to 40 percent of the commercials tested are not in finished form. They are presented by still photos, illustrations, or an inexpensive, "rough" film that conveys the concept of the finished commercial. The commercial must be accompanied by a finished sound track.

Before writer's cramp sets in, the audience is treated to another television program or a couple of short film features. Then, a supposedly embarrassed master of ceremonies apologizes to the audience, saying that the staff has goofed and handed out the wrong form for indicating preferences in the door prize drawing. Since an entire category was left out, could they please fill out this new form? Door prizes include items like $10 worth of pain relief products, a year's supply of tea, a three-month's supply of low calorie colas, and so on. Preferences must be checked by *brand name,* and the purpose of this little charade is to measure brand switching after exposure to the commercials. The staff reports that it is almost always less than 10 percent, usually about 4 percent to 5 percent of the audience.

Another control vehicle is presented, and then members of the audience are asked to write down brands and product categories of commercials that they saw earlier, plus anything they remember about them.

Once this recall measure is administered, the standard session comes to a close. However, there are evenings when a client may wish to obtain additional diagnostic information that was too extensive to ask earlier in the session. If so, the audience is shown that commercial again and asked to answer in-depth questions. When this phase is completed, door prizes are given away, All in all, the evening's entertainment takes about two hours, and about one hour is devoted to actual viewing. A great deal of effort is expended to make the audience feel welcome and comfortable and leave thinking that it has been a fun and worthwhile evening.

In addition to theater testing, ASI also offers commercial testing via cable TV, called Recall Plus. ASI uses a number of cooperating cable systems across the country and telephones a sample of subscribers. They are invited to watch a 30-minute "special" that evening and told that they will be called the following day to obtain their reactions. (The procedure is very similar to one used by Gallup & Robinson, Inc., which is covered later in this chapter.)

Using a program with general family appeal that has not previously been aired on TV, ASI inserts four commercials in the show. The next day, the ASI staff makes its calls until a total of 200 interviews are completed. This sample will yield approximately 180 who were in the "commercial audience"—respondents who actually saw the test commercials. In addition to questions about the program, respondents are asked to recall, unaided, the products they saw advertised and, with prompting, particular brands. A variety of questions is asked to test responses to various elements of the commercials.

The "plus" portion of Recall Plus is similar to the refocus procedure used in the theater when a test commercial is shown a second time. Because ASI leases unused cable channels, the company is able to run these test commercials every few minutes while postviewing telephone interviews are in progress. The interviewer asks respondents to turn on their TV set, view the test commercials again, turn off the set, and then answer detailed diagnostic questions.

When all the testing is completed, whether in the theater or through Recall Plus, a mountain of questionnaires must be keypunched and programed into computers. The data must be analyzed and evaluated, and a written report is prepared for clients. An extensive report is ready in a month, but for anxious clients willing to pay the extra fees, "fast tabs" of top-line scores can be available in a couple of days.

Staff assessment of a commercial's impact is grouped in three areas: (1) *interest and involvement,* reflected in the Instantaneous Response Profile from the theater device. The adjective checklist is also an indicator of interest; (2) *communication,* in which both the quality and quantity of recall is measured by the recall questionnaire administered at the end of the session; and (3) *effectiveness,* in which the persuasiveness of the commercial is evaluated, principally by the brand-switching test.

Burke Marketing Research

One evaluation system that uses an on-air testing technique is offered by Burke Marketing Research. It's called the DAR (Day-After Recall) and provides clients with

9.3/Conducting Interviews on Day-After Recall

Courtesy of Burke Marketing Services, Inc.

a 24-hour recall test of TV commercials. The commercials to be tested are placed in time slots bought from a local TV station. Burke operates in approximately 25 major markets, and 3 cities are typically used for each test.

Beginning in the morning of the day following the telecast of test commercials, viewers are interviewed by telephone (see 9.3). The sample to be called is drawn by a random technique from telephone books. Interviews with housewives are usually concluded by about 4:00 P.M., and then interrogators concentrate on reaching men, working women, teenagers, and children—if they are required for the test. Clients may specify the demographic makeup of the sample used to test their commercials.

When approximately 200 viewers of the test program have been reached, the interviewing is over. Interviewers must determine whether the respondent watched the test program and whether he or she remembers a commercial for the test product. This latter category puts respondents in the "claimed recall" category, and from there more questions follow. The interviewer asks about details from the test commercial. Cues may be provided to aid recall. ("Did you happen to see a commercial for any laundry starches, or not?" If yes, "What brand was that?") Burke considers claimed recall alone to be a poor measure of a commercial's communications effectiveness, because some viewers may remember a different commercial or a commercial for a competitive brand, or they may say that they saw the commercial but not be able to remember a thing about it. They may declare that they saw the ad just to please the interviewer. To guard against inaccuracies, respondents who say they have seen the test commercial are given the opportunity to substantiate their claim. They are asked to describe any specific audio or video elements they remember. ("They said it was good for your clothes and made ironing easier.") All these "related recall" verbatim responses are organized into codes and then quantified to show what Burke calls the "sales messages registration" (copy points) and "situation/visual" elements (details of the commercial's story line.) Scores on these items are very helpful to advertisers who want to know whether the message they are trying to deliver was actually perceived and remembered. In other words, did the commercial fulfill the advertising objective?

Only those interviewees who actually had a chance to be exposed to the commercial, which is substantiated by their confirmation of having viewed the commercial time period, are included in the *commercial audience*. This audience category is a refinement of the program audience category, for it eliminates viewers who head for the refrigerator when the commercial break begins. Recall scores on the test commercial are shown as a percentage of the commercial audience. The size of this commercial audience in comparison to the program audience can vary greatly. Burke reports that most of the time, the commercial audience runs between 66 and 78 percent of the program audience.

Burke clients receive tabulations of the commercial audience, a report on the verbatim responses regarding the commercial, and the related recall scores. Flash top-line scores may be telephoned to a client on the day following the interviews. As an example, such a report might state that 209 viewers were in the program audience; 166 viewers were in the commercial audience; and 46 viewers provided related recall, which translated to a score of 28 percent of the commercial audience.

The final and more elaborate report is in the hands of clients in two or three weeks. (See 9.4.) Recall scores have quite a spread. Burke uses a norm of 24 percent on related recall scores, based on the testing of more than 2,500 commercials. The company notes that this percentage has remained virtually constant for many years. The lowest score ever recorded was 2 percent (apparently an unbelievably innocuous commercial); the highest was 72 percent. Burke believes that these scores indicate communications effectiveness — the degree to which a *memorable* impression was achieved, in addition to the substance of that impression. (If viewers cannot remember the ad, the product is unlikely to appear at the top of a shopping list.) The Burke technique, however, is not a measure of persuasiveness; it does not reflect changes in predisposition and a commitment to purchase. Such information, of course, would be difficult or impossible to obtain in a telephone interview, especially since most advertising does not achieve a dramatic, bolt-out-of-the-blue impact.

For clients who wish to test commercials in unfinished form, Burke provides what it calls the RCR (Rough Commercial Recall), introduced in 1977. This pretest is designed for use by advertisers before substantial sums are spent in final production. (The DAR system is considered a posttest, because it uses only finished commercials.) As in the Gallup & Robinson system (to be described later), a sample of households is telephoned the day before the telecast of the program that contains the test commercials. Approximately 400 people are recruited to watch the program (usually a half-hour situation comedy), and Burke reports that normally, about 150 of those recruited actually view the program. All those recruited are told that they will be phoned the day after the telecast to obtain their opinions. When these subsequent interviews are conducted, respondents are asked about both the program and the commercials. The questioning procedures are patterned after those used in the standard Burke DAR test.

The basic Burke methodology is relatively simple and has not been changed since its inception in the early 1950s. The home viewing environment is a natural one, and Burke believes that its research data give clients a valuable measure of the extent of recall and of the communications effectiveness a commercial will enjoy when launched in a major campaign.

Gallup & Robinson, Inc.

One of the most interesting methods used by Gallup & Robinson, Inc., to test commercials is called the In-View service. The research is designed to either pretest or posttest television commercials. Gallup & Robinson, headquartered in Princeton, New Jersey, reserves time for its clients in a prime-time program shown on a UHF station in Philadelphia or Pittsburgh. On the day of the program, 300 men and 300 women between the ages of 18 and 49 are telephoned and invited to view that evening's episode of the program. Several of the commercials shown in the program will normally be under test.

Approximately 150 men and 150 women who watched the episode are called 24 hours later. The qualified viewers — those who were able to convince the interviewer that they did see the program — are presented with 15 brand name cues (8 real, 7 phony) and asked which commercials they recall. Detailed questioning is conducted on all commercials for which recall is claimed. The results of these interviews are tabulated and presented to clients.

9.4/An Example of a Burke Marketing Research Analysis

This is an abbreviated example of a Burke analysis, rewritten to disguise the actual client.

Burke Marketing Research Inc.

ANALYSIS

Conclusion

"Picnic Time," the 30-second commercial for Mrs. Jones' Mustard, is a below average communications vehicle. From the standpoint of both overall memorability and delivery of key sales messages, it proved to be less effective than the majority of commercials tested by Burke.

Overall Memorability

The basic measure of overall memorability is Related Recall (i.e., "communications effectiveness"). The Related Recall Score of 13% for "Picnic Time" represents the percentage of respondents exposed to the commercial who were able to correctly remember a sales message and/or a situation/visual element from the execution. This retention level of 13% is significantly below the corresponding Burke female norm of 24% and represents a score which has been exceeded by 86% of the commercials tested in the past three years.

Sales Message Registration

"Picnic Time" not only failed to create a memorable impression but also failed to communicate its primary sales messages. In fact, only one out of ten respondents (10%) exposed to the commercial mentioned one or more of the primary messages. Thus, "Picnic Time" did not meet its communication objective of convincing potential customers that Mrs. Jones' Mustard:

- tastes better than the leading brand;
- is enjoyed by children;
- has all natural ingredients.

ANALYSIS

Point of View

From Burke's point of view, the following are <u>possible</u> reasons
why "Picnic Time" scored below average. One should bear in mind
that, although this is a subjective interpretation, it is based
on our years of experience with commercial testing. From this
perspective, we see the following as potential problem areas:

- The audio portion is hard to understand--both the jingle
  and the children talking are somewhat indistinct.

- The video portion of the commercial doesn't necessarily
  reinforce the audio--i.e., if one doesn't understand the
  audio, the video alone does not convey the copy points.

- The dominant visual impression is the interaction between
  the children, which draws attention away from the product
  and package.

- The brand name is not visually dominant. The Mrs. Jones
  name is shown quickly at the beginning and end of the commercial and, while there is a package on the table where
  the children are eating, the brand name is not distinct.

- The product shot of the complete line of foods made by
  Mrs. Jones may be confusing the issue and detracting from
  the association of the brand name with mustard.

Regarding these points, one should bear in mind that the respondent's "cues" for giving recall are the product category
and brand name--i.e., we asked if the respondent remembers
seeing a commercial for Mrs. Jones' Mustard. While a respondent may in fact remember elements of the commercial, if she
doesn't associate them with the brand name, she will not be able
to give recall and the commercial has not suceeded in conveying
the brand name.

The chief advantage of this system is that viewers see the commercials on their own TV set and in a normal viewing environment. With a 24-hour delayed-recall telephone technique, results can be tabulated quickly and provided to clients within three working days. The client receives data on group norms for the product category in which the test commercial falls and more elaborate detail on the test commercial.

As an example of the kind of report a client receives, portions of one are excerpted below. A 30-second Coast Deodorant Soap commercial was shown, and interviews were held the following day with 176 men and women who had seen the commercial. These viewers are included in the Proved Commercial Registration (PCR) base. Answers to questions about the various copy points are listed below as Idea Registration scores. As a measure of persuasiveness, 31% of the respondents indicated a "favorable buying attitude," significantly above the score for most other bath soaps, according to Gallup & Robinson.

Idea Registration

PCR base (number of persons — men and women combined)	(176)
One or more copy points	99%
Picks you up/wakes you up	94%
Refreshing	35%
Makes you feel good	19%
Pleasant fragrance/scent	18%
Makes you clean/feel clean	12%
Lathers well	11%
Quality/better/best	11%

Mentions

Man	99%
Black man	28%
Dog	93%
Wants to go for a walk	71%

Persuasiveness

Favorable buying attitude	31%
Average copy points for respondent	2.2

To give the client direct feedback from respondents, Gallup & Robinson passes along all verbatim testimony taken from the telephone interviews. Here are two "verbatims" on the Coast commercial:

There's a black guy and a dog and the dog wanted to go for a walk. The guy takes a shower and starts to wake up fast with Coast Soap. It's an eye-opener. It smells nice and keeps you fresh. The sales point is that it's a deodorant soap that smells good and refreshes you and helps wake you up. I thought it sounded like a good soap. It was cute. I liked it. My interest was increased. If it smells nice, I'd like it. I last bought Lifebuoy.

Someone was in bed. It showed a guy, and a dog barking to go out. He used the soap and woke up, and took the dog out. It was a cute commercial. The point was that it's supposed to wake you up to be more alert. I already use it and I learned nothing new. I enjoyed it. It's a cute commercial. I like commercials with action and lots of color. The advertiser increased my interest because it was a good commercial and caught my attention. I bought Coast the last time.

In addition to the In-View testing service, Gallup & Robinson also provides other commercial evaluating services, including what is called On-Air Custom Single Show Surveys. This service is available in 39 metropolitan areas across the United States and employs some delayed-recall measurements also used in the In-View technique. The research can be tailored to a client's needs by testing commercials on individual programs, in markets of the client's choice, on any desired day, and targeted to a variety of special audiences (mothers, teenagers, dog owners, weight watchers, and so on). Data provided to clients include PCR scores, verbatim testimony, Idea Registration scores, and Favorable Buying Attitude percentages, which reflect the persuasiveness of the commercial.

Gallup & Robinson has also conducted research into animated commercials, humor in commercials, the best use of station breaks, the importance of audio-video synchronization in commercials, "winning" and "losing" presentation approaches, and other areas of special concern to advertisers who want to maximize the effectiveness of their television investments.

Mapes and Ross, Inc.

A competitor to Gallup & Robinson, also headquartered in Princeton, New Jersey, is Mapes and Ross, Inc., which has been providing a TV commercial evaluation service since 1972. There are similarities between the two in methodology. Scores on both day-after recall and brand preference are measured under what are called "battlefield" conditions—the normal viewing environment of the American household. A sample audience is recruited by telephone operators calling a randomly selected sample of male and/or female viewers in each of three major markets. An invitation is extended to watch a program scheduled in prime time on a UHF or independent station. (Mapes and Ross handles all arrangements with the stations.) For their cooperation, respondents are given the opportunity to participate in a drawing for three cash prizes.

As part of the invitation phase, respondents are asked their preferences in various product categories. (Some of the products will be advertised in the test program, and some will not.) The questions cover whether the respondents think that one brand in a product category is the very best, that two or three brands are better than the others, or that all brands are about the same. The interviewer asks only about product categories; respondents provide any brand names on an unaided basis. Mapes and Ross reports that, because these preexposure questions do not direct attention to any particular brands, patterns of day-after are not biased. Interviewers set up appointments with respondents for a telephone interview the following day.

The subsequent interviews begin by asking respondents which half-hour segments they watched and how much they enjoyed the programs. Next, the product group attitude and brand preference questions—the same ones used in the initial interview—are repeated, to measure the extent to which viewers changed their preferences for the brand in the test commercial. Aided recall for each of the commercials run in the program is then obtained. Sample questions:

"You may be familiar with other commercials for [brand name], but thinking only of last night's commercial, will you describe specifically what they did? Please describe as much of what took place on the screen as you can."

"What did they talk about and show?"

"What was the main idea the commercial was trying to get across to you?"

Clients of this research company can arrange to have optional questions asked. For example, respondents can be asked to provide ratings on a 10-point scale on statements about the test brand or test commercial. Concluding questions pertain to the respondents' demographics and the brand bought last in the test categories.

In an interesting validation study, Mapes and Ross reported that test results from its system provided an opportunity to discover the relationship between day-after recall and changes in brand preference. They concluded that there is a very low correlation between the two measures; each measures different things.[1] High recall of a commercial is no guarantee that a consumer will subsequently buy the brand.

Reports to clients are ready in a few weeks, based on samples of 200 program viewers of either sex or 250 men and women combined. Included in the reports are:

•   proven recall score—reported separately for the entire sample, for users of the product category versus nonusers, and so on

•   preexposure and postexposure brand preference levels—for the entire sample, for recallers versus nonrecallers, for users versus nonusers, and so on

•   verbatim testimony of all recallers

•   a profile of how well ideas were communicated to recallers—including identification and importance rating of the idea perceived by each recaller to be the *main* idea of the commercial

•   demographics—age, education, income, use of product category, and brand bought last

McCollum/Spielman/& Company, Inc.

A competitor similar to ASI also utilizes a test-screening situation, but with a number of differences in methodology. McCollum/Spielman/& Company, Inc., offers clients what it calls Advertising Control for Television (AC-T). The standard AC-T test takes place simultaneously in four parts of the country—the East, the north-central area, the south-central area, and the West Coast. Test facilities in each of these locations include a closed-circuit videotape system.

A random sample is drawn from telephone directories. The chosen households are mailed a short explanatory letter and tickets to attend a session at Prevue Studio, where AC-T testing is done. The company states that its samples are balanced by region, sex, and age. AC-T does recruit special audiences with controlled demo-

---

[1]Harold L. Ross, Jr., "Recall Versus Persuasion: An Answer," *Journal of Advertising Research* 22, no. 1, February-March 1982, p. 13.

graphics for clients who wish to test their advertising with target audiences. Cigar smokers and businessmen who rent trucks are two examples.

A typical session will bring 100 to 150 people into each of the AC-T facilities. They are seated in groups of about two dozen around TV monitors, and here they watch a sequence of programs and commercials. AC-T differs from the ASI system in that instructions to the participants come from an on-screen host who asks viewers to complete a variety of evaluation forms. All question-and-answer alternatives are pre-taped and appear on the TV screen. Respondents record their answers on a special numerical questionnaire.

The normal sequence runs something like this: the host orients the viewers by explaining why they are there and what they will see. They are asked to complete a questionnaire yielding data on demographics and brand product usage. Viewers then watch a program consisting of auditions of young performers. Halfway through, there is a "station break," and seven noncompetitive commercials are played back to back to simulate a commercial clutter sequence. Four test commercials are separated by three control commercials. Then, the viewers watch the remainder of the program and are asked for their opinions on the talent they've just seen. Next, on an unaided basis, participants complete an open-end recall questionnaire that measures their awareness of the brand, product types, and main ideas of the commercials they viewed some minutes earlier. By now, the subjects are about halfway through the AC-T test.

Since many commercials are not telecast in such a cluttered environment, the second half of the program is changed so that the ads can be tested in a spot situation. Respondents watch a second TV program. The same four test commercials are shown again, but this time they are placed in isolated positions within the program. They are reshown primarily to focus attention on the test commercials, so that the measurements will be based on the maximum number of respondents aware of the commercial. In other words, after first exposure to the commercial, the average level of awareness runs about 50 percent for established brand commercials in a 30-second format. The second time around, the awareness level usually jumps to better than 90 percent. AC-T much prefers to base its diagnostics on a 90 percent sample rather than a 50 percent sample.

After this second TV program, a postmotivation measure is administered in the form of an ingenious pseudo shopping trip to a supermarket via videotape. Participants are given a series of shopping lists and told to fill their "market baskets" with $25 worth of products. The idea, of course, is to see how many subjects switch to brands advertised in the test commercials. Their selections are compared with the brand usage information they recorded on the questionnaire.

To conclude the test, viewers answer questions designed to obtain diagnostic information about such things as jingles and presenters, comprehension of demonstrations, perception of product, and company image. Clients can design almost anything they want into this last section of the test.

Executives of McCollum/Spielman/& Company believe that the AC-T methodology is superior to its competitors' for a number of reasons. Participants view programs and commercials in small groups on TV monitors, not on a theater screen as a member of a large audience. Since the AC-T on-screen host is the same in every location and at every test, the potential problem of emcee bias is eliminated. The diagnostic data are based on the analytic sample from all four testing facilities. The company feels that one of its greatest strengths lies in the ability to use a preproduction commercial. These are inexpensive spots, which may cost only a few thousand dollars. Since they are played back on a TV monitor and not a large theater screen, the differences in quality are not as noticeable. Thus, the information gained in the AC-T test can be diagnosed, and changes can be made in the commercial, before $60,000 or $70,000 is spent in final production. The most suitable forms for this kind of inexpensive preproduction commercial seem to be live action with simple sets, simulated backgrounds, and those that use nonprofessional actors. Still photos or finished artwork (more elaborate than the typical storyboard) can be presented on videotape or 16mm film in rapid sequence, with zooms or with other simple effects. Some clients use actual storyboards in rough form on film or tape, but AC-T emphasizes that these are not reliable predictors of audience response to the finished commercial; live action, still photos, and finished artwork seem to be better indicators.

Based on its experience, McCollum/Spielman can draw a number of interesting conclusions. The company notes that the average commercial leaves about half the audience unaware of the brand advertised. The range is great. As an example, some commercials test with a 90 percent score on brand recall, whereas others test as low as 15 percent. In the clutter test, the position of the commercial apparently is not very important. The first and the last commercial in the sequence often test slightly better. In awareness tests, AC-T reports, a 30-second commercial tests on the average about 75 percent as effective as a 60-second commercial, but the range for all commercials can vary greatly. Many of the commercials tested by AC-T present a number of creative advertising techniques. Tests designed to measure the value of different techniques often reveal fascinating data. In some cases, a commercial may score very high in awareness because of unusual visual devices but unfortunately fail in presenting a basic selling story in a convincing manner. Conversely, some dull and visually uninteresting commercials do not distinguish themselves in generating awareness but clearly contain a potent selling message. AC-T advertises itself as particularly designed to help clients pinpoint problems that may spell disappointment or failure in the marketplace unless identified and corrected.

Radio commercials are also tested in the four McCollum/Spielman locations. The test pattern is somewhat similar to the television commercial testing procedure. Participants are exposed to both radio and television programs and commercials during a session that runs approximately two hours. Following the first TV program (about one-third of the way through the session), respondents are exposed to a test commercial and a control commercial inserted within a six-minute radio program. About three-quarters of an hour later, on an unaided basis, respondents are asked what brand names they remember being advertised in the radio spots and what they remember about them. Toward the end of the session, the commercials are played a second time, and then respondents are asked what they think the main idea of the radio commercial is, how it compares with other radio commercials they have heard, and how they feel about the commercial. Their responses are recorded by a rating scale and an adjective checklist. The test purportedly measures the communicative attributes of the commercial in terms of brand name and sales point recall, and the overall reaction and interest of consumers in purchasing the product advertised.

Tele-Research, Inc.

A significantly different testing procedure is used by Tele-Research, Inc., headquartered in Los Angeles, in markets across the country. This research method, developed in 1964, measures what actually occurs in the real-life marketplace. Over 2,800 supermarkets and drugstores, through exclusive arrangements with Tele-Research, provide their facilities for conducting tests under actual shopping conditions.

Three interviewers are assigned to question a sample of 600 shoppers outside the selected stores. Respondents are asked about 10 questions related to their use of the product and brand, their frequency of purchase of certain products, and some basic demographics. As a control sample, 300 are given a small booklet of cents-off coupons that can be redeemed in the store on that day only. The remaining 300 shoppers constitute the test sample. As the day progresses, they are recruited and then escorted in small groups into a trailer parked at the store site for a testing procedure that lasts about 12 minutes. The subjects view up to five commercials (one is always a control commercial), answer questions about what they have seen, and receive the same cents-off coupons given to the control group.

At the end of the day, Tele-Research tabulates the redeemed coupons from each group. (In a booklet of 10 coupons, 3 to 6 may be for brands advertised in the test commercials.) The accompanying diagram shows how the procedure works (see 9.5). In order to eliminate bias, the test commercials are rotated so that they are not always seen in the same order. Likewise, the position of the various coupons in the booklet is rotated. In order to measure recall, 150 subjects in the test group are telephoned 24 hours later and asked questions about the previous day's viewing of the test commercials.

Tele-Research can identify each cooperating subject throughout the procedure with the use of a number code. That code is associated with answers to the preliminary questions, the postviewing questionnaire, the redemption of coupons, and the recall telephone inquiry a day later. Thus, clients can request separate scores for particularly important demographic groups.

Tele-Research reports that purchase of brands in the test commercials is usually "hyped" 1 percent to 2 percent because of the cents-off motivation and because of exposure to the test commercials. Therefore, redemption scores cannot be projected to consumer behavior in the marketplace. Of particular importance to clients is the "selling effectiveness" score of the test commercial in comparison with norms established by Tele-Research. (See 9.5.)

In addition to the tabulation of actual consumer purchases based on coupon redemptions, clients are provided with scores on answers to various questions asked of respondents who viewed the test commercials, with the company's own diagnostic data, and with results of the 24-hour delayed recall questionnaires. Tele-Research maintains that its method yields an excellent correlation between its findings and subsequent sales performance in the marketplace.

9.5/How Tele-Research Pretests Advertising

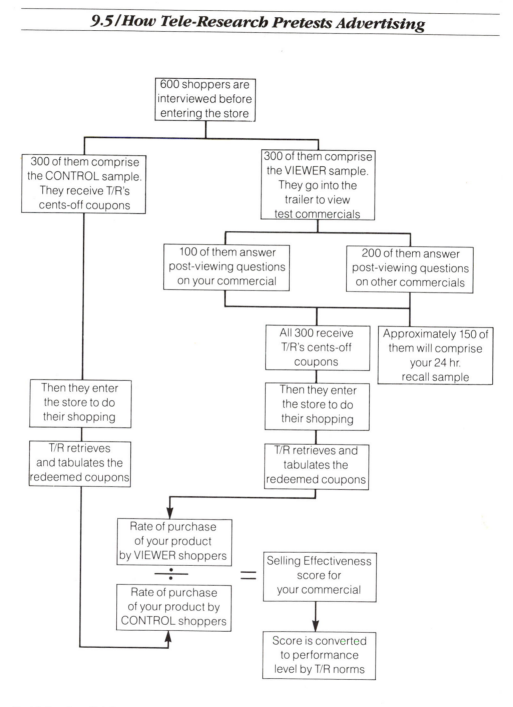

600 shoppers are interviewed before entering the store

300 of them comprise the CONTROL sample. They receive T/R's cents-off coupons

300 of them comprise the VIEWER sample. They go into the trailer to view test commercials

100 of them answer post-viewing questions on your commercial

200 of them answer post-viewing questions on other commercials

All 300 receive T/R's cents-off coupons

Approximately 150 of them will comprise your 24 hr. recall sample

Then they enter the store to do their shopping

Then they enter the store to do their shopping

T/R retrieves and tabulates the redeemed coupons

T/R retrieves and tabulates the redeemed coupons

$$\frac{\text{Rate of purchase of your product by VIEWER shoppers}}{\text{Rate of purchase of your product by CONTROL shoppers}} = \text{Selling Effectiveness score for your commercial}$$

Score is converted to performance level by T/R norms

Reprinted courtesy of Tele-Research, Inc.

Conclusions

The research companies described in this chapter are seven of the major commercial evaluation services. There are others. A few have flashed on the horizon, causing great excitement in the advertising world, but they have since plummeted into oblivion. Laboratory experiments that measure subjects' physiological responses while they are viewing test commercials were summarized in Chapter 4. The gadgetry measures autonomic or involuntary responses through the use of psychogalvanometers, pupillometers, eye cameras, and the like. These laboratory experiments are not in common use in evaluating commercials.

Because of the costs involved, the testing of commercials is usually confined to major advertisers and agencies, and they may not be inclined or equipped to handle such research themselves. (Even at major companies, these ancillary services may be the first to get the axe when budgets are cut and times are tough.)

The strengths and shortcomings of testing commercials have been debated for many years. Is the testing of programs and commercials in a theater setting a valid form of evaluation? The environment is not typical for TV viewing. The setting is a darkened theater, and the object of "forced attention" is a huge screen. To beat the problem of the "theater bias," viewing can be done with smaller groups around individual TV monitors, but the setting is still not natural. Most test commercials have never been on the air and are new to the audience, so the effect of repetition over a period of time cannot be measured. A number of research experts are also skeptical of recruitment procedures for the samples. Audiences recruited in shopping centers are not a microcosm of the total population. Too many people never go to shopping centers, or they go so infrequently that they are never included in a sample. Direct mail solicitation of subjects also suggests a bias, because many of the people contacted are unwilling or unable to participate.

Cable TV systems that insert test commercials in regular programing and then monitor purchase diaries do have obvious advantages. However, such systems are pretty expensive, and many advertisers find that they cannot afford them.

Telephone interviewing to test recall of commercials yields interesting data. Such a methodology has the advantage of obtaining responses from people who are not under a microscope at the time they view the commercial. A telephone sample, however, automatically eliminates homes without phones or with unlisted phones, and those of new residents who are not yet listed in a telephone book.

Some advertising agencies with an adequate research department prefer to conduct their own tests. They may bring in small groups of people to view test commercials. A research director can then conduct an in-depth discussion with these consumers to study perceptions, attitudes, and inclinations to buy a particular product or brand. If an advertiser first runs commercials in a test market, it's not too difficult for the agency to train telephone interviewers to conduct a 24-hour recall survey. This process may be less expensive than retaining an outside research organization.

All the independent research companies offer expertise and try to give clients the most useful information possible. The data, reported down to the last decimal point, and the accompanying diagnoses are all based on sampling. But because samples cannot measure the "universe," they're not foolproof. Further, data are often reported on the basis of what people *said* they thought or did. The researchers do not claim that their data are infallible, of course, and they would admit that they do not know the client's market as well as the advertising agency.

Commercial evaluations are useful in providing guidelines—clues about a commercial's strengths and weaknesses. Research will not tell if a consumer will buy a product. It will, however, indicate viewer or listener interest, perception, attitude change, recall, and the like. It's difficult to measure sales against a specific commercial or group of commercials. The sale of a product is not consummated in a 30- or 60-second commercial; it is consummated at the point of purchase. *Commercials, therefore, must be evaluated on how successfully they communicate what was intended to be communicated.* The advertising may be designed to introduce or acquaint, build images, shift attitudes, compare a product favorably with the competition, build dealer support, impress stockholders, or fulfill other marketing functions. The commercial is the outgrowth of the basic advertising objectives, and it must be evaluated in terms of its communications function. An advertising campaign does not begin and end with the commercial. The commercial is the most important ingredient, but it must function *with* the media buys, the program environment, the impact of repetition, the timing of the campaign, and all the other factors constantly in flux in the marketplace.

part three

Buying and Selling Time

chapter ten

Audience Research

We Must Be Number Two — Everyone Else Says They're Number One

The value of audience research to networks, stations, cable operators, advertisers, agencies, and station reps is incalculable. They all put audience estimates, or ratings, to a number of uses. But in general, ratings are used in two important ways — by broadcasters in making programing decisions and by those who buy and sell advertising time.

The activity surrounding audience research is usually outside the spotlight of public attention — until, that is, a favorite show is canceled. The press may report that its demise was caused by low ratings, and howls of protest have sometimes saved shows from the programer's axe. Usually, however, executions carried out because of low ratings are well deserved and are a mercy to the audience.

Complaints that the broadcast advertising industry relies too much on the little numbers printed in the ratings books have been heard ever since the system of ratings began. Although the criticism may be valid, the broadcasters and advertisers who invest millions of dollars in formal audience research do not agree. They consider their expenditures good investments, for the data they are buying are certainly more reliable than even their best guesses. The ratings are consulted in many programing and advertising decisions, but the research companies that syndicate the audience research can hardly assume responsibility for how the ratings are used.

The ratings have been around for a long time. Beginning in 1929, the first formal network audience measurements, supported by major advertisers, were initiated by the research company of Archibald M. Crossley.[1] It used a telephone survey recall

[1]Robert J. Landry, *This Fascinating Radio Business* (Indianapolis: Bobbs-Merrill, 1946), p. 143.

technique to measure the program popularity of network radio programs. The official name of the service was the Co-operative Analysis of Broadcasting, but the industry simply dubbed these ratings "the Crossley."

In the mid-1930s and through the 1940s, the C. E. Hooper Company dominated radio audience measurements. A telephone interview technique was used in which respondents were asked if their radio was in use and, if so, what program was tuned in. The respondent was also asked if other family members were listening to radio and what the age and sex of all listeners was. If an interviewer phoned a sample home and no one answered, that household was counted as not listening to radio. Later, as out-of-home listening increased, as the number of sets per home increased, and as radio became a more personal medium often used on an individual basis, this kind of telephone interviewing was eclipsed by other methodologies. (Accurately measuring out-of-home listening has always been extremely difficult.)

In 1941, personal interviewing was introduced to radio audience measurement when Dr. Sydney Roslow, a New York psychologist, started The Pulse. House-to-house interviews in selected blocks were conducted by Pulse employees. All family members age 12 and over were asked about their radio listening in the previous 24 hours. The Pulse operated successfully for many years, reporting radio ratings in more than 160 markets, but the high cost of this methodology caused the failure of the company in 1978.

Over the years, the techniques and scope of audience measurements have grown into a complex and sophisticated business. Some neophytes in the broadcasting business invariably say, "Oh, I understand the ratings. It's easy—nothing to it!" As a matter of fact, however, it isn't easy, and there is a lot to it.

"Oh, oh; it looks as if the ratings are starting to come in."

Drawn for *Broadcasting* by Jack Schmidt.
Copyright, *Broadcasting* magazine; reprinted by permission.

To understand the research, what is really needed is a little study and a determination to use terms accurately. The words of audience research language are not usually interchangeable; they must be defined explicitly. Standard definitions have been established through the cooperation of a number of groups — including the National Association of Broadcasters, the Committee on Local Television Audience Measurement, the Electronic Media Rating Council, the Advertising Research Foundation — plus representatives from stations, networks, representative firms, and trade associations. Published by the NAB in 1970 as *Standard Definitions of Broadcast Research Terms,* they spell out the specifics so necessary to understand audience research. (A special glossary of broadcast research terms from this document has been compiled at the end of this chapter. It is designed to be used as a reference for further study.)

Several companies syndicate audience research data to subscribers. Their best customers are the broadcasters, who carry most of the cost. Advertising agencies, which pay proportionately much less than the stations for the same research data, often seem to be in the driver's seat. They decide whether to base their buys on one service or another; stations and their representatives are obliged to present "avails" and accompanying ratings in the form requested by the time buyer.

There is no perfect system for measuring broadcast audiences that is also economically feasible. There are advantages and disadvantages to every system in use. It is important to understand the basic methodologies used by these companies in order to evaluate the research data they generate.

A. C. Nielsen Company

In 1936, a group of engineers at the Massachusetts Institute of Technology invented a mechanical recorder that could be attached to a radio to measure the tuning of the set. The A. C. Nielsen Company, a marketing research company headquartered in Chicago, was sufficiently interested in the gadget and bought the patent. By 1940, it was in the

10.1/The First Audimeter

This photograph shows the first of a succession of Audimeters used by Nielsen to measure radio, and later TV, audiences. This 1936 model contained a 16mm film cartridge that traveled at 1 inch per hour. A beam of light on the film was triggered every time the set was turned on and off, and so the cumulative time of set use was actually "photographed" on the film. The light beam also moved from left to right, and when decoded, the film revealed set tuning. Once a week, the cartridge had to be replaced and mailed to Nielsen headquarters for decoding.

radio audience measurement business and offering the first national radio audience measurements based on a mechanical device, the Audimeter. (See 10.1.)

Measuring audiences by Audimeters was quite an innovation, and the Nielsen radio audience measurements were sold as syndicated research across the country to broadcasters, agencies, and advertisers. In the late 1940s, when the television boom was on, Nielsen moved into TV audience measurement and adapted the Audimeter to television. By 1964, the company had completely withdrawn from radio.

Nielsen today is one of the largest marketing research companies in the world, operating in two dozen countries. Its activities in television audience measurement result in many kinds of reports. The major reports are the *Nielsen Television Index,* which measures national audiences' viewing of ABC, CBS, NBC, the Public Broadcasting Service, and most of the cable network services, and the *Nielsen Station Index,* which measures viewing in 220 individual TV markets across the country.

Nielsen Television Index

Issued on a year-round basis, the Nielsen Television Index (NTI) reports a national sample's viewing patterns. The sample consists of approximately 1,700 households, distributed across the United States, whose network viewing habits are projected to a national population of over 84 million households. How can this be? The Nielsen company explains it this way:

Try this interesting experiment. (Hypothetically — unless you happen to have 100,000 beads handy.) Imagine 100,000 beads in a washtub; 30,000 red and 70,000 white. Mix thoroughly, then scoop out a sample of 1,000. Even before counting, you'll know that not all beads in your sample are red. Nor would you expect your sample to divide exactly at 300 red and 700 white.

As a matter of fact, the mathematical odds are about 20 to 1 that the count of red beads will be between 270 and 330 — or 27 to 33 percent of the sample.

So, in short, you have now produced a "rating" of 30, plus or minus 3, with a 20 to 1 assurance of statistical reliability.

These basic sampling laws wouldn't change even if you drew your sample of 1,000 from 84 million beads instead of 100,000 — assuming that the 84 million beads had the same ratio of red and white.

This is a simple demonstration of why a sample of 1,000 is just as adequate for a nation of 84-million households as for a city of 100,000.[2]

Estimating the error factor is strictly a matter of statistical probability. The amount of error could be reduced, of course, if the sample size were increased — but here the cost factor becomes critical. Professionals in the business understand that the audience research companies provide *estimates,* not exact numbers. What are important are the trends — the performance of the network programs on a week-to-week basis. If a prime-time program drops two rating points in a week, statistical error is such that this drop means nothing. If, however, the program drops two rating points every week for six weeks, it's a safe guess that the series is headed for the film vaults.

---

[2]*Everything You've Always Wanted to Know About TV Ratings* (Northbrook, Ill.: A.C. Nielsen Company, n.d.), p. 13.

How are the all-important 1,700 households—in cities and towns and on farms—selected by Nielsen for inclusion in the NTI sample? Census records of all U.S. households are the basis for establishing survey areas, and the sample is then selected from these areas. Nielsen uses an area probability sample, and field surveyors are sent to computer-selected households where they explain the purpose of the research and ask for permission to install an Audimeter. The cooperation rate is better than 70 percent. Compensation rates are modest and do vary. Because of family moves and deaths and for other reasons, the sample has an annual turnover of approximately 45 percent. This change prevents the sample from aging faster than the total population. In any event, no family is kept in the sample longer than five years.

Each Storage Instantaneous Audimeter (SIA), an electronic device that is about the size and shape of a cigar box (see 10.2), is wired directly to Nielsen's office in Dunedin, Florida, via telephone lines. A small computer in each SIA records the time the set is turned on, the channel tuning, and the time the set is turned off. Twice every 24 hours, Nielsen "calls" and interrogates each set equipped with an SIA. Data from the entire sample of approximately 1,700 homes can be collected in slightly less than

10.2 / Storage Instantaneous Audimeter and Recordimeter

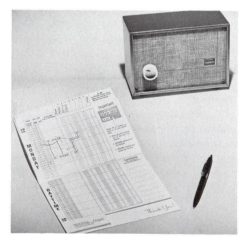

The Storage Instantaneous Audimeter (above) measures TV set usage and stores the information in its electronic memory. At least twice a day, an NTI central office computer dials up each unit and retrieves the information via special telephone lines. In addition to measuring the tuning to conventional TV and cable channels, the unit also records use of pay TV, video cassette recorders, and video games.

The NTI uses Recordimeters and Audilog diaries (above) to determine who is viewing television. The Recordimeter readings are entered into the Audilog as verification of TV set usage. The households in the sample provide demographic information that accompanies the set usage data reported by the SIA households.

Photos courtesy of A.C. Nielsen Company.

two hours. This new system greatly speeds up the NTI reports, and clients can receive preliminary information the following morning, including average audience ratings, share of audience, and station count and circulation for each program's total duration by each half-hour. Households using television are also reported for each half-hour as a percentage figure. (See 10.3.)

Electronic devices, of course, do not record viewing—only set tuning. Who's watching? That's the critical question. To obtain the answer, the NTI uses a matched sample drawn from 3,600 households. For every home equipped with a Storage Instantaneous Audimeter, there are two homes in a matched sample that provide audience composition data for viewership of network programs. During specified weeks, Nielsen asks participating households to keep a diary of family viewing by each quarter-hour, and in addition, a Recordimeter is attached to each household set (10.2). The Recordimeter measures cumulative set use. Also cigar-box size, it operates something like the speedometer in a car. Digital numbers are displayed, and one digit turns over for every six minutes the set is in use. Households in the Recordimeter sample have the device in use all year, but they are asked to keep diaries for only 38 weeks. The number showing on the Recordimeter is to be entered at the top of each day's diary. When the TV set is in use, a signal is emitted every 30 minutes as a reminder to keep up diary entries. The cumulative viewing time decoded from the Recordimeter is checked against the diary as verification of total viewing. From this matched sample, Nielsen issues the NTI's *National Audience Demographics Reports,* which indicate audience composition in terms of age, sex, and a few other basic categories.

Based on all the data collected from the national sample, Nielsen issues a wide variety of reports to aid its clients covering viewing of particular types of programing, such as sports, syndicated programs, network specials, weekday daytime, and the like. Other special reports cover child and teenage viewing, program cumulative audience estimates, cable viewing, and tracking studies of programs by both households and persons.

Nielsen Station Index

Four times a year, the 220 markets in the Nielsen Station Index (NSI) are measured in national "sweeps." Bigger markets are measured more often—up to seven times a year. In seven centers around the country, groups of telephone operators employed by Nielsen face an enormous task. In a year's time, 200,000 diaries must be placed to measure TV viewing in the individual markets. (Only about 100,000 diaries are eventually returned.) Operators must telephone a list of selected households and ask if members would be willing to keep a diary of television viewing for a week.

Nielsen has established Designated Market Areas (DMAs)—specific geographic areas that do not overlap. A county is assigned to a particular DMA when 50 percent or more of the viewing in that county is to a home-county TV station or stations. (The DMA is the counterpart of the Arbitron Ratings Company's Area of Dominant Influence, and the Nielsen Station Index is directly competitive with Arbitron television reports.)

A random selection of households, containing both listed and unlisted telephones, is drawn by computer for each DMA, and operators begin their recruiting assignments. In order to reduce sampling errors, diaries are mailed to all of the "no answers" and "refusals" anyway, and a fair number are returned completed. Operators are instructed to try a no answer three times over a two-day period in an effort to make contact.

The diary sent to each household contains explicit instructions on how to report on each day's viewing activity. A questionnaire asks for some basic demographic information on the age and sex of household members and education and employment of the "lady of the house." The diaries provided for each set in the home are set up to begin on a Thursday and run for seven days. Years ago, both Nielsen and Arbitron sent out diaries that began with Monday entries. It was discovered that a diary-keeping fatigue factor set in by Saturday or Sunday, and thus, on the weekends, the diaries only reflected a portion of total viewing. Since weekend time is so

10.3/Sample NTI Report

February 28, 1983, became part of television's history when the final episode of M*A*S*H was aired. The beloved characters from this hit series said goodbye to each other and headed home. CBS was left with an average audience rating of more than 60 percent. (Note the figures for the competing networks.) This is a sample page from the bi-weekly *National TV Ratings* report issued by the Nielsen Television Index.

Nielsen NATIONAL TV AUDIENCE ESTIMATES

WEEK 2

TIME		8:00	8:15	8:30	8:45	9:00	9:15	9:30	9:45	10:00	10:15	10:30	10:45
ABC TV	TOTAL AUDIENCE (Households (000) & %)	18,160 21.8				10,410 12.5							
	Program	← THAT'S INCREDIBLE →				← ABC MONDAY NIGHT MOVIE AMERICAN GIGOLO (OP) →							
	AVERAGE AUDIENCE (Households (000) & %)	11,000 13.2	16.5*		9.8*	6,410 7.7	8.3*		7.9*		7.4*		7.4*
	SHARE OF AUDIENCE %	17	22 *		12 *	10	10 *		10 *		10 *		10 *
	AVG. AUD. BY ¼ HR. %	16.6	16.4	10.5	9.2	8.3	8.2	7.8	7.9	7.6	7.2	7.5	7.3
CBS TV	TOTAL AUDIENCE (Households (000) & %)	29,650 35.6		57,560 69.1									
	Program	ALICE		← M*A*S*H SPECIAL (OP) →									
	AVERAGE AUDIENCE (Households (000) & %)	25,570 30.7		50,150 60.2	57.9*		61.5*		61.7*		60.8*		59.2*
	SHARE OF AUDIENCE %	41		77	72 *		76 *		78 *		79 *		79 *
	AVG. AUD. BY ¼ HR. %	28.1	33.3	55.8	60.0	61.4	61.5	61.9	61.5	61.3	60.3	59.8	58.5
NBC TV	TOTAL AUDIENCE (Households (000) & %)	14,330 17.2											
	Program	← NBC MONDAY NIGHT MOVIES THE NIGHT THE BRIDGE FELL DOWN (OP) →											
	AVERAGE AUDIENCE (Households (000) & %)	6,750 8.1	10.5*		8.1*		7.9*		7.2*		7.3*		7.6*
	SHARE OF AUDIENCE %	10	14 *		10 *		10 *		9 *		9 *		10 *
	AVG. AUD. BY ¼ HR. %	11.0	10.0	8.4	7.9	7.9	8.0	7.3	7.1	7.3	7.4	7.6	7.7
TV HOUSEHOLDS USING TV (See Def. 1)	WK. 1	68.4	69.6	69.2	70.2	72.0	72.6	71.6	70.3	66.7	65.2	63.4	61.4
	WK. 2	72.5	75.9	80.2	81.6	81.2	81.0	79.6	78.9	78.3	76.5	75.4	73.8

U.S. TV Households: 83,300,000

For explanation of symbols, See page A.

EVE. MON. FEB. 28, 1983

Courtesy of A. C. Nielsen Company.

important to both programers and advertisers, the starting date for the diaries was changed. Reported weekend viewing levels promptly went up. Like Arbitron, Nielsen usually encloses two quarters with each diary as an extra incentive. These little cash rewards can run higher in difficult-to-recruit areas, such as in some minority neighborhoods or in poor urban areas. The placement of diaries, however, is predicated on a plea that cooperation provides an opportunity to express likes and dislikes and to help the TV industry better understand viewers' preferences.

Households in the 18–25 age group account for the poorest return rate of diaries; the ones in the 35–49 age group have the best cooperation rate. The higher both the education and the income level, the more conscientious family members are in completing diary entries. Not all the diaries will be returned, obviously, and so Nielsen must oversample in order to obtain an adequate sample—particularly in poor urban areas where the return rate is very low. The returned diaries are checked, and unless all the days are filled in ("no viewing" is an acceptable entry), the diary is rejected. All the handwritten entries must be keypunched for computer digestion. In approximately two weeks, the first of the NSI reports will be ready to mail to subscribers, and they are all distributed within four weeks. Television stations pay approximately 80 percent of the cost of the NSI reports. The rates charged are based on market size, the number of reports issued each year, and the station's rate card. The costs to advertising agencies, which are proportionately much less for the same reports, are based on a sliding scale related to the agency's spot expenditures.

The NSI report, called *Viewers in Profile,* contains the following basic information: each station's average quarter-hour audience throughout the week broken down in terms of Metro Area, DMA, ratings, shares, total households, total persons, and demographic (age and sex) breakouts (see 10.4). Additional information includes an Alphabetical Program Index, which allows a user to find a specific program quickly; a Share Trend Guide, which details seasonal variations for a program continuing in the same time period; and audience estimates, which indicate the number of viewers per DMA Household Rating Point. Program Audience Averages are also reported, which indicate viewing levels for regularly scheduled programs. For example, a program "stripped" (in the same time period) Monday through Friday may, for one reason or another, have higher ratings on a Tuesday than on any other day of the week. All these data expedite the work of time buyers, who constantly consult the rating books. At the front of each NSI report, there is detailed information on the size and makeup of the sample, plus basic information on numbers of households with color TV, with more than one set, and with cable TV. Statistical tolerances and relative error are explained in detail for those who read and understand the fine print.

NSI Metered Markets   A quarter of the nation's TV households are in New York, Los Angeles, Chicago, San Francisco, Philadelphia, and Detroit—markets of immense importance to the networks, local stations, and advertisers. In these six areas, Nielsen has replaced a pure diary methodology with Storage Instantaneous Audimeters to obtain local market reports. Diaries from a matched sample are used to obtain audience demographics—a system similar to that used in the NTI.

When the service, which is very costly to subscribers, was initially set up, it was largely underwritten by the independent TV stations in these markets. They were convinced that their audience levels were shortchanged in estimates based exclusively on diaries. Research, compiled from both diaries and meters, bears out that belief. Daytime and early and late fringe viewing are invariably underreported when diaries are compared with actual set tuning on meters. Meters also show that there is much more tuning to independent stations at all hours of the day than is ordinarily reported in diaries. Apparently, the fatigue factor, which causes people either to forget to fill in

10.4/Sample Page from a Cleveland NSI Report

Nielsen measures each of the nation's 220 local television markets four to seven times a year, using diaries placed in sample house-holds. The information, once processed, is re-leased to clients in this form as a *Viewers in Profile* report.

JANUARY 1983   TUESDAY   6.30PM– 9.00PM

Courtesy of A. C. Nielsen Company.

diaries or to try to remember their viewing two days later, particularly works against the independent stations. When advertisers buy only by the numbers — and many of them do — these stations are often left out. The independent stations feel better equipped to fight the network affiliates for a share of the advertisers' dollars with a report based on meter readings. They have paid dearly for it, however, because they were the only ones willing to pay for the cost of this new methodology in the beginning. In the 1970s, one independent station in Los Angeles was paying more than $40,000 a month until many of the other stations in that market subscribed to the service and helped share the cost. Other areas will undoubtedly become Nielsen SIA markets when the stations are willing to underwrite the cost. In the meantime, they will continue to rely on the NSI and Arbitron reports compiled from diaries.

Arbitron Television

In 1938, a young psychology major at George Washington University embarked on a project to measure radio listening in the nation's capital. James W. Seiler's success in this venture eventually encouraged him to establish the American Research Bureau in 1949. Today, that firm is known as the Arbitron Ratings Company and is a subsidiary of the Control Data Corporation, a large computer company. Arbitron measures both radio and television audiences in markets across the country.

In television, Arbitron surveys more than 210 markets each year, with national sweeps in February, May, July, and November. Larger markets are measured more frequently — up to seven times a year. Arbitron has carved the nation into what it calls Areas of Dominant Influence (ADIs), which corresponds to its competitor's Designated Market Areas. With the use of a computer, both listed and unlisted telephones are drawn for each ADI, and Arbitron begins the work of establishing its samples for upcoming surveys. A letter is first sent to the household, and then an interviewer calls to ask for cooperation in keeping a TV diary. Diaries are mailed from the headquarters in Beltsville, Maryland, and contain a small cash incentive. A diary is provided for each TV set in the home, rather than each person. An interviewer phones the household on the day the survey begins to remind participants to keep the diary and calls again several days later to answer any questions and to thank the respondents for their cooperation.

The diary (see 10.5) covers viewing of all family members to each set in the house. Columns are indicated for male head of house, female head of house, other family members, and visitors. Entries are made by the quarter-hour, and diary keepers are asked to indicate the time the set is turned on, channel number and station call letters, and program name. Entries are to be completed for seven days. At the back of the booklet, there are questions on family size, city and county of the household, and the television set(s) — whether they are color sets and can receive UHF, cable TV, or a pay TV service. Respondents are also asked their racial background and whether or not there are working women in the household. Arbitron reports that there has been little static over these requests; in fact, the cooperation rate has been high. In markets with high ethnic concentrations, these special data are useful in planning both programs and advertising buys.

10.5/Arbitron TV Diary

Leaving this portion of the page open will assist you in keeping the diary.

What TV stations (channels 2-83) can you receive
clearly enough for viewing on this set? (Fill in below)

Channel Number	Station Call Letters	City		Channel Number	Station Call Letters	City

MALE HEAD OF HOUSE	**FIRST NAME ONLY:**
FEMALE HEAD OF HOUSE	**FIRST NAME ONLY:**

OTHER FAMILY MEMBERS

NAMES

Accurate station identification is very important. Please use both the station call letters and channel number in your viewing entries.

TIME	TV SET		STATION TUNED IN		NAME OF PROGRAM	AGE →										V I S I T O R S	V I S I T O R S	V I S I T O R S
QUARTER HOURS	OFF	ON	CALL LETTERS	CHAN. NO.		SEX →	M	F										
6:00- 6:14																		
6:15- 6:29																		
6:30- 6:44																		
6:45- 6:59																		
7:00- 7:14																		
7:15- 7:29																		
7:30- 7:44																		
7:45- 7:59																		
8:00- 8:14																		
8:15- 8:29																		
8:30- 8:44																		
8:45- 8:59																		
9:00- 9:14																		
9:15- 9:29																		
9:30- 9:44																		
9:45- 9:59																		
10:00-10:14																		
10:15-10:29																		
10:30-10:44																		
10:45-10:59																		
11:00-11:14																		
11:15-11:29																		

6:00 A.M.

WEDNESDAY

Courtesy of Arbitron.

The percentage of usable TV diaries runs about half of all diaries mailed out. Entries in diaries returned from multiset households are edited so as to provide unduplicated viewing information for a given household. Completeness of the entries is also carefully checked. Some researchers consider the "functional illiteracy" of a portion of the population as part of the reason for poor diary entries. Carelessness or lateness in completing the entries may also be reasons. The diaries ask for information by quarter-hours, yet few people sit down to watch TV, or leave the set, on the quarter-hour mark. A situation comedy may be tuned in at 8:04 and watched until 8:26 P.M., and the viewer may dutifully enter her viewing as 8:00 – 8:30 P.M.. Although she did view each quarter-hour long enough to qualify for inclusion, she did not, however, see either the opening or closing commercials. It's impossible to establish the exact tune-in and tune-out time with either a diary or a personal interview. Only a meter will reveal that. As for the absenteeism rate while the set is on, no methodology can supply that information.

After the Arbitron computers have processed all the data gleaned from the diaries, local market reports are mailed to clients. (See 10.6.) The earliest ones are out a couple of weeks after the survey is completed, and for major markets, they run to more than a hundred pages of numbers. All the little numbers translate into stations, time periods, ADI households reached in terms of both ratings and shares, and audience composition for each quarter-hour reported by age and sex. Program averages are shown for shows that are stripped Monday through Friday. A station-break estimate simplifies the time buyer's work by providing an average audience for the preceding and following quarter-hours. Information in the front and the back of the Arbitron books (nicknamed the "Boiler Plate") includes the sampling method, the degree of sample error, a glossary, information on the survey area, demographic characteristics, sample size, households accepting diaries, and so on.

Arbitron Metered Markets

Like Nielsen, Arbitron has introduced the use of meters into major markets. Its method is similar. The metered sample provides data on HUT levels (percentage of households using TV during any given quarter hour) and individual program ratings.

Early every morning, between 2:30 A.M. and 4:00 A.M., the Arbitron computer retrieves the data from each household meter via telephone lines. The information is immediately relayed to a computer at Arbitron headquarters. By 9 A.M. local market time, a 24-hour report is released for clients and is available at any of the seven Arbitron local offices. Weekly and monthly printed reports are also available, including demographics obtained through a matched diary sample. Arbitron's metered households are used in New York, Chicago, Los Angeles, San Francisco, Philadelphia, and Dallas, and the company expects to add additional markets.

Arbitron Radio

Arbitron has dominated radio audience measurements for many years. A number of other research companies have challenged the leader, and several have gone out of

10.6/Sample Page from a Dallas–Fort Worth Arbitron TV Report

Weekly Program Estimates　　　　　　　**Time Period Average Estimates**

DAY AND TIME (STATION / PROGRAM)	WK1	WK2	WK3	WK4	RTG	SHR	JAN '83	NOV '82	MAY '82	FEB '82	RTG	SHR	TV HH	18+	12-24	12-34	TOT 18+	18-49	12-24	18-34	25-49	25-54	WKG WMN 18+
	1	2	3	4	5	6	58	59	60	61	8	9	11	13	15	16	18	19	20	21	22	23	24
RELATIVE STD-ERR 25% THRESHOLDS (1σ) 50%	6 / 1	6 / 1	5 / 1	5 / 1	1 / -						2 / -		14 / 3	21 / 5	24 / 6	22 / 5	16 / 4	15 / 3	22 / 5	17 / 4	14 / 3	14 / 3	15 / 3
SUNDAY 4:30P-5:00P (CNTD)																							
KTXA GT SP MOVIE	4	7	5	6	6	15	7	10	15	10	7	18	80	124	47	84	79	71	29	49	50	53	24
KTWS STV	-	-	-	1					2	3			4	10	4	8	5	5	2	4	2	2	3
KNBN NO TOCA BOTN	1	1	-	1	1	2			**	**	1	2	8	15	6	11	8	7	6	5	3	4	1
KXTX RAWHIDE SU	6	5	4	4	5	12	4	14	13	10	4	12	94	128	25	71	70	47	14	35	39	40	27
KERA PTV	-	-	2	-	1	2	2	2	2	2	1	2	12	18	4	7	7	5	2	4	3	4	
HUT/TOTAL	52	33	35	29	37		45	30	27	33	36		597	846	214	430	426	263	121	187	184	218	139
5:00P-5:30P																							
KDFW B CROSBY GLF	3				3	6					3	6	47	85	5	49	49	16		1	16	22	20
4CNTRY RP SU	3	10	8	7	7	20					7	20	116	170	11	35	92	28	5	15	26	36	23
--4 WK AVG--					7	18	38	17	18	22	7	18	108	159	10	32	87	27	4	14	25	34	23
KXAS SUN ACTN NWS	9			8	8	19					9	20	121	148	5	14	86	14	2	4	13	23	19
HAWAIIAN OPN		8			8	21					7	19	115	141	27	38	44	5	2	2	2	4	9
SN DIEGO OPN			6		6	19					6	19	96	166	21	45	57	16	8	5	11	24	17
--4 WK AVG--					8	20	35	34	31	25	7	20	113	151	15	28	68	12	4	4	10	18	16
WFAA SUN WRLD SPT	23				23	44					24	46	362	570	158	255	279	157	81	109	99	140	108
SHOP SMART		1	3	2	2	6					2	5	32	46	9	14	27	13	9	6	10	11	5
--4 WK AVG--					7	19	4	6	7	4	7	19	115	177	46	74	90	49	27	32	32	43	31
KTVT FUGITIVE SU	6	4	5	4	5	13	9	14	11	20	5	13	102	129	37	83	77	57	27	41	43	45	31
KTXA GT MOV FVRTS	3	6	3	6	5	12	5	12	17	12	5	13	63	92	36	67	50	47	25	33	29	29	15
KTWS STV									**	**			3	7	2	5	3	3	1	2	2	2	1
KNBN NO TOCA BOTN	1	1	1	1	1	2			**	**	1	2	10	17	8	11	7	6	5	4	3	4	
KXTX BIG VALLE SU	6	3	4	4	4	11	3	13	9	9	4	11	91	132	42	78	76	53	24	39	33	36	28
KERA PTV	-	-	1	2	1	3		2			1	3	14	16	2	6	6	5	1	4	4	4	1
HUT/TOTAL	53	36	33	35	39		52	37	33	35	38		619	880	198	384	464	259	118	173	181	215	147
5:30P-6:00P																							
KDFW NWS 4 SU 530	6	13	13	10	10	25	39	22	23	29	10	26	163	248	19	49	143	41	10	23	34	49	33
KXAS NBC SUN NEWS	10			9	9	20					9	21	138	164	8	27	85	15	1	6	15	22	18
SUN ACT NW L		8	7		8	20					6	17	113	181	23	35	74	22	4	6	18	28	18
--4 WK AVG--					9	20	36	32	27	19	8	19	125	173	15	31	79	18	3	6	16	25	18
WFAA SUN WRLD SPT	22				22	40					23	41	337	534	134	230	273	153	67	106	98	130	103
BLCK HORIZON		1	2	1	1	3					1	3	20	31	6	11	16	6	3	4	4	2	2
--4 WK AVG--					6	15	2	4	8	8	6	16	99	156	38	66	80	43	21	29	28	36	27
KTVT FUGITIVE SU	6	5	5	5	5	12	9	13	10	18	5	12	106	140	40	91	83	62	29	45	46	49	37
KTXA GT MOV FVRTS	3	7	2	6	4	10	5	11	16	12	5	12	61	92	35	63	48	44	22	31	25	25	15
KTWS STV	-	-	-	-					**	**			1	4	2	2	2	2	1	1	1	1	
KNBN NO TOCA BOTN	1	1	1	1	1	2			**	**	1	2	10	17	8	11	7	6	5	4	3	4	1
KXTX BIG VALLE SU	6	2	5	4	4	10	4	12	9	8	4	10	91	135	41	79	78	54	25	40	33	37	28
KERA PTV	-	-	1	2	1	2		2			1	3	12	14	3	7	6	5	1	3	3	3	
HUT/TOTAL	55	38	38	38	42		53	39	35	39	41		668	979	201	399	526	275	117	182	189	229	159
6:00P-6:30P																							
KDFW 60 MINUTES	19	31	30	29	27	48	48	48	51	51	28	51	409	637	68	176	346	155	37	86	127	153	111
KXAS CHIPS	12				12	20					11	19	171	240	93	176	121	89	31	77	64	69	59
SMURFY VAL		11			11	18					9	16	155	170	78	142	81	61	44	46	48	57	35
VOYAGERS			6	5	5	10					6	11	81	70	36	45	45	24	19	10	18	24	20
--4 WK AVG--					8	15	30	13	16	12	8	14	122	140	61	102	73	49	28	36	37	43	34
WFAA SUN WRLD SPT	18				18	30					19	32	288	491	139	241	258	167	71	97	113	126	85
BELVE IT NOT		6	9	8	8	14					7	14	124	228	83	154	103	75	29	48	58	67	32
--4 WK AVG--					10	18	9	20	8	14	10	19	165	294	97	176	142	98	39	60	72	82	45
KTVT SU SUPER MOV	3	1	3	5	3	5	5	5	7	7	3	5	61	92	35	62	43	31	21	27	13	17	18
KTXA GT MOV FVRTS	3	5	1	5	3	6	3	5	11	8	4	7	48	76	35	55	41	38	21	27	22	23	13
KTWS STV	-	-	-	-					**	**			1	4	2	2	2	2	1	1	1	1	
KNBN SOLEDAD	-	1		1	1	1	1		**	**	1	1	9	14	4	7	7	5	4	2	4	6	1
KXTX WRLD CLS WR2	3	1	1	2	2	3	2	3	2	2	2	3	41	45	19	31	25	16	10	9	11	13	6
KERA PTV	2		1	1	1	1	2	2	1	1	1	1	16	26	2	7	14	4		3	4	6	4
HUT/TOTAL	60	58	52	54	56		62	53	43	55	56		872	1338	323	618	693	398	161	251	291	344	232
6:30P-7:00P																							

DALLAS-FT WORTH　　　　　TPA-83　　SUNDAY　　　　FEBRUARY 1983 TIME PERIOD AVERAGES

* SAMPLE BELOW MINIMUM FOR WEEKLY REPORTING
** SHARE/HUT TRENDS NOT AVAILABLE
- DID NOT ACHIEVE A REPORTABLE WEEKLY RATING
‡ TECHNICAL DIFFICULTY
+ COMBINED PARENT/SATELLITE
▲ SEE TABLE ON PAGE iv

business. As a result, the Arbitron methodology deserves careful review. More than 250 individual radio markets are measured each year in the spring. Larger markets are measured more frequently—up to four times a year. This is how it's done: Arbitron first determines the geographic limits of each survey area by establishing both a Metro Survey Area (MSA) and a larger Total Survey Area (TSA). In general, the MSA corresponds to the Standard Metropolitan Statistical Areas as defined by the U.S. Office of Management and the Budget, but because of its experience, Arbitron does make some adjustments. When first surveyed, a TSA usually includes every county that is covered by the O.5 MV/M signal (meaning a field strength meter reading of one-half milovolt) for at least two AM stations licensed to the metro area of the market. This area of coverage is determined by a radio engineering test of actual station signal strength. Later, in subsequent reports, Arbitron may adjust the TSA on the basis of reported listening to stations heard within that area. In a local market report, for example, the MSA might cover 5 counties, and the TSA, 16. Listening data for both are reported side by side. In the metro area report, low-power stations can enjoy more favorable comparisons with high-power stations because the measurements are confined to a relatively small geographic area. In the TSA report, a low-power station often will not compare favorably with powerhouse competition. For the local advertiser whose market is confined to the metro area, these data are very helpful. The total survey area may be more important to other advertisers whose product distribution does not stop at the metro boundaries and whose advertising goals therefore are not confined to the metro area.

The Arbitron Radio report sent to clients contains average and cume persons for each station on the basis of time periods, Monday-through-Friday averages, Saturday-and-Sunday listening, out-of-home listening, and, of course, audience demographics in terms of age and sex. All this information is reported for both the Metro Survey Area and the Total Survey Area. (See a sample report in 10.7.)

For each market, Arbitron establishes what will be necessary for an Effective Sample Base. Then it uses the services of the MetroMail Company, which supplies nationwide mailing and telephone lists in the form of magnetic tapes. In many markets, because of the high proportion of unlisted telephone numbers, an "expanded sample frame" is used. A computer eliminates known listed telephone residences, businesses, nonresidential exchanges, and the like, and the remaining numbers then have an opportunity to be included in the total sample. When the sample has been selected, Arbitron personnel go to work. A letter sent to each home in the sample states that the household has been selected for inclusion in a radio study and that an interviewer will be calling to request cooperation in the survey. When the interviewer phones, he or she explains the purpose of the study, determines the number of persons in the household 12 years of age and older, and then asks that these members keep an individual diary of radio listening for one week. In order to reach as high a percentage as possible of the households selected by the computers, interviewers are instructed to make at least five attempts to contact a "no answer" household. Diaries are mailed from Arbitron headquarters, and a cash incentive is normally included. It's usually 50 cents, but sometimes, in order to stimulate interest and cooperation, a bit more is enclosed for age groups that historically have a poor diary return rate—teenagers, for example.

10.7/Sample Page from a Boston Arbitron Radio Report

Average Quarter-Hour and Cume Listening Estimates

BOSTON
WINTER 1983

MONDAY–SUNDAY
6.00AM–MIDNIGHT

STATION CALL LETTERS	ADULTS 18+ TOTAL AREA AVG PERS (00)	TOTAL AREA CUME PERS (00)	METRO AVG PERS (00)	METRO CUME PERS (00)	METRO AVG PERS RTG	METRO AVG PERS SHR	ADULTS 18-34 TOTAL AREA AVG PERS (00)	TOTAL AREA CUME PERS (00)	METRO AVG PERS (00)	METRO CUME PERS (00)	METRO AVG PERS RTG	METRO AVG PERS SHR	ADULTS 18-49 TOTAL AREA AVG PERS (00)	TOTAL AREA CUME PERS (00)	METRO AVG PERS (00)	METRO CUME PERS (00)	METRO AVG PERS RTG	METRO AVG PERS SHR
WBCN	523	5851	388	4299	1.5	7.5	475	5043	369	3792	3.5	18.4	521	5739	388	4248	2.4	12.4
WBOS	52	1750	43	1328	.2	.8	45	1561	36	1143	.3	1.8	47	1704	38	1282	.2	1.2
WBZ	759	11346	497	6784	1.9	9.6	97	2920	55	1578	.5	2.7	311	6026	196	3454	1.2	6.2
WCAP	18	508	14	433	.1	.3	4	158	1	117			8	301	4	226		.1
*WCAS	18	234	17	217	.1	.3	11	123	11	123	.1	.5	17	180	16	163	1	.5
*WCCM	32	369	29	298	.1	.6	3	43	2	38		.1	2	67	2	62		.1
WCGY	112	1561	51	908	.2	1.0	82	894	33	517	.3	1.6	109	1464	48	850	.3	1.5
WCOZ	276	4930	185	3188	.7	3.6	241	4230	156	2729	1.5	7.8	266	4792	175	3092	1.1	5.6
WCRB	147	2641	105	1799	.4	2.0	17	651	16	603	.2	.8	61	1482	42	1126	.3	1.3
WDLW	63	943	63	932	.2	1.2	11	233	11	222	.1	.5	43	573	43	562	.3	1.4
WEEI	316	6136	289	5269	1.1	5.6	34	1172	33	1077	.3	1.6	89	2301	87	2087	.5	2.8
*WESX	48	698	48	698	.2	.9	1	61	1	61			7	174	7	174		.2
WEZE	22	604	21	544	.1	.4	3	166	3	166		.1	12	314	12	314	1	.4
WHDH	468	6422	403	5373	1.6	7.8	78	1773	54	1358	.5	2.7	240	3787	194	3062	1.2	6.2
WHTT	215	5180	147	3712	.6	2.9	170	3779	112	2640	1.1	5.6	206	4673	139	3327	.8	4.4
WHUE	23	803	22	721	.1	.4	1	73	1	73			4	273	4	236		.1
WHUE FM	238	3522	175	2736	.7	3.4	15	410	10	360	.1	.5	71	1276	46	908	.3	1.5
*WILD	95	863	95	798	.4	1.8	58	522	58	487	.5	2.9	75	666	75	631	.5	2.4
*WJDA	59	518	59	482	.2	1.1		14		14			11	132	11	115	1	.4
WJIB	308	4789	240	3553	.9	4.7	34	580	22	365	.2	1.1	112	1851	83	1325	.5	2.6
WMJX	300	5045	237	3770	.9	4.6	205	3781	154	2768	1.5	7.7	281	4667	223	3515	1.4	7.1
WMRE	66	1419	61	1280	.2	1.2	4	217	4	202			18	573	16	507	.1	.5
WRKO	328	4920	263	3802	1.0	5.1	43	1270	34	981	.3	1.7	111	2256	93	1709	.6	3.0
*WROL	71	1187	53	956	.2	1.0	9	143	7	96	.1	.3	23	467	19	391	.1	.6
WROR	268	5150	202	3652	.8	3.9	168	3282	124	2327	1.2	6.2	247	4681	182	3310	1.1	5.8
WSSH	256	3503	148	2011	.6	2.9	65	1176	52	783	.5	2.6	173	2298	92	1306	.6	2.9
WSTD	28	611	15	352	.1	.3	1	47		25			5	172	4	119		.1
WVBF	192	3067	135	2263	.5	2.6	150	2215	102	1603	1.0	5.1	188	2918	132	2179	.8	4.2
*WXKS	181	1345	178	1278	.7	3.5	4	73	4	73		.2	50	374	50	341	.3	1.6
WXKS FM	365	5689	290	4309	1.1	5.6	301	4508	235	3259	2.2	11.7	351	5390	276	4010	1.7	8.8
WAAF	86	2086	36	815	.1	.7	73	1906	35	785	.3	1.7	85	2051	35	799	.2	1.1
WOKQ	136	1953	30	429	.1	.6	36	688	2	97		.1	91	1343	15	207	.1	.5
WPLM	36	424	10	142			1	68		21			8	153	7	89		.2
WPLM FM	82	1277	45	530	.2	.9	3	125	3	90		.1	18	389	10	187	.1	.3
TOTAL	118	1451	55	551	.2	1.1	4	179	3	97		.1	26	457	17	208	.1	.5
WSRS	154	1593	26	288	.1	.5	20	194	6	57	.1	.3	54	687	11	138	.1	.4
WHJY	136	2251	11	306		.2	126	2023	11	295	.1	.5	133	2202	11	306	.1	.4
METRO TOTALS			5152	25141	20.0				2006	10435	18.9				3141	16159	19.1	

Footnote Symbols: (*) means audience estimates adjusted for actual broadcast schedule
ARBITRON RATINGS

Courtesy of Arbitron.

10.8/How to Fill in an Arbitron Radio Diary

HOW TO FILL IN THE ARBITRON DIARY

Please carry the Arbitron diary with you wherever you go during the seven days of the survey. <u>Then, each time you listen to radio</u> —

❶ Please fill in the time you start listening and the time you stop. Be sure to check (✔) the AM column to indicate morning and PM column to indicate afternoon and evening. For times that begin or end at 12 o'clock, please use Noon (PM) or Midnight, "Mid" (AM). Whenever you change stations, please start on a new line.

❷ Fill in the "call letters" of the station you are listening to. If you don't know the call letters, fill in the name of the program — or the dial setting.

❸ Check (✔) either the AM or the FM column to indicate whether you are listening to the AM radio dial or FM radio dial.

❹ Check (✔) to show whether you are listening at home or away from home.

❺ If you don't listen to radio on a certain day, check (✔) the circle at the bottom of the page for that day.

HERE'S WHAT A SAMPLE PAGE MIGHT LOOK LIKE —

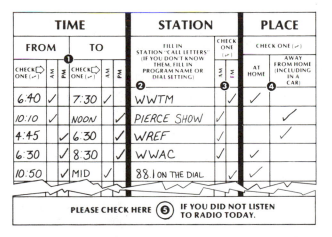

IMPORTANT — Many stations broadcast on both AM and FM. For this Arbitron survey, it is important to correctly identify whether you are listening on AM or FM (even though the station may use the same call letters and broadcast the same thing over the air).

In order to have an accurate record of your radio listening, please fill in your own diary regardless of your age or handwriting ability. To keep your Arbitron diary from getting mixed up with any others in your household — please fill in your initials (or first name) here.

The day before the survey week begins, the telephone interviewer again calls the home with a reminder to begin diary entries the next day. (See diary, 10.8.) A few days later, the household is called again—as another reminder and to see if there are any difficulties in keeping the diaries. At the same time, respondents are encouraged to mail in their diaries immediately after the survey's conclusion. Despite this effort, Arbitron reports that only about half of the diaries are returned and are usable.

In order to adequately measure radio listening in predominantly black and Hispanic communities, Arbitron uses a special methodology. In markets with a large black population there is an additional step in the initial interview. The interviewer asks a question about race or nationality. If the response is "black," Arbitron includes a higher cash incentive for cooperation. There are then three follow-up calls, rather than the usual two.

To measure predominantly Hispanic populations, telephone calls are not used. In order to reduce the potential for communications problems, bilingual Arbitron employees visit selected households in order to place diaries. Follow-ups are also handled by personal contact, including the final call to pick up the completed diaries. Cash incentives are also higher than those for households selected by standard placement techniques.

Proponents of the diary method point out that the diary is designed to travel with the person, not stay with a particular radio. It contains very specific, easily understood instructions. Respondents are asked to fill in individual listening on a day-by-day basis, indicating time of listening and call letters of the station—or, if call letters are not known, program name or dial setting. The diary also asks that respondents indicate either "at-home" or "away-from-home" listening, as well as FM listening. (Away from home is subdivided into "in a car" and "some other place." If they did not listen to radio on a particular day, they are asked to check a special box. The back of the diary asks for age, sex, and, if the respondent works, place of residence—by city, county, state, and ZIP code.

Arbitron believes that its method is superior to other ones, because the diary is personal, portable, and covers seven days of listening on a 24-hour basis. As a result, it's economical. Diaries, of course, can go anywhere the U.S. Postal Service goes and can be used to obtain not only radio listening information but also a wide variety of marketing information. The names and street addresses of respondents are not released, and so there is a cloak of anonymity for those who cooperate.

No method is perfect, and the diary method has been criticized on a number of bases. Respondents' lack of cooperation is probably the biggest bugaboo for research companies that use diaries. Even though the return rate seems fairly low, many research authorities consider a 50–60 percent response pretty good. How conscientious people are in keeping accurate daily entries is open to speculation. In large markets where perhaps three or four dozen radio signals are available, people may not know what they're listening to or may report incorrectly. This is the sort of error that constitutes an unknowable factor. Placing diaries on the basis of a sample drawn from telephone lsitings obviously excludes new residents and unlisted and non-telephone homes. Using the Expanded Sample Frame does permit the inclusion of these homes, and Arbitron now uses it in all markets.

One of the frustrations faced by Arbitron has been the "hypoing" problem. A number of stations in given markets have launched intensive promotion campaigns, elaborate contests, and the like in order to boost their ratings during an Arbitron sweep. Arbitron then expanded its sweeps to cover longer time periods—from 10 weeks up to 44 weeks. This procedure is designed to diminish the problem so that the company's reports reflect more "normal" listening behavior.

Radio's All Dimension Audience Research (RADAR)

To meet the needs of the radio networks and their advertisers, RADAR (Radio's All Dimension Audience Research) was launched in 1968. These rating reports, published by Statistical Research, Inc., of Westfield, New Jersey, are issued twice a year, generally in February and July. They are based on continuous sampling of listening to more than a dozen radio networks. (Because of the proliferation of radio networks, this list will probably be expanded.) RADAR data are gathered by telephone interviewing. A national sample of 6,000 households is balanced by region, size of household, age, sex, and ethnic group.

From a half-dozen centers across the country, interviewers call selected households. (A random digit dialing system allows the inclusion of unlisted households.) A single respondent, age 12 or older, is selected for each household, and the interviewer calls that person each day for the seven-day survey period to inquire about radio listening habits. (RADAR researchers believe that use of a single respondent per household eliminates the so-called "yea-saying" or "me-too" problem that is sometimes encountered when more than one member of a household is interviewed.)

Interviewers are instructed to probe for the exact starting and ending times for the respondents' radio listening for the previous 24 hours. The response rate runs about 75%—a higher cooperation rate than even the Nielsen Television Index. RADAR believes that its methodology provides better representation of younger adults and eliminates the "literacy bias" that bedevils the diary method.

In tabulating the data, RADAR extensively checks network clearances on hundreds of affiliates. This procedure verifies when and if an affiliate broadcasts a network program. Not all stations carry every network-fed program and commercial, and in many cases, broadcasts are delayed. Newscasts tend to have a better clearance than other kinds of programs. Each of the networks cooperates by providing RADAR with broadcast clearance data as reported by its individual affiliates. It is important that the information cover both programs and network commercials, because the size of the audience of a network affiliate is immaterial to an advertiser whose commercial has been "bumped." Thus, RADAR collects clearance information on commercials that were broadcast with the program at the time of the network feed, commercials that were extracted from a program and carried later, and those that were not carried at all.

RADAR audience estimates are published in three volumes. Volume 1, *Radio Usage,* provides estimated total audiences of all AM and FM network radio stations, reported in terms of audience demographics and various dayparts. Volumes 2 and 3 provide estimates of *Network Audiences to Cleared Programs (plus Commercial Exposures)* and *Network Audiences to Cleared Programs (excluding Commercial*

Exposures). Additional detailed information provides breakouts in terms of demographic characteristics, geographic areas, quarter-hour ratings, reach and frequency estimates, and the like.

The voluminous RADAR report is the only rating service that measures national radio network audiences. Because the surveys have been conducted for many years, RADAR has been able to track some very interesting changes in radio listening patterns. For example, FM listening has been growing steadily, and 1979 was the first year in which it exceeded AM listening. The heaviest usage of radio is by men 18–34 and women 18–49. Both groups average about three and three-quarters hours per day. It is interesting to note that teenagers and women 50 and older are the lightest radio users, but they still manage to spend about three hours a day with radio. Another surprising RADAR statistic, tracked since 1976, shows that working women spend more time with radio (about four hours a day) than do nonworking women (three and one-quarter hours). Automobile listening accounts for 16 to 19 percent of total radio listening.

Other Radio Audience Research Companies

The preeminence of Arbitron in measuring *local* market radio audiences has been challenged by a number of companies over the years. Several research companies have introduced various methodologies, only to go out of business because of the high cost of their service and lack of support from the industry. Two research companies now challenging the leader are described below.

The Birch Report   From its headquarters in Coral Springs, Florida, the Birch Report measures individual radio markets through telephone interviews. Like the other rating services, Birch uses telephone listings provided by the MetroMail Company. Household listings are sorted into ZIP codes in order to balance the sample geographically. A dialing procedure is used that allows unlisted households to be included in the sample.

Birch interviewers place their calls in the evening hours Sunday through Friday, with interviews evenly distributed across each night of the week. If a busy signal or no answer is encountered, up to two additional attempts are made to reach the household. Respondents are asked about their radio listening for the previous 24 hours and about their age, sex, and ethnic group.

The telephone recall methodology was selected by Birch because it allows the entire sample to respond to exactly the same survey questions. Confusion over station identification is normally resolved by the respondents—not a diary editor. Birch maintains that telephone interviews reveal significantly more time spent listening to radio than ever shows up in a one-day or one-week diary.

Sample sizes vary by market size, ranging from approximately 1,050 in most medium to large cities to 1,570 in major markets. In New York and Los Angeles, the sample covers approximately 2,350 interviews each.

Reports issued to clients include each radio station's average quarter-hour ratings and shares, daily and weekly cumulative estimates, age and sex breakouts, daypart summaries (morning drive time, for example), and listening estimates by location (home, car, and other places). Monthly Birch reports cover two months of sampling—the current and preceding month. Quarterly and semiannual summaries are helpful in tracking trends. Clients may also subscribe to the Birch Demand Data (BiDD) service, which reports ethnic listening data, audience estimates by county, ZIP code, or city area, and other specialized information.

RAM Research Company   Headquartered in San Diego, the RAM Research Company measures radio listening in individual markets via use of a one-day diary. The company's individual markets generally conform to recognized Standard Metropolitan Statistical Areas. In every market surveyed, measurements are for 50 weeks a year; the weeks containing Christmas and New Year's Day are skipped. RAM selects a geographically balanced sample from residential households with listed telephone numbers, and operators call to solicit participation. A one-day diary—a simple single sheet of paper—is mailed for each member of the cooperating household age 12 and older. Respondents are asked to enter each radio station listened to during the survey day and the time of day each period of listening started and ended. They are also asked to indicate age, sex, the time they awakened, the date they kept the diary, and whether during that day they read a local daily newspaper.

The number of diaries sent out obviously varies with the market size. The smallest markets average 2,500 diaries, and the largest market, 14,000. A small cash incentive is enclosed with each diary. Follow-up calls are made by RAM operators to remind members of participating households that the diaries will be coming in the mail, to answer any questions, and, later, to encourage the return of completed diaries. The returned diaries are edited, coded, and finally entered into a computer.

In order to reflect the constant changes in most radio markets, RAM (like Birch) issues its reports monthly. These reports are based on listening data from the previous three months of surveys. The reports contain estimates of each station's quarter-hour share of audience for various dayparts, average persons per quarter-hour, cumulative daily ratings broken down by daypart, and average daily cumulative persons listening to each station. Data are reported in terms of age and sex.

In addition to its standard ratings report, RAM also issues a Qualitative Usage Estimate. Prepared twice a year, this report covers approximately four months of diary measurements. Data are obtained from questions listed on the back of the one-day diary. ("How many out-of-state airplane trips do you take per year? How many soft drinks do you drink per week?") Questions cover product consumption, travel, visits to various kinds of stores, movie attendance, dollars spent annually in various categories, and the like. The qualitative report is correlated by age and sex for each station, so that an advertiser can identify those stations that deliver the greatest number of people who drink beer regularly, for example, or buy new cars.

Electronic Media Rating Council

Confidence and credibility are essential for all the ratings services. Because so many decisions, often involving millions of dollars, are based in part on the little numbers printed in the ratings books, the broadcast advertising industry must be able to rely on the accuracy of the information. The responsibility for reliability in audience measurement falls to the ratings services themselves and also to the Electronic Media Rating Council (EMRC).

In 1963, following a congressional committee investigation that revealed a number of serious shortcomings in audience measurements, industry leaders organized the Broadcast Rating Council, which in 1982 was renamed the Electronic Media Rating Council. The job of the EMRC is to *monitor, audit,* and *accredit* the various ratings companies. It has established minimum standards of performance and has also developed a procedure to check adherence to these standards. Companies that meet the standards are awarded EMRC accreditation.

The most important and time-consuming work of the EMRC is the auditing of the various audience research companies. Independent certified public accounting firms are retained by the EMRC to:

1.　check the sample design, the universe sampled, and other initial specifications in the research methodology.

2.　check the implementation of the sample and the extent to which the designated sample is achieved.

3.　check the interviewers—their experience, training, and supervision and the controls placed on them.

4.　verify the fieldwork of interviewers and confirm a company's internal verification procedures.

5.　check all procedures for handing questionnaires and meter-generated data.

6.　audit the editing and coding of data and the controls used to guard against errors of omission or commission.

7.　examine data processing, weighting procedures, keypunch verifications, computer programs, and so on.

8.　check published reports and procedures to ascertain the accuracy of printed output.

Costs for the audits are borne by the ratings companies and may reach almost half a million dollars annually. The result of these auditing labors, however, has been audience estimates that meet (or exceed) the minimum standards of the EMRC.

Conclusions

This chapter surveys the methods used by the best-known audience research companies. Through the years, other companies have flourished and then passed from the scene, primarily because of economics. The cost of research, paid primarily by the broadcasters, has been a significant expense to the industry, but modern broadcast advertising simply could not function without audience research.

There is no perfect methodology for measuring audiences. Each system—one-day or one-week diaries, personal or telephone interviewing, or meters attached to receivers—has its advantages and disadvantages. The voluminous data gathered by the ratings companies provide tremendous help to advertisers attempting to put together media executions that achieve "the biggest bang for the buck." To the uninitiated, the ratings often seem incomprehensible, but computers have simplified their use, and with some study and determination, just about anyone can grasp the meaning of the numbers published in the ratings books. Any intelligent person, whether a professional or a neophyte, realizes that the ratings are always *estimates* — they are not carved in stone. The numbers are based on samples of a larger universe and are therefore subject to error. The Electronic Media Rating Council serves the industry by auditing and accrediting the various ratings companies. The watchdog role of the EMRC is an important one, because audience research has a far-reaching impact on the advertising industry, the broadcasting community, and the public.

10.9/Glossary of Broadcast Research Terms

Audience   A group of households or a group of individuals that are counted in a television or radio audience according to any one of several alternative criteria.

Audience measurements are generally expressed in two ways: as percentages, in which case they are called ratings, and as absolute quantities, in which case they represent either a number of households or a number of individuals.

Audience Composition   A term that refers to a classification of the individuals or the households in a television or radio audience into various categories. Common categories for individuals are age and sex groupings (e.g., men, women, teenagers, and children). Common categories for households are based on the number of members of the household, age or education of the head of household, household income, and so forth.

Circulation Area   Conceptually, a geographic area within which a television or radio station actually obtains audiences.

A circulation area for a television or radio station is often described in terms of a group of counties, or perhaps, a group of minor civil subdivisions. One commonly used criterion for inclusion in such a circulation area is whether at least some specified percentage (e.g., 5 or 10 percent) of the households or the individuals

in the county, or the minor civil subdivision, is estimated to be in the audience of that station during a specified period of time.

A circulation area is defined on a "do-receive" basis and should not be confused with a coverage area, which is defined on a "can-receive" basis.

Cost Per Thousand   The ratio of the cost of a television or radio advertisement (in dollars) to a number of households (in thousands) or to a number of individuals (in thousands) estimated to be in the audience at the time the advertisement is broadcast. The term is more fully referred to as "cost per thousand households (or homes)" or as "cost per thousand viewers." Often abbreviated CPM.

Not all cost per thousand ratios are comparable. Some ratios may be computed by using all households or individuals in an audience, while others may be in terms of some specified subgroup, such as the number of households with children, or the number of teenagers in an audience. Further, while a ratio may be computed for a single announcement, the announcement may be a 20-second, 30-second, or full-minute commercial. In addition, the ratio may be expressed per commercial minute of advertising, rather than per announcement. For example, the cost per thousand households for an entire television program is sometimes divided by the number of minute-long commercials on that program to arrive at a ratio called the "cost-per-thousand per-commercial minute."

From *Standard Definitions of Broadcast Research Terms*, (Washington, D.C., National Association of Broadcasters, 1970). Reprinted by permission of the National Association of Broadcasters.

Coverage Conceptually, the number of households or individuals, regardless of where located, that are able to receive a given television or radio station, or group of stations.

Coverage is measured on the basis of a survey, which may determine reception either by field tests of television sets or radios that ascertain whether a station can be received, or by interviews with persons that ask them whether they can receive a station.

When coverage figures are given for a limited geographic area rather than on the basis of "regardless of where located," the limited area should be clearly stated.

Coverage, as defined, is on a "can-receive" basis and should not be confused with circulation which is defined on a "do-receive" basis.

Cumulative Audience A term that refers to the net size of a television or radio audience during two or more time periods. That is, a household or an individual will be counted as part of a cumulative audience only once, even though the household or the individual appears in audiences during two or more time periods. Also called "net audience" or "unduplicated audience."

One may compute a cumulative audience figure for time periods during the same day, on different days within a week, or over a period of several weeks.

Cumulative audience figures are often used as a measure of the circulation of a network or a station and as a measure of the reach of a television or radio program, or group of programs. The concept of cumulative audience also may be used for different combinations of media. In all cases duplications are eliminated in the computations.

Frame A list, file of cards, map, or some other form that identifies all sampling units that are to be given some chance of appearing in a statistical survey, and also describes the location of these sampling units. One frame commonly used is a set of telephone directories. Another is a set of maps showing housing units.

A frame provides a working definition of the statistical population in a study, and a means of access to the elementary units selected for study. However, in practice a frame may only represent a statistical population imperfectly. That is, a frame may be subject to various imperfections such as incompleteness, or duplication, or both.

A frame is as essential for a complete census as it is for a sample study.

Frequency The average number of time periods, out of a set of specified time periods, in which households or individuals are in the audience of a given television or radio network, station, or program. This type of average is normally computed only for those households or individuals that are in the audience during at least one of the time periods. Also referred to as "average frequency."

Gross Rating Points The simple total of television or radio ratings during two or more time periods, or for two or more programs. Normally this sum should be taken only of ratings with the same base.

Gross rating points represent the size of a gross audience expressed as a percentage of the base used in developing the particular ratings included in the gross total. Thus, multiplying gross rating points by that base yields a gross audience figure.

Households Reached The number of households that are estimated to be in the audience of a television or radio network, station, or program during a specified period of time, regardless of where located. Also called, inexactly, "homes reached."

Households-Using-Television Rating A type of rating for television in general, rather than for a specific network, station, or program. The base is households with one or more television sets, in a specified area. A households-using-television rating shows the percentage of these households that are estimated to be in the audience of any one of a group of television stations, at a specified time.

The term "households using television" without the word "rating" attached should be used to refer to the actual number of households in television audiences rather than to this number expressed as a percentage.

A household should be counted as using television only once in the computation of this type of rating even if it is using two or more television sets simultaneously.

Often referred to as "HUT rating." Also called, inexactly, "homes-using-television rating." A households-using-television rating should not be referred to as a "sets-in-use rating."

Individuals Reached The number of individuals that are estimated to be in the audience of a television or radio network, station, or program during a specified period of time, regardless of where located.

Rating The size of a television or radio audience expressed in relative or percentage terms.

A rating represents a percentage of some base. This base must always be stated explicitly. The base may be a number of households or a number of individuals, but in any case a rating shows the percentage of this number that is estimated to be in a television or radio audience.

A number of different types of ratings are widely used. First of all, there are several alternative criteria used for counting a household or an individual in, or out of, a television or radio audience. Second, ratings may measure the audience of a network or of a station, or of a program, or of a group of stations or programs. Third, ratings may represent only audiences in homes, or audience in homes and away from home as well — for example, radio audiences in automobiles. Fourth, ratings may reflect audience at an instant in time, average audience over several points in time, or an accumulation of audiences over several points in time. Hence, any rating must be accompanied by a careful definition of the nature of the audience that it measures. (Five different kinds of ratings are defined below.)

1. *Average Audience Rating* A type of rating computed for some specified interval of time, such as for the length of a television or radio program or for a 15- or 30-minute period.

Conceptually, it is possible to compute a rating as of any given instant, or point in time. An average audience rating may be thought of as the average of such instantaneous ratings over a number of points in time. In all cases, exactly which values are used in computing the average must be made clear.

Thus, this type of rating is more precisely called an "average instantaneous-audience rating," though in practice the terms "average audience rating" and "average minute rating" are more frequently used.

In practice, average audience ratings are almost always calculated from sample data collected either by coincidental interviews or by meters.

2. *Instantaneous-Audience Rating* The size of a television or radio audience as of a given instant, or point in time, expressed as a percentage of some specified base.

3. *Metro Rating* A rating computed for the households or the individuals in a well-defined metropolitan (metro) area.

The term should normally be used to refer to a rating computed for a standard metropolitan statistical area, as defined by the U.S. Bureau of the Budget. However, sometimes it may be used to refer to a rating for an area that is geographically broader or narrower than the corresponding standard metropolitan statistical area, or to refer to a rating for an area for which no standard metropolitan statistical area at all has been defined. In these cases, the special use of the term should be indicated.

4. *National Rating* Any rating calculated for a television or radio network or program over the United States. In general, this kind of rating shows the percentage of television or radio households, or the percentage of a group of individuals, that is estimated to be in the audience of a network or a program over a specified time.

The base for a national rating is normally all television or radio households, or all individuals, in the United States. In some cases, however, the base used for a national rating may be limited to all television or radio households, or all individuals, in those geographic areas to which a program is being broadcast. In such cases, the exact base to which the rating is projectable should be clearly stated, and the rating labeled "national rating (program are a basis)" or "national rating (program station basis)."

5. *Total Audience Rating* A type of rating computed for some specified interval of time, such as for the length of a television or radio program or for a 15- or 30-minute period.

To be counted in the audience for purposes of a total audience rating, a household or an individual must be in the audience for some consecutive period of time during the interval (e.g., for five consecutive minutes or more). To calculate a total audience rating, the number of households or individuals that are counted in the audience is expressed as a percentage of some specified base. The base may be a group of television or radio households, or a group of individuals.

A total audience rating is commonly interpreted as a cumulation of instantaneous audiences, excluding, however, those that are in the audience for less than a specified time.

To the extent that it excludes those members of an audience that are in the audience for less than a specified time, a total audience rating reflects something less than what is literally the "total" audience.

In practice, total audience ratings are frequently calculated from sample data collected either by diaries, by recall interviews, or by meters.

Reach The number of households, or individuals, that are estimated to be in the audience of a given television or radio program, or group of programs, at least once over some specified period of time. Thus, reach is simply a term used to describe the cumulative audience of a program, or group of programs. The term is also used frequently to describe the cumulative audience of a commercial announcement or a series of commercial announcements, as well as that of programs. Also called "net reach."

Sample Elementary units that have been selected from a statistical population according to some specified procedure. By definition, a sample is intended to serve as a basis for generalizing to a statistical population.

A sample must be selected according to some sampling plan or sample design, which is a complete set of instructions on how to construct a frame, on how to define a sampling unit, and on how to choose sampling units from the frame for a survey.

There are many different methods of sampling, which result in different kinds of samples (Six of the most common samples used in audience research are defined below.)

1. *Area Probability Sample* A probability sample for which the sampling units are well-defined geographic areas, for example, city blocks. It is also possible to choose a

sample of areas on a nonprobability basis, but in this case the term "area sample" should not be applied without qualification.

2. *Cluster Sample* A type of probability sample. The distinguishing feature is that the sampling unit is defined as a group, or cluster, of elementary units, rather than as an individual elementary unit. A cluster sample is a simple random sample of clusters.

In a given survey, for example, clusters might be defined as groups of neighboring housing units, and a simple random selection of such groups would constitute a cluster sample.

Estimates based on a cluster sample will normally be subject to larger standard errors than estimates based on a simple random sample of the same number of elementary units. However, the extent of the difference between the two methods of sampling will depend on the extent to which the process of clustering results in clusters that are relatively homogeneous with respect to the characteristics of interest in a study. The more homogeneous clusters are, the larger is the standard error of an estimate based on a cluster sample. In any case, the standard error of each estimate based on a cluster sample can be ascertained by application of the appropriate formula.

A main advantage of a cluster sample, as opposed to a simple random sample of elementary units, is that it assures some geographic clustering of elementary units, and thereby assures some reduction in travel time and costs, which can, at least in part, be used to increase the size of the sample.

3. *Probability Sample* A sample drawn by a procedure that has the following properties: (1) selection of sampling units is from a frame and is accomplished mechanically, generally with random numbers, and (2) the probability of selection of any individual sampling unit, and of any combination of sampling units, is ascertainable from the nature of the procedure. Also called "random sample."

There are several different methods of probability sampling, which result in different kinds of probability samples.

The special feature of all methods of probability sampling is that they permit use of the theory of probability for the computation of limits on the margin of error that is attributable to the use of sampling, rather than attempting a complete census.

Use of probability sampling does not, in itself, guarantee a reliable result, nor one that is accurate or useful. Estimates based on a probability sample will be subject to nonsampling errors as well as to sampling error.

4. *Quota Sample* A particular type of nonprobability sample. In its design, quotas are set as to the number of respondents of various types that interviewers are to obtain. For example, quotas may be set for various geographic areas, for various age and sex groupings, for different economic levels, and so forth. The aim in setting such quotas is to insure that the sample is distributed, with respect to these characteristics, in proportion to presumably known population totals.

Once quotas are set, they are generally assigned to interviewers to fill as best they can — by searching out people with the appropriate characteristics. No frame is employed, nor is the sample selected on a probability basis. Thus, in the selection of the sample, quota sampling is always a type of judgment or convenience sampling.

Setting quotas and then filling them by judgment, convenience, or otherwise, provides no assurance of a reliable and accurate sample result. The result of a quota sample will still be subject to some degree of sampling error with respect to the characteristics that the study is supposed to measure. In any case, there are no formulas for calculating standard errors for the results of a quota sample because there are no ascertainable probabilities of selection.

Quota sampling should not be confused with stratified sampling, which is a method of probability sampling.

5. *Simple Random Sample* The simplest and most basic type of probability sample. It must be selected by a procedure that gives (1) every elementary unit equal probability of being selected for the sample, and (2) every possible combination of the predesignated number of elementary units to be chosen the same probability of being selected.

Other methods of probability sampling differ from simple random sampling only in that the probabilities of selection may vary from elementary unit to elementary unit, or from one combination of elementary units to another.

To select this type of sample in practical operation, one must first construct a frame that identifies every elementary unit individually. Thus, elementary units represent the possible sampling units. Then, with the aid of random numbers, sampling units are chosen one at a time from the frame until a predesignated number of elementary units are selected. Each selection must be in such a manner that all sampling units not previously selected for the sample have equal probability of being chosen. That is, each selection must be independent of previous selections except to the extent that previous selections are not given a chance to be reselected.

6. *Stratified Sample* A type of probability sample. The application of stratified sampling requires that sampling units be classified into various categories, or strata, according to one or more criteria; for example, according to geographic location, or according to size of household or according to both of these criteria. The over-all sample is divided among these strata for purposes of calculating estimates from the sample.

There are several versions of stratified sampling. For example, in some problems, one will classify all sampling units in the frame before the sample is selected. Then one selects a simple random sample, of predesignated size, from each stratum. This is called stratification before selection. Another version of stratified sampling involves selecting a sample from the entire frame, after which all elementary units chosen for the sample are classified into strata. This is a form of stratification after selection.

Estimates based on a stratified sample will normally be subject to smaller standard errors than estimates based on a simple random sample of the same number of elementary units. However, the exact gain will depend on the extent to which the process of stratification results in strata that are relatively homogeneous with respect to the characteristics of interest in a study. The more homogeneous the strata are, the smaller is the standard error of an estimate based on a stratified sample. The gain from stratification will vary from an estimate of one characteristic to another. In any event, the standard error of each estimate based on a stratified sample can be ascertained by application of the appropriate formula.

Stratified sampling is a method of probability sampling and should not be confused with quota sampling where the final choice of sampling units is normally left to the interviewers.

Share of Audience   Generally, the percentage of the aggregate television or radio audience in some specified area at some specified time that is in the audience of a given network, station, or program. Frequently referred to simply as "share."

A share may be computed on a household basis or on an individual basis. The base for a share on a household basis is normally households using television or radio in a specified geographic area, over a specified time. Thus, a share on a household basis shows the percentage of those households using television or radio that are estimated to be in the audience of a given network, station, or program, over a specified time.

The base for a share on an individual basis is normally individuals using television or radio in a specified geographic area, over a specified time. The base may include all such individuals, or perhaps some specified group of individual persons (such as those who have attained a specified age) that are using television or radio. Thus, a share on an individual basis shows the percentage of these individuals using television or radio that are estimated to be in the audience of a given network, station, or program, over a specified time.

Turnover   The ratio of a cumulative audience over several periods of time (e.g., four weeks) to the average audience per period of time (e.g., per week). This ratio serves as an indication of the relative frequency with which the audience of a program, or of a station, changes over a period of time. The greater the turnover in audience, the higher is the ratio.

chapter eleven

Network Sales

The Moguls of the Biz

There's a long shopping list of media available to advertisers, and yet most major advertisers automatically gravitate to the broadcast media. For mass-marketed consumer products and services, the networks offer many advantages, the foremost being instantaneous coverage of mass national audiences.

The three dominant television networks provide major advertisers with a quality environment that reaches large markets quickly, efficiently, and successfully. Options for advertisers are now increasing with new technologies available and new networks being formed. Using satellite links, many cable networks deliver specialized programing to particular audience segments. Radio networks have multiplied, likewise offering special programs and audiences.

Huge investments are made by the various networks in their efforts to provide a variety of programing to audiences and in turn deliver these audiences to advertisers. The business of buying and selling network time is a fascinating one. It is complicated by constantly fluctuating program schedules, shifting audience patterns, and an unpredictable level of new competition.

Radio Networks

No advertising medium in the United States has undergone more spectacular changes than network radio. When television bloomed like a hot-house rose in the 1950s, the radio networks faced a devastating desertion of audiences and advertisers. It's been a long difficult road back, but they have survived and proliferated.

The term *network radio* is used to apply only to the traditional line networks interconnected by AT&T circuits — ABC, CBS, NBC, and Mutual. In recent years, these networks have spawned multiple services, and newcomers have joined this increasingly competitive marketplace — RKO Radio, the Sheridan Broadcasting Network, the National Black Network, and others.

Another kind of radio network — the *unwired,* or *rep,* network — was inaugurated in the early 1970s. Organized by station representative firms, these networks carry no common programing but are sold as a package to advertisers. (This kind of buy is more fully described in the next chapter.)

A third kind of radio network has evolved, offering various syndicated programing services. These organizations provide programing to subscribing stations that contain commercials sold to national advertisers. The majority of the commercial positions is reserved for the station to sell to local and spot advertisers.

With more than 8,000 commercial radio stations in this country, there is no shortage of potential affiliates. Most of the radio networks have positioned themselves to serve rather narrow target audiences, and an affiliation with a similarly programed local station makes a happy marriage for both parties.

Network programing is available in virtually every market in the country, and this widespread distribution constitutes an attractive advertising opportunity. The advantages offered to advertisers are impressive. Network radio is efficient and inexpensive, and with one simple buy an advertising message can be fed to several hundred affiliates and to their thousands of listeners. This national coverage is most attractive to advertisers who do not have budgets large enough to meet the costs of network television, as well as to advertisers who wish to augment major advertising buys in other media. The medium is considered an excellent complement to either network or spot TV, and for advertisers who buy a lot of radio time, network is often combined with spot. Since commercial production costs are low, copy can be constantly changed.

Network radio is sometimes used as a *reach* extender, but advertisers are particularly pleased with network radio's ability to deliver *frequency*. (See Chapter 5.) A desired target audience may be reached many times at an efficient cost-per-thousand. Somewhat elusive or demographically narrow audiences — working women, high-income men, teenagers, blacks, and Hispanics — can be reached by various radio networks with relatively little "waste circulation."

Buying opportunities are extremely flexible in network radio. Advertisers can buy on a year-round basis, or they can buy a schedule that runs less than one week. "Drive time" (6:00 – 10:00 A.M. and 4:00 – 7:00 P.M.) is the most sought-after network buy.

Like network television, most network radio is bought by New York advertising agencies, but a significant amount of business comes from advertisers and agencies in Chicago, Detroit, Los Angeles, and San Francisco. Although buys are usually made a month or so in advance of the air date, the network can accommodate advertisers on very short notice.

The standard unit in network radio is still the 60-second commercial, although 30-second units are available and usually cost half the minute rate. It is worth noting that in spot radio, 30-second commercials often cost approximately 80 – 85 percent of the 60-second rate. Availabilities are often sold on a fixed position basis, in which the advertiser is guaranteed a particular time period. Less expensive positions are available on a run-of-schedule basis and may be moved or preempted without notice.

The costs for network radio are very low compared with those of network television, and they are even low compared with the costs of print ads in national consumer magazines. The prices vary from daypart to daypart and are predicated on a number of factors: the number of affiliates in a network lineup, the competitive picture, the general state of the economy, the size of the networks' inventories, the size and demographics of the audiences and—therefore—the cost-per-thousand.

Radio has not been considered a glamour medium for many years, and so network account executives find that it's an uphill fight to win new clients. Some advertisers are too preoccupied with their television investments to give radio the time and attention it deserves. A common complaint among account executives is that agencies ignore or neglect radio because the 15 percent commission from this low-cost medium "isn't worth the trouble." If they do use radio, many advertisers and their agencies prefer to use spot instead of network.

Network account executives constantly strive to make radio more visible and important to advertisers. Most agencies, however, remain relatively uninterested in network buys. They feel that spot radio will remain their primary vehicle in this medium, because they are able to place schedules on *only* those stations that present the best reach and frequency figures for prime prospects.

In the eyes of agency buyers, several problems plague the radio networks and make it an unattractive buy. *Wild-spotting* by local affiliates discourages some prospective network advertisers. The term refers to the practice of lifting a network commercial from a newscast, for example, and replacing it with a local spot. The network commercial is played later, not always at the time or in the program environment the network advertiser wants. Some of the networks forbid, or closely monitor, these practices and do guarantee rebates to advertisers if station clearances for a particular schedule do not meet a satisfactory level. Station clearances have been, and continue to be, a headache for several of the radio networks and for their clients.

What is probably the single most important limitation of the networks becomes apparent in a market-by-market analysis. Invariably, a network has some very weak affiliates and some very strong ones. This lack of uniform performance in the ratings makes it necessary to do one or both of the following: augment network buys with spot buys in particular markets, or make multiple network buys to offset lineup weaknesses. This kind of cut-and-fit buying strategy is the only way to achieve adequate reach and frequency goals in the various markets. In addition, audiences are fragmented in radio, and affiliates of the same network may broadcast greatly differing local program formats.

Time buyers use network radio audience measurements as reported by RADAR (Radio's All Dimension Audience Research), augmented with individual market reports from the syndicated research companies, primarily the Arbitron Ratings Company (see Chapter 10).

Satellites have invigorated the world of network radio in recent years. The advantages to the traditional line networks of using satellite "birds" are twofold: the fees for the use of a transponder are less than those charged for AT&T circuits, and audio quality via satellite transmission is superior. As more and more stations invest in earth station dishes, the flexibility of radio will increase. Many stations are affiliated with more than one network, and it is a relatively simple matter to put an ad hoc network together for some special event—a major rock concert fed live to affiliates, for example.

There are really five basic elements to radio programing—news, features, music, sports, and talk. What an affiliate seeks from a network is the kind of programing it either cannot produce or would find too costly to produce. News and features have been the meat and potatoes of most of the radio networks, but that is changing, too. Even talk shows have worked successfully on network radio. With a live satellite feed and the use of a toll-free telephone number, a talk-show host can field questions and comments from around the country.

Statewide, line-connected networks have been in existence for decades and offer excellent opportunities for regional advertisers. There are now more than two dozen, most located in the Northwest, Midwest, and Southeast.[1] These networks may provide regular programing, such as regional and agricultural news, or special-events programing, such as a popular regional sports franchise.

With expanding network radio services and the new technologies, stations will find better opportunities to choose network programing compatible with their own format. Advertisers as well as audiences will benefit.

In the complex world of network radio, who pays whom? For affiliates of the traditional networks, remuneration for carrying network programs is very modest. Stations are usually paid on the basis of the number of commercials carried from network feeds and according to particular dayparts. Important affiliates in large markets are paid proportionately more than small affiliates. It depends on the market, the importance of the station to the network, and a variety of other circumstances. Some affiliates receive no compensation at all, only free programing. (In certain cases, very small affiliates must pay their own telephone line charges in order to pick up a network feed.) In return, the network has a lineup of several hundred affiliates that constitutes a salable commodity to advertisers.

In the case of the unwired, or rep, networks, the stations, sold as a package to advertisers, are remunerated for the commercials they air. No programing is involved.

In the case of syndicated programing services that provide the bulk of a subscriber's programing, the stations pay for the service. The fee depends on the station's coverage area and the market in which it is located. These programing services share the commercial positions with their subscribing stations, so that some positions are sold to national advertisers by the network and some are assigned to the local station for sale to spot or local advertisers.

Television Networks

Every day of the year, tens of millions of American households tune their TV sets to one of the three giant networks. The Great Triopoly—ABC, CBS, and NBC—has

---

[1] Richard Hammer, "Network Radio: She Ain't What She Used to Be," *Broadcasting*, February 26, 1979, p. 14.

monopolized the nation's viewing for more than three decades. With the advent of the new technologies, the networks have experienced a slight but steady decline in their share of the total television audience. Independent stations, pay TV, the proliferating cable networks, videodiscs, and video cassettes offer alternatives, but the result has not been a wholesale desertion of network viewers. As a result, the three networks constitute an advertising medium that delivers huge audiences on a day-in, day-out basis. No other advertising medium can match these audience figures, and so network television is still number one for the top 100 advertisers. Many of them invest more than 90 percent of their advertising budgets in TV. Only about 600 advertisers are large enough (both in terms of product distribution and advertising budget) to use network television. All are represented by advertising agencies, and it is interesting to note that the top 10 ad agencies control about half of all the expenditures on network television. Considering the billions of dollars involved, the buying and selling process is confined to a fairly small number of professionals, mainly in New York (where most of the buys are handled), Chicago, Detroit, Los Angeles, and San Francisco.

ABC, CBS, and NBC maintain large sales departments devoted to selling and servicing national advertisers. Each network must operate in the marketplace against two strong competitors, and all the networks operate on a 100-percent sales philosophy. Unsold time cannot be warehoused and sold at a later date. The buying and selling of an intangible, perishable commodity like time, often priced at tens of thousands of dollars per commercial unit, makes TV network sales an intriguing but hectic business.

To the nation's viewers, a network is really no more than a program schedule — to be perused and evaluated before a program choice is made. Over the years, the competition for audiences has been a major factor in escalating program costs as the networks search for the best possible programs to reach and serve the demands of the public. The time and financial investment are almost incalculable. To support this kind of investment, the network sales departments must sell, and sell hard, to the only buyers who will foot the bill — the nation's advertisers.

The price for commercial units in network programing is predicated on a number of important considerations:

1.   the marketplace situation. How much money is available at any given time of the year for investment in network TV advertising? This situation will fluctuate with all the variables that affect the national economy and the sale of products and services to the nation's consumers.

2.   the estimated size and demographics of the audience for any given program. Audience reach and composition can vary greatly throughout the day, during the week, and by season.

3.   the competitive challenge of the other two networks

4.   the size of the inventory. How much unsold time does the network have on its hands? The length of "avails" sheets quickly indicates whether, at a particular moment, a buyer's or a seller's market exists.

5.   the network's requirements for revenue. A network sales department must generate the income that will meet the costs of operating a huge programing service,

maintaining an enormous payroll, compensating several hundred affiliates that carry network programs, and returning a profit to the network's shareholders.

Because of these important variables in determining network time charges, prices for commercial positions constantly change. "We deal in a commodity," said one network executive, "and the name of the game is supply and demand." Network time is sold in four ways: *up front, scatter, opportunistic,* and *program sponsorship.*

Up-Front Buying

Every year in the early spring, the three television networks announce their fall prime-time schedules for the upcoming TV year, which runs from mid-September through Labor Day of the following year. The excitement and speculation that surround the announcements keep the lights burning late in major advertising agencies, for that's when the up-front buying begins. The buyers usually represent advertisers who spend in excess of $5 million annually and who buy two or more quarters in network television. (Quarters refer to three-month periods: first quarter, January– March; second quarter, April–June; third quarter, July–September; fourth quarter, October–December.) Using network TV to reach large audiences on a regular basis is crucial for their marketing plans. The significant sums invested up front guarantee access to important target audiences.

Up-front buying is usually made in prime-time shows, in some sports programing, and in certain particularly popular daytime shows. Pilot previews for the new fall shows are arranged for major advertisers and top media buyers. These special screenings may be spread across a couple of weeks, and the network buyers can expect to be bleary-eyed after viewing new programs hour after hour. The screenings are strictly business, because the buyers will carefully evaluate each program based on very practical buying considerations—what kind of audience will that program attract and in what kind of numbers? Many variables are at work, but the three most important are the time slot, the program lead-in, and the programs scheduled in the same time period on the two competing networks. From previous track records, their own expertise, and perhaps some good hunches, the buyers estimate audience shares for each program on each network. At 8 o'clock on a particular evening, for example, a buyer may estimate that CBS will earn a 35 percent share, NBC a 25 percent share, and ABC a 40 percent share of the total audience viewing *network* television. (Everyone realizes, however, that once the programs are aired in the fall, independent stations, cable networks, pay TV, and other viewing options will siphon off a portion of network audiences, and thus, the estimated network shares will total less than 100 percent.) These estimates are not just a guessing game but a serious business, because it is from estimated shares that subsequent negotiations are launched for up-front buys.

The negotiation process is sometimes fast and furious, and supply and demand dictate the prices. The agency will estimate, based on the market for a particular season, what cost-per-thousand (CPM) it expects to pay for a particular client. Experienced buyers are always pretty close, and the CPM becomes the primary negotiation point between agency buyer and the network account executive. The buyer will tell the account executive the budget and the demographic requirements for each buy, and the network sales department will put together a package of programs that best fits those requirements.

Individual prices are not quoted for each commercial in the package — only a total price. Buyers will obviously try to obtain the very best price possible, thus receiving the lowest possible CPM. The networks often hold back a few particularly attractive positions in case they need to "sweeten" a deal with an important advertiser. Sharp buyers always want to know what's in the "bottom drawer." As one top media executive said, "Our goal is top quality programing at a rock bottom price."

Because CPM is the critical factor in the purchase of network time, up-front buyers who regularly invest millions of dollars are usually given a CPM guarantee by the network, which may be based on total households or on a specific demographic target. This guarantee is verbal and never committed to writing. Neither buyer nor seller has a perfect crystal ball, and when the fall programing season rolls around, a program that was predicted to be a hit may turn out to be a flop. The loss of audience will raise the CPM for the advertiser who bought into that show. If the CPM on the total up-front package rises significantly above the verbal guarantee, the network always provides some bonus spots in order to make up for the audience loss. There is no charge to the advertiser for these bonus commercials.

Severe criticism has been directed at the networks by advertising agency executives in recent years because of constantly changing prime-time schedules and incessant preemptions. Changing a program's time slot or canceling a show creates a ripple effect, and carefully laid plans must be reviewed. New series are often abruptly canceled. The chairman of the board of the nation's largest advertising agency, Young and Rubicam, has criticized the instability generated by a frantic ratings competition. "Some experts contend it is easier to slip a sunrise past a rooster than it is to slip a turkey past a six-week Nielsen."[2]

Buyers, however, can be wily in the network negotiating game. By demanding a series of counteroffers in order to squeeze the best possible deal, they may prompt round after round of competitive offers by the networks. Hour-long phone conversations are common between a buyer and a network account executive. Changing a date or a position in a certain program may be the decisive stroke in closing a deal. When one buy is completed, and some tension relieved, it may be time for the buyer to begin network negotiations for another client. Simultaneous negotiations for several clients' network schedules are common, and also nerve-racking.

For the advertiser who elects to "lie back and wait," the risks of not buying up front are obvious. On the one hand, if it's a seller's market, the buyer may be virtually shut out. On the other hand, if it's a buyer's market, the advertiser may be able to place commercials at a bargain when the networks "break price." Timing is all important, for buying too early or too late may affect the CPM more than any other factor. And if it happens to be a real seller's market, the best availabilities may quickly vanish from the networks' inventories. It is not uncommon for each of the three networks to sign more than a billion dollars in business during the brief up-front season.

---

[2] Edward Ney, "Agency/Advertiser Hostility Toward Networks Surfaces at ANA Workshops," *Broadcasting,* March 6, 1978, p. 38.

Because the buyers and sellers constitute a relatively small and closely knit fraternity, the network salesperson tries to help his or her clients make the best possible buys. A top agency buyer will ordinarily deal with one account executive from each network. But since no one account executive can be conversant and expert in the total programing lineup of a network, each is backed up by a sales force of specialists who can serve the buyer's special needs. A particular client may be interested in buying a sports package, for example. The regular network account executive will enlist the services of the sports sales specialists to provide information on these availabilities. Like all time salespeople, the network account executive earns a commission on sales.

The negotiations and compromises between buyer and seller may go on for a week or so before a typical up-front buy is sealed. People outside the broadcast advertising industry are sometimes stupefied to learn that such a buy, representing perhaps a $10-million investment, could be agreed to in such a short period of time and finalized by nothing more than a phone call. But that's really all it takes. The call is usually followed by an order letter that spells out only these essentials: dates and programs in which commercial positions have been bought and the total price. Up-front buys are usually for no less than 26 weeks, with options to renew.

Between buyer and seller, their word is their bond. This trust is mandatory, because the formal legal contracts sometimes exchanged between network and agency are almost never signed. Their respective legal departments are rarely able to agree on the specifics of contract language. Since the advertising business cannot grind to a halt for this reason, millions of dollars in network time are bought each year without the exchange of any formal contracts.

After an up-front buy is made, the network prices out each individual unit for the advertiser. Unit pricing is necessary for accounting purposes, especially if a commercial is preempted by a news event, for example. If an advertiser's commericial is not aired, the company must be either credited or given a "make-good," which is essentially replacement time.

During the up-front season, the network account executives are tremendously busy. They must stay on top of a constantly fluctuating market for network time. For the rest of the year, these salespeople are selling *scatter*.

Scatter Plan Buying

In the early years of television, many major clients invested their advertising dollars in sponsorships. In many cases, the advertisers held the rights to the program. Some advertisers entered into cosponsorship arrangements or alternating week sponsorships. As network time and production costs escalated, however, it became clear that putting all or most of the advertising eggs in one basket was not only expensive but also risky and inefficient.

About the same time — in the late 1950s following the quiz show scandals — the networks extended their control of programing. Programs were now either wholly owned and produced by the networks or had substantial network money invested in their development. Advertisers and their agencies found the costs of producing their own programs prohibitive. Thus, they withdrew from an active role in program development and sponsorships and at the same time began to modify buying criteria. Sheer ratings were no longer so important as they once were. Clients were increasingly interested in demographic breakouts and the cost efficiency factors reflected in CPMs. Spreading their dollars across the weeks, across the three networks, and across many different programs maximized total audience reach and minimized waste circulation.

Prices for network programs vary in a supply-demand market and also in relation to viewing levels and advertisers' marketing needs. As a result, prices are highest in the fourth quarter of the year, October through December. This is the season of heavy Christmas gift advertising, new car introductions, and cold remedy advertising. The second highest-priced season is usually the second quarter, April through June. The first quarter is less expensive than the second quarter, and the summer quarter, when viewing levels are lowest, can be bought at the year's lowest prices.

The networks' basic inventories vary not only with the time of the year, but also within the broadcast day. The frequent TV viewer knows that many more commercials are carried in daytime than in prime time. Time standards for the networks permit six commercial minutes per hour in prime time and twice that number in daytime. Late-night and weekend dayparts are separate categories. The early evening half-hour network newscasts, to give another example, usually carry five commercial minutes. These minutes represent commercial time in *network* programs and do not represent locally inserted commercials at station breaks.

Other valuable minutes are assigned to local affiliates for station identification and for locally originated commercials. The commercial time within a broadcast hour is negotiated between the network and all of its affiliates acting together as a group. Each affiliate has the same amount of time to sell during network breaks, and the stations attach a high price tag to these attractive positions.

Each of the various network dayparts offers the advertiser special advantages and opportunities. For example, prime time and the early evening network newscasts offer huge audience reach. Women are still a primary target, but prime-time shows can deliver working women and men — people who are not available in other dayparts.

Daytime TV is incredibly efficient in delivering the all-important demographic of women 18–49 years old. Soap operas and game shows are relatively inexpensive to produce, and the networks have twice as much time available for sale in daytime as they do in prime time. Even though some advertisers still buy minutes, the standard commercial length is 30 seconds. Thus, in daytime, the networks' logs might show 24 30-second commercials per hour. Advertisers have learned that daytime programs are excellent vehicles for introducing consumer products.

Late-night network programs efficiently deliver audiences composed of urban men and women. Network sports of all kinds attract men in large numbers and therefore constitute an important sales opportunity for products for which the man makes the buying decision or is the primary user.

Saturday morning children's programs deliver an almost pure demographic audience based on age. Thus, they constitute efficient buys for manufacturers of toys and certain edibles for which children have a strong voice in brand selection.

Charges to advertisers are based on the time of the year, the audience (and therefore the CPM) the network thinks it can get, the total expenditure under consideration, the "softness" of the market, and the negotiating skill of buyer and seller. Time costs on the networks have been increasing at a rate exceeding the national inflation rate for several years, reflecting a limited three-seller market. Prices, however, must be competitive and in line with what advertisers are willing and able to pay. With very few exceptions, time charges are commensurate with audience delivered and are *not* directly related to the production costs of any given program. For example, if a dramatic series that costs $800,000 per episode to produce is doing poorly in the Nielsen Television Index, the cost to the advertiser may be significantly less than the cost of a commercial position in a highly rated but fairly low-cost comedy series.

Besides regular time costs, network advertisers are also billed for *color commercial insertion charges*. These are charges for the actual physical handling of the commercial tape or film by the engineers who insert it in the programing sequence. Prime-time charges run about $500 per insertion; daytime charges are approximately half this figure. Since these amounts are gross charges per insertion, the networks pay advertising agencies a 15 percent commission.

Opportunistic Buys

Because the networks operate on a 100 percent sales philosophy, a top agency buyer will occasionally be called by a network account executive who is anxious to peddle some "distress merchandise." The program offering may be a Friday "fire sale" of weekend avails, such as a sports event or sometimes a prime-time movie. As the air date draws closer, the network may find itself with a number of unsold availabilities. Courage in the face of controversy is not a common trait among advertisers. In the face of a hard-hitting documentary on an explosive subject or a TV movie considered by some to be too violent or sexually explicit, many advertisers head for the hills. Strict

"Let's skip all the commercials tonight."

buying guidelines have been issued to ad agencies by many clients outlining what kinds of program are "acceptable." As a result, these "acceptable" programs often command premium prices. (The problems encountered by advertisers in buying controversial network programs are the subject of 11.2 at the end of this chapter.)

Eleventh-hour "relief requests" by advertisers are accepted by the networks as a matter of policy. An advertiser released from a program because of its content is obliged to reinvest those dollars in a make-good spot in another program. The networks, however, may find themselves with a number of unsold commercial positions. Prices drop dramatically as the network tries to recoup as much as it can from a losing situation. It's called an opportunistic market by the buyers. For advertisers who feel a program is acceptable or who don't care about possible criticism, these buys are a fine opportunity to reach a large network audience at a bargain rate. Many advertisers keep a reserve account available for just such situations.

Throughout the year, the advertising agency that handles network advertisers will constantly monitor the performance levels of each client's network buys. These "stewardship" reports track audience levels and demographic breakouts as reported in the bible of network buyers and sellers — the Nielsen Television Index. (The NTI was described in Chapter 10.) A dog-eared copy of the latest NTI report is always in the top desk drawer or briefcase of agency buyers and network account executives. Audience levels are scrutinized to the last percentage point.

The NTI, as the only continuing national survey of television network audiences, is tremendously important to the broadcast advertising industry. The millions of dollars that are spent as a result of advertising decisions made at the agencies and programing decisions made at the networks are predicated largely on the numbers printed in the NTI books. (See 11.1.)

Buyers keep track of ratings levels based on both households and target demographic groups in order to see if verbal cost-per-thousand guarantees will be met. If the stewardship report shows that a particular schedule is falling below estimated audience levels, the agency buyer will start requesting (then screaming for) bonus spots before the advertising campaign ends.

11.1/A Sobering Reminder

In accepting the National Association of Broadcasters' Distinguished Service Award at an NAB convention, Jack Harris, president of KPRC and KPRC-TV in Houston, issued a reminder to fellow broadcasters:

Our priorities are too often dictated by the seemingly eternal struggle for that extra rating point, translating into that extra dollar. We compete with each other, not always to offer the best service, but too often to deliver the most bodies all day every day, all night every night. We have become captivated by and enslaved in the numbers game. And, in the process, good judgment and a pursuit of excellence has been subverted. The challenge to this maturing industry is to break the shackles that bind us to the ratings game, to reach upward toward new plateaus of achievement that will make us all proud as well as profitable.

Television Digest, April 2, 1979, p. 2.

Program Sponsorships

Most network buying is on a participating, or scatter, basis, but major advertisers are sometimes interested in sponsoring specials. Sponsoring a high quality program may not only deliver large numbers of a target audience but also bring an important measure of prestige to the advertiser. Other attractive aspects of such sponsorships are the excellent merchandising and promotional opportunities possible when one advertiser enjoys close association with a well-publicized special. The advertiser also knows that the commercial messages can be "isolated" in the program and that they will not have to compete with other commercials for viewers' attention.

Specials are usually bought by advertisers who market mass consumer goods or who wish to improve their corporate image. Planning and development begin far in advance of the air date, regardless of whether the special is supplied by the network itself or by an advertising agency.

If the special is network supplied, the host or stars of the program are usually under network contract, and the entire program is developed and produced under network auspices. It's the job of the network sales department to find an advertiser or advertisers interested in a special totally packaged by the network.

If the special is supplied by the advertising agency for its client, negotiations may begin a year before the air date. All three networks may be approached. Specials are usually scheduled just preceding or during an advertiser's peak sales period. Since it is increasingly difficult to negotiate a good time period, particularly in either the second or fourth quarter, the special had better be a blockbuster. The advertiser has to be prepared to pay a premium in order to place the special, because the network will not preempt regular programing (and advertisers) unless it is sure the special will more than make up the loss of revenue.

The number of requirements for a network special or miniseries and the details that must be attended to are mind boggling. To acquire scripts, talent, studio facilities, and personnel for the production of top network specials takes months of organized effort. Costs for time and production can run anywhere from $500,000 for a news documentary to $2 million or more for an entertainment special. (Specials are rarely sold on a CPM basis; as J. P. Morgan once said, "If you have to ask the price of a yacht, you can't afford it.") Promotion and merchandising are additional costs. For the client, the special must fit the marketing strategy and be a "merchandisable" program. Huge promotion campaigns are always prepared to publicize the special to dealers, retailers, and the viewing public. The agency may turn out dozens of different merchandising aids, point-of-purchase materials, shelf talkers, and so on. The development of both the program and the promotion requires a tremendous coordinating job.

The advertising agency normally does not handle the actual production of a television special but usually negotiates with an experienced independent producer who has a long and reliable track record. It's to the advertiser's advantage to buy this kind of special, versus one produced by the network, because program content can be controlled through script approval and talent selection. Some advertisers are wary of news documentary sponsorships produced solely by a network, because the subjects are frequently controversial. They are afraid that, if such a program is heavily criticized, they will also receive a share of the brickbats.

Affiliates are usually pleased with a strong lineup of network specials. They can often stimulate advertising activity from a local retailer who stocks the product advertised on such a special. Because the programs are always heavily promoted, they are almost always good audience builders.

Affiliate Compensation

Time costs on the networks always seem astronomical to the uninitiated, but the networks are huge enterprises that must support major facilities (offices, studios, and equipment) and meet an enormous payroll. In addition, 15 percent of all time sales goes to the advertising agency as the standard commission. The network affiliates must also be paid. Each year, according to Federal Communications Commission figures, about 10 percent of the total revenue from network time sales is disbursed to affiliates as payment for carrying network programs. The percentage has declined over the years; in the early 1960s the figure was approximately 25 percent.[3]

The three television networks have approximately 200 to 250 affiliates apiece, spread across 50 states in both large and small markets. Obviously, a station in New York is not in the same league as an affiliate in Billings, Montana; thus, the networks negotiate a network hourly rate with each affiliate. This rate is based on a number of factors: the size of the market, the total circulation of the station, and performance levels of network programs on that station, the quality of the local programing, the station's image in the community, and last but not by any means least, the competition in that market. The broadcast day is divided into a number of time classifications, and the station is paid a sliding percentage of the standard hourly rate for carrying network programs. The affiliate is paid more for carrying prime-time programs than for daytime fare. In recent years, as the costs of TV rights for sports events have increased, the networks have not compensated affiliates for carrying these events. Instead, the affiliate must rely on the income from local spots sold in and around the events.

The FCC requires that network-affiliate contracts be negotiated every two years, but negotiations frequently take place more often than that. The competitive challenge of other TV stations in a market greatly affects network-affiliate relationships. In a three-station market, a network usually has no choice but to stay with its current affiliate. In a four-station market, however, the presence of a hungry independent seeking network affiliation will keep the other stations on their toes and detract from the leverage they have in negotiating remuneration levels. In contrast, if there are only two stations in a market, or only two VHF stations, the network that wants to keep an important affiliate may find it must raise its payments.

Affiliates send monthly reports to the network detailing every network program and commercial carried. If programs are preempted for some reason and commercials are not aired, payments are adjusted accordingly. The networks keep their affiliates constantly apprised of what commercials will be aired in which programs so that the stations can give both network and local advertisers competitive clearance (or "product protection.") A network automotive advertiser, for example, doesn't appre-

---

[3]*Television/Radio Age,* February 4, 1974, p. 22.

ciate having a commercial followed at the station break with a spot for a local car dealer selling a competitor's model. Unfortunately, this does happen, and too often it goes unreported to the network.

Program clearances by affiliates, particularly ones in major markets, are crucial to the network's economic survival. Every nonclearance reduces the audience potential for a show, and this may force the network to reduce its selling price for advertising on that particular program. Sometimes, stations refuse clearance of new shows they consider weak, and this action may doom the show from the start. Clearances have also been a problem on controversial programs that the affiliates thought included too much sex and violence. (See 11.2 at end of chapter.) On a number of occasions, affiliates have refused to clear network movies and instead have run a local movie or syndicated program. The audience may be just as large as it would be for the network program, and it is obviously more profitable to the station to sell all, and not just some, of the commercial positions within that time period.

Another problem that plagues the networks is called *clipping,* wherein a greedy local station cuts away from the network a few precious seconds early so that it can squeeze in an extra commercial. Sometimes, only closing credits are lost on a network show, but sometimes portions of network commercials are not aired locally, or the opening billboard to the following network program is missed. Solutions to these problems lie with network-affiliate negotiations and good communications. Potential violations of FCC rules on clipping are discussed in Chapter 17.

Cable Networks

When Satcom 1 was launched in 1975, the skies were opened for the development of the cable networks. Home Box Office, a subsidiary of Time, Inc., was first on the "bird." Other services, both subscriber-supported and advertiser-supported, quickly followed, all hoping to capture large audiences through the medium of cable. Major cash-rich corporations and some ambitious entrepreneurs, such as the flamboyant Ted Turner, announced new networks and rushed to make them operational. By uplinking programing to a satellite transponder, these networks could supply thousands of individual cable companies spread across the country.

Cable networks fall into two categories: pay TV services such as HBO and Showtime, primarily showing movies, and advertiser-supported services such as the Cable News Network, the USA Network, ESPN, and dozens of others. These specialized networks carry everything from cultural programing, health news, and religious programs to services for specific audiences such as children and Hispanics.

Despite their small, fragmented audiences, the cable networks did not escape the notice of Madison Avenue. All the major agencies now have units that are accumulating information and expertise in the various new technologies, cable in particular. Clients have asked their agencies to provide advice on how best to use cable advertising, and many have made significant investments. Bristol-Myers, Procter & Gamble, Colgate-Palmolive, Datsun, Campbell Soup, American Cyanamid, Levi-Strauss, Anheuser-Busch, and many other major national advertisers have signed on the dotted line. They consider the money spent an investment in the future — an effort to get into cable from its start and stake out a measure of exclusivity. These clients are particularly interested in sponsorships that closely align the advertiser and the program. Creative input in program development is common, and the final product is perfectly tailored to the target audience a particular advertiser wants to reach. For example, in producing a cable network program entitled *Better Homes & Gardens Idea Notebook,* the Sherwin-Williams Company joined with the magazine of the same name to produce a five-day-a-week series of special interest to women.

Cable offers a video option to those advertisers who cannot afford the high costs of the big three networks. In addition, the "superstations" such as WTBS-TV in Atlanta and WGN-TV in Chicago, which are fed to cable systems around the country via satellite links, provide a way to reach national audiences. Superstations, invariably independent, are an attractive buy for advertisers with limited budgets or for larger advertisers who want to augment buys in conventional TV.

Some advertisers have developed barter shows to offer to a cable network. Such a program is designed as an ideal vehicle for the sponsor's message and is provided free to the network. In turn, the network can sell some remaining commercial positions to noncompeting advertisers. Advertiser or barter syndication is described in greater detail in Chapter 12. In most cases, the frustrations of a clutter of competitive commercials are not present in the cable networks when an advertiser negotiates exclusivity in sponsored blocks of programing.

What else makes the cable networks attractive to advertisers? With dozens of networks available, specialized programs attract distinct target audiences. Therefore, unlike conventional TV, the cable audience has less "waste circulation." Although reach is limited, cable networks build frequency, and for many advertisers that constitutes an ideal time buy. Audiences to the cable networks tend to be "upscale," and research has proved that cable households watch TV more than noncable homes. Cable audiences are small, and therefore CPMs tend to be high, but this is not considered a major problem. As cable expands, CPM will undoubtedly become a more important buying consideration, but for now the cable networks are not, or should not be, bought on a CPM basis. The sponsor buys the programing environment — whether it be 24-hour news, sports, cultural programing, or whatever — and does so at a relatively low price. Cable costs are closer to those of radio than to those of TV, and the various networks encourage advertising agencies to include cable in their early media planning. It simply doesn't cost that much more to buy cable, and the results for certain advertisers have been impressive. Some of the most successful commercials have been those of direct response advertisers. Selling everything from magazine subscriptions to kitchen knives, these advertisers often use a toll-free telephone number to accept on-the-spot orders. They don't care about CPMs — they only care about ringing telephones. (Direct response advertising campaigns are discussed in greater detail in Chapter 14.)

The flexibility of cable is very attractive for certain kinds of advertisers. Standard 30-second TV commercials are often used, but advertisers can also buy 60-, 90-, and 120-second lengths. "Infomercial" is the label for longer commercials that enable an advertiser to present an expanded sales pitch. If ad agencies plan for the use of longer commercials when they shoot regular ones, production costs for cable can be kept quite low. A standard 30-second commercial can easily be turned into a direct response advertisement with the addition of a toll-free telephone number or a mailing address.

Cable networks are also useful to advertisers in testing campaigns or copy themes, because of the low time costs. Such campaigns may later be expanded and placed on the conventional television networks.

Every cable network seeks to carve out a unique position by programing news, sports, performing arts, ethnic programs, children's shows, women's programing, music, or other forms of entertainment. In addition to the dozens of advertiser-supported networks, many pay-TV networks are also competing for attention. Not all these cable networks, whether subscriber- or advertiser-supported, will survive. How many cable networks will find sufficient support to stay in business is anyone's guess. The experts certainly don't agree.

If the cable networks are so attractive, why haven't advertisers deserted the high-cost major networks? The answers are quite obvious. Cable penetration is still fairly low, particularly in the top 25 markets, which are of great importance to national advertisers. Coverage is a patchwork. One area may be fully covered by cable, and an adjoining area may have no cable service whatever. Audiences are small, and with dozens of channels available, measurement of cable viewers is difficult and often unreliable. Advertisers who traditionally buy on a CPM basis, seeking the largest possible audience at the lowest possible price, are not conditioned to evaluate cable on its own terms. But as cable penetration grows in the coming decades and as some of the problems mentioned above are eventually resolved, the cable networks will offer important options for a wide variety of advertisers.

Conclusions

The United States is one of a relatively few countries serviced by very large, corporate-owned commercial broadcasting networks. Stations, not the networks, are licensed by the government. Because Americans spend so much time and attach so much importance to their use of the broadcast media, the business of buying and selling network time is a truly fascinating enterprise. The nation's advertisers, big and small, have gladly paid the bill. They know that only the networks can deliver national audiences in large numbers on a consistent daily basis. The buys are relatively simple to negotiate, and the advertisers' commercials are aired simultaneously on hundreds of affiliates to an audience that may number in the millions. Costs are reasonable in terms of audience delivered, and this efficiency constitutes one of the networks' greatest attractions to the national advertiser. The impact of a commercial schedule launched on a network basis is often dramatic. A successful one in terms of subsequent sales may mean that the advertiser will regain the cost of a network advertising investment many times over.

Until recent years, buying network time was confined to a handful of major radio and television lineups. That is no longer the case, because both radio and cable networks have proliferated. In radio, the traditional line networks must now compete with unwired, or rep, networks sold on a tailor-made basis by station representative firms. In addition, ad hoc and regional networks can be organized fairly easily to offer listeners and advertisers attractive programing. The increase in the number of radio stations has encouraged new networks, and so have satellite interconnections, which are less expensive than AT&T circuits.

The numerous cable networks have captured the fancy of many advertisers interested in specific target audiences. The costs are low, and there is great flexibility in buying programs and commercial schedules. Those clients that have invested in cable hope to be in on the ground floor of an exciting new communications industry.

Some advertisers invest virtually their entire budget in broadcast advertising, with most of the money ear-marked for network buys—whether radio, TV, or cable. It must be remembered, that, although a network buy may appear relatively simple to make, the success (or failure) of advertisers, agencies, and—most importantly—people involved in buying and selling network time rides on almost every buy.

11.2 / A Difference of Opinion

Advertisers who make television network buys often face a dilemma. On the one hand, operating in a marketplace that is often brutally competitive, they feel that it is crucial to maximize the effectiveness of their advertising dollars. Prime-time network buys in widely viewed programs are extremely important. On the other hand, complaints about sex, violence, and profanity in programing have increased in recent years. Programs that are considered objectionable by some are often winners in the ratings and attract prime demographics—that is, young adults. Many advertisers are concerned about their association with this kind of programing. Critics of every stripe have voiced their protests and gained considerable attention.

Feeling that the networks were ignoring their complaints, several organizations have focused their attention on major network advertisers. By monitoring television and identifying sponsors of what they consider to be objectionable programs, these groups have used the threat of organized consumer boycotts of these sponsors' products. Various opinion leaders and broadcast and advertising executives are quoted below from trade publications and the public press, both print and broadcast. Their views on this subject are strong and diverse. In the years to come, the cast of characters will undoubtedly change, but it is unlikely that the controversy will go away. Readers are invited to draw their own conclusions.

The Reverend Jerry Falwell, Moral Majority: The people own the airwaves. Don't ever let anyone tell you that there's a knob on there, that you can turn it on or off. You should not have to turn it on or off, you own the airwaves. Let the networks do the turning on the other end before they dump the garbage in your living room. They have the responsibility. So, here we are today, year after year, becoming a little more permissive than the year before, dumping four-letter words, and suggestive and risqué settings right into your home, until television has virtually become unfit for human consumption.

The Reverend Donald Wildmon, Coalition for Better Television: If it sells products, it sells values, ideas, morals, motives, attitudes. It sells everything, and it does, and it can't keep from it, by its very nature. To say that violence on television doesn't affect us, you'd have to say that the sex on the television doesn't affect us or profanity on television doesn't affect us, or anything else on television doesn't affect us. It *does* affect us. The networks can show what they want to show, the advertiser can sponsor what he wants to sponsor, the viewer can view what he wants to view, and the consumer can spend his money where he wants to.

William Rusher, publisher, National Review: What is this religious right up to with respect to television? As far as I can see, they are proposing a simple economic boycott of sponsors of television programs that indulge in explicit sexual references or violence or what have you that is not to their taste. I ask you, what's wrong with that? As far as I can see, there isn't anything wrong with it.

Alfred Schneider, vice president, broadcast standards, ABC: By attempting to coerce advertisers into supporting only programs they deem "morally acceptable," these groups are trying to subvert the programing choices available for a national audience. This effort to impose their values on others through television is antithetical to the principles governing a free society. In our present system of television, the ultimate choice of a program rests with the individual viewer.

James H. Rosenfield, president, CBS-TV: Family stability, societal violence, cultural values: these are overwhelming human concerns. Yet how can these concerns be addressed by throttling freedom of expression, as some of our otherwise well-meaning censors would do? Such efforts invariably bring with them larger threats to freedom of expression, much as attempts to inhibit movies, television and, yes, even comic books, were corollaries of the incredible climate of the repression America experienced during the McCarthy era in the 1950s.

Nicholas Johnson, former FCC commissioner: I think it's time we in Washington say out loud the truth that all of us read in our mail from Americans in all walks of life: the men who are currently running commercial network television in this country are a vicious, evil influence.

Howard Cannon, former U.S. senator from Nevada: There is an ominous resurgence of book-burnings through the country and increased cries for censorship and control of the media. The daily programing decisions must be left up to you — the broadcasters, and not the government or self-appointed special interest groups.

Peggy Charren, president, Action for Children's Television: ACT doesn't think censorship and limiting options is the way to make change. We believe efforts should be aimed at what should be added, not what should be taken off. We oppose hit lists. I worry that this thing could accelerate, maybe news will be next.

Michael Ross, producer, Three's Company: I think the networks are very careful of what they are accepting for future air. I think they have been affected. That's the beginning of the terror. Because if they are truly affected, and they really are being ultra careful, we're back to *Father Knows Best, Ozzie and Harriet,* "Hello Mom, hello Dad, have a cracker."

Open letter to television writers and producers, Clean Up TV Campaign: You, of course, remain completely free to produce the most degrading of material if you choose to do so, but while new shows are still being planned you should be aware that the ultimate syndication of such material will not be financially supported by a sizeable portion of the public. Although this announcement will undoubtedly be met with a chorus of "censorship" accusations from some within the television industry, it is clear that the public is not nearly so naive as those opposing our efforts would apparently like to believe. Thoughtful people will be able to distinguish the difference between "censorship" (which involves authoritative restrictions) and the simple exercise of our basic Constitutional rights to say what we think and to decide from whom we will or will not buy products.

Dr. Everett Parker, United Church of Christ: [If the networks listened] they wouldn't be in the trouble that they are now from the threats of boycott from these fundamentalist groups. And of course, they don't know how to judge the power of the fundamentalists, because they don't know anything about religion.

Roy Danish, director, Television Information Office: Advertisers look at programs differently than broadcasters. Those who buy time have a single obligation, that is to seek suitable audiences for their commercial messages. Broadcasters have different objectives. Not only must they attempt to please large audiences much of the time, they must also offer a balanced schedule of entertainment and information. It includes programs that deal with controversial matters. It includes programs that annoy or offend some people, without being either overly violent or permissive. In other words, programs that are not expected to please everyone, but which do meet specific needs. Unlike the broadcaster, no advertiser is accountable to your community or the Federal Communications Commission for the balance and quality of a broadcast schedule.

James R. Block, general advertising manager, Kraft Retail Food Group: Kraft is not about to impose or pass judgment on the moral or social mores of our customers. We buy a lot of television, including specials and participations, as well as spot. We invest millions of dollars yearly, but we never consider ourselves censors. That is not our right as an advertiser. We merely follow our standing practice of placing our advertising in programing that is compatible with our marketing objectives, advertising standards, and commercial strategy.

Al Hagen, corporate marketing manager, Toyota Motor Sales: We feel threatened because we view this as a potential violation of freedom of speech. We feel vulnerable because we have no choice but to advertise on TV.

Owen Butler, chairman, Procter & Gamble: For sound commercial reasons, we are not going to let our advertising messages appear in an environment which we think is distasteful for many of our potential customers.

Advertising Age, editorial: P&G has a $200,000,000-plus investment in the half-dozen daytime soap operas it produces, and may have felt the need to protect that investment. The soapers are a vulnerable genre that must come under the coalition's [Coalition for Better Television's] scrutiny sooner or later, but it has, for now, given P&G's soaps a pass. With the P&G decision leaving a big hole in the ranks of advertisers who must face the assault of the crusading coalition, the feeling persists that the No. 1 advertiser was simply looking out for No. 1.

Gail Smith, director of advertising, General Motors Corporation: We [the advertisers] got in the middle of this goddamn thing, and we're innocent victims. We'll have to see what happens in this boycott area. If it fails, the organization can go belly up. If it succeeds, you've got a different horse to deal with as we look at television in the future.

chapter twelve

Spot Sales

But My Station Is a Mustbuy!

Several billion dollars are invested each year in spot advertising in radio, television, and cable TV. This huge expenditure is a tribute not only to the selling power of these media but also to their flexibility and versatility. A specific campaign can be ordered in just the markets and on just the stations important to an advertiser. For many clients, spot augments network buys to "heavy up" advertising weights in particularly important markets. Other advertisers, however, use spot as their primary buy in the broadcast media, especially if an advertised product has limited distribution. And for other advertisers, who may have achieved national distribution of their product but still operate within extremely limited budgets, a network buy may be too expensive. Thus, spot may be the best option for them.

The term *spot* does not refer to an individual commercial but to advertising schedules bought on stations in selected markets. Although spot buys are usually for commercial announcements, an advertiser will occasionally buy program sponsorships on a spot basis. A campaign may be ordered for just a few days or weeks or for several months.

Many advertisers invest in both network and spot buys, and the way they allocate their budget depends on the marketplace and the advertising opportunities available at a given moment. From the broadcasters' viewpoint, spot revenues are affected greatly by supply and demand. Investments may vary dramatically from quarter to quarter. In many cases, the sums spent on spot fluctuate accordingly with those spent on network buys. If the networks are sold out or close to it, spot will prosper, because advertisers who are unable to get what they want on the networks will move their dollars into spot. If the networks "break price," advertisers may sometimes move spot dollars to the networks to take advantage of the rate reductions. Many spot advertisers, however, are not network customers; their use of spot depends on the strategy of their particular advertising program in any one year and the geographic distribution of their products.

An advertiser headquartered in Chicago who wants to place a schedule of radio commercials in 150 markets obviously needs an efficient system for time buying. The time-buying responsibilities will be handled by the advertising agency or, possibly, by a media buying service. (Some ad agencies do not maintain fully staffed media departments, and this kind of specialized work is farmed out to the experts in an independent company who specialize in media planning and buying.)

The nation's commercial stations, which number almost 9,000, depend on their station representatives to solicit national spot business for them. Since any one station would find it impossible to maintain account executives in all the major buying centers, most stations rely on representative firms that maintain offices in these cities. Rep firms may handle a dozen or several hundred stations. It's their job to keep up-to-the-minute information on their clients' commercial availabilities, rates, audience estimates, and so on.

If an agency time buyer in Chicago wants information on a station in Phoenix, he or she need only pick up the telephone to call a rep whose office is just a block or two away. Within 24 hours, the buyer will have the information. The accompanying diagram (12.1) shows the interrelationships of the various enterprises involved in spot buying.

Spot Time Buying Procedures

There are several stages in spot time buying from the inception of a campaign until the day the commercials are last aired and all the bills are paid.

Step One. In the early stages of planning, the advertising agency's media department develops a media strategy designed to meet the client's objectives. (See Chapter 5.) With client approval, that plan will be carried out when it is time to begin the actual

12.1/Relationships in the Spot Buying Process

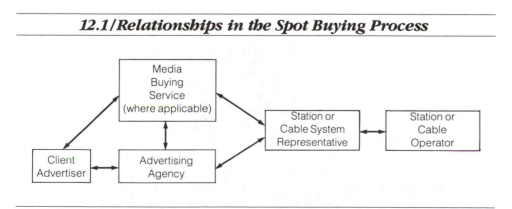

time buying. The time buyer assigned to a particular client must work with the station representatives to make the best and most efficient buys possible. The markets to be bought, the demographic objectives, and the budget are all specified.

Buys are too hectic and confusing to attempt to buy a dozen markets at once. With few exceptions, therefore, time buyers will buy the most important markets first (usually the largest) and then proceed down the list. A rep with stations in a number of different markets may have to come to the agency or media buying service several times to see the same time buyer on the same campaign. Since the rep is primarily concerned that his or her stations be included in the campaign, these occasional extra visits represent only a minor inconvenience.

Step Two. The station rep, after a telephone request from the time buyer, will put together a package of station availabilities and prices. The more the rep knows about the objectives of the campaign, the better job he or she will do in preparing avails. Avails will usually include the following data:

- programs or commercial positions available
- times and dates
- prices
- program ratings
- total households (or data on a particular demographic group)
- cost-per-thousand or cost-per-point estimates for each availability
- gross rating points
- reach and frequency estimates

Rating levels, household estimates, and demographics are based on the audience research service preferred by the agency or advertiser. (In the case of radio, Arbitron audience estimates are usually quoted; in television, data come from either Arbitron or the Nielsen Station Index.)

Step Three. The rep will usually deliver all the information to the buyer in person and discuss the options. On the same day, of course, the buyer may be discussing similar opportunities with other station reps for the market under consideration. In a four-station market, for example, the advertiser may be buying only two stations for a particular campaign. Thus, a rep's sales ability, the attractiveness of programs and prices, and the rapport established (often over many years) between buyer and seller are of great importance. It's a negotiating game, and supply and demand control the expenditure. Naturally, the time buyer will try to get the best possible buy for the advertiser, and the rep will try to "bring in the order" for client stations. Negotiations usually take place under some rather horrendous deadlines, because most spot schedules are bought just a few weeks before air dates.

With a limited budget and the pressures of a major buy, the time buyer must establish standards for evaluating all the proposals. Buyers and sellers agree that demographic and cost-efficiency estimates (cost-per-thousand or cost-per-point) constitute the major criteria. In essence, such criteria mean that the aim is to reach the target audience (defined in terms of sex and age) at the most efficient price. Clients sometimes impose spot-buying guidelines. Buyers may have instructions about minimum ratings levels for any particular commercial position, the dayparts to be bought, and the types of program to be considered. If clients are concurrently running network schedules, they may specify a time separation between their network and spot commercials. All these requirements complicate spot buying.

Another criterion for making buying decisions is a TV program's environment (in the case of radio, the programing format of the station). Some advertisers are very particular about the qualitative aspects of the programs in which their commercials appear. A bank, for example, may not want to run commercials in, or adjacent to, some of the more raucous game shows. Other advertisers have instructed their agencies to reject certain programs considered to be too violent or sexually suggestive.

All buyers are well aware that the television viewer selects the program and that the radio listener selects the station. Because of the vast proliferation of radio programing formats, the buyer needs to know the specific programing policy of the station under consideration. The demographic makeup of that station's audience reflects its programing policy. Stations that constantly change formats build and destroy audiences, and for this reason, many radio time buyers are interested in long-term ratings as part of their buying criteria. In a large, very competitive market, the audience pie is sliced a bit differently every time a station changes format. Information provided by the reps is invaluable, because the common handicap of all spot buyers in most cases is that they cannot see or hear what they are buying.

Still another basis for spot buying is estimated *gross rating points* (GRP). For example, a client may plan a spot schedule that is expected to achieve 200 GRP in the top 50 markets and 100 GRP in the second 50 markets. Average quarter-hour ratings are used, and the ratings for each commercial position are added up. A gross rating point represents 1 percent of all the television (or radio) households in a given geographic area. Four well-placed prime-time TV positions that achieve a 25 percent rating each will add up to a weekly GRP of 100; or 20 positions that deliver a rating of 5 percent will also attain 100 GRP. The figures represent varying amounts of duplicated audience, for no advertiser can hope to reach every household in a market in one week, regardless of the number of commercials run. Estimates of gross rating points have no connection to costs but simply indicate the impact a schedule may have on a market during a one-week period.

Time buyers always try to obtain the best possible schedule at the lowest possible price. Spot buying is like network buying in that supply and demand greatly affect the prices. Selling "off the rate card" is common in spot buying, and buyers frequently ask station reps to "break price" for their clients. If business is booming and a station is practically sold out, the rep would not consider asking a station to cut its rates. When the market is "soft," stations will sometimes offer a client "bonus" spots that are free if a certain minimum number of commercials are ordered. Running free spots rather than cutting prices is considered a dodge by some people. For many stations, however, spot business makes the difference between red and black ink on the financial statement, and they are willing to make deals off the rate card in order to bring in extra business.

Spot buying in cable TV is in its infancy, but a promising future is suggested. Until cable expands to achieve adequate penetration of households on a national basis, spot activity will be limited.

The obstacle of patchy geographic coverage can be overcome to some extent by advertisers who buy cable on an *interconnected* basis. Eastman Cable Rep, the largest cable rep firm, has developed a marketing plan for the cable systems it represents that allows an advertiser to buy a specific area through an interconnection of local cable systems. The programing may be regional spots, for example, or one of the national cable networks. In the latter case, the networks allocate some commercial positions for sale by local cable operators so that commercials from spot and local advertisers can be inserted. Spot buys on cable TV are not based on the nitty-gritty details of ratings and CPMs but rather on programing environment, the number of subscribers to each cable system, and a total negotiated price.

Step Four. When a representative gets an order from a time buyer, he or she will usually telephone or teletype the station (or cable system) to ask for a confirmation. (If an order is not placed, the time buyer should provide a courteous explanation that can be relayed to the station.) Inventory control at the station level is crucial for broadcasters who hope to reap profits in national spot business. The station must keep careful track of what is currently available for sale and what will soon be available for sale (following advertisers' expiration dates). The station must also supply these data on a continuing basis to the national representative. The same availabilities offered to an agency time buyer in New York may be concurrently offered to other agency buyers in major cities around the country and also to local advertisers in the broadcaster's hometown. "Avails" are sold on a first-come, first-served basis.

As soon as the station receives an order from its representative firm, the inventory will be checked and a confirmation sent to the rep. If all times ordered are still available, everything is rosy. If not, the station will identify which positions are already sold and offer alternatives.

Step Five. The time buyer receives an order confirmation from the station representative. If substitutions must be offered, they can usually be negotiated very quickly, for the time buyer is anxious to move on to other markets and stations on the list. The station rep issues a written confirmation of the final order and sends a copy to the station.

Step Six. The agency's traffic department is notified immediately after a buy is confirmed and told the starting date and the length of time that commercials will run on each station. It's the job of this department to handle the shipment of the commercials (films or tapes) to each station, along with explicit instructions for rotating them.

Step Seven. During the course of an advertising campaign, the agency is billed on a monthly basis by the stations. Station accounting departments prepare the billing and forward invoices and notarized affidavits of performance to the agency. The affidavit enumerates every commercial run for a particular client during the past month. "Final Sunday Billing" was inaugurated some years ago to handle the problem of the last day of the month's falling in the middle of the week. Most time buys are made weekly, not monthly, and it is infinitely easier to handle billing on a Monday-through-Sunday basis. Stations now submit their invoices through the final Sunday of any given month. If commercials are run after that Sunday, they are included in the next month's billing.

Step Eight. When the accounting department at the agency receives the station invoice and affidavit, it will check it against what the time buyer ordered. If everything agrees, the bill should be promptly paid. The standard 15 percent agency commission is reflected in the billing. For example, if a TV station has run $10,000 worth of time for a given advertiser, the advertising agency commission of $1,500 will be shown on the bill. The agency pays the station $8,500 and bills its client $10,000.

The times, dates, or actual schedule on the affidavit may not always coincide with the times ordered by the buyer. In such cases, the result is the most vexing, time-consuming and complained-about problem in spot business. The accounting department sends the bill to the time buyer, who by now is busy with something new. The time buyer must decipher the problem, notify the station rep, and ask for an explanation. By the time the station rep secures an explanation from the station and relays it to the time buyer, more time has passed. The buyer may or may not accept make-good commercials run at times other than the ones ordered. Commercials may have been preempted, or the rates on the invoice may not be correct. Commercials may not have been aired in compliance with the rotation schedule. Resolving all of these problems takes time, and all the while the station is wondering when it will be paid. Buyers and sellers of time all agree that paperwork is the number one problem in the industry, and station business managers sing the "slow-pay" blues in unison. Billing problems are more prevalent in TV than in radio, because in television, specific times rather than general time blocks are usually ordered. The consolation to the station, of course, is that there is little direct sales cost in bringing in spot business — just the commission to the rep firm.

Commissions to station representatives obviously come from their client stations, and they are based on a percentage of the gross after the 15 percent advertising agency commission has been deducted. Radio reps generally earn 15 percent. The following example shows how commissions work in a typical radio spot buy.

4-week schedule on Station A for Client X:	$4,000
Less 15% ad agency commission:	600
	3,400
Less 15% station rep commission:	510
	$2,890 net to station

Commissions for television reps vary, but they are commonly between 5 percent and 10 percent. The TV percentage is lower because of the high dollar volume involved in the buys.

Radio Rate Cards

The rate cards published by radio stations across the country are as diverse as the stations themselves. In New York City, a top-rated station may charge $500 for a 60-second announcement. A small station in Wyoming may charge only $10. Although the rates vary tremendously, the pricing and discounting structures used to determine them are based on two premises: (1) in general, prices are established in relation to audience delivered, and (2) the more the advertiser buys, the less it costs per unit.

In establishing prices, a radio station manager must first determine the various rate card time classifications, generally on the basis of the station's audience size throughout the day. For most stations, but not all, commute hours (or drive times) are prime time and often designated as AAAA or AAA time. The next lower classifications are usually the daytime hours, followed by evening hours, and finally the graveyard period, midnight to dawn. (Some stations, particularly contemporary and rock stations, reverse these time classifications, because estimates show their largest audiences tuning in during the afternoon and evening hours.)

The ideal rate card is easy to read and is structured in a logical progression, such as by time classification, including the range of discounts. Different advertisers obviously have different objectives, and the intelligently planned radio rate card provides flexibility for these different needs. Some advertisers are interested in long-term campaigns that will continuously maintain consumer awareness. Other advertisers buy short flights to publicize a special sale. Certain advertisers seek a male audience or want to reach housewives or teenagers. If a rate card offers all these opportunities, it makes the selling job much easier for the national rep or the station account executive.

A great variety of discounts is available on rate cards. The most common are weekly discounts, with descending prices based on the number of commercials bought each week. Other discounts, offered for long-term advertisers, are often called consecutive week discounts. For big spenders, some stations offer a *bulk,* or *volume, discount* based on annual expenditures. For advertisers on limited budgets, *best-times-available* (BTA) or *run-of-station* (ROS) packages are usually available. In BTA or

---

12.2 / Sample Radio Rate Card — Hometown Radio, U.S.A.

Time Classifications		:60	:30
AAAA	6:00–10:00 A.M. Monday thru Saturday	$84	$64
AAA	3:00–7:00 P.M. Monday thru Saturday	75	60
AA	10:00 A.M.–3:00 P.M. Monday thru Saturday	65	52
A	7:00 P.M.–midnight Monday thru Saturday, all day Sunday	55	44

Total Audience Plan (TAP) #1	Total Audience Plan (TAP) #2	
1/3 AAAA	1/4 AAAA	1/4 AAA
1/3 AAA	1/4 AA	1/4 A
1/3 AA		

Weekly	:60	:30	Weekly	:60	:30
6X	$72	$58	6X	$63	$50
12X	65	52	12X	58	45
18X	63	50	18X	56	43
24X	61	48	24X	54	41

For fixed position in any time classification, add 15%.

Yearly Run-of-Station Bulk Rates (run at any time on a best-time-available basis)

	:60	:30
500 per year	$31	$25
1,000 per year	28	21

ROS buys, the station sells positions at a lower rate but does not guarantee the time of day the spots will run. (For a glossary of rate card terminology, see 12.4 at the end of this chapter.)

Because so many advertisers want their commercials run in drive times and in daytime periods in the latter part of the week, many radio stations offer a *total audience plan* (TAP). (See 12.2.) The TAP discounts are attractive, but the advertiser must agree to have commercials run throughout the broadcast day and across the days of the week. The station decides where each announcement will run within the time blocks ordered. Advertisers are told that a TAP will improve their reach, which is valid enough, but it also frees a number of commercial positions on a station's log and thus permits more time to be sold throughout the week.

In many markets, especially larger markets, it is increasingly common for stations to adopt a price *grid*. For any particular daypart there may be half a dozen different prices—Grid I, Grid II, and so on. (See 12.3.) Depending on the supply and demand on a particular station, an advertiser may buy higher or lower on the grid. Some stations will sell lower on the grid with the understanding that those commercial positions can be preempted by another advertiser who pays the higher rate. In the fourth quarter, at Christmas time, advertisers usually must buy near the top of the grid in order to get a schedule on the air. Grids reflect the acceptance of both buyer and seller that schedules must be negotiated. Stations always try to sell as high on the grid as possible and still get the business. Sometimes, commercials are sold at the preemptible rate, but advertisers are given a verbal guarantee that their announcements will not be preempted. These matters are always at the station's discretion.

Radio stations offer both 30-second and 60-second rates, and many also carry 10-second commercials on a "rates-on-request" basis. Commercial time standards vary from station to station, but virtually every station in the country abides by a policy of not exceeding 18 commercial minutes per hour. This standard was established years ago by the Radio Code of the National Association of Broadcasters, although today

---

12.3/Sample Radio Rate Card—Radio Megalopolis, U.S.A.

Time Classifications

(Monday thru Sunday)
AA   10:00 A.M.–3:00 P.M.
A   3:00 P.M.–midnight
B   5:00–10:00 A.M.

Rates for 60/30 Second Announcements

	Grid I	Grid II	Grid III	Grid IV	Grid V
Class AA	300/240	280/224	260/208	240/192	220/176
Class A	250/200	230/184	210/168	190/152	170/136
Class B	200/160	180/144	160/128	140/112	120/96

Consecutive Week Discounts: 13 weeks 5%   26 weeks 7-1/2%

these Code standards are no longer in formal effect. To reduce clutter, many stations are now limiting commercial time to 8, 10, or 12 minutes per hour, and both advertisers and listeners have been pleased.

Television Rate Cards

Years ago, television rate cards seemed hopelessly complicated. Various dayparts, grids, discounts, and the like ran for pages. Nowadays, the unnecessary complications have been phased out. Most TV stations issue a simple card with a single price for each commercial position available. These cards are revised constantly, often every week. There are two basic reasons why the industry changed to simplified pricing. First, audience ratings from Arbitron and Nielsen are issued much more frequently than in the past. Because rates are based on the audience delivered, a new rating book means a new rate card. Second, the industry has accepted the fact that TV buys are the result of *negotiation*. It is not uncommon, and also widely accepted, that two commercials that run back to back may be billed at different rates. There are a number of factors that account for this difference:

1. the supply and demand on a particular station and in a particular market. Stations must price themselves against competing stations, by their own status in the rating books, and in accordance with demand for that particular time of year. Fourth-quarter rates are always the highest of the year, even though the first quarter historically reflects the heaviest viewing levels.

2. the time when the buy was made. Stations discount commercial positions as the air date draws near.

3. the volume of the buy. A buyer who is responsible for a large expenditure from a major client over the course of a long campaign should be able to negotiate a better deal than a small-budget client buying on a one-time-only basis.

4. the skill of the buyer. Experienced buyers know the television marketplace. They are totally conversant with audience research and are familiar with the stations and markets they buy. After making hundreds of buys for all kinds of clients, each with different goals and budgets, they know what kind of negotiations to pursue. Their job is to bring in the best possible schedule at the lowest possible price.

One of the fascinating aspects of time buying is the analysis of audience behavior. Television absorbs the greatest portion of Americans' leisure time, and buyers must be knowledgeable in the way in which audiences *use* the medium and know when their target audience is viewing in maximum numbers. The households-using-television (HUT) level may be 10 percent at 8:00 A.M. and 60 percent at 8:00 P.M. Viewers may desert a station in droves at the conclusion of a popular program, and the rating book may reflect a real see-saw pattern through the day. Even in prime time, a station's rating may increase or decrease dramatically from one hour to the next. A blockbuster special on a competing network may reduce a program's rating by 30 or 40 percent. The growth of cable TV promises viewers greater options that will inevitably eat away at the networks' share of the total audience. Pay TV, offering uncut, uninterrupted movies, has been shown to have a significant impact on commercial television's prime-time audience levels.

Some TV stations offer opportunities for clients to save a few dollars with time buys bought on a *fixed, semifixed,* or *preemptible* rate. The lower rates are available to advertisers who have limited dollars to spend and who are willing to risk being preempted by a higher-rate advertiser. Depending on the specifications in the station's rate card, these lower-rate advertisers may be preempted on two weeks' notice, one week's notice, or no notice at all. The station will obviously do its best to reschedule this advertiser in other time periods. Although this buying procedure may be satisfactory for local advertisers who can't afford fixed time rates, national spot advertisers usually do not want schedules subject to preemption. As a result, time buyers try to get fixed times at preemptible rates.

Because individual pricing units are increasingly used in TV rate cards, discounts are not as extensive as they are in radio. Many stations, however, will offer a dollar volume discount for major advertisers spending a significant sum over a one-year period. Others will offer a discount to short-term heavy advertisers who buy, for example, at least 25 announcements per week. Some rate cards contain a discounted package offering.

The term *rotations* (or orbits) is common on TV rate cards, and it refers to a scheduling system that distributes an advertiser's commercials on either a horizontal or vertical basis. A *horizontal rotation* is common in stripped programs, meaning the same program scheduled on a Monday-through-Friday basis, such as soap operas, game shows, and afternoon movies. In a horizontal rotation, the advertiser's commercials are rotated in the same program across the days of the week. A *vertical rotation* places the advertiser's commercials in a time block of programs. For example, one day the commercial may be run at 10:00 A.M., the next day at 10:30 A.M., and the following day at 11:00 A.M. The reason for these rotations in TV is the same as the reason for the total audience plans in radio: they increase advertiser reach and open up more availabilities for the station to sell.

Roadblocking merits attention as a time-buying tactic used to launch a new product or introduce a new campaign. The time buyer negotiates the purchase of a commercial position in the same station break on all three network affiliates in a given market. Independent stations may also be included. For example, Coca-Cola may buy 9:00 P.M., when the HUT level is at or near its maximum. Only viewers who have retreated to the kitchen will escape the message. Roadblocking builds tremendous reach in a very short period of time, and the strategy is obviously employed by advertisers with a significant budget, working far in advance of the air date. It should be remembered that the viewers at home are not necessarily the only target audience the advertiser has in mind. Advertisers compete in all the media and also in retail outlets. An important secondary audience may include retailers and sales representatives. The goal is a "share of mind" and merchandising support at the point of purchase. Advertisers often publish and distribute their TV schedule to this "secondary audience" in order to make a positive impression and prove the company's advertising commitment.

The 30-second commercial is the standard in TV. Occasionally, 10-second and 60-second units are sold. Since 60-second commercials cost twice the 30-second rate, there are few spot advertisers who buy them. These longer messages are more often seen on network TV, where a major company may wish to present a corporate-image commercial.

Barter and Tradeouts

"To trade by exchange of commodities rather than by the use of money," is the way one dictionary defines *barter*. Bartering broadcast time for goods and services has been a common practice for decades. In recent years, barter activity has become big business.

Almost every radio and television station in the country has been involved in a barter or tradeout arrangement at one time or another. Few stations are ever completely sold out, and their unsold time represents a loss never to be recovered. Because it would infuriate their regular full-rate advertisers, broadcasters are reluctant to unload unsold time at greatly discounted prices. They are, however, willing to trade it for goods and services.

Tradeouts are made at the local level between station management and local businesses. When the station manager needs new office furniture, when the news department needs a remote truck, or the sales department must entertain a multitude of clients, tradeouts can be arranged. In return for merchandise or due-bills, the station will run a certain number of commercials. The number will obviously be negotiated, but in most cases the retailer will not be exchanging merchandise for the card rate value of the commercials. The cost of new furnishings for the station lobby may be $5,000, and the card rate value of time traded to a local furniture store may be $8,000. In most instances, tradeout commercials are arranged on a best-time-available (or run-of-station) basis. Tradeouts usually do not include production costs.

In some instances, however, particularly with top-rated stations, tradeouts may be arranged in which the time is not discounted. A refrigerator for the station's employees' lounge may be traded for time valued at no less than the retail price of the refrigerator. Additionally, the deal may specify that the commercials run in designated time periods, not on a best-times-available basis.

Barters usually take place at the national level and are a bit more complicated than a local tradeout deal because of the presence of a middleman. There are a number of barter houses, and one of the largest and best known is the William B. Tanner Co. of Memphis. Its catalogue is distributed widely to both print and broadcast media management. Barters usually involve "big-ticket" items—automobiles, major vacation trips, and the like. The salesperson representing the barter house negotiates with the station for what is needed. It may be prizes for a promotional contest or premiums for the station sales staff to use as giveaways. A rock station, for example, may want to secure a half-dozen motorcycles as contest prizes. The value of the time is always discounted; an automobile may be worth $12,000, and the value of the bartered time as shown on the rate card could be two or three times that sum.

In most instances, the barter house negotiates for a certain number of commercials. (If a barter were based on a total price, a station might raise its rates and dramatically reduce the number of commercials owed to the barter house.) Expiration dates are usually indicated in a barter deal, and a station may impose restrictions on the kinds of advertisers it will accept. Prosperous, top-rated stations commonly will not engage in barter deals.

Once a barter arrangement is negotiated, the barter house will peddle the time to whoever wants it. Large national advertisers often avoid these opportunities, because the barter commercials are occasionally in poor time periods and are constantly preempted. The bargain simply isn't worth it if the national advertiser is trying to coordinate a major multimedia promotion. Sometimes, however, advertisers can arrange excellent schedules that will not be preempted.

It is difficult to estimate the volume of barter business conducted each year in the broadcasting industry, but a safe guess is that it runs into the tens of millions of dollars. It is an opportunity market for all concerned.

Advertiser, or Barter, Syndication

A special form of barter has become increasingly popular in television—barter syndication. The station trades time for a *program* rather than for goods and services. The advantages to the advertiser of such an arrangement are:

1. The advertiser can develop a program that is tailored to the interests of a target audience, and the proper programing environment can provide an excellent show-case for the sponsor's message.

2. The costs of such a program are invariably less than those of full sponsorship of a network TV series.

3. Because of lower costs, the advertiser can stretch a budget to build frequency and high sponsorship identification among a target audience.

4. The series is syndicated on a spot basis in just the markets of prime importance to the advertiser.

5. Good time periods can be negotiated with stations or cable systems interested in carrying such a series.

6. Large corporate manufacturers can advertise many different products in the commercial positions within the series.

7. With high identification between the sponsor and the program, the series can be merchandised to dealers, retailers, and the public.

For the station that accepts a barter syndication series, there are two major advantages:

1. A time period is filled at no charge, and the station does not have to produce programing or buy regularly syndicated programing.

2. Several of the commercial positions in the program are "given back" to the station and can be sold to noncompetitive national or local advertisers.

Barter syndication is not without its problems for both advertisers and stations. Some of the disadvantages are:

1. Production costs must be kept in line, or all the savings can be quickly lost.

2. Negotiating a good time slot on an important station in a major market is not always easy, and major market clearances are the whole idea behind barter shows.

3. Although some programs have been widely syndicated, most can probably expect to reach no more than 60 percent to 70 percent of U.S. households, compared with network television's penetration of well over 90 percent.

4. In general, barter programs do not achieve the ratings a network program can expect. An average TV household rating between 10 percent and 15 percent is considered typical. A station may eschew the risk and instead pay the premium price for a guaranteed winner such as a syndicated sitcom that enjoyed a long network run.

5. A barter program that performs poorly is more difficult to cancel than one purchased outright in ordinary syndication. The distributor of a bartered program may beg for a few more weeks, hoping that the show will catch on. Options are reduced for the station that is locked into a commitment.

6. There's plenty of competition from other program producers also trying to obtain one of the relatively few good time periods available on top stations.

7. Time periods and day of broadcast often vary from market to market, complicating the business of merchandising the program.

8. "Bicycling" of programs (the shipment of films or tapes from station to station) can pose problems in timing and in the coordination of promotion campaigns for a series. (The wave of the future will eliminate this problem with satellite distribution of syndicated programs for both radio and TV.)

These disadvantages have not discouraged advertisers from entering the barter programing business. In fact, barter has grown significantly. In 1976, only 10 percent of the top 100 advertisers were engaged in barter programing, but by 1981 the figure had grown to 60 percent.[1]

When the Federal Communications Commission adopted the Prime Time Access Rule, effective in 1971, the net effect was a tremendous boost to barter syndication. The three commercial TV networks were required to cut back their programing in prime-time hours from three-and-a-half to three hours. The FCC's purpose in adopting this rule was to encourage programing diversification and to provide both local-station and independent producers the opportunity to create new programs that might better serve the public. The rule was less than a total success. Stations looked around for low-cost and high-profit shows to fill the 7:30–8:00 P.M. time period (one hour earlier in the Central time zone).

On a barter basis, game shows, wild-animal series, and a variety of other entertainment programs were launched. Some of the most popular (not necessarily shown in the prime-time access period) have been *Hee Haw, Donahue, John Davidson, Sha Na Na, Wild Kingdom, In Search Of,* and *Hollywood Squares*. Many of these series are owned by advertisers and provided to stations on a barter syndication basis.

Time banking is a variation on the traditional barter syndication. An advertiser,

---

[1]*Broadcasting*, September 14, 1981, p. 9.

through its agency, provides a program to stations in exchange for a dollar amount of advertising that is credited to the advertiser's "account." At some time in the future, the advertiser can use this accumulated time. In most cases, an advertising agency will handle arrangements. The "credits" accumulate in the agency's time bank and are eventually sold to one or more of its clients. The flexibility of such a system is an obvious advantage, but there is also the potential for incredible problems.

One of the nation's largest advertising agencies, the J. Walter Thompson Company, discovered that its syndication unit was so poorly managed that the company would have to write off more than $30 million in time-banked advertising. Fictitious entries over more than four years were discovered in the agency's computerized accounting system. The embarrassed agency reported that a survey of stations participating in the time bank had disclosed substantial discrepancies between their records and the inflated entries made in the agency's records. The computer shenanigans resulted in a scandal that hit front pages across the country.[2]

The growth or decline of barter syndication is dependent on the state of the economy, the costs of network and spot television, stations' costs in buying programing, the general supply and demand of the programing marketplace, and the ultimate status of much-debated Prime Time Access Rule.

Unwired, or Rep, Radio Networks

National station representatives who sell spot radio time to advertising agency time buyers know all too well that one of their biggest problems is just getting radio included in a media strategy! The radio industry has continuously sold the medium as being efficient, effective, and excellent for a media mix. Television, however, is a tough competitor, and many times, radio has almost been written off by clients who invest all of their budget in TV and the print media.

One way to get more advertisers to invest their money in radio is by making the medium easy to buy. Certainly, that has always been the case in network radio. Now, however, the "wired webs," or traditional line networks, have a strong competitor: unwired radio networks.

In the 1960s, many stations, particularly in small markets, were available to advertisers as a group buy, but major stations in major markets were not. As a new business venture, the Blair Radio Network was established in 1970 and is considered the first of the modern rep networks.[3] Other unwired networks, organized by representative firms, have also become available to advertisers.

Unlike affiliates to a regular line network, stations in rep networks do not carry common programing. They are not linked together; they carry only the commercials mailed to them by the advertiser, who has bought a large group of stations participating in a spot network. The nucleus of any network is the rep's list of represented stations. For buys extending beyond this list of basic markets, the rep arranges with

[2]*Wall Street Journal,* March 30, 1982, p. 1.

[3]*Broadcasting,* October 14, 1974, p. 36.

stations in other markets and thus can provide a tailor-made list to fit an advertisers's needs. Stations usually serve as outlets for only one network.

Rep networks offer a very attractive flexibility to advertisers. An advertiser may buy a list of markets such as the top 50 or 100. The starting dates of the campaign may be staggered, if necessary, to accommodate various marketing requirements. The advertiser can "heavy up" the schedules in particularly important markets. Different commercial lengths can be used, or various dayparts can be ordered. The traditional line networks cannot provide this flexibility.

In order to make unwired networks as attractive and easy to buy as possible, the rep firms assume responsibility for coordinating the schedules and handling the billing. Thus, instead of the advertising agency receiving 200 separate invoices from as many stations, it receives one bill—from the Katz Radio Network, the Blair Radio Network, the Eastman Network, or whatever network has landed the order. The agency pays the rep firm, which then compensates all the stations in the network and deducts a commission for its services.

Not everyone is enthusiastic about rep networks. The regular line networks must certainly sell hard in order to offset this strong competition for radio advertising budgets. Many buyers believe that a rep network buy is more expensive than a line network buy on the same number of stations and that it requires a substantial budget. It may be that smaller advertisers are better off using regular spot buys.

Conclusions

Radio, television, and cable spot sales offer advertisers of all sizes many important and attractive options. Campaigns can be placed in a tailor-made list of markets and on just the stations or cable systems of the buyer's choosing. Advertising weights can be varied, starting dates can be staggered, and the advertiser can run regionalized copy to achieve greater impact. Long-term commitments are not necessary. Schedules can be bought on relatively short notice and, if necessary, canceled or modified.

For large advertisers, spot schedules can augment network buys in particularly important markets. Spot is an ideal advertising vehicle for test-marketing new products or for launching new campaigns. Large advertisers can quickly add spot to their advertising program to meet a strong competitive challenge or other unexpected development.

For small regional advertisers, spot buys can be tailored to fit product distribution patterns. The buys may be heavy or light, but what is important is the opportunity to stretch advertising budgets for maximum efficiency.

Barter for products, services, or programing presents an opportunity market for both advertisers and broadcasters. Another flexible possibility is the unwired, or rep, radio networks. Station representatives have increased revenues for themselves and their stations by taking over the paperwork chores and selling spot radio in group-station buys.

Account executives from rep firms sell spot time to time buyers in agencies and media buying services across the country. The budgets may be large or small, but these two key people—the rep and the buyer—facilitate the flow of buying and selling between advertisers and stations.

The advertisers' investments in spot buys add up to billions of revenue dollars each year for the nation's broadcasters. Since spot represents a major vehicle for selling goods and services, the nation's advertisers consider the expenditure well worth it.

12.4 / Glossary of Rate Card Terminology

Annual Discount A reduction offered to advertisers who buy a 52-week schedule. It is sometimes based on the total number of commercials purchased or on the total annual expenditure. (See Bulk, or Volume, Discount.)

Best Times Available (BTA) A "pot luck" advertising schedule offered by many stations, often at the lowest rates. It is usually sold as a package and scheduled at the station's discretion. (Also called Run of Station or Run of Schedule.)

Bulk, or Volume, Discount A reduction offered to advertisers who either buy a large volume of commercials (perhaps 1,000 or 1,500) or spend a specific minimum amount of money over a one-year period.

Consecutive Week Discount (CWD) A reduction for long-term advertisers who run continuous schedules of 13, 26, 39 or 52 weeks. Discounts usually range from 5 percent to 15 percent off the station's regular rates.

Fixed Position A commercial position guaranteed by the station to run at a particular time. These are the most expensive rates.

Frequency Discount A reduction based on the total number of commercials run on a station during a one-year period. Often shown on a rate card as 13× (times), 26×, 52×, 104×, 156×, 312×, and so on.

Grid A pricing system that may show a variety of prices for each daypart. The station will sell near the top of the grid when business is very good and near the bottom of the grid when business is "soft." (See Sections.)

Orbit (See Rotations.)

Preemptible A commercial position

bought at a rate lower than the full advertising rate and subject to preemption by an advertiser who wants the same position and is willing to pay the full rate.

Product Protection A guarantee by a station that the advertiser will be "protected" from the commercials to competitors by a minimum amount of time. Product protection may be for 10 minutes, 15 minutes, a half-hour, or whatever the station may designate.

Rate Protection A station's guarantee against rate increases for advertisers buying a schedule. Rate protection may be offered for a specific number of weeks or, often, for just the duration of an advertiser's schedule. (If a station *lowers* its rates, the advertiser may immediately switch to the less expensive rates.)

Rotations a scheduling system that rotates an advertiser's commercials either horizontally or vertically. A horizontal rotation moves the commercial in the same time period across the days of the week, such as 3:00 P.M. Monday, 3:00 P.M. Tuesday, 3:00 P.M. Wednesday, and so on. A vertical rotation moves a commercial throughout a general time period, such as 10:00 A.M. Thursday, 10:30 A.M. the following Thursday, 11:00 A.M. the following Thursday, and so on.

Run of Station (ROS) (See Best Times Available.)

Sections Price designations on TV rate cards for fixed positions and preemptible positions. For example, the top-priced fixed-position rate may be designated Section 1 at $300; a position preemptible on two weeks' notice may be designated Section 2 at $275; and a position that is preemptible with no notice may be designated Section 3 at $250.

Short Rate   A rate charged to an advertiser who cancels or changes a schedule. For example, if an advertiser buys a schedule and earns a 5 percent discount for 26 consecutive weeks and then decides to cancel at the end of 20 weeks, the CWD will not apply. This advertiser will be short-rated and must pay an additional 5 percent for all the commercials run during the 20-week period.

Total Audience Plan (TAP)   A package plan offered by many radio stations. A TAP distributes an advertiser's commercials over several dayparts and across the days of the week for a reduced rate.

Weekly Discounts, or Plans   A reduction offered to advertisers based on minimum weekly buys. It is often offered as a plan of 10, 20, 30, or more announcements per week.

chapter thirteen

Local Sales

We Have a Problem — Now the Boss Wants to Be in the Commercial

Each year local advertising revenues for the nation's radio and TV stations make impressive gains. Broadcasters consider such accounts vital. In radio especially, local advertisers are a station's bread and butter, accounting for approximately three-fourths of total radio industry advertising revenues. In television, local advertising has also made consistent increases from year to year. (Cable revenues from local advertisers at this point are very modest indeed. The specialized nature of cable, however, promises good opportunities for adventuresome local advertisers.)

Local advertising in the broadcast media usually means retail advertising, but not always. The major spenders include:

- department and discount stores
- financial institutions
- automobile and truck dealers and related services
- restaurants and fast-food outlets
- supermarkets and other food stores
- entertainment and leisure activities
- specialized stores selling clothing, furniture, appliances, carpeting, or jewelry

The big local advertisers noted above are also heavy print users, but these clients consider the broadcast media to be wise investments. Other local advertisers, however, are reluctant to spend much money in the broadcast media. Their reasons are varied; some are valid, and others are not.

Retailers who deal with tangible merchandise and are used to the tangible qualities of print advertising are often unfamiliar with the advertising possibilities of radio or TV. On the one hand, they are comfortable and complacent reading their favorite newspaper. They can pin up their ads on a bulletin board. On radio or TV, on the other hand, an ad is an abstraction that exists only momentarily. Further, since commercials are often not conducive to selling a large number of individual items, many retailers still cling to print advertising. Newspapers do this job superbly, and an immediate response in sales may be very easily traced to print ads. The broadcast media are best suited to promoting events and building a store image. It is difficult, however, to convince a retailer weaned on item selling in newspapers that a blind medium such as radio can effectively generate store traffic.

Many retailers have told station account executives, "I tried radio (or TV) once, but it didn't work." The chances may be good that the retailer succeeded in breaking every rule of good broadcast advertising. (The ultimate ridiculousness of some retailers in "testing" the broadcast media is reflected in a story about a store manager. He bought radio time to feature one product that he had never before advertised, and then he hid it under the counter to see if anyone would ask for it!)

The reluctance of some retailers to make major commitments in the broadcast media, especially TV, has been greatly reduced as more and more of them successfully test the waters. All the entreaties of TV account executives cannot match the impact on retailers when they see a major competitor launch a winning TV campaign. At that point, the account exec should have an easy sell. This situation has occurred so regularly that most retailers with an advertising budget of any size are no longer intimidated by television. They are attracted to the medium for the same reason that the Procter & Gamble Company is: TV provides mass coverage, delivers an "intrusive" message, and does so with a depth of impact and persuasion that is difficult to duplicate in a static medium such as print.

Analysis of the Local Client

Few retailers use the services of advertising agencies. Most of them develop their advertising "in-house," and they may use an agency only for special assignments — creative and production work, for example. Retailers often prefer to negotiate their own media buys. With a limited staff, many retailers depend on the assistance of local stations in developing their broadcast campaigns and in constructing a media plan. For those involved in making these decisions, it is necessary to begin at the beginning by answering the following questions:

1.   What attributes and liabilities are inherent in the store's *physical facility?* Is the store attractive, inviting, clean, and well lighted? Are parking accommodations adequate? Analyze the immediate neighborhood.

2.   What constitutes the store's *shopping area?* Define it in terms of geography and transportation patterns. How far will most customers travel to this advertiser's outlet(s)?

3.   What kinds of *goods and services* are sold? Is the emphasis on quality, price, or some other attribute? How is merchandise stocked and displayed? Is there a broad

selection? Are there any lines available or services rendered that are not available elsewhere?

4.   Is the *sales staff* competent, knowledgeable, friendly, and available? Do customers help themselves and go to a checkout stand, or do they need a salesperson? Does the staff relate to the customers? (Some retailers that cater to young adults, selling everything from water-beds to stereo systems, invariably hire clerks who are contemporaries of their customers.)

5.   Who are the retailer's *customers?* Define them in terms of demographics and shopping patterns. Is the range of customers and potential customers very broad or rather narrow? *Why* do they select this particular store rather than a competitor? (This is the key question to be answered in this entire analysis.) Are ethnic considerations important? In many markets where there are significant minority populations, retailers may cater exclusively to a particular ethnic group. Advertising to such a market must be "on target."

6.   What are the *shopping patterns* at this store? When do customers shop, in terms of days of the week and hours of the day? (This is important in timing the placement of both print and broadcast ads.) Are there many repeat customers? (Supermarkets, for example, attract a great number of faithful customers; other retailers that sell "big-ticket" items such as cars and appliances are constantly seeking new customers.)

7.   What are this store's *pricing policies?* Does this retailer price goods or services at, below, or above prevailing rates set by competitors? If goods are priced higher, is there a significant offsetting store attribute that is obvious to the customer? What are the store's credit policies?

8.   What is the *competitive situation?* Are there a significant number of competing stores? If so, how near are they? What are their attributes and liabilities in appealing to the same customers? Does the competition conduct aggressive advertising and promotion campaigns?

9.   What is the *advertising history* of this retailer? Is the store well known? Has the image projected in previous advertising been appropriate? Has the budget been spent in print, broadcast, direct mail, or some other medium? With what results? What has worked well, and what has failed?

10.   What is the *reputation* of this retailer? Is the store known for its quality, pricing, expert sales staff, attractiveness, generous credit policy, or other attribute? What are the shortcomings? (Glossing over a tarnished reputation is a mistake in conducting such an analysis.)

11.   What are the *problems?* Do they include location, quality of merchandise or service, store personnel, facility and parking, aggressive competition, and so on? A candid analysis of the problems—and every retailer has them—gives those who plan an advertising program a much better chance of achieving positive results. An advertising campaign may or may not be able to do anything about the problems.

Although the analysis above deals with retailers, the same sorts of questions should be answered by any other local advertiser—a bank, restaurant, real estate company, or whatever.

Radio and television are not replacements for print advertising, of course. A store that moved all its advertising budget from newspapers and direct mail to the electronic media would be very foolish indeed. Broadcast advertising, however, has proved itself most effective in a media mix, because of its flexibility, coverage, and speed. For example, radio's coverage may be more select than newspaper coverage, depending on the nature of the time buys and the target audience sought. Radio is very competitive with newspapers in terms of cost-per-thousand estimates. The versatility and immediacy of broadcasting can benefit the retailer in other ways. Commercials can point out newspaper ads or direct mailings. Copy can be changed quickly, which is important to retailers who may need to make a fast change in sale items or in pricing. Television can take the viewer on a store tour and display merchandise, friendly clerks, ample parking lots, and other store attributes. In addition, the broad circulation of radio and television within any given market is a definite plus in merchandising.*

These advantages of the broadcast advertising media can be very attractive to local retailers. Newspapers present a number of problems, even though they have been the traditional retail medium. Rates have been rising in recent years, along with cost per-thousand estimates. In most markets, circulation in proportion to population has been declining. Given the large number of pages in many daily newspapers, retailers often wonder if their ads are so buried that they are lost to a number of prospective customers. Another factor is that newspapers constantly reach the same audience. Since young people are not heavy newspaper readers, certain retailers (contemporary clothing stores and fast-food outlets, for example) have found the broadcast media increasingly appropriate for their needs.

If a retailer's broadcast campaign is a failure, the reason is often inexperience. Many hold unrealistic expectations and wonder why customers aren't breaking down the doors. The station's account executive who sold the schedule should share the blame, however, since it is his or her job to help the retailer use the broadcast media properly. Some store managers with a severely limited advertising budget say that talk is cheap but television is not. They are concerned that their low-cost TV commercials will look pathetic run back-to-back with slick, expensive national commercials. The station account executive can show the retailer how a good, high-impact commercial can be produced on a modest budget and still be original enough to constitute a source of pride for store personnel.

Budgeting

For local advertisers, the broadcast media seem to work best as part of a well-planned media mix. The broadcast budget, properly developed and executed, should be considered an *investment* that pays off, not an out-of-pocket expense. Probably the

---

*It should be noted that the term *circulation* means different things in newspapers and in broadcasting. For newspapers, the term means the number of copies distributed. On the one hand, it is obvious that more than one person may read the same copy of the paper. On the other hand, a page containing a retailer's ad may never be opened by many who receive the paper. In broadcasting, *circulation* refers to the geographic area in which some specified percentage of the households or people are estimated to be in the audience of a particular station during a specified period of time. (See the glossary at the end of Chapter 10.)

most common approach used by retailers is to simply allocate a percentage of the advertising budget for the broadcast media on the basis of judgment rather than formula.[1] Other budgeting systems may (1) reduce the size of newspaper ads or eliminate print ads that are perceived as "weak," and put the dollars saved into radio or TV or (2) develop specific objectives with an accompanying cost estimate (advertising a special sale, for example, or the opening of a new store).

Budgeting methods that should be avoided, but are too commonly used, include (1) the garbage budget—made up of leftover monies from various activities, (2) the me-too budget—which copies a competitor's advertising program, and (3) the carbon-copy budget—which repeats last year's advertising program without regard to its success or appropriateness.[2]

One way to stretch a meager advertising budget is with the use of cooperative advertising allowances, by which a manufacturer shares in the expense of advertising at the local level. Co-op advertising is described in detail later in this chapter.

A final broadcast budget should include not only the time charges and production expense but also additional costs that are easy to overlook: talent residuals, any special agency fees or commissions, extra photography or graphics not included in a station's production fee, and the expense of dubbing multiple copies.

Creative and Production

The distinct differences between local and national advertising are most obvious in the creative and production work. For national advertisers, radio and TV stations simply broadcast commercials supplied by advertising agencies. For local advertisers, the station is often involved not only in producing commercials but also in handling the creative work. Retailers know their business, and broadcasters know what can and cannot be done in radio and TV within a given budget. What is necessary is a strategy meeting to develop effective commercials that don't send the retailer to the poorhouse.

Such a meeting would include one or more members of the retailer's staff. Those representing the station should be the account executive, the production supervisor, the TV director (or radio producer-engineer), and any other key station people who work regularly with local advertisers. In such a brainstorming session the retailer should present the store's advertising strategy—exactly what is to be communicated to the target audience. The station personnel can then make suggestions for production techniques, studio settings or locations, talent selection, use of graphics, and the like. Communication and cooperation are the key ingredients. Retailers should not be "snowed" with production gimmicks that eclipse the selling message.

In retail campaigns, store managers are concerned with communicating to prospective customers one or more of the following features: (1) specific items and prices; (2) events such as an end-of-the-month sale, January white sale, or, most importantly,

---

[1]*Profitable Retail Television Advertising* (New York: National Retail Merchants Association, 1977), p. 53.

[2]William L. McGee, *Building Store Traffic with Broadcast Advertising* (San Francisco: Broadcast Marketing Co., 1978), p. 167.

the Christmas season; and (3) store image and services. Obviously, it is not possible to squeeze very much information on all these features into one 30- or 60-second commercial; thus, a commercial will usually concentrate on just one or two aspects.

Item selling has enjoyed some spectacular successes in the broadcast media, but the selection of the item or items to be featured and the manner of presentation must be carefully considered. First of all, the retailer should select a popular item that is timely and is stocked in large quantities. The news value of the item should be exploited. The item should represent the merchandise carried in the store and be an attractive value to prospective customers. The commercial should provide sufficient information to interest the viewer, and the number of items featured should be limited, or else the trees will be lost in the forest. An exception to this guideline is shown by the huge success of some commercials that simply use a panning camera to survey a tremendous selection of one item — perhaps cameras, ladies' handbags, or toys.

Event selling is an excellent way to use the broadcast media to support print advertising. Special selling periods (Christmas, back-to-school, Mother's Day) are likely to find the retailer involved in heavy newspaper and direct mail campaigns. Radio and television can complement such campaigns by generating interest and excitement for an upcoming event. Ten-second announcements run in a "saturation buy" a day or two before a major store event are particularly effective (and inexpensive). "Donut" commercials are increasingly used in both radio and TV. A generic opening and closing (often using a musical theme) is developed, and the "hole" in the middle can be constantly changed with updated information on particular merchandise or store events.

In *image and service selling,* the retailer must look beyond the merchandise. Managers often think of their store almost solely in terms of what it sells, but the customers' involvement is deeper. A store is size, selection, decor, sales personnel, free delivery, shopping bags, parking, credit and return policies, and a host of intangibles. The broadcast media, with their exceptional creative capacities, are able to build a store's image in a way the retailer cannot achieve in the print media. Music, sound effects, lights, movement, excitement — these cannot be captured by ink on paper. But they can be built into a radio or TV commercial. The results may be new prestige and wider customer acceptance and store loyalty. Overzealous store advertising managers have sometimes, unfortunately, produced image commercials based not on what the store actually represented but on what they wished it did. Such advertising can puzzle regular customers and mislead prospective customers.

No matter what commercial strategy is employed — item, event or image — it should be remembered that *all* commercials contribute to the customer's total impression of a store. That image should be carefully constructed, because once it is established, it is difficult and expensive to change.

All creative work designed for broadcast advertising should be coordinated with the print campaign, and the two can effectively reinforce each other. Commercials can promote a full-page ad detailing an end-of-the-month sale, for example, or preview a store's Christmas catalogue. ("Coming soon. . . . Watch your mailbox.")

On a limited budget in particular, the best commercials are usually straightforward and simple and use radio and TV in what they do best — personal selling. Straight announcer ads in radio can be very effective, but they depend on good, flowing, uncluttered copy and a skillful announcer who sounds as if he or she *cares* about the message. In TV, a standup pitch is sometimes considered "quick and dirty" selling. As a matter of fact, a standup pitch in TV is one of the hardest commercial formats to bring off. Unless the setting and lighting are right and the actor is a skillful communicator, it should not be attempted. (Every reader has seen commercials that presented a spokesperson who was immediately disliked in the opening seconds.) A stumbling block in using a popular disc jockey or other personality may be the policy of the station where that person is employed. Many stations do not permit their on-air talent to appear on competing stations, and that includes commercials.

Production costs in radio are generally not a problem, but in TV, cost controls are essential. Any TV director worth the title can suggest numerous ways to cut costs and not sacrifice effectiveness. Music and sound-effects libraries are available in most stations, and many TV stations have access to "wild footage." This kind of generic film or tape may include anything from sizzling steaks on a barbecue grill to a Fourth of July parade. If necessary, a good director can make ingenious use of still photographs.

Two major national trade organizations, the Television Bureau of Advertising and the Radio Advertising Bureau, provide extensive sales assistance to their member stations. These organizations are described in greater detail in an appendix to Chapter 2 (see 2.5). To stimulate creative ideas, sample reels or tapes in particular product or service categories are available. Success stories, gathered from around the country, can give both stations and retailers ideas about how to use the broadcast media effectively, not only in the creative execution but also in buying broadcast time.

In TV, when a final commercial or commercials are agreed on, storyboards should be sketched. These do not have to be the elaborate boards that are often prepared for national clients. Simple illustrations will do. In this way, the director has a clear idea of what the client expects, and an inexperienced client, in particular, will be able to visualize the finished commercial. A clear written estimate of production costs should also be provided so that a local advertiser understands exactly what is involved.

Sales Procedures

Selling time at the local level requires much more versatility on the part of the account executive than it ever does at the national level. (Station reps call on experienced time-buyers; preliminaries are skipped, and negotiations proceed promptly.) Television attracts such heterogeneous audiences that the list of likely local advertisers is always extensive. In radio, however, because of the fragmentation of audiences, the station's format and its audience really dictate the sales list. A country music station will pursue one set of advertisers, a "beautiful music" station another. Still, both will seek common clients — financial institutions and the like. Thus, no matter how specialized the program format, there is always a diverse list of clients and prospective clients.

The most successful local broadcast account executives will attest to the following procedures for selling retail accounts.

Step One. The purpose of the advertising salesperson's first call should be simply to get acquainted and gather information. A good salesperson will not attempt to sell time from the station's viewpoint but rather from the retailer's assessment of advertising needs. To do so, the salesperson must understand the prospect's hopes and expectations and learn as much as possible about that local business. The section earlier in this chapter on the Analysis of the Local Client poses the questions that need answers.

Step Two. The second call is for the purpose of making the sales pitch. There are no hard and fast rules on the best procedure for selling time, even though some account executives think they have a magic formula. The salesperson's presentation is obviously based on the information gathered in the first call, the subsequent homework, the personality and the advertising knowledge of the store manager, and some old-fashioned sales techniques. Some account executives simply move down through a list, first selling their medium, then selling their station and its audience, next talking availabilities, and then finally mentioning costs. This procedure may work very well for the large retail store heavily involved in all facets of advertising. For the relatively inexperienced advertiser, however, the first concern is, "How can I reach my customers? How can I get people into my store?" The account executive who has correctly analyzed the prospect will understand these concerns and may use a variety of approaches. He or she will discuss the retailer's needs and create a desire for the station's "product" by revealing some lack in the store's advertising program. One approach is to present station success stories. These successes can be attested to by letters to the station from satisfied advertisers, or more elaborate presentations can be used that show sample commercials and then quote sales results. Either method is a powerful tool, for each provides solid evidence of the station's impact in the community.

For some retail accounts with little or no broadcast experience, the salesperson will do well to talk commercials first and time buying last. Unless the store's management people can become excited about what their commercial will say or look like, they won't take much interest in the station's rate card. To generate that interest, many radio account executives bring in a spec commercial—a 30- or 60-second ad produced on speculation that can be played for the advertiser. If the commercial is good and appealing, the retailer may be eager to sign on the dotted line. Spec commercials aren't economically feasible in TV, but one standard ploy often works. As a last resort, the station salesperson who is anxious to close a sale may urge the store manager to serve as talent. "You'd be just great on television, and who knows more about this store than you? Besides, you won't have to pay an announcer." The ego trip is often irresistible and, unfortunately, often results in some of the worst advertising on television.

Step Three. After the account executive has made the pitch, he or she should leave a program schedule, a coverage map, and a rate card with the store's advertising manager. Unless the client is an experienced broadcast advertiser, many account executives leave behind little or no audience research data. Such statistics are often too confusing for the uninitiated, and smart salespeople know that if they sell by the figures, they will have to live with them later. Selling the station's personalities is often easier to do and more personally relevant to the client than selling audience statistics.

Step Four. When an order is secured, it is the responsibility of the account executive to see that the advertiser is making an intelligent buy. The salesperson knows and understands the program schedule, audience research data, and costs. From this knowledge a carefully constructed schedule should be plotted. A clever commercial is not enough. It must be scheduled on the right days and at the right times, with sufficient frequency to reach the advertiser's best prospects. Underselling is as great a disservice to the client as overselling.

Almost every retailer runs a number of sales during the year. Newspaper and direct mail should advertise the items, but the broadcast media should be utilized to promote the event. Because the retail business flows in peaks and valleys, the advertising time buys of most stores should probably be developed on a flight basis. It may not be necessary, or even desirable, for a retailer to run commercials every day of the year. Retailers who use broadcasting for short-lived campaigns and who are off and on in flights will do well to develop a thematic approach for all broadcast commercials in order to maximize the reinforcement value. A theme may be established with nothing more complicated than a store slogan or a special musical refrain.

Radio and television should be used to support major events or to promote particularly current items. For example, radio's tremendous flexibility can benefit both the broadcaster and the retailer who cooperate in an arrangement to run commercials for sunglasses only on bright sunny days or to advertise air conditioners when the temperature reaches 85 degrees. Much versatility is possible. The account executive's skill and imagination can be put to work for the retailer inexperienced in the broadcast media, and campaigns can be designed to fulfill the objectives of each advertiser. As retailers discover their own best uses of the broadcast media, the results are sometimes spectacular.

Step Five. Once a schedule is running, the station account executive should remember the obligation to service that account. (Computers can help provide good service — see 13.1.) This can be accomplished by keeping in touch to find out whether the client is satisfied with the results, striving to improve the schedule, and generally expressing interest and a willingness to help. The retailer expects results from the advertising investment. Poor servicing is one common reason for retailers saying, "I tried it once."

Remuneration for station account executives usually takes one of the following forms:

Straight commission. In this case, the account executive is paid an agreed-on percentage of his or her sales. The percentage varies from station to station. TV account execs usually earn a lower percentage than radio salespeople, because they deal in a higher priced commodity. In radio, a salesperson for a low-rated station may earn a higher commission than A.E.'s at other radio stations, because the selling job is tougher and the rates are lower.

Draw against commission. An agreed-on sum of money, called a draw, is pledged by the station to the account executive each month. This draw is deducted from the total earned commissions. The advantage of this system is that the salesperson can count on a certain minimum sum each month.

Guarantee plus commission. This system guarantees a fixed sum each payday to the account executive. This guarantee, however, is *not* deducted from commissions. As a result, a lower commission rate is established because of the sum guaranteed up front.

It should be noted that, no matter what form of compensation is used, an account executive who doesn't deliver is soon looking for other employment. Commissions paid to salespeople are always based on the net—the amount the station collects after granting the 15 percent agency commission. In addition, commissions are based on *paid-up* accounts. (As in any other business, broadcasters must deal with delinquent accounts.) Bonuses to provide an incentive for exceptional performance are common, and so are sales contests. The sole source of income for most stations is the sales department. A happy, motivated staff can make the difference on a profit-and-loss sheet.

Local Rates

Because local newspapers are formidable competitors to broadcasters, many stations offer a special rate to hometown clients in order to obtain some of the retailers' advertising allocations. Station managers realize that their coverage of outlying areas often constitutes "waste circulation" to the local merchant. Customers are not likely to travel miles into the city just because a retailer has advertised a sale. (This waste circulation usually does not exist for the national spot advertiser, who wants widespread broadcast distribution to match product distribution patterns.)

Local rate cards are common in small and medium-sized markets but not too prevalent on top-rated stations in major markets. The reason is twofold. Some top stations are so close to being sold out that they don't have to offer a local rate. Other

13.1/Chores for a Computer

To ease the paperwork burden of stations, computers are now firmly established to handle work in traffic, accounting, and sales. A computer's most important attribute in this role is its memory, which is far more accurate than the human kind. Thus, depending on the system, a station's computer program may be used to:

• keep track of the station's inventory of availabilities

• record the commercial schedule for every client, including starting and ending dates

• track commercials that are moved from their regular position or are missed or "bumped" for one reason or another

• flag competitive spots (rejecting a commecial that is scheduled too close to that of a competitor)

• print past-due accounts and flag perpetually delinquent accounts

• record and print all commercial contracts

• print invoices and affidavits of performance

• print separate billing lists by station account executive, individual ad agencies, individual client, and product type

• print the daily log (in most cases in less than 10 minutes)

• prepare sales proposals that fit an advertiser's specifications, enumerating availabilities by programs and times, demographic breakouts, the cost of each commercial, and computations of cost-per-thousand and cost-per-point for each availability

• process accounts payable

• issue the station's payroll

stations, located in the largest markets, have difficulty separating local from national advertisers and determining which ones would earn the lower rates. It is easier and less complicated for these major stations to use one rate card.

Radio stations use local rates more frequently. In many instances, the local or retail rate cards are structured identically to the national rates. The prices are simply lower. Television stations usually don't publish local rate cards, because rates and schedules are usually negotiated on a single buy basis. The local retailer who is a "TV believer" and uses the medium a great deal may earn some sort of discount or drive a very good bargain. Such retail business is as prized as national spot business by station management. (In spot business, the station may deal through a station representative with a time buyer 2,000 miles away, and the station obviously has little control of the situation.) Station sales managers know that many retail accounts are excellent prospects for sponsorships of regularly scheduled local programs. Retailers who sponsor daily newscasts, traffic or weather reports, school sportscasts, or other events of local importance usually do so on a long-term contract. These sponsorships are an excellent advertising investment, because the advertiser is closely associated with an important community service.

Co-op Advertising

Literally thousands of manufacturers have a cooperative advertising budget available to local retailers for sharing in the expense of advertising a product at the local level. Everything from underwear to vacuum cleaners to ice cream is advertised in co-op arrangements. The commercial (often provided by the manufacturer) is tagged with the store name, and the manufacturer and the retailer split the costs of broadcast time or print space. Because the ad is placed by the retailer, who is often able to buy radio time and newspaper space at local rates, the cost may be particularly attractive to the manufacturer.

The lion's share of available co-op allowances is spent in newspapers. To compete for these dollars, many stations employ a co-op specialist assigned to assist retailers in using the broadcast media and subsidizing the cost with co-op monies. Small retailers are often abysmally ignorant of co-op arrangements and need all the help they can get from a local station. Both the Radio Advertising Bureau and the Television Bureau of Advertising provide extensive information on co-op programs for use in pitching retail accounts.

For the retailers, co-op money permits them to expand their total advertising program and to feature popular items in commercials and print ads without carrying the total cost. In many instances, the manufacturer will provide ready-made radio or TV commercials that help keep production costs in line and permit the retailer to tie into a high-quality, professionally prepared advertising program. TV commercials are usually on 16mm film, and they are often provided at no cost or for the cost of the film print. Store identification can be added at the beginning of the film, the end, or both. The film can be cut and reassembled to suit the store image. Sound tracks can be replaced or modified. Manufacturers vary in what they will permit retailers to do with the film, but the store can always build its own identification into the commerical.

Although some store managers are delighted to use co-op monies, they prefer to produce their own commercials that feature particular products.

Numerous retailers are not enchanted with co-op programs for several reasons. They say, "Why should a local department store share 50–50 in the cost of a minute TV commercial for a nationally distributed line of men's shirts when the store may get only 10 seconds as a tag?" A customer may be able to find this brand at a dozen different stores. The store manager wants to promote the store, not help the competition get sales. Another reason for dissatisfaction is that co-op programs at the store level usually mean that advertising dollars are being diverted to participate in these plans. Thus, the store is restricted in the amount of money delegated to its own advertising program.

Co-op is used most extensively in newspaper advertising in composite ads, wherein a drugstore, discount house, or supermarket may take out a full page ad and feature dozens of items. Each manufacturer is then billed for a portion of the ad. The store usually ends up paying little or nothing.

Many manufacturers are reluctant to reveal their co-op allowances to the media, not only because co-op programs have been exploited by retailers but also because many manufacturers do not want to encourage an increased use of such programs. On the other hand, the media (radio in particular) are always anxious to learn about available co-op programs, because they represent opportunities for new business. The manufacturers remain notably close-mouthed.

Many retailers don't really know how to use co-op allowances effectively. They often simply work out an arrangement with the manufacturer to forego co-op monies and instead take a discount on the wholesale price of the goods. Manufacturer's representatives sometimes use the inducement of co-op allowances to secure shelf space in retail outlets. It provides a sweetener for expanding distribution. Co-op allowances have been both used and abused by all the parties concerned.

In order to protect themselves, manufacturers always set a limitation on the amount of money to be used. In addition, they usually require that the retailer use the allowance within a one-year period or else forfeit it. The *Robinson-Patman Act,* which is administered by the Federal Trade Commission, specifies that a manufacturer's co-op arrangements be equitable among retail outlets so that big store chains will not gain an unfair advantage. The legal requirements are complicated but were clarified to some extent in 1972, when the FTC issued *Guides on Cooperative Advertising.*

The Federal Communications Commission has also involved itself in broadcast co-op advertising by issuing rules pertaining to fraudulent billing.[3] Covered are such abuses as providing an inflated bill to a local dealer to pass on to a manufacturer, billing for commercials that did not run, and billing for commercials that promoted only the store and not the manufacturer. (In these cases, the fraudulent bill is passed along to the manufacturer by the retailer.) These are serious offenses, not taken lightly by the FCC. (These problems and others are discussed in Chapter 17.)

To help eliminate billing problems, the Cooperative Advertising Committee of the Association of National Advertisers has developed a "tear-sheet" procedure for stations

---

[3]*Applicability of the Fraudulent Billing Rule* (Revised), FCC 76-489.

to follow. This is a system for certifying to the retailer (who in turn reports to the manufacturer) exactly what was aired, when it was aired, and how much it cost.[4] The procedure is similar to the long-time newspaper practice of providing a tear sheet of the ad that ran when submitting a co-op claim.

Sample radio co-op commercials for the Monroe Auto Equipment Company, promoting automobile shock absorbers, are shown in 13.2. These recorded commercials permit the local dealer to insert copy between musical jingles. Suggested copy is provided. The script also shows the format for verification that the commercials ran a particular number of times and the rates being charged. This form must be notarized before payment is processed.

Many manufacturers require that co-op bills be sent to the Advertising Checking Bureau, which maintains a half-dozen offices around the country. The stations' invoices and affidavits are carefully checked before payment is approved. The bureau works on a fee basis for manufacturers whose co-op programs are in widespread use. Its procedures help protect the manufacturers from dishonest co-op claims. (The growth potential for broadcast co-op advertising is tremendous. The Advertising Checking Bureau reports that 80 percent of the advertising it checks for clients is in the print media.)[5]

Conclusions

The multiple facets of local broadcast advertising can provide invaluable experience to a young station account executive. The client list for any salesperson may include a number of highly experienced and successful advertisers, as well as a number of prospects who have never before used radio or television. The challenges are as diverse as the advertisers themselves.

Selling time to local retailers is truly a business of "trying on the other fellow's shoes." Station account executives not only must know their own business but also must often take a self-taught crash course in retailing. Unlike some national station representatives, they are not just taking orders but really *selling* the medium and their station to a retailer who wants and needs help. Simple selling, however, is not enough at the local level. In these times of increasing competition among all the media, it is absolutely necessary for stations to *service* their accounts. Commercials and schedules can always be improved.

At the local level, salespeople are often involved in not only the creative planning but also the actual production of a campaign. That sort of activity is unheard of for account executives working in network or national spot business. Helping a local advertiser launch a successful campaign can be a tremendously satisfying endeavor.

Co-op advertising offers special opportunities to initiate local advertisers to radio and television. With the financial subsidy of a national manufacturer, along with some

---

[4]William L. McGee, *Broadcast Co-op, the Untapped Goldmine* (San Francisco: Broadcast Marketing Co., 1975), p. 76.

[5]*Broadcasting,* March 30, 1981, p. 63.

13.2/One Company's Co-op Radio Scripts

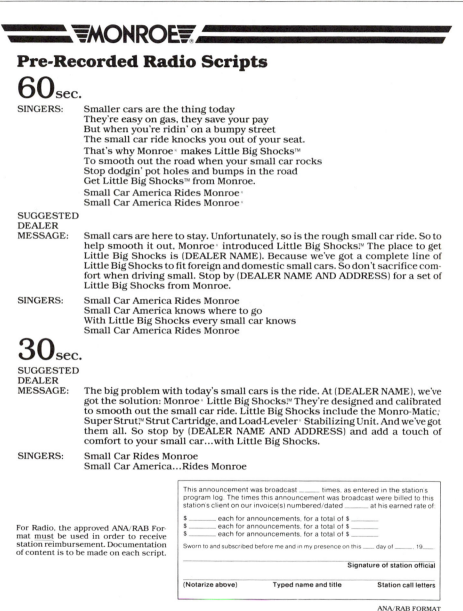

⇒MONROE⇒

Pre-Recorded Radio Scripts

60 sec.

SINGERS: Smaller cars are the thing today
They're easy on gas, they save your pay
But when you're ridin' on a bumpy street
The small car ride knocks you out of your seat.
That's why Monroe® makes Little Big Shocks™
To smooth out the road when your small car rocks
Stop dodgin' pot holes and bumps in the road
Get Little Big Shocks™ from Monroe.
Small Car America Rides Monroe®
Small Car America Rides Monroe®

SUGGESTED
DEALER
MESSAGE: Small cars are here to stay. Unfortunately, so is the rough small car ride. So to help smooth it out, Monroe® introduced Little Big Shocks™ The place to get Little Big Shocks is (DEALER NAME). Because we've got a complete line of Little Big Shocks to fit foreign and domestic small cars. So don't sacrifice comfort when driving small. Stop by (DEALER NAME AND ADDRESS) for a set of Little Big Shocks from Monroe.

SINGERS: Small Car America Rides Monroe
Small Car America knows where to go
With Little Big Shocks every small car knows
Small Car America Rides Monroe

30 sec.

SUGGESTED
DEALER
MESSAGE: The big problem with today's small cars is the ride. At (DEALER NAME), we've got the solution: Monroe® Little Big Shocks™ They're designed and calibrated to smooth out the small car ride. Little Big Shocks include the Monro-Matic, Super Strut,™ Strut Cartridge, and Load-Leveler® Stabilizing Unit. And we've got them all. So stop by (DEALER NAME AND ADDRESS) and add a touch of comfort to your small car...with Little Big Shocks.

SINGERS: Small Car Rides Monroe
Small Car America...Rides Monroe

For Radio, the approved ANA/RAB Format must be used in order to receive station reimbursement. Documentation of content is to be made on each script.

This announcement was broadcast _____ times, as entered in the station's program log. The times this announcement was broadcast were billed to this station's client on our invoice(s) numbered/dated _____ at his earned rate of:

$ _____ each for announcements, for a total of $ _____
$ _____ each for announcements, for a total of $ _____
$ _____ each for announcements, for a total of $ _____

Sworn to and subscribed before me and in my presence on this ___ day of _____, 19___

_____
Signature of station official

(Notarize above)   Typed name and title   Station call letters

ANA/RAB FORMAT

Talent disclaimer for television and radio.

IMPORTANT NOTE: The usage of this commercial is strictly limited by law. Specifically, this commercial may only be broadcast during the specified Co-op dates. In the event you fail to observe this important limitation you will be responsible for any damages including, but not limited to attorney fees incurred by J. Walter Thompson and/or Monroe Auto Equipment Company as a result of the prohibited uses.

hand holding from a station account executive, many small retailers have built highly successful businesses.

The variety of clients, the marketing problems encountered, and the opportunity to develop creative selling programs furnish the salesperson with an interesting and challenging career. It's no secret to the ambitious young people in the broadcasting business that most station managers attain their positions by coming up through the ranks of broadcast sales departments.

chapter fourteen

Direct Response Advertising

Just Enter Your Credit Card Number...

This offer will expire soon, so telephone this toll-free number now. *Operators are waiting to take your call.*

This is the ending of a two-minute, direct response commercial. These sales pitches have played a role in broadcast advertising for many years, although never placed at center stage and often relegated to fringe and late-night time periods. Commercials of this genre are designed to put buyer and seller in direct contact. (The middlemen present in most marketing situations — wholesalers, retailers, and dealers — simply do not exist in direct response advertising.)

The print media enjoy the greatest use of direct response advertising. Recently, however, radio and television — and cable in particular — have been obtaining their share of an industry that is growing at a phenomenal rate. Total expenditures for direct response advertising (which includes direct mail) are estimated at more than $25 billion a year.[1] The potential for the broadcast media appears to be enormous, because of a number of forces at work in the marketplace.

1. The convenience of shopping at home has great appeal to working adults. With more women in the work force, there is less time for leisurely shopping.

2. Shopping at home eliminates travel time, gasoline expense, and (for some people) freedom from concerns over street crime.

3. Major companies with excellent reputations have turned to direct response

---

[1]*Advertising Age,* January 18, 1982, p. S-1.

advertising. Their presence in the media provides some assurance to consumers that this kind of advertising is trustworthy and merits attention.

4.   The soaring costs of direct mail have provided an impetus to try the broadcast media. Many marketers have tried it and liked it. Cable TV, especially, has been a boon to some direct marketers. The specialized audiences and low costs are a perfect media fit for many of them.

5.   Many direct response advertisers sell products that are purchased on impulse and do not represent a major expenditure. Placing an order will not devastate the family budget.

6.   From the marketer's point of view, maintaining a central point of inventory keeps the lid on marketing costs and also allows a broader selection to be offered to the customer. Shoplifting, a major loss for many retailers, is virtually eliminated.

7.   For the seller, there are no problems in achieving distribution, and it is unnecessary to hire and train a field sales force.

8.   Some of the most attractive sales offers are for products and services that are not readily available in the open marketplace.

9.   Ordering directly from a marketer is a familiar transaction. In a year's time, it is estimated, 72 million adults (or almost half the adult population) order items through the mail.[2] Ordering in response to a commercial is no more complicated than using a catalogue or a direct mail piece. It is, in fact, more convenient. With a toll-free number, all the customer needs is a telephone and a credit card.

10. Videotex, a system for delivering textual data to the home screen (discussed in depth later in this chapter), will open vistas for both consumers and marketers. Extensive information can be presented to the viewer, who sometimes has the option of ordering on the spot. A new generation of consumers who cut their teeth on electronic calculators and similar gadgets is not intimidated by the keypad console used in placing orders.

Direct response advertisers use radio, television, and cable in several ways:

They sell products and services directly. The most common items are records and tapes, books, magazines and other subscriptions, tools, and appliances. But anything else that entrepreneurial imagination dictates can be sold.

They sell tickets to events. The electronic media are splendid vehicles for marketing tickets to sporting events, concerts, theater productions, and any other kind of attraction with wide appeal. Computerized systems for selling tickets can readily process credit card orders. For the customer whose tickets subsequently arrive in the mail, the convenience is obvious.

They generate leads and conversions. The purpose of this advertising is to solicit a request for more information. This puts an interested possible customer into contact with a salesperson (either in person or on the telephone) or results in a sales brochure or similar information being sent out. This kind of advertising has been used by the U. S. Army to put potential soldiers into contact with a recruiting officer. Other

---

[2]Ibid.

advertisers seeking leads or conversions may be marketing big-ticket items that are unlikely to be sold in only one or two minutes. These items include real estate, insurance, correspondence courses, and the like.

They use support advertising. This special category is used to "soften up" prospects and pave the way for a subsequent sales pitch. Publishers Clearing House and Reader's Digest are two companies that use extensive support advertising for their massive mailings. The commercials point out a mailing due to arrive very shortly or a major newspaper supplement. ("Watch your mailbox for this special offer.") These support commercials are usually 30 seconds or, sometimes, 60 seconds rather than the typical longer direct response commercials.

Creative Considerations

Creative planning in direct response commercials often follows a formula. The formula is based on the *communications purpose* of the ad: to motivate the listener or viewer to respond *now*. General consumer advertising is often attitudinal, being designed to build favorable impressions, brand awareness, and the like. But most direct response advertising strives to turn the passive viewer into an active customer—one who is on the phone, credit card in hand.

Two minutes is a common length for direct response commercials, giving copywriters some elbow room in developing a sales story. A typical format for such a commercial follows:

• *5 to 10 seconds.* This is the attention step, which may include exciting visual material or compelling copy. ("In the next two minutes, I want to tell you about something that may change your life.")

• *65 to 75 seconds.* In this portion the product or service is described, with benefits, features, demonstration, and testimonials. There is a complete arsenal of persuasion packed into a fast-paced pitch.

• *15 seconds.* Next comes an action device to motivate the consumer immediately. (Procrastinators tend to lose interest and never order.) Premium offers often increase the response. Usually free, these premiums are designed to win over the half-hearted consumer.

• *20 to 30 seconds.* Finally, ordering information, including the terms of the offer and the telephone number or mailing address, is given. If the product or service is not available through any other means, this is the place to hammer home that information. Ordering information must be repeated.

Variations on this format certainly exist, and the growing sophistication of direct response advertising will begin to move some commercials away from the hard-sell diatribe. In most cases, long teasers are not suitable. What is being sold should be presented as quickly as possible—in the attention step or immediately following. The most effective direct response commercials are simple, straightforward, and very aggressive. Quite a bit of information must be packed into two minutes. "Show and tell" is the technique, and the copy should flow smoothly from beginning to end. (A photoboard for a TV commercial soliciting subscriptions to *Outdoor Life* magazine, shown in 14.1, follows this basic commercial format.)

Even in longer commercials, it is necessary to limit the number of sales points. Clutter should be avoided; repetition is advisable. To anticipate and neutralize natural consumer reservations, a portion of the commercial should contain information on guarantees, refunds, and the like. The approach on most of these commercials is very personal, almost eyeball-to-eyeball selling, and the momentum is designed to arouse enthusiasm, even to the point of urgency. Free premiums may not be necessary, especially if the basic offer is one of obvious quality. Time-Life Books have attained a fine reputation; bonuses are not required to sell the product.

Ordering information should be phrased in the imperative ("Call now") and presented in both audio and video. In radio, it is crucial to repeat instructions.

For marketers of fairly complicated products that require a rather lengthy explanation, the research on time-compressed TV commercials (noted in Chapter 8) may be of particular interest. A commercial can be speeded up as much as 25 percent, still sound natural, and actually elicit greater interest and recall than one run at normal speed.

It should be noted that professionals in direct response advertising are keenly aware that their industry's reputation has been somewhat sullied. One direct response expert has written that

Abuses were rife in the early buccaneering days. Products sold through television might arrive months after they were ordered, while others never arrived at all. A lot of merchandise that did show up was third rate. Some commercials were vicious come-ons for shark-toothed salesmen with shady real estate deals, phony freezer food plans, overpriced house siding, fake diet pills, and junk encyclopedias at premium prices. The principles of truth in advertising and a full disclosure of the terms of the sale were often disregarded. The TV audience was finding out the hard way that an offer that sounded too good to be true really was too good to be true.[3]

Today, direct response marketers must—and do—work to build public confidence in an industry that has initiated many reforms.

Time-Buying Strategies

Most direct response marketers buy time at discounted prices that are negotiated with each station, cable operator, or cable network. For these bargain rates, the advertiser must accept preemptible TV time and the perpetual problem of being "bumped." In radio, run-of-station commercials encounter the same problems. Because of their longer length, direct response commercials are invariably placed late at night or in other dayparts that do not attract a large audience. Cable television advertising, however, is still in its development stage and is fighting to attract advertisers, so direct response clients can buy into just about any daypart.

[3]John Witek, *Response Television: Combat Advertising of the 1980s* (Chicago: Crain Books, 1981), p. 8.

14.1/A Direct Response Commercial

TIMES MIRROR MAGAZINES
OUTDOOR LIFE

TITLE: "MOST DANGEROUS GAME"   COMM'L. NO.: XXGR 0222 (:120)

(MUSIC UNDER)
MAN: You can see it in their eyes. They are some of the most dangerous animals in the world.

The lion -- if it's hungry, it will eat you.

The leopard -- it's a deadly killer because it's small and almost totally silent.

The grizzly -- it stands nine feet tall. Now you can come face to face with them in this special gift from Outdoor Life.

Incredible stories on the animals that strike the deepest terror in man.

It's the Most Dangerous Game -- from the editors of Outdoor Life --

a special free gift for you with a low cost introductory subscription. A full year of Outdoor Life for only $6.97.

Call this number, 1-800-228-2080 and bring home the great outdoors. The action. The information. The pride...

Outdoor Life. I'm talking about hunting and fishing the way you like it --

pages of tips and tactics you can use to enjoy the outdoors even more. Articles on fish and game in your neck of the woods...

on the big ones that didn't get away and the little secrets that make it happen.

Outdoor Life. It's all you need to know -- from what's new in hunting equipment to where the bass are hitting big.

Lures. Boots. Boats. Fathers and sons. Adventure. Close calls and long shots.

That's the Outdoor Life for you. Equipment. Camping. Hunting. Field guides and updates and special reports on everything

from trout to turkey to white tails to mallards.

It's the tradition of caring for the wilderness, of making it on your own, through strength and smarts.

Outdoor Life. It's the man's magazine you can depend on -- every month, every issue. Come with us today and get Outdoor Life's Most Dangerous Game -- free with your paid subscription.

Call now. 1-800-228-2080 and save 53% off the $15.00 cover price. That's 40% off the regular subscription rate of $11.94.

So you get 12 great issues -- for just $6.97.

1-800-228-2080. For the Most Dangerous Game. For the great outdoors. For Outdoor Life. (MUSIC OUT)

Courtesy of Grey Direct and Times Mirror Magazines.

Small audiences are not necessarily a disadvantage to these advertisers. For example, the households-using-television level in a given market may be 75 percent at 10:00 P.M. and 25 percent at 10:00 A.M. In spite of the significant difference in audience, the morning time period may generate a better response than the prime-time position because of the kind of product or service advertised and because of the more narrow demographics of the morning housewife audience.

Low-rated programs also win favor with direct response advertisers, not only because of the cheaper time costs but also because of the nature of the programing. One marketing expert believes that "the higher the rating, the higher the attentiveness level. Conversely, the lower the rating, the lower the viewer attentiveness."[4] In other words, an exciting, first-run prime-time network program is engrossing enough to completely eclipse the commercials sandwiched in the station breaks. But a bored insomniac watching reruns of a too-familiar situation comedy may pay more attention to a direct response commercial than to the program.

Time-buying strategies vary for each client and circumstance. For example, support commercials are usually a standard length, which makes them easier to place. They must, however, be carefully scheduled to air just a day or two before a major printed piece reaches the consumer. Preemptible time, therefore, may not be feasible. Costs quickly escalate when direct response advertisers have to pay regular rates.

Per inquiry (PI) advertising schedules may occasionally be negotiated with the media. The commercials are really direct response ads, but the customer sends the order to the station, not the advertiser. The station may broadcast as many PI ads as it cares to, but it is not compensated for the commercial time. Instead, the station receives a predetermined amount for every inquiry the advertiser receives. Obviously, each inquiry or order must be funneled through the station in order to monitor the response. Because the station gambles that it will receive *some* remuneration for the PI schedule and because of the paperwork involved, very few stations accept PI advertising. Those that do are usually doing poorly in the ratings and are hurting for revenues. In the future, cable may offer brighter prospects for PI advertisers.

Evaluating most direct response commercials does not involve the kinds of research discussed in Chapter 9. Measuring recall and persuasion are unimportant subtleties for many direct marketers, who are primarily interested in knowing how a particular commercial "pulls" and how it performs when aired in various dayparts. Thus, one method is to rotate various commercials and compare responses based on similar dayparts.[5] Conducting a test to find the optimum offer is best done in similar markets. For example, in Market A the product may be priced at $14.95, and in a matched market it may be priced at $19.95 accompanied by an attractive premium. To test the efficiency of a broadcast schedule, it's a simple matter to track the response for commercials tagged with a toll-free telephone number. Since most calls are made within 10 minutes of the airing, a marketer can quickly tabulate what hours of the day and what kinds of program produce the best results.

---

[4]Bob Stone, *Successful Direct Marketing Methods,* 2nd ed. (Chicago: Crain Books, 1979), p. 144.

[5]Diane Brady, "Direct Response TV: A Growing Alternative," *Broadcasting,* November 16, 1981, p. 22.

Videotex as a Direct Response Medium

The jargon that has been spawned by the new technologies would have been totally baffling to most professionals in broadcasting and advertising 10 years ago. Today that vocabulary is still Greek to the lay public, but anyone working in the industry needs to be conversant with the new technologies. A bandwagon enthusiasm for technology has swept the industry with the development of broadband cable, direct broadcast satellites, videodiscs and videocassettes, superstations, and assorted computer linkups with home TV sets. As these technologies develop, the industry must seek answers to some important questions: What does the public want? Who will pay for it? How will they pay?

Many advertisers who rely on direct marketing methods have already successfully tested the waters in cable television. Some of them are now looking at other technologies that will suit their marketing needs. Videotex may be an exciting option for many of them.

Videotex is the most commonly used generic term for all the electronic systems that transmit computer-stored frames of textual and graphic information to remote video screens. No matter which of the several technologies is used, videotex involves transmitting "pages" of information. A "black box" next to a television receiver stores the digital information, and the videotex viewer can call up a full page of numbers, letters, and relatively crude multicolor graphics. This call-up process involves the use of a keypad that looks something like a small handheld calculator. Depending on the technology, it can take anywhere from a fraction of a second to many seconds for the desired information to appear. (See 14.2.)

Teletext is the general term for a one-way information service delivered to the home screen via a broadcast signal. That signal, in most instances, utilizes the unused picture linage of a regular TV signal, called the *vertical blanking interval*. The regular TV picture is delivered by an electronic beam that, in effect, "writes" the information horizontally across the screen, line by line, at a speed that gives the viewer the impression of movement. When the beam reaches the bottom of the screen there is a fraction of a second during which the beam carries no video information as it returns to the top of the screen. When the vertical blanking interval is used for teletext purposes, part of this brief instant is filled with "pages" of textual information in digital form.

Not all teletext systems use the vertical blanking interval. A one-way system occupying a part or all of a complete cable video channel is also possible. These systems can deliver many more pages of information with a very short waiting time than can vertical blanking interval systems.

There are two basic types of teletext service—business information and consumer information. A subscriber to a business service might retrieve information on the stock market, commodity prices, airline flights, and business news, usually in his or her office. Consumer services include headline news, sports scores, entertainment information, weather reports, restaurant guides, and shopping information, received on the home TV set.

In either case, the viewer "grabs" the desired page by punching three or four numbers on the keypad. The user is really tapping into a kind of endless loop of pages.

By first punching up an index on the screen, the viewer can select from many options. "Branching" is the technique for organizing the vast amount of specific information available to the user in a way that allows easy and quick retrieval. Here's an example of how it works in a marketing application.

Mr. Suburbanite is interested in buying a lawn trimmer. On his TV screen he punches up the index on the teletext system. From his many choices he selects "shopping" and sees a list of retailers. He selects "general retailers" and finally "Sears." Next, the index to the Sears catalogue appears. "Lawn and garden" is selected. Mr. Suburbanite then selects "hedge and lawn trimmers," and finally he is down to descriptions and prices on two weed whackers. On a teletext system, which is one-way, this customer will then either have to phone Sears or go there in person to

14.2 / Videotex Material Is Prepared for Delivery

Videotex pages are composed on a modified computer terminal using a keyboard similar to that of a standard typewriter.

Courtesy of Mycro-Tek Products Division of Mergenthaler Linotype, an Allied Company.

place an order. A two-way interactive system could allow him to complete the transaction and never leave home.

Interactive videotex (sometimes called *viewdata*) systems use wire connections to the home, contain more information pages, and require less waiting time. The user, via a keypad, taps into a computer at a central location. Some kind of interaction with the system, which stores alphanumeric information (letters and numbers) and graphics, is always possible. The two-way system operates through the same cable that brings regular TV or cable programing to the home screen, or through regular telephone lines after the user dials a special number. As with a teletext system, the user punches a keypad, but instead of grabbing pages as they go by over and over again, as in a teletext system, the user selects materials from a data bank. Incredible quantities of information are available. With the keypad, the user can ask for additional information, complete a simple banking transaction, or place an order. The implications for marketers are significant. Sample videotex pages are shown in 14.3.

Mr. Suburbanite and Sears could complete their commercial transaction, de-

14.3/Sample Videotex Pages

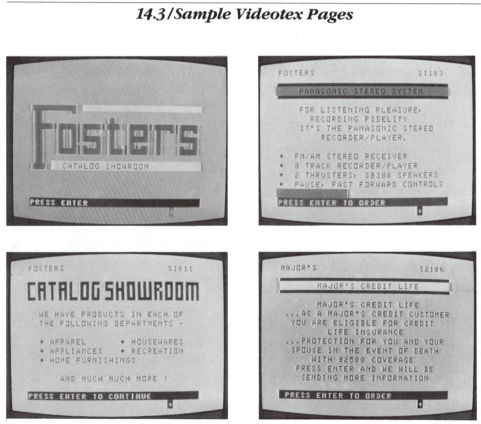

Courtesy of ViewMart, Inc.

scribed previously, on a two-way interactive videotex system. The buyer selects the lawn trimmer of his choice, enters his order, and then punches in his credit card number. Next, the TV screen displays the order with the buyer's name and address and details of the purchase. When Mr. Suburbanite presses "send" to confirm the purchase, the TV screen tells him, "Thank you for shopping at Sears!" In a few days, the lawn trimmer is delivered.

Widespread growth of interactive videotex in marketing transactions is clouded by a number of obstacles. The high cost of installing equipment is a formidable problem. The vast majority of present cable households has only a 12-channel one-way system. Replacement with two-way systems that are capable of handling many channels is a costly proposition and will take years to complete. In addition, TV set manufacturers must be confident that there is a sizable market before they build sets that incorporate the microelectronic circuits that convert computer signals into a readable display on the home TV screen.[6] In the meantime, many experts think, the greatest growth in electronic shopping will develop in households that have both a touch-tone telephone and cable TV service. Millions of consumers already have both, and little additional hardware is needed to make this existing equipment a two-way system.

Besides the example of Mr. Suburbanite cited above, there are other less expensive marketing opportunities for the use of videotex. An advertiser may simply "sponsor" pages of textual information. On some systems, for example, the stock-market report will show that it is being presented courtesy of a particular brokerage house. The company logo is included on the screen. Other possible sponsorships include sports scores from a sporting goods manufacturer, airline schedules from a travel agent, houses for sale from a real estate company, health and first aid tips from a drugstore chain, and so forth. Classified ads, the yellow pages, real estate listings, and voluminous store catalogues are likely candidates for adaptation to videotex.

All these data, delivered to the home in the form of alphanumerics and graphics, obviously offer the consumer information in quantity, but with extremely limited visual detail. Advertisers can use various colors for numerals, letters, and backgrounds, but that's about it.

Probably the most sobering problem facing the growth of videotex lies not with the broadcasters, advertisers, or equipment manufacturers, but with the consumer. One videotex expert put it this way:

Consumers do not want, nor can they afford, every possible gadget. They will pick and choose. The choice of a video recorder may mean the rejection of a videotex decoder — not consciously, but because the individual is going to spend his time watching old movies or tennis lessons on the tube, not scanning news bulletins. Getting hundreds of thousands, or millions, of consumers to adopt a new piece of equipment takes more than manufacturing and technical know-how. It demands a marketing campaign to make people aware of and disposed to purchase the device.[7]

---

[6]Efrem Sigel, ed., *Videotext: The Coming Revolution in Home/Office Information Retrieval* (New York: Harmony Books, 1980), p. 131.

[7]Sigel, *Videotext,* p. 130.

Infomercials

Videotex may offer exciting applications, but most consumers want to *see* what they're buying. As a result, direct response advertisers may find *infomercials* more promising because of the greater visual possibilities. Infomercials are extensive product demonstrations and sales pitches produced on tape or film and lasting anywhere from 3 to 15 or more minutes. On cable systems, infomercials can be presented alone, but they are especially effective when presented in conjunction with videotex systems. In such an application, the viewer can find out specific information about a product, see a demonstration, and perhaps order the product through interactive videotex.

Depending on the elaborateness of the infomercials, production costs can be significant. The sales they generate must justify the expense. If an advertiser is already shooting commercials for conventional TV, costs can be controlled by shooting the footage for the infomercials at the same time.

For the convenience of the viewer, a cable shopping channel may present infomercials and demonstrations around a particular theme. A local cable company (or an interconnection of several systems) can present a reasonably simple program using a kitchen set, for example, in which various products related to food are demonstrated. Fashion shows have been presented on cable systems by a number of department and clothing stores, and other possibilities lie ahead. The restraining force in such program development is obviously the production cost. These demonstrations must attract sufficient viewers who will *buy*.

Many people might like to view such demonstrations but are not available when they are presented. To deal with this common problem, Adams-Russell, Inc., and the giant advertising agency the J. Walter Thompson Company have developed a pilot program. For a cable system in Peabody, Massachusetts, infomercials ranging from three to seven minutes have been developed. Product demonstrations, recipes, and

"We get 104 channels."

retail shopping features can be selected by a viewer on a home telephone that activates a computer and feeds the desired information to the viewer's home screen.[8] If it is successful, and not too expensive, the system may be expanded to major multisystem operators.

All the new technologies offer possibilities to advertisers. Some pay TV premium movie services have considered accepting a limited number of commercials. More and more cable systems are developing interconnections. Videodiscs and cassettes containing special interest programs and commercials may be sold, rented, or loaned at no charge. The growth of cable networks, low-power TV stations, and direct broadcast satellites will offer more opportunities—and will further fragment audiences. Many of the innovations are engineering marvels, but their success in the marketplace is not a foregone conclusion, because consumers have limits on both their time and their budget. People must believe that a service is truly worthwhile, or they won't pay for it.

Major advertising agencies today are assigning personnel to track the new technologies in order to answer their clients' questions about marketing and media trends. A senior vice president and media director at N. W. Ayer, a major advertising agency, has written:

People are running out of time. There are 168 hours in a week. Let's take a look at how adults may allocate them: working and traveling to work—45; sleeping—56; eating—20; watching TV—27; reading—10; total hours per week—158. Since there are only 168 hours available, this leaves 10 hours per week for everything else; running, shopping, fighting, helping with homework, visiting family, friends, doing laundry, going to a ball game or movie, etc. Therefore, advertising to people in the future will be more difficult. Not only because of the increasing number of programs and options available, but because there will be increasing competition to make the consumer aware each option even exists. Americans are changing their priorities, as well as their lifestyles. Media people will have to understand these changes affect the ability to reach the consumer.[9]

Conclusions

Direct response advertising has grown significantly in recent years, and the field offers expanding career opportunities. For advertisers, the fragmentation of audiences means that time costs are lower in some media and that specialized audiences are available in sufficient numbers. Well-known national advertisers are getting their feet wet now in direct response advertising. Creative and production work offer opportunities to construct expanded commercials—even special programs catering to select audiences. Time-buying strategies for direct response advertisers usually strive for discounted time.

The new technologies, cable and videotex in particular, will offer opportunities for advertisers to experiment with new, efficient advertising strategies. The abundance of computer-stored data that can be delivered to the home TV screen via videotex has

---

[8]"Satisfied Shoppers," *Broadcasting,* September 27, 1982, p. 8.

[9]Marcella Rosen, "The Media Person of the Future," *Marketing & Media Decisions,* December, 1981, p. 164.

exciting possibilities. Besides having the convenience of ready access to information, the videotex user can also use the system to bank, shop, and conduct other commercial transactions. The obstacles to the growth of videotex lie primarily in the high cost of the equipment and in the need to market the system for ordinary consumer use.

The convenience of in-home shopping may be increased with the expanding use of infomercials on cable shopping channels. These longer commercials, which fully demonstrate a product and deliver a full-fledged sales pitch, may be welcomed by the consumer who has limited shopping time.

All the new technologies, including cable, low-power TV stations, direct broadcast satellites, video cassettes and videodiscs, and others, will change the complexion of broadcast advertising as we know it today. In the 1980s and 1990s, professionals will find broadcasting and advertising evolving in ways not yet fully understood. The industry's future may be somewhat uncertain, but it can never be expected to be dull.

part four

Social Responsibility

chapter fifteen

Truth in Advertising

Your Mileage May Vary...

Appearances to the mind are of four kinds. Things either are what they appear to be; or they neither are, nor appear to be; or they are and do not appear to be; or they are not, and yet appear to be. Rightly to aim in all these cases is the wise man's task.

In this way the Greek philosopher Epictetus summarized one problem in finding elusive truth almost 2,000 years ago. The phrase *truth in advertising* has been the object of respect and scorn and thoughtful analysis and inflamed rhetoric. It is certainly a source of confusion to the consumer and consternation to the advertising industry. What is truth in advertising? What criteria should be used as measures of truth? Who should establish the criteria? Where should the lines be drawn? Who should bear responsibility?

To begin at the beginning is to recognize that advertising is a powerful tool of persuasion in guiding consumer purchase decisions. The way consumers respond to advertising messages is fraught with complexities. If analyzed as a simple process, this response might be divided into (1) attention, (2) perception, (3) belief, (4) motivation, and (5) purchase. But consumers do not progress through these steps like so many robots. Gaining the attention of consumers through advertising does not imply that their feet are irrevocably set on the path of ultimate product purchase. Each receiver will decode the advertising message in his or her own unique way. How that message is perceived and subsequently believed provides opportunities for the misinterpretations, deceptions, and frauds that continuously plague the advertising process.

People's predispositions are a major factor in whether they pay attention to something—a fact advertisers have known for years. Interest is usually heightened when predispositions are strong. They may be either positive or negative, but obviously the advertiser's objective will be simplified if a receiver already feels strongly about, or is concerned with, a product or promise conveyed in the advertising. Gaining attention is the first goal of advertising—a difficult task when consumers are bombarded with messages. Shaping the perceptions of those who do notice an advertisement is the next step.

Consumers, consciously or unconsciously, look for things that are relevant to them. Their perception of stimuli is based in a mind set that sifts and then accepts, rejects, or simply ignores the message. But since attitudes are not carved in stone, advertisers have learned that a skillful campaign with high repetition can not only make the unaware aware but also achieve an attitude shift. Certainly, individual perceptions are not a reliable diagnosis of "truth," however defined. The complex psychological makeup of each consumer makes it possible for some advertisers to manipulate some consumers' predispositions and attitudes and to exploit their foibles and even their gullibility. Unfortunately, in the marketplace as in the political arena, history has shown that, when one is gullible, one is also vulnerable.

Most people quite willingly accept deception in certain forms, such as in entertainment. The magician who makes the visible invisible and the circus side show barker who lures in customers with promises of strange and wonderful things have fooled people for centuries, and people love it! In these instances, the deception is harmless. In the political arena, however, people's vulnerability and their subsequent deception have resulted in some of history's tragedies. The unswerving loyalty of ignorant masses has led to disastrous wars, and the blind acceptance of religious faiths has sometimes resulted in persecutions and genocide. The sins of the marketplace in deceiving gullible customers are modest in comparison. That does not excuse them, of course, but perhaps the comparison will help to establish a reasonable perspective on the problems.

"Truth in advertising" will not be found unless the problems are first identified and understood. Exactly how is the consumer misled in advertising? What specifically are the areas of complaint? A number of deceptive practices, misleading advertising techniques, or general areas of consumer complaint are discussed below. Some of these practices are illegal, and some are not. Many occupy the gray area that prompts the question of what criteria should be used to evaluate advertising—what the admaker puts into the ad, or what the consumer may take out of the ad?

Bait and Switch

"This brand new deluxe vacuum cleaner with all the attachments is yours for only $49.95, and you'll get our exclusive guarantee. Hurry in today, folks, because this offer will end soon." The bait is irresistible! A deluxe vacuum cleaner for $49.95? What a bargain! This old gimmick still bilks the consumer with the "bait" of a tremendous bargain and the subsequent "switch" to a much higher priced model. The store has no intention of selling this bargain, but it uses such advertising to lure in prospects. Then, the salesperson persuades them that the bargain is really no bargain at all, because a much bigger and better model is what they really deserve. Before the customers can collect their wits, the slick salesperson has the poor suckers signed up for a financial commitment many times the price of the original bait. It may be a vacuum cleaner, sewing machine, TV set, major home appliance, or a series of dance lessons. The possibilities are numerous, but these products have most commonly been the objects of bait-and-switch frauds. Although this trick is practiced most extensively by unscrupulous small retailers, large chains of stores have also been charged with bait-and-switch advertising. It's strictly illegal but often hard to prove. The victims are usually poorly educated and ignorant of their own rights in the marketplace. They may not even fully realize the nature of their involvement. If they do, they may be too embarrassed to complain, or else they may feel that protest would be useless.

Bait-and-switch practices have been found in direct mail advertising, door-to-door selling, on the airwaves, and in newspapers and magazines. Realistically, the media would be hard pressed to check every advertiser for the possibility of bait-and-switch tactics. Usually, however, they know which businesses have indulged in unscrupulous practices and can watch out for ads publicizing spectacular "savings." Such a screening process by responsible media constitutes the first line of defense. The second line of defense lies with the consumer, to whom common sense should speak.

"Scientific" Claims

Americans greatly respect science and technology, and a product whose advertising claims are wrapped in the evidence of "scientific" tests may prove tremendously attractive. The problem of presenting the results of valid scientific tests in advertising messages is horrendous. Testing may involve complicated methods and analysis conducted by a team of scientists. Their findings may appear as so much mumbo-jumbo to the advertising agency seeking to translate extensive scientific data to consumer language. Because the task is almost hopeless in a 30-second commercial, it is easy to see why advertising has perpetrated glib little phrases that may sound reassuring to the consumer but are actually meaningless. What does "doctor-tested" mean? What does "scientific tests prove" prove? The claims communicated in the advertising may or may not be valid. The consumers don't know, since there is no way all the data can be conveyed to them. Even if it were possible, a consumer might need a Ph.D. in chemistry to analyze the findings.

In recent years, the Federal Trade Commission has become increasingly interested in advertising claims based on scientific tests. It has requested a multitude of advertisers to substantiate their claims. The commission subsequently receives reports that require another battery of scientists to interpret. The task of determining the veracity of those claims is further complicated by vigorous disagreement within the scientific community. The consumer does not benefit very directly from such controversy, but the FTC's interest has served to caution reckless advertisers. They are increasingly hesitant to perpetrate fraudulent advertising based on phony or nonexistent testing with the knowledge that the FTC, local authorities, and the media are increasingly concerned and alerted to this problem.

In the area of broadcast self-regulation, extensive guidelines have been developed over the years in the so-called "men-in-white" provisions. Because dramatizations with actors playing physicians, dentists, and pharmacists have been used and abused, a number of guidelines (sometimes ignored) have been established. Third-person representations of professional advice are unacceptable. (For example, the actress may not say, "My doctor told me …") The following phrases are likely to raise eyebrows in the broadcast standards departments at the networks: "Many doctors prefer …" "… tested in leading hospitals …" "medically proven …" "Doctors know about Product X."

The problem of communicating scientific data to the public through advertising messages is not confined to proprietary products. Automobiles, tires, gasolines, laundry detergents, and a vast array of cleaning products have all been advertised in a cacophony of claims and counterclaims. The resulting confusion and consumer complaints are understandable. But because the data presented are often truthful and useful, banning or severely curtailing the reports of scientific testing in advertising would hardly be a service to the consumer. An amputation is not a reasoned cure for a sore toe.

One common and fairly safe technique for suggesting a scientific context is to verbally manipulate the advertising claim. A product may not "cure" a problem but may be touted to "help prevent" or "help relieve" some malady. A commercial may proclaim that a product "can be effective" or even "virtually foolproof." These qualifiers—dubbed *weasel words*[1]—may keep an advertisement on the safe side of the law, but they do not constitute candor with consumers. Most people, unless they are trained in semantics, do not pick up the nuances.

What the distortion of scientific tests indicates, in both direct and implied claims, is the need for strong, cogent self-regulatory guidelines and clear legal delineations issued by the appropriate regulatory bodies and upheld by the courts.

Manipulated Statistics

Disraeli's oft-quoted observation "There are three kinds of lies: lies, damned lies, and statistics" applies to many industries, including advertising. Statistical manipulation will permit the advertiser to "prove" just about anything. Technically, the bits and pieces that make up an advertising claim may be truthful, but as a whole, the advertising may be misleading. "Two out of three doctors prefer …" may sound to the consumer as if $66\frac{2}{3}$ percent of the membership of the American Medical Association endorses a particular brand of laxative. Perhaps only three doctors were interviewed. Although that would be unlikely, the advertising does not say what kind of "doctors" they were.

The *biased sample* is the most common form of statistical manipulation in advertising. The basic and most scientifically valid sample is the random sample, wherein everyone or everything in the population has an equal opportunity to be included. A true random sample, however, is a pretty rare thing because of the great expense and the time required. As a result, most samples cited in advertising claims

---

[1]Carl P. Wrighter, *I Can Sell You Anything* (New York: Ballantine, 1972). This paperback contains a fascinating study of manipulative techniques. Many examples are given to illustrate various distortions of fact in advertising copy.

are based on a stratified random sample. This means that the sample is designed to include the appropriate characteristics that are believed to be in the "total universe." This includes proportioning a sample by sex, age, income, education, ethnic grouping, and so on. The trouble can begin right here. The selection of this stratified sample may not be based on valid information, and thus, there is a built-in bias before the data collection even begins. Many people are simply unwilling or unavailable to be included in a sample. Others are eager to participate. Securing honest answers to questions is a further complication. Annual income, for example, may be stated as one figure to an interviewer and quite another to the Internal Revenue Service.

The degree of bias the above problems represent is impossible to measure. A television commercial with wide exposure cited the great relief from pain that a sample of patients had found by taking a particular brand of analgesic. What the commercial did not state was that the sample was composed only of new mothers, still in the hospital and suffering from postnatal discomfort. They hardly qualified as a stratified random sample. Other shortcomings can increase problems of bias in sample selection. In some cases, the sample may be too small. In other cases, data may be procured from only one testing procedure. In either event, results will be biased. If a coin is tossed 10 times and comes up heads 8 times, it would be ridiculous to proclaim to the world the results of that one sample. Proclamations based on similar nonscientific samples have been made many times in advertising claims, however, and consumers are usually unaware of the deception. They are led to believe that the product will perform as stated in every instance.

The averages quoted in advertising offer another opportunity for statistical manipulation. Most college students know the difference between the mean, median, and mode, but consumers who have been out of school for a few years may have forgotten. They presume that the number quoted is an arithmetic average. The advertising doesn't tell them, anyway. The mean may be too high or too low for an advertiser's purposes, and so a deceptive commercial may replace that figure with the *median* or *mode* and still proclaim stunning results for the product.

Secret Ingredients

Akin to the matter of scientific testing is the fascinating world of secret ingredients. Advertising claims of a secret ingredient are obviously intended to provide a sharp competitive edge. The advertiser hopes that consumers will perceive a unique advantage in the product — one that will result in a stampede of brand switching or that will reinforce consumers' sense of self-satisfaction for selecting the superior product. For many excellent patented products available on the market, product efficacy depends on a unique and valid ingredient or manufacturing process. Unethical advertisers whose products are not similarly blessed are not reluctant to manufacture a claim of a secret ingredient.

In the nineteenth century, advertisements for a wide assortment of tonics and "youth restorers" promised to cure everything from falling hair to the gout. This kind of advertising has all but disappeared, but the public is still offered the allure of secret ingredients. Now, however, the pitch is much more sophisticated. Cosmetics, over-the-counter drugs, detergents and soaps, toothpastes, mouthwashes, and gasolines have all been touted to contain an ingredient or additive that makes the product superior. The ingredient may be a figment of the advertiser's rich imagination, or it may be an ingredient also found in the competitors' products. Both cases reflect advertisers' problems in marketing parity products. Advertising copy is rife with claims that Product X contains Placebo! The illusion of uniqueness may also be created by substituting some scientific-sounding formula for the generic name. Many believing consumers do not know what's been done—or even care—in their pursuit of the golden promise held out to them by the product with the secret ingredient.

Phony Demonstrations

The production problems of TV and the opportunities for visual deception have worked hand in glove on many occasions to execute some frauds as phony as Piltdown Man. Many misleading demonstrations have been impossible to detect on the home screen. Evidence of a product's superiority has sometimes been so convincing that consumers thought the "proof" was irrefutable. In all cases, the victims were the viewing public and honest competitors.

One of the most famous cases arose from the Colgate-Palmolive Company's Rapid Shave television commercial, produced by the advertising agency Ted Bates & Company. "To prove Rapid Shave's super-moisturizing power, we put it right from the can onto this rough, dry sandpaper." Swish, on it went, and off came the sand in clean,

'FIRST I'D LIKE YOU TO KNOW THAT I'M 5 FOOT 2, I WEAR ELEVATED SHOES AND A TOUPEE...'

Cartoon by Sidney Harris. Reprinted with permission.

smooth strokes. What the viewer didn't know was that it was not sandpaper but a sheet of Plexiglas covered with sand. The FTC first initiated action in 1960 by charging the advertiser and the agency with perpetrating false and deceptive advertising. After a full investigation and hearing, the FTC finally issued a cease-and-desist order in 1961 requiring Colgate-Palmolive to withdraw this advertising from the media. The respondent chose to pursue the case in the federal courts, and after years of litigation the U.S. Supreme Court agreed to hear the case. The landmark decision against Colgate-Palmolive was handed down in 1965, and in it Chief Justice Earl Warren declared:

We agree with the Commission, therefore, that the undisclosed use of plexiglas in the present commercials was a material deceptive practice, independent and separate from the other misrepresentation found. We find unpersuasive respondents' other objections to this conclusion. Respondents claim that it will be impractical to inform the viewing public that it is not seeing an actual test, experiment or demonstration, but we think it inconceivable that the ingenious advertising world will be unable, if it so desires, to conform to the Commission's insistence that the public be not misinformed. If, however, it be impossible or impractical to show simulated demonstrations on television in a truthful manner, this indicates that television is not a medium that lends itself to this type of commercial, not that the commercial must survive at all costs. Similarly unpersuasive is respondents' objection that the Commission's decision discriminates against sellers whose product claims cannot be "verified" on television without the use of simulations. All methods of advertising do not equally favor every seller. If the inherent limitations of a method do not permit its use in the way a seller desires, the seller cannot by material misrepresentation compensate for those limitations.[2]

Advertising agencies and their television producers are now extremely cautious in developing demonstration commercials. Affidavits are signed, and witnesses who are present during production will testify, if necessary, to the legitimacy of the demonstration. TV producers who are foolish enough to "doctor" up the product, setting, or lighting or to perpetrate a fraud through deceptive tape or film editing are courting trouble.

A few advertisers, however, still can't resist the temptation to use the devices of a phony demonstration. What are these devices? An old-timer in commercial production can recite them all: whipped detergent suds make a delectable looking head on a glass of beer; vegetable shortening is a wonderful stand-in for ice cream, and it won't melt under the lights; a cleaner will miraculously penetrate the dirt on a kitchen floor if the floor is first covered with powdered graphite; soap chips glisten on breakfast cereal even when sugar doesn't; a soft drink will sparkle if the ice cubes in it contain a wad of aluminum foil; beaten egg whites make a gorgeous lather of "shampoo" and won't turn the model's eyes red; a fine mist of water on cake frosting will make it look like a scrumptious masterpiece; and shaving cream is a good substitute for whipped cream, because it won't melt as easily and the TV crew won't eat it!

The Campbell Soup Company found itself in the soup with the FTC over an advertisement that used glass marbles in the bottom of the bowl. The problems for the producer were evident: all the goodies sank to the bottom, and on camera, the soup appeared to be thin and rather unexciting. When marbles were added they supported

---

[2]FTC v. Colgate-Palmolive Co., 85 S.Ct. 1035 (1965).

the edibles and made them visible on camera. The Federal Trade Commission was unsympathetic. No one adds marbles to soup.

In many cases, these bits of visual legerdemain are harmless enough. They are prompted by the exigencies of a deadline, a budget, and a need to show a product as it really is. Long before television arrived on the scene, photographers working on magazine advertisements used a multitude of studio tricks to improve the looks of a product. No one worried about regulatory actions. Times change, however, and now government officials have little sympathy for the problems of a TV producer who must create a commercial that makes a product look as attractive as possible. Sometimes a perfectly superb product may look impressive on the studio set but it appears as a visual disaster on a camera viewfinder. Naturally, the crew is tempted to "dress" the product in colored lighting, dilute or strengthen it, or do whatever else experience and imagination dictate. Most producers today, however, conscientiously abide by the rules of legitimate demonstrations. The product can still be made to look good on camera, but it usually takes more time to light and stage when the delusory little shortcuts cannot be employed.

One of the most reprehensible tricks of phony demonstrations involves deception not in how the advertiser's product is presented but in how the competitor's product is portrayed. A side-by-side comparison of almost any two brands can hoodwink the viewer into believing that the competitor's product is truly inferior. Seeing can be deceiving. The competitor's hair spray may be used on a model whose hair is hopeless anyway, for example. All the devices that are used to make a product look appealing can also be used to make it appear a disappointing second choice. The advertiser and the agency that unfairly compare their product with that of a competitor are guaranteed a chance to play defendant in a lawsuit.

False Analogies and Dangling Comparisons

Symbols are a legitimate and effective advertising device. They can create high audience interest and more clearly communicate a function for a product or service. The problem for the advertising agency is to find the right analogy. To properly represent a product, the analogy should be intellectually valid. Is the on-camera torture testing an accurate indication of a product's durability in routine use over the span of several years? Wristwatches and automobile tires have been put through a battery of Spanish Inquisition techniques that make unforgettable TV commercials. Are the comparisons valid? Maybe yes, maybe no, but it is very clear that depicting the product in normal use would put an audience to sleep. Although the analogy should be interesting, it should also be accurate and not mislead the viewer into believing that the product is stronger, bigger, better, or longer lasting than it actually is.

"Happy ending" commercials usually tie the product to a social or personal dilemma. Listeners or viewers may be so absorbed in some problem that they are unable to separate the make-believe situation from product reality. Will gargling with Brand X mouthwash double the salesman's orders? Will Susie land the star quarterback by using a certain shampoo? No one consciously believes these implications, but appeals to security and personal acceptance still sift through. Advertisers may argue that the psychological boost of confidence provided by using certain products will help Susie and the salesman achieve success. These comparisons are not really destructive, but ones in the area of health and safety generate greater concern. Toothpaste commercials that promise sex appeal are only silly; toothpaste commercials that imply that product use will eliminate dental caries are misleading. The nutritional value of food products should be fairly presented and not linked with spectacular growth in children or with a bloom of good health that strains credulity. Over-the-counter drug advertising should comply with governmental and self-regulatory guidelines and not suggest that a product will restore vigorous health and youth. Tire advertising should not imply that a certain magic foursome will equip a car with the stopping power of a Siberian tiger.

Dangling comparisons are the result of clever semantic manipulation. "Hospital tests prove Brand X kills 35 percent more germs!" "Nostrum A goes to work twice as fast!" "Get 50 percent more power with Whizbang Gasoline!" "You'll earn twice as much in half the time." "Our widget is whiter, brighter, smoother, stronger, easier, cheaper, better." Than what? One advertiser did elucidate: its detergent is stronger than dirt! The technique is not confined to product advertising. A corporate advertiser bragged in TV commercials that "Esso is doing more."

Like is commonly used in advertising copy to accomplish a comparison. This popular weasel word implies, but stops short of, a guarantee. "Feel like a tiger." "Smell like a rose garden." "Sleep like a baby." The phrases promise everything but are actually meaningless.

Other dangling comparative techniques may be extremely subtle in suggesting a comparison with competitors' products. "Bufferin doesn't upset your stomach!" This is a simple declarative sentence, and yet the hidden meaning is more important than the overt. Does this claim imply that other analgesics *will* upset the stomach?

A non sequitur in advertising copy can slip past the consumer's ear to implant an idea that is not really valid. "This household cleaner is used every day in City Hospital. To sanitize your bathroom and keep it 'hospital clean,' use Brand X!" "Football star Bob Halfback runs five miles every morning and then eats a big bowl of Krunchy Munchees. Build your stamina and strength and make the team with Krunchy Munchees!" The conclusions seem to be based on a valid premise, but they are not.

William James once observed, "There is no worse lie than a truth misunderstood by those who hear it."

Deception by Omission

Deception by omission is a subtle and insidious device often developed on a purely emotional base, and it's one that exploits the immature consumer. "Go now—pay later" glorifies the going and seems somehow to suggest that later payment will be painless and so far into the future that customers need not concern themselves. Since immediate gratification is the theme, the product's shortcomings and the buyer's responsibilities are glossed over. Correspondence schools with their "free talent tests," for example, recruit pupils on a wave of enthusiasm for the profits and fame that await them. Needless to say, the school's successes are few, but these exceptions are presented as typical to prospective students. The work, the time, and the expenditures required are only alluded to or are completely omitted in the school's advertising. A battalion of lawyers is available to assure the advertiser that no law is being broken and that the contract signed by the new student is irrevocable. A student who wants to wiggle off the hook finds it either impossible or not worth the time and expense to wage a fight.

In broadcasting, the time limits of a commercial mean that much information must be omitted. The advertiser is certainly not going to use those precious and expensive seconds to announce to the world any drawbacks in the product or service.

Consumer-protection laws now help to protect the buyer who purchases products with a guarantee or warranty. In many cases, these laws extend to advertising copy, and the advertiser can no longer simply proclaim, "It's guaranteed!" If mention of a guarantee is included in an advertisement, the basic provisions of that guarantee must be presented.

Stereotypes

Advertising stereotypes have been around much longer than the electronic media. Years ago, magazine and newspaper readers were accustomed to a number of easily recognizable stereotypes in print ads. Benign Mother, warm and affectionate, served oatmeal to her healthy cherubs. Father, tired after a long day's work, daydreamed in a chair by the fire and indulged in self-congratulation over the life insurance he had bought to protect his familial responsibilities. The Young Man (handsome devil) smoked his favorite cigarette to project an image of success and sophistication. The Sweet Young Thing, of course, was dependent, shy, and indecisive. Her primary concern was the proper choice of complexion soap. All these images, common in early print advertising, show up in modern broadcast commercials. They are simply redressed and updated. Although the portrayals attempt to be consistent with contemporary society, they are invariably throwbacks to an earlier time when stereotypes were routinely accepted.

Why do advertisers and their agencies create commercials that perpetuate stereotypes? The most common explanation arises from time limits. Advertisers maintain that to inform and indoctrinate a consumer in 30 to 60 seconds, they must make symbols and images immediately understandable. There is no time for lengthy exposition or characterizations that break the mold.

Stereotyping may be by age, sex, ethnic grouping, or occupational status. Even though the possibilities are diverse, the same old demeaning aspects of stereotypes emerge. Children are presented as precocious brats or as unbelievably sweet and well-behaved. Teenagers are usually shallow and preoccupied with their own insecurities (which can be miraculously eliminated by some product purchase). The elderly—women especially—are invariably doddering, confused, and humorously endearing. Both men and women are presented in a number of standard roles. Men are usually portrayed as bright, intelligent, successful, and competent. The "father-knows-best" image is not useful for all advertisers, however. Some prefer the "father-knows-nothing" portrayal, wherein the wife-spokeswoman preaches the merits of a product (usually a personal product) and solves her mate's problem.

Women and women's groups have complained loud and long, often to little avail, about the roles that females play in commercials. There are many stereotypes of women, but the most common (and the most objected to) are (1) the simple-minded housewife who needs the authoritarian spokes*man* to show her how to perform some household chore a better way, (2) the working woman (usually a flighty, befuddled secretary or store clerk) who likewise needs the advice of a male authority figure, and (3) the beautiful sex bomb who adorns the ad (and the product), but appears to be a virtual mental defective. She sometimes carries a briefcase designed to transform her instantly into a successful "professional woman." Two major objections arise from these portrayals. First, the stereotypes do not accurately reflect social reality. Second, the extensive distribution and repetition of these commercials tend to reinforce destructive and demeaning images of women.

Designing creative approaches for advertising directed at women has caused some consternation. Because of the changing status of so many women, is there a distinct difference between the response of, for example, a stay-at-home housewife who has no intention of working outside the home and that of a dedicated professional woman? A major advertising agency, the J. Walter Thompson Company, conducted a proprietary research study that explored this question and many others related to advertising aimed at women. The results were reported in a fascinating book written by JWT's senior vice president, Rena Bartos. She reported that the traditional approaches used to present women in TV commercials were mutually disliked by a wide variety of women.[3] Obviously, advertisers need to update their approaches and make conscientious efforts to avoid stereotyping.

The nation's seniors also have justified complaints about their presentation in advertising, because of the patronizing tone and the impression given that this group's needs and buying patterns are entirely different from those of the general population. Census data show that slightly more than 25 percent of the nation's population is age 50 or older, but this group accounts for far more than that percentage of discretionary income. Older people are an important market, yet even major advertisers have completely bungled advertising programs designed, in part, to appeal to this group. For example, a classic mistake in a TV commercial for Country Time Lemonade Flavor Drink Mix showed a somewhat deaf and befuddled grandpa repeating incorrectly what people were telling him about Country Time. General Foods withdrew the commercial after receiving a deluge of complaints.[4]

Greater sensitivity and improved communication are obvious remedies to some of the stereotyping problems. Review by a variety of people at both the agency and

---

[3]Rena Bartos, *The Moving Target, What Every Marketer Should Know About Women* (New York: Free Press, 1982), p. 251.

[4]Theodore J. Gage, "Ads Targeted at Mature in Need of Creative Hoist," *Advertising Age,* August 25, 1980, p. S-5.

client level can identify these problems before an ad goes into production. This requires input from both men and women, of all ages, with diverse backgrounds and attitudes. No wonder focus groups have been popular in unearthing responses to products and advertisements!

Testimonials

The testimonial radio or television commercial may be just as effective as the door-to-door salesperson who drips sincerity. But although the householder who answers the door knows and understands the motives of the salesperson on the threshold, this same householder often fails to perceive that a product testimonial on television is paid for. It seems so honest, so genuine! Or, at least it did until the testimonial format was beaten into the ground and consumers began to view many of these ads cynically.

In the past, commercials with actors and famous celebrities proclaiming their enthusiasm for every imaginable product reached some preposterous levels. Most often, such commercials today are innocuous and simply amusing. When the actor or celebrity slips into a role that suggests some special expertise, however, the commercials can no longer be considered harmless. Medical opinion, scientific data, engineering competence, or investment acumen should be presented only by those genuinely qualified.

Pat Boone, in a celebrity testimonial with his daughter, Debbie, endorsed Acne Statin, an acne medication that allegedly caused skin burns on one user. The FTC filed charges of false and deceptive advertising. The unusual business arrangement between Boone and the product manufacturer attracted further attention. Rather than being paid a fee for his endorsement, Boone received 25 cents for every $9.50 bottle of the product that was sold. (Consumers, of course, had no idea from the advertising that the celebrity had "a piece of the action.") A consent order was negotiated, and for the first time in FTC history, a product endorser agreed to be personally accountable for representations made in advertising.[5] (Consent orders are explained in Chapter 16.)

In a somewhat similar case, former astronaut Gordon Cooper was the target of an FTC investigation for his endorsement of a gas-saving device for cars. The FTC charged that Cooper had presented himself as an expert on automotive engineering when he endorsed the "GR Valve" in TV and newspaper ads in the late 1970s. The commission charged that he had no such expertise, had misrepresented test data and consumer results, and had failed to disclose that he had a direct financial interest in the sale of the product.[6] The case was finally settled in a consent order. Subsequently, the FTC expanded its guidelines for testimonial advertising. (They were summarized in Chapter 6.)

---

[5] Federal Trade Commission, *Annual Report of the Federal Trade Commission for Fiscal Year 1978,* Part II, Sec. 15.

[6] Richard L. Gordon, "FTC Hits Astronaut for Deceptive Ads," *Advertising Age,* July 16, 1979, p. 1.

Selling Status and Building Bandwagons

In the seventeenth century, the religious philosopher Benedict Spinoza wrote, "None are more taken in by flattery than the proud, who wish to be the first and are not."

Advertising that is directed toward status seekers—however one defines them—is inevitable in a capitalistic society that tends to measure its wealth in material possessions. The great increase in discretionary purchasing power in the last quarter-century has made more and more money available for luxury purchases. Advertising copy for expensive cars, furs, jewels, fine furnishings, and clothing are replete with appeals to snobbism. Although one might contend that this kind of advertising promotes a shallow sense of values, making such a moral judgment is a dangerous and too often hypocritical response. Who is to say how consumers should best spend their money? The techniques used to sell a product or service should not, of course, subjugate human values for material ones; beyond that, the only real cause for alarm is the advertiser who insidiously exploits the insecurities and naiveté of children by unduly emphasizing status. A toy or a bicycle should not be touted as a status symbol. Children should not be led to believe that, if they do not possess a particular product, they are early failures or their parents don't love them.

Bandwagon advertising techniques were a major subject of Vance Packard's book *The Hidden Persuaders.* In the 1950s, this best-seller was termed an exposé of the manipulative advertising industry. The barons of Madison Avenue were portrayed as victimizing a gullible and helpless public with advertising that pandered to their irresistible emotional impulses. Their goal was to build a bandwagon effect. Now as then, a common technique is to use a hortatory statement: "Join the Pepsi generation!" (or be left out!). Commercials are filled with imperatives. The impression left with the listeners is that everybody is indeed doing it, or eating it, or wearing it—and certainly buying it. The device is obviously more prevalent and effective in selling nonessentials than in selling needed goods and services.

Because most national consumer advertising is attitudinal, substance is often superseded by presentation. Too little information is provided, and yet advertisers hope that consumers will hop on their bandwagon. Many do. Still, the good sense and intellectual independence of the American consumer have prevailed. The failure every year of hundreds of test market products is proof that the public will not be coerced or hornswoggled into buying everything it is told to buy. Accusations of selling the unnecessary to the unwitting are probably overestimated, and they belong with the myth of Americans as sheep. Americans are not congenitally naive.

Puffery

If all the exaggerated superlatives were struck from commercial copy, the nation's audiences would probably be bored to death with advertising. A copywriter with a rich imagination and a well-thumbed thesaurus is bound to exaggerate, because hyperbole attracts attention for the selling message. A strictly factual, rational, and nonemotional ad would probably fail. Where, then, should the ethical line be drawn for permitting exaggeration in advertising?

As a rule of thumb, the courts have held that "puffery," as an expression of an advertiser's high opinion of a product or service, is acceptable. It is considered legally to be a legitimate opinion, obviously biased but not a false claim. Puffery claims are legally regarded as opinions rather than factual claims, which, though not proved true, are not proved false.[7]

The question inevitably arises whether consumers may interpret an advertiser's "puffed" opinion as a factual product claim. The debate often boils down to a distinction between what the admaker put in the ad and what a consumer took out of it.

Most puffery is probably relatively harmless, and it is interesting to speculate whether it is axiomatic in many product categories (notably cosmetics) that, the more overblown and outrageous the claim, the more acceptable it is. Who believes that a new hair color will transform Miss Dowdy into a raving beauty or that an aftershave cologne will find the hero with a harem on his hands? No one; but if the commercial is well done, it's fun, and viewers will like the advertising and the product. Lesser exaggerations, however, can be misleading, because they are offered as literal truth even when the product cannot live up to the claim. "You'll find a million uses for this polish" is probably acceptable; but "You'll never have to polish your floor again" is not.

[7]Daniel Morgan Rohrer, ed., *Mass Media, Freedom of Speech, and Advertising* (Dubuque, Iowa: Kendall/Hunt, 1979), p. 269.

"He's worked in so many of those irritating-type commercials, the public is beginning to recognize him."

Drawn for *Broadcasting* by Sid Hix.
Copyright, *Broadcasting* magazine; reprinted by permission.

The creative team writing the advertising puffery should conscientiously evaluate its efforts on the basis of what the consumer will take out of the ad. Whatever the product promise, it should be extended as a reasonable expectation of performance; the product should be able to live up to the promise in normal use. Even if the FTC doesn't crack down, the advertiser who makes an exaggerated promise will be punished in the long run, because disappointed consumers will never again buy the product.

Poor Taste

There's nothing illegal about poor taste in advertising. Many people, both inside and outside the industry, think that poor taste is like the weather — everybody talks about it, but no one seems to be able to do anything about it. There is no shortage of commercials that violate good taste and assault the audience's sensibilities with the shrill, the obnoxious, and the downright stupid. The aggravation of program interruptions is compounded when the messages boast and brag, chant ridiculous jingles, or launch into a hard sell or "you-dumb-jerks" approach. These travesties on good taste are not confined to low-budget fender-thumping retail commercials. Large national advertisers are responsible for equally vulgar commercials. They reason that, if loud, repetitive, and annoying commercials will stick like a burr in viewers' minds, there will be a subsequent ring of coins in the cash register. Making a sale is all they care about.

Gresham's Law that the bad drives out the good is not necessarily valid in advertising. Standards are constantly rising, and a survey of advertising practices over the decades would provide ample proof of improvements. In the broadcasting industry, improvements in taste can be traced to two factors. The first is increasing advertising budgets, which now allow agencies to hire top writers, musicians, photographers, and other professionals who take great pride in their work and often turn out advertising that far exceeds broadcast programing in charm, taste, and aesthetic appeal. The second factor is stringent self-regulation by broadcasters, particularly at the network level. Their standards are filled with prohibitions related to taste. Although the prohibitions are sometimes labeled arbitrary by advertisers, broadcasters have succeeded in banning from the airwaves a host of techniques considered in poor taste. Live models cannot be used in commercials for foundation garments unless they are fully clothed. Commercials for feminine hygiene products are confined to certain daytime periods and late-night television. In addition, these personal products and others are severely restricted in what may be presented visually and aurally. Liquor advertising is not seen or heard on the vast majority of stations, not because of a government ban but because both broadcasters and the distilling industry realize that the use of hard liquor is an extremely sensitive issue with a great many people. Advertising for beer and wines is acceptable but is subject to strict guidelines.

Until 1982, when the Code Authority of the National Association of Broadcasters was phased out as the result of an unfavorable court decision based on antitrust charges, subscribing stations were provided with reams of Code requirements covering a wide variety of "problem" products and services. With the demise of the Code, the networks and individual stations assumed sole responsibility for their own acceptance policies. All these efforts on the part of advertisers, the media, and a number of self-regulatory groups have contributed to a rising standard of taste in advertising. This subject is explored in depth in Chapter 18.

Conclusions

Truth in advertising, even after careful analysis, still escapes concrete definition. The problems that surround this goal are like the patterns of a changing kaleidoscope. Solutions are elusive. One thing is clear, however: the responsibility for establishing and maintaining truth in advertising must be shared. Government regulation, self-regulation, and consumer education must work in harmony to achieve high standards. To abdicate all responsibility to government is to invite eventual censorship, an anathema in a free enterprise system. Yet in order to protect the health and safety of the consumer, regulatory bodies at the local, state, and federal level do have a legitimate interest in enforcing the law and prosecuting advertisers guilty of deceiving and cheating the public. The main problem in legislating advertising practices is to strike a workable balance that permits honest advertisers to function competitively and that also enables the appropriate regulatory body to protect the consumer from dishonest advertisers.

The appropriate and practical limits of government regulation are the object of intense debate in the advertising industry. Many advertising practitioners — including advertisers, agencies, and media — feel that a number of regulatory proposals are either unwieldy or punitive to advertisers with integrity. They pay lip service to the tenets of self-regulation and express horror at extended government regulation. Regrettably, they back up their protestations with precious little time, money, or staff for building an effective self-regulatory mechanism.

One problem with self-regulation, of course, is getting everyone concerned to accept and adhere to such regulations; another is the difficulty of establishing fair standards. Some critics say that if the justices of the Supreme Court cannot agree on the standards established in the Constitution, it would be folly to expect less gifted people to agree to an interpretation of standards for truth in advertising. This argument, however, is no excuse for not attempting self-regulation. Self-imposed standards work best with ethical businesspeople and with those who have inadvertently strayed into gray areas. To date, the successes far outnumber the failures.

As for the unscrupulous advertisers, they will never understand moral preachments. Appeals to ethical standards by well-intentioned advocates of self-regulation will fall on deaf ears. Such advertisers are the vampires of business, who victimize the poor, the elderly, and the uneducated. Eventually, they press the self-destruct button of *caveat emptor.* Then, and only then, do they understand the clout of government regulation. They richly deserve whatever is dealt to them in punishment by the legal system (and probably more).

Particularly in large corporations, responsibility for truth-in-advertising claims is dissipated at the executive level. Brand managers may live or die by their success or failure in meeting goals. Thus, they often do nothing more than perfunctorily review the veracity of advertising claims. Too many other things require the attention of those who run to stay in place.

The stereotype of advertising agency account executives as fearful, sniveling "yes men" who would sell their soul to placate the client gets tiresome, and yet a number of agencies have compromised whatever ethics they might have held. The client and the agency share legal responsibility for advertising claims. In the best of scenarios, this joint obligation accomplishes two things: an agency will not knowingly create deceptive advertising if it knows it cannot pass the buck, and the client will not be able to threaten the agency with loss of the account for refusing to perpetrate dishonest advertising.

Within the province of government regulation and through self-regulatory efforts lie many of the solutions to deceptive and misleading advertising. But what is the consumer's responsibility? In an interdependent society, people naturally delegate portions of their personal decision making to others. They do not have time, nor have they found it necessary, to master many skills. A relatively abundant economy has provided most consumers with all the basics of life and a great deal more. Consumers cannot and will not become expert on every subject involving a purchase decision. Even though they have become accustomed to the authoritarian voice of advertising, the advertising industry should not have to bear full responsibility for consumer education. Neither should the government quarterback every purchase decision, even though it should protect the consumer from illegal and deceitful practices. At all times, consumers should be treated with respect. The advertising they see and hear should be honest, factual, and useful. Beyond that, the consumer — as the recipient of a public education who can study a wealth of information on products and services — must function as a free agent in the marketplace.

In a 1919 Supreme Court decision, Chief Justice Oliver Wendell Holmes wrote:

When men have realized that time has upset many fighting faiths, they may come to believe even more than they believe the very foundations of their own conduct that the ultimate good desired is better reached by free trade in ideas – that the best test of truth is the power of the thought to get itself accepted in the competition of the market, and that truth is the only ground upon which their wishes safely can be carried out. That at any rate is the theory of our Constitution. It is an experiment, as all life is an experiment.[8]

---

[8]*Abrams* v. *United States,* 250 U.S. 616, 630 (1919).

chapter sixteen

Government Regulation — The Federal Trade Commission

Somebody's Watching

The Federal Trade Commission is a controversial and unusual agency. Other governmental agencies, such as the Food and Drug Administration, the Federal Communications Commission, and the Securities and Exchange Commission, operate under specific congressional mandates to perform specific regulatory functions. The FTC's mandate is to prohibit "unfair or deceptive acts or practices in or affecting commerce" — broad and vague terminology. This largely undefined responsibility is subject to the interpretation of whatever political appointees happen to hold seats on the FTC at any point in time. Because its far-reaching powers are largely unrestrained,[1] the FTC has at times been the center of a maelstrom of criticism. Even the creation of the agency originated in a confrontation between government and business.

In the early years of the twentieth century, many burgeoning monopolies killed off their competition with unscrupulous business practices. The situation was so serious that alarmed members of Congress proposed the establishment of a federal bureau to regulate business and prevent the formation of monopolies. The Federal Trade Commission Act, passed in 1914, created a needed antitrust instrument to maintain a free, competitive marketplace. The legislation provided that the FTC would

---

[1]Kenneth W. Clarkson and Timothy J. Muris, eds., *The Federal Trade Commission Since 1970: Economic Regulation & Bureaucratic Behavior* (Cambridge: New York, Cambridge University Press, 1981). This excellent reference analyzes restraints on the FTC from Congress (which passes legislation, approves budgets, and exercises oversight powers), the courts (which may review on appeal various commission actions), the White House (which appoints the five commissioners), and various other executive agencies (which may exercise various constraints in specific areas of responsibility).

be composed of five commissioners appointed by the President and subject to the consent of the Senate. No more than three of the five could be members of the same political party, and each commissioner was to be appointed to serve a seven-year term. (Over the years, many commissioners have been reappointed when their terms expired.) The Federal Trade Commission Act has been amended a number of times over the years. The most important amendment, the Wheeler-Lea Act of 1938, brought consumer protection squarely under the jurisdiction of the FTC and added new weapons to the commission's arsenal.

1.　The FTC could protect consumers against deceptive advertising no matter what effect, if any, such advertising had on competition.

2.　False advertising of foods, drugs, devices, and cosmetics was brought under the FTC's jurisdiction.

3.　The general rule of *caveat emptor* shifted toward *caveat venditor* — let the seller beware. Business would be held responsible for its actions, including advertising practices.[2]

The wellspring of the commission's power to regulate advertising comes from three main sections. Section 5 prohibits "unfair methods of competition in or affecting commerce, and unfair or deceptive acts or practices in commerce." Section 12, which was added with the Wheeler-Lea Amendment, contains a strict prohibition against any "false advertisement" for the "purpose of inducing or likely to induce purchase of food, drugs, devices or cosmetics." Section 15, added at the same time, defines false advertising as follows:

The term "false advertisement" means an advertisement, other than labeling, which is misleading in a material respect; and in determining whether any advertisement is misleading, there shall be taken into account (among other things) not only representations made or suggested by statement, word, design, device, sound, or any combination thereof, but also the extent to which the advertisement fails to reveal facts material in the light of such representations or material with respect to consequences which may result from the use of the commodity to which the advertisement relates under the conditions prescribed in said advertisement, or under such conditions as are customary or usual.

These duties — to serve as a watchdog on competition, to help enforce the antitrust laws, and to assume the major government responsibility for consumer protection — presented an awesome task to the FTC. Many critics have charged the agency with failing to fulfill these responsibilities over the course of its history. The commission, sometimes referred to as the "Old Lady of Pennsylvania Avenue," was alleged in one study to be "steeped in political patronage" and to be a political dumping ground where "positions were openly given because of personal connections and political patronage."[3]

Seven young law students, known as "Nader's Raiders," launched an aggressive

[2]William E. Francois, *Mass Media Law and Regulation,* 2d ed. (Columbus, Ohio: Grid, 1978), p. 393.

[3]Senate Committee on Government Operations, *Study on Federal Regulation: The Regulatory Appointments Process,* vol. 1, 95th Cong., 1st sess. (1977), S. Doc. No. 25, p. 205.

investigation of the FTC in 1968. The consumer protection advocate Ralph Nader, who had championed reforms of unsafe business practices, then developed a keen interest in the organization and activities of the federal agency responsible for regulation in this area. Nader's published report contained a devastating indictment of the FTC.[4] The staff was labeled lazy and incompetent; guilty of political cronyism, and absenteeism; fearful of both big business and Congress; responsible for discriminatory hiring and illegal secrecy; dependent on "voluntary" compliance rather than pursuit of legal remedies; slow to initiate actions; preoccupied with trivial cases; and too timid to seek from Congress the necessary additional powers to adequately protect consumers' interests. Officials at the commission were outraged and condemned the report as unfair and inaccurate.

Soon after the report came out, the Antitrust Law Section of the American Bar Association, at the behest of President Richard M. Nixon, investigated the structure and activities of the FTC. The results of this investigation were released late in 1969.[5] The rhetoric was not as sensational as that of the Nader group, but the conclusions were essentially the same.

As a result of the criticism and political pressures, the FTC was extensively reorganized in the early 1970s. Some of its activities were consolidated, and new duties were given to two major bureaus, the Bureau of Competition and the Bureau of Consumer Protection. The former is primarily concerned with enforcing antitrust laws and preserving free and fair competition. The Bureau of Consumer Protection is of primary interest and concern to the advertising industry. In a number of bold, aggressive moves, the revitalized commission stepped up its regulation of advertising, credit practices, and warranties. Prompted by increasing complaints from aggrieved consumers, American business was put on notice that the FTC would seek out and prosecute violations of the law. What follows summarizes some of the FTC activities and powers that particularly affect advertising practices.

Industry Guides

The Bureau of Consumer Protection develops and distributes industry guides related to a variety of products, services, and marketing practices. These little brochures are simply statements explaining the FTC's opinion on how certain products should be marketed. Guides have been issued, for example, for marketing dog and cat food, feather and down products, and private vocational and home study schools. A guide is not a treatise but a position paper on the state of the law at a particular time. Although these advisory interpretations do not have the force of law, they help determine the meaning of certain industrywide terms and the circumstances under which such words as *gold-filled* or *water resistant* might be construed as deceptive. Conscientious members of the business community are careful to consult these guides when planning an advertising strategy.

---

[4]Edward F. Cox, Robert C. Fellmeth, and John E. Schultz, *The Nader Report on the Federal Trade Commission* (New York: Richard W. Baron, 1969).

[5]*Report of the Commission to Study the Federal Trade Commission* (American Bar Association, 1969).

As a help to the advertising industry, the FTC issued *Guides for Advertising Allowances* in 1972 and *Guides Concerning Use of Endorsements and Testimonials in Advertising* in 1975 and 1980 (see Chapter 6). Another useful FTC publication, *Guides Against Deceptive Pricing,* issued in 1964, contains a number of opinions related to misleading advertising of so-called bargains, retail price comparisons, and the use of advertising that states, "Formerly sold at $_____." The fact that the media are filled with proclamations of spectacular "savings" under the "regular" price is evidence that many advertisers either don't know about the FTC guides or ignore them because they have no regulatory teeth. Perhaps because there is no legal backing for them, the commission has issued only a very limited number of these industry guides.

Advisory Opinions

The FTC gives an advisory opinion in response to a query from a person or a company. The opinion does not prejudice the commission if it wishes to reconsider the matter or revoke the opinion. The opinions are not binding, but they help business people determine where the limits of the law may lie. The commission is selective in responding to requests, and its advisory opinions are not always made public, in order to protect confidential information (such as trade secrets) that may be revealed in the request. (There is hardly a stampede of advertisers seeking commission comments on proposed campaigns. "Why bring this to the FTC's attention? We're not looking for trouble.")

Trade Regulation Rules

The Bureau of Consumer Protection is also authorized by the Federal Trade Commission Act to issue trade regulation rules (TRR). These rules differ from industry guides in that they declare what will constitute an unfair or deceptive practice in the opinion of the commission. Violation of a TRR is considered by the Commission as a *prima facie* violation (meaning a violation at first appearance) of Section 5 of the act, which is concerned with unfair methods of competition and unfair or deceptive acts. The rules are considered by the commission to be legally binding on all parties within the intended scope of the stated principles.

Because TRR carve out *new* legal parameters and requirements, the advertising industry has responded to proposals for new rules with everything from quiet suspicion to outrage. (Advertisers much prefer the FTC's industry guides, which are advisory, established after hearings, and adhered to on a voluntary basis.)

Before rules are adopted, the commission holds open hearings in which interested parties may present their views. The hearings, research, and investigations that contribute to establishing new TRR can span several years.

TRR were not issued until the decade of the 1960s, and the dozen or so existing rules are concerned, in almost all cases, with matters not related to advertising. (TRR, for example, have been issued for putting care instructions on textile wearing apparel and for eliminating the misbranding and deception about the leather content of belts.) The advertising industry's interest in the FTC's power to issue trade regulation rules has, to date, been based on principle and on proposals to issue such rules, not their actual adoption. Because advertising is a creative process, TRR directed specifically toward advertisers would, of necessity, have to deal in broad principles. It would be impossible for the FTC to write detailed rules and attempt to enforce them on such a fluid industry.

To date, the commission has proposed a multitude of rules affecting various kinds of businesses — everything from used car dealers to funeral home operators. Those most affecting the advertising industry cover advertising directed at children (discussed later in this chapter), food advertising, performance claims for over-the-counter drugs, and advertising by professionals (doctors, lawyers, and the like).

For all the time, money, and activity poured into the deliberations over rule making, relatively few rules have been adopted. These include *Advertising of Ophthalmic Goods and Services* (the "eyeglasses rule"), *Franchising Business Opportunity Ventures,* and *Proprietary Vocational and Home Study Schools,* all adopted in the late 1970s. The impact of these rules was to correct abuses in specific industries. For example, restrictions on price advertising were lifted, allowing consumers to shop for the best buy; and certain kinds of disclosure were mandated before a sale can be made.

Other proposed rules, such as the ones pertaining to children's advertising and those dealing with nutritional and "natural" claims for food products, were greeted by howls of protest from affected companies. These companies organized considerable lobbying to exert maximum pressure to kill the proposed rules. Since Congress ultimately controls the FTC's purse strings and exercises oversight powers, the displeasure of a number of important members in the House and Senate can have considerable effect in defusing rule-making. Accusations were made that the FTC was trying to restructure the business world and inaugurate an expensive and unnecessary burden on business. In the blunt words of some, the "consumer crazies" at the FTC had run amok and were trying to engineer society.

Proponents of rule making, however, have always pointed out that advertising too often sells products on a basis that is irrelevant to the attributes of the product or the ways in which it is actually used. Consumers are entitled to disclosure of relevant facts. Rules provide *prior notice* to advertisers of what the commission considers unlawful. Everyone plays by the same rules, theoretically, and both consumers and business have some degree of protection from unscrupulous competitors.

The clamor over a variety of TRR was quieted when Congress passed the *FTC Improvement Act of 1980*. This legislation contains a number of temporary restraints that will eventually expire unless Congress renews them. The single most significant change from the advertising industry's point of view was the removal of the FTC's use of "unfairness" as a criterion for industrywide rules.[6] The commission may not accept staff recommendations for investigations on the basis of unfairness where a record of deception does not exist. (The FTC is, as we have seen, empowered to move against "unfair or deceptive" acts or practices, and a number of proposed TRR, particularly the rules affecting children's advertising, were based on unfairness, not deception.) Any

---

[6]William J. McDonough, Jr., "New FTC Law Clarifies Ad Rules," *Advertising Age,* June 23, 1980, p. 51.

proposed TRR must be published in a notice that announces the rules the commission intends to propose, a legal justification, and an analysis of the projected costs and benefits of the rules. If TRR are adopted, they must pass congressional review by the Commerce Committees of both the House and Senate. This review process, known as the legislative veto, can nullify rules before they are promulgated.

With considerable cold water thrown on the commission's rule-making activities, the FTC staff turned to other activities to handle advertising problems—the Advertising Substantiation Program, increased monitoring by the Division of Advertising Practices, and the pursuit of individual lawsuits in adjudicated cases.

Advertising Substantiation Program

Back in 1971, as a result of a petition filed by Nader and his Center for the Study of Responsive Law, the FTC adopted a resolution that requires all advertisers to be able to substantiate any claim about a product's performance, quality, effectiveness, safety, or comparative price.[7] A convincing case was made that business was not voluntarily providing this information to the public. Soon afterwards, the FTC began the Advertising Substantiation Program, ordering that certain advertising claims be backed up. Targeted were products related to public health and safety—automobiles, dentifrices and toothpastes, soaps and detergents, hearing aids, electric razors, cough and cold remedies, tires, air conditioners, and TV sets. The FTC maintained that public disclosure would be of direct benefit to consumers and public interest groups but also to business competitors, who might challenge advertising claims that had no basis in fact.

Advertisers not sufficiently prepared to back up their claims had to scramble to find convincing substantiation. As the requested data began stacking up in the commission's offices, so did the problems of finding staff, budget, and time to analyze the materials. A very small number of formal complaints were filed by the FTC in response to staff evaluations of the submitted data. In many cases, the substantiation was just placed on public file, and the few people who did consult the information came either from the academic community or from consumer groups.

In an effort to make the program more useful to consumers, the FTC changed a number of procedures in 1973. As a result, advertisers who are asked to submit substantiation now have 30 days instead of 60 days in which to reply, which obviously speeds up the review process. The FTC asks that the information be written in plain language, because previously the average layperson was not able to decipher the voluminous and technical submissions.

By changing the substantiation program from a shotgun to a rifle approach, the commission was more selective in seeking data from advertisers it considered the most likely offenders. In an attempt to organize and standardize the evaluation process, the FTC staff now follows the *Deceptive and Unsubstantiated Claims Policy Protocol* developed in 1975. (See 16.4, at the end of this chapter.) The protocol outlines information that must be sought and questions that must be answered in evaluating advertising claims.

---

[7]*Federal Trade Commission Annual Report,* 1971, p. 11.

Many commission staff members and advertising professionals consider the substantiation program to be the best device to date to encourage honest advertising claims. It is essentially preventive rather than corrective, and it is a tremendous deterrent to false or misleading advertising. Advertisers are encouraged to do their homework before an ad is created. Although many advertisers consider the program a nuisance at best, the result has been better, more honest, and more informative advertising. The commission has a legal right to request these data, and the lesson for the advertising industry has been very clear. The prudent advertiser must have adequate and reasonable proof of claims before the claims are made.

Division of Advertising Practices

As a result of the Advertising Substantiation Program, the FTC staff realized that it needed a rational method of selecting claims for substantiation. It was clear that such a program needed to focus on specific problem areas.

Under the Bureau of Consumer Protection, the Division of Advertising Practices was established and assigned two primary functions: to monitor advertising in both the print and broadcast media and to evaluate claims and substantiating materials. The monitoring program involves clipping ads from magazines with national circulation and monitoring television commercials. As a result of this viewing, the staff may ask one or more of the networks for commercial storyboards. Obviously, the best this unit can do is to employ a sampling technique for monitoring. Beyond this, it must rely on the alertness of other commission staff members and on the active interest of consumers and competitors.

Questionable advertisements are carefully analyzed in terms of the *Deceptive and Unsubstantiated Claims Policy Protocol.* If a significant problem presents itself, the Division of Advertising Practices may refer it to the Bureau of Consumer Protection, which may either initiate a lawsuit or seek a nonadjudicated settlement.

Adjudicated and Nonadjudicated Settlements

The Bureau of Consumer Protection receives complaints about advertising from a great variety of sources. Some complaints may be referred by the Division of Advertising Practices. Others may come from a competitor who believes that a particular advertising technique is an unfair or deceptive business practice. A complaint may be filed by a consumer group or by a product purchaser who feels he or she has been exploited unfairly. Whatever the source, the thousands of complaints that pour into the FTC cannot all be accommodated. With a limited staff and budget, only a small number of cases can be pursued through either adjudicated or nonadjudicated settlements. FTC settlement procedures are shown in 16.1. The most important and time-consuming step is the first one — the assessment and investigation of a complaint. A stringent cost-benefit consumer injury analysis is conducted to identify those cases that have the greatest consumer impact and represent the most serious violations of Section 5.

If, after evaluating a complaint, the commission feels that there is substantial reason to believe that an advertiser has violated the law, it may initiate action. This action may result in voluntary compliance, in a consent order, or in a full-fledged lawsuit.

Voluntary Compliance

If a practice has already been stopped (perhaps because an advertising campaign has run its course) or will shortly be stopped, the advertiser may be permitted to file an assurance of voluntary compliance. The advertiser agrees not to continue the advertising practice that has been questioned by the commission. Such an assurance is not allowed in every case, but the commission will consider the gravity of the matter, the past record of this advertiser, and whether an assurance is suitable in a certain case. This voluntary promise is not legally binding, but if it is violated, the FTC may resume proceedings against the advertiser.

Consent Orders

In more serious cases, if the commission is not satisfied with voluntary assurance, it prepares a formal complaint if there is reason to believe that a particular practice violates a provision of the Federal Trade Commission Act. The advertiser will be notified of the commission's intention to institute formal proceedings charging violation of one or more of the statutes administered by the FTC. The party has 10 days in which to

---

16.1/Federal Trade Commission —
Settlement Procedures

1. FTC staff assesses and investigates complaint with commission approval.
2. Complaint *or* Consent order *or* Voluntary *or* Investigation closed — recommended negotiated compliance no action.
3. FTC issues *or* Commission rejects complaint or accepts order.
4. Administrative law judge hears case.
5. Administrative law judge issues initial decision and order or dismisses complaint.
6. Either FTC staff or respondent appeals, as appropriate.
7. Commission hears case on appeal.
8. Commission makes decision.
9. Case may be appealed to U.S. Circuit Court of Appeals.
10. Court of Appeals hears case and renders decision.
11. Case may be appealed to the U.S. Supreme Court.
12. Supreme Court hears case and renders decision; or it refuses to hear case, which means Circuit Court of Appeals decision stands.

---

respond and state whether it is interested in having the proceedings disposed of by the entry of a consent order between the party and the commission. It is at this point that the case becomes either an adjudicated or nonadjudicated matter. (It is estimated that in four out of five cases, the advertiser takes the latter option of a consent order.)

An advertiser who elects to seek this nonadjudicated settlement may appear or be represented by counsel to negotiate the matter. The consent order will spell out in detail the facts of the case, conclusions of law, and requirements to be binding on the party, which usually means that the advertiser agrees with a commission order to sin no more. What is important, however, is that the consent order is legally binding. "In addition, the agreement may contain a statement that the signing thereof is for settlement purposes only and does not constitute an admission by any party that the law has been violated as alleged in the complaint."[8] After the consent order is drawn up, it is put on public record for 30 days, which permits interested parties to comment on it. Then, the consent order is forwarded to the five commissioners, who usually accept it. In unusual cases, they may reject it and issue a complaint that will turn the case into an adjudicated matter. Unlike voluntary compliance, a consent order is binding on the respondent, and a violation of the order will subject the party to the same penalties as those for violating a cease-and-desist order.

Adjudication Procedures

In adjudicated matters, the procedures are more formal, lengthy, and costly to both the advertiser and the government. Adjudication requires that specific legal steps be followed. It begins with the issuance of a complaint by the commission, and it may end with a cease-and-desist order. The initial complaint must contain, among other things, a clear and concise factual statement of the practices alleged to be in violation of the law, a recital of the commission's legal authority in relation to the matter, and a notice of the time and place for a hearing, which must be at least 30 days after the complaint has been served. This provision allows a 30-day negotiation period in which the commission staff and advertiser may work out a consent order.

If the party elects to contest the allegations, the matter is put on the commission docket, and one of the administrative law judges is assigned to hear the evidence. Formerly called hearing examiners, these judges make the initial decisions in contested cases involving alleged violations of laws administered by the FTC. The setting and procedures are similar to those of a federal district court. The respondent is represented by legal counsel, and the judge hears testimony of witnesses, cross-examination, and oral argument and accepts depositions, documents, and other evidence. After all the evidence has been received, the administrative law judge considers it and files an initial decision within 90 days of the hearing. He or she may dismiss all of the charges or some of them. The judge may issue a cease-and-desist order or another order, such as for corrective advertising. At this point, the judge's jurisdiction ends.

Before the decision is carried out, however, it must go to the five commissioners.

---

[8]*FTC Organization, Procedures and Rules of Practice,* August 15, 1971, rev. February 3, 1973, Sec. 2.33, p. 37.

If neither the FTC legal staff nor the respondent files an appeal of the judge's decision, the commission will confirm that decision in almost every instance. Both, however, are permitted the absolute right of appeal. A brief must be filed within 30 days of the service of the initial decision. If this happens, the commissioners will sit as judges to accept evidence and hear oral argument. The commission may uphold or reverse the decision of the administrative law judge, or it may modify or remand the decision. The final order of the commission is not effective for 60 days. (A cease-and-desist order, for example, would not create a burden for an advertiser whose campaign had run its course by the effective date of the order.)

The 60-day grace period permits time for the respondent to seek review of the case in the U.S. Circuit Court of Appeals. If the respondent decides to appeal, it may continue business as usual, and this includes perpetration of whatever practice has been part of the commission's cease-and-desist order. Matters of this sort can go on for years, and in the meantime, the allegedly illegal advertising practice continues. (The manufacturers of Regimen, a reducing aid, and Geritol, a tonic, fought commission decisions for years in the federal courts. Sixteen years elapsed in the commission's efforts to force Carter's Products, Inc., to drop the reference to liver in Carter's Little Liver Pills.)[9]

Violation of a cease-and-desist order not on appeal in the federal courts will subject the party to a civil penalty of not more than $10,000 for each violation. Violations of the Wheeler-Lea Act involving false and misleading advertising may subject the party to a fine, six months' imprisonment, or both. If the respondent pursuing the case is dissatisfied with the decision of the Court of Appeals, it may seek final review in the U.S. Supreme Court. The high court may hear the case and render a decision, or it may refuse to hear the case, in which case the decision of the appeals court stands.

Other Remedies

In either adjudicated or nonadjudicated settlements, the FTC's legal machinery suffers from two major shortcomings built into the regulatory system. Because the FTC cannot exercise prior restraint or censorship, the perpetrator of false and misleading advertising may exploit thousands of consumers before being called to account. The second problem, evident in so many cases, is that years can elapse while matters are in litigation. In many instances, regardless of the final settlement, an advertiser can reap enormous profits from allegedly deceptive practices while a case is in the courts, and those profits can far exceed litigation costs.

New FTC Powers

During the 1970s, Congress passed several bills designed to expand the commission's powers. An amendment to the Alaska Pipeline Bill in 1973 authorizes the commission

---

[9]Carter Products, Inc., v. FTC, 268 F.2d (9th Cir.), cert. denied, 361 U.S. 884 (1959).

to go to court to seek preliminary injunctions against unfair or deceptive acts or practices. This weapon has rarely been used. It is issued only when a federal court is convinced that the FTC's evidence is substantial enough to warrant such an emergency measure, for a preliminary injunction stopping some sort of business practice is a rather drastic move. Most often, allegedly false or misleading advertising simply does not call for this kind of action.

When the Magnuson-Moss Warranty-Federal Trade Commission Improvement Act was signed into law in 1975, the commission gained many new powers. The law expanded and reinforced the FTC's authority to promulgate rules that would specify new regulatory areas and define with the force of law what is "fair" and what is not. A number of due process provisions were also added to hearing procedures on rule making. If the Justice Department fails to act within 45 days of receiving an FTC request to do so, the FTC can now represent itself in court in civil action. The FTC's jurisdiction has been expanded from matters "in commerce" to matters "affecting commerce." Through a consumer redress provision, the commission may now go to court on behalf of consumers injured by violations of FTC regulations. Extensive new disclosure and content standards for warranties have also been established. (The FTC Improvement Act of 1980, discussed earlier, does not affect the commission's powers granted by the Magnuson-Moss act.)

Restitution

The commission is empowered to seek redress of consumer injuries in certain cases involving unfair or deceptive acts or practices.[10] Remedies include the refunding of money or property, the rescission or reformation of contracts, and damages or other appropriate relief. The theory is that the rustlers should not be allowed to keep the calves. But restitution is obviously a complicated matter to adjudicate, especially in view of today's mass marketing practices. (A next-to-worthless ointment sold to thousands or millions of arthritis sufferers at $1.49 a tube presents a hopeless prospect for restitution.) By definition, restitution would require administration on a case-by-case basis, a lengthy process. It has been invoked in only a few cases, primarily those involving refunds for diet plans, vitamin supplements, and other products for which advertised claims were not adequately substantiated.

Corrective Advertising

To protect consumers from false and deceptive business practices, another recourse is available to the commission —corrective advertising. This regulatory innovation, introduced in 1971, involves advertisements designed to correct the impression left by previous advertising alleged by the FTC to have been false or misleading. The first corrective advertising was run by Profile bread, owned by the ITT Continental Baking Company. It resulted from FTC complaints about the advertisements for this product and for two other products of ITT Continental—Wonder Bread and Hostess snack

---

[10]Earl W. Kintner, *A Primer on the Law of Deceptive Practices,* 2nd ed. (New York: Macmillan, 1978), p. 88.

cakes. Specific copy claims were cited for all three products, particularly in the area of nutrition. Profile bread was allegedly advertised as a diet product, purported to be less fattening than ordinary bread because it contained fewer calories per slice. After some complicated bargaining, the Profile bread case was resolved in a consent order, a nonadjudicated matter. (The Wonder Bread and Hostess snack cake cases were heard by an administrative law judge.)

For Profile bread, ITT Continental agreed to devote 25 percent of its advertising expenditures for the following 12 months to running corrective advertising. Television commercials were produced for this purpose after the FTC approved the following copy:

I'm Julia Meade for Profile bread. And like all mothers I'm concerned about nutrition and balanced meals. So, I'd like to clear up any misunderstandings you may have about Profile bread from its advertising or even its name. Does Profile have fewer calories than other breads? No, Profile has about the same per ounce as other brands. To be exact, Profile has seven fewer calories per slice. That's because it's sliced thinner. But eating Profile will not cause you to lose weight. A reduction of seven calories is insignificant. It's total calories and balanced nutrition that counts. And Profile can help you achieve a balanced meal. Because it provides protein and B Vitamins as well as other nutrients. How does my family feel about Profile? My children love Profile sandwiches. My husband likes Profile toast. And I prefer Profile to any other bread. At our house delicious taste makes Profile a family affair.'' [11]

A consent order in 1972 with Ocean Spray Cranberries, Inc., settled the second corrective advertising case. Ocean Spray agreed that it would no longer advertise its juice product as being as nutritious or more nutritious than orange or tomato juice unless this was proved to be true. Of the advertiser's expenditures, 25 percent was to be devoted to this TV message:

If you've wondered what some of our earlier advertising meant when we said Ocean Spray cranberry juice cocktail has more food energy than orange juice or tomato juice, let us make it clear; we didn't mean vitamins and minerals. Food energy means calories. Nothing more. Food energy is important at breakfast since many of us may not get enough calories, or food energy, to get off to a good start. Ocean Spray cranberry juice cocktail helps because it contains more food energy than most other breakfast drinks. And Ocean Spray cranberry juice gives you and your family Vitamin C plus a great wakeup taste. It's . . . the other breakfast drink. [12]

A careful analysis of these two corrective advertisements clearly reveals how subtle the message can be. In the Profile bread commercial, especially, it is interesting to note that the copy implies that the viewer misunderstood the earlier advertising. "I'd like to clear up any misunderstandings you may have about Profile bread." The advertiser did not mislead; the consumer misunderstood. The Ocean Spray commercial is an example of how a scientifically meaningless phrase ("food energy") can be used to suggest to the consumer that a product has high nutritional value.

In both of the above cases, the agreement to run corrective advertising was part of a consent order. The concept of forcing, or at least pressuring, an advertiser to

[11]*Advertising Age,* May 8, 1972, p. 133.

[12]*Consumer Reports,* February, 1972, p. 64.

publicize past wrongdoing brought vehement protests from the advertising industry, which expressed doubts that the FTC had the legal authority to *order* corrective advertising. Major advertisers in particularly competitive markets would not be likely to roll over and play dead without challenging such an order. That challenge came in the famous Listerine case.[13] As one observer put it:

For over 50 years, Listerine was advertised as a cold and sore-throat remedy, based on tests made long ago showing that Listerine killed the germs causing colds and sore throat. The FTC long had questioned these findings, but Listerine stuck to its advertising. Finally, the FTC was able to prove the invalidity of the tests on which Listerine claims were made. More than that, medical science found that colds are not caused by bacteria, but by viruses that enter through the nose and the eyes, not through the mouth. To the commission, all the evidence was against the Listerine claim, and the court held that during all those years the advertising had been false.[14]

[13]*Warner-Lambert Co. v. FTC,* 562 F.2d 749 (CADC 1977).

[14]Otto Kleppner, *Advertising Procedure,* 7th ed. (Englewood Cliffs, N.J.: Prentice-Hall, 1979), p. 552.

"DESPITE THE FACT THAT THE FEDERAL TRADE COMMISSION COMPELS US TO ADMIT THAT ALL WE'VE SAID ABOUT PELL'S PILLS FOR THE PAST 38 YEARS IS FALSE AND MISLEADING, WE'RE SURE YOU'LL CONTINUE TO BUY AND TRUST THEM JUST AS YOU ALWAYS HAVE."

The defendant was ordered to allocate $10.2 million worth of ads that contained the following corrective statement: *"Contrary to prior advertising, Listerine will not help prevent colds or lessen their severity."* In TV commercials, the FTC ordered that this disclosure be presented in both audio and video and that in the audio portion no other sound, including music, was permissible.

Warner-Lambert appealed the FTC order to the U.S. Court of Appeals for the District of Columbia Circuit. With great interest, the advertising industry watched this confrontation between the commission and a major advertiser. In a two-to-one decision, the Appeals Court upheld the commission order, but it eliminated the language the FTC had ordered included in the disclosure: "Contrary to prior advertising. . . ." The court said that such a requirement could serve only two purposes: either to attract attention that a correction followed or to humiliate the advertiser. The court determined that the latter purpose would be called for in only an egregious case of deliberate deception, and that this was not the case.

As a last-ditch hope, Warner-Lambert exercised its right to appeal the case to the U. S. Supreme Court. In 1978, the highest court in the land denied certiorari—which meant that it refused to hear the case and left the decision of the Appeals Court standing as legal precedent. Advertising executives considered the decision a significant setback to the industry; the FTC had court recognition of a powerful and punitive weapon in dealing with deceptive advertising.

A Special Problem—Children's Advertising

Few issues in television advertising have been more emotionally and politically charged than the controversy over advertising aimed at children. The conflict has simmered since the earliest days of TV and has boiled over in various confrontations involving government regulators (primarily the FTC and the FCC), Congress, commercial interests, and consumer groups. In the last decade, the FTC's actions and proposed actions have resulted in "the strongest lobbying pressures in the history of advertising regulation being brought to bear upon Congress in an effort to have it enjoin, limit or veto" such actions.[15]

The Child Viewer

To better understand the controversy, one must first appreciate the characteristics of child viewers and their relationship with the television set. Children devote a tremendous amount of time to watching television. Research indicates that most of them spend more time with the tube than with the teacher. Nielsen reports that children aged 6 to 11 spend about 29 hours a week with TV; children aged 2 to 5 spend about 33

---

[15] Gerald J. Thain, *Television Advertising to Children & the Federal Trade Commission: A Review of the History & Some Personal Observation,* Advertising Working Papers, No. 9 (University of Illinois, 1981), p. 1. Professor Thain formerly served as assistant to the director of the FTC's Bureau of Consumer Protection.

hours. Although much of the debate over children's advertising has focused on the Saturday and Sunday morning children's TV "ghetto," the audience research shows clearly that both age groups allocate only about 12 or 13 percent of their total TV viewing to weekend mornings. The remainder is spent viewing TV in other dayparts, when programing is theoretically designed for adults or for the "family audience." (Nielsen also reports that between midnight and 2:00 A.M., there are nearly a million children aged 2 to 11 in the viewing audience.) What all this viewing means is that in the course of a year, a child under 12 may see 22,000 to 25,000 or more commercials.

Although much of what children view is designed for adults, children are not miniature grown-ups. Their perceptions and interpretations of everyday occurrences can be markedly different from those of adults. Their world is very small, and every experience and object can assume monumental importance. Youngsters are constantly testing new ideas and searching for reliability. The familiar and repetitious nature of much children's programing and advertising may content them because it is predictable. They *know* what the outcome will be.

Children's mental capacities are constantly developing. The ability to reason, to think abstractly, to compare, to evaluate, and to reach rational judgments comes only with a long maturation process. During that process, children are very susceptible to appeals of short-term gratification.

The vulnerability of children has long been recognized in social customs and in the law. Compulsory education provides them an avenue by which they can escape from ignorance and immaturity. As they are growing up, the law protects them in many ways. Child labor laws, special categories of criminal law (a child, for instance, may not fully understand the ramifications of violating a trespass law), and exemptions from many legal obligations are just a few examples. Adult society is held reponsible for

"I don't understand all that fuss about commercials. I like 'em!"

protecting, safeguarding, and nurturing the growth of children. The FTC has felt that its responsibilities in this area are in exercising controls over the businesses that market and advertise their products to children. Heavy TV advertisers have been the target.

Commercial Content: Toys and Edibles

It's no secret to any adult who takes the time to eyeball the set on Saturday morning that most commercials directed toward children are for toys and "edibles." In terms of product categories, only a relatively few advertisers want to reach children. That, of

16.2 / Toy Commercial Requirements

Since the demise of the Code Authority (see Chapter 18), the toy manufacturers must deal directly with broadcasters, specifically the three major TV networks. Their guidelines and assorted requirements fill many pages and must be met before toy commercials will be "cleared." Mattel, Inc., and its advertising agency, Ogilvy & Mather, Inc., developed the following reminder list for their creative people. The dos and don'ts are extensive and may vary from network to network. The accompanying photoboard for the Barbie Electronic Piano proves that requirements can be met. Note the disclosures that the doll and piano are sold separately and that a battery is not included. Frame number 11 is nicknamed the "five-second island." With a static camera shot and a neutral background, the viewer can see exactly what this toy consists of.

Must do

1. Represent toy accurately (appearance, movement, sound).

2. Show product in safe play situation.

3. Demonstrate toy on merits as plaything.

4. Disclose exact method of toy operation.

5. Disclose assembly requirements.

6. Disclose what is inside package (five-second island).

7. Disclose battery requirements.

Can't do

1. no fantasy

2. no animation

3. no endorsements

4. no puffery

5. no overglamorization

6. no frightening situations

7. no exaggeration

8. no asking parents to buy

9. no fast cuts (scene to scene)

10. no slow motion

11. no speeding up

12. no comparatives

13. no superlatives

14. no camera distortion

15. no dazzling visual effects

16. no volume augmentation

17. no attention-getting devices

18. no real-life counterparts

19. no special lighting

20. no unusual props

21. no costumes on children

22. no irritating techniques

23. no special lenses

24. no "heroic" shots

25. no stock footage (last two-thirds)

26. no trick camera angles

27. no supers (except batteries)

course, is to be expected. Children have little or no financial resources, and their interest in products is confined to what they can personally use or consume.

Toy advertising, over the years, has been a continuing subject of controversy. Toy manufacturers, their agencies, and broadcasters cannot be proud of some of the early advertising techniques they used. The quick cuts, the exaggerated camera angles, the doctored sound tracks, and a dozen other tricks up the sleeve of an adroit director could make a toy absolutely irresistible to a child. The razzle-dazzle techniques of some toy advertising created such howls of outrage that the industry mobilized to initiate self-regulatory reforms. For many years, the National Association of Broadcasters Code Authority served as "central clearance" in reviewing all toy commercials

OGILVY & MATHER
5900 Wilshire Blvd., Los Angeles, Calif. 90036
(213) 937-7900

Client: MATTEL
Product: BARBIE
Title: "BARBIE ELECTRONIC PIANO"
Commercial No.: MABL 7123

JOB NUMBER: 1F 0136

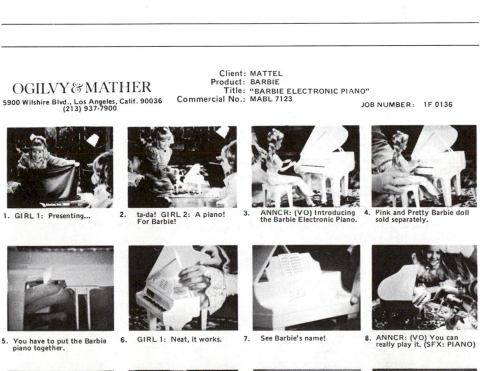

1. GIRL 1: Presenting...

2. ta-da! GIRL 2: A piano! For Barbie!

3. ANNCR: (VO) Introducing the Barbie Electronic Piano.

4. Pink and Pretty Barbie doll sold separately.

5. You have to put the Barbie piano together.

6. GIRL 1: Neat, it works.

7. See Barbie's name!

8. ANNCR: (VO) You can really play it. (SFX: PIANO)

9. Or help Barbie play it.

10. GIRL 2: She's playing her song! ANNCR: (VO) 9-volt battery not included. (SFX OUT)

11. The Barbie Electronic Piano comes with bench, music book and 2 playing wands. Barbie doll sold separately.

12. New from Mattel.

directed at children. With the end of the Code in 1982, the responsibilities for screening these messages fell to individual stations and, most especially, to the three TV networks' broadcast standards departments. The restrictions the toy manufacturers and their ad agencies must live with are extensive. (See 16.2.) In general, the toy manufacturers seem relatively satisfied with and supportive of the strict guidelines. The restrictions not only help to keep government regulators off their backs but also help to equalize a very competitive market. All advertisers have to play by the same rules.

The extensive self-regulatory reforms in toy advertising that have evolved since the early 1960s have neutralized many of the complaints. As a result, attention has shifted in recent years to the other major product category in children's advertising — edibles. Edibles, as identified by researchers in children's advertising, can really be translated as: candy, cookies, cakes, salty snacks, heavily sugared dry cereals, ice cream, puddings, soft drinks, and fast-food restaurants.

"Junk food," declare the consumerists, who accuse the broadcast advertising industry of presenting a course in gluttony every Saturday morning. They charge that such foods are about as nutritious as the packages they come in and that children are being taught the worst kind of eating habits. Actually, the controversy is more legitimately centered on the products themselves, not on the advertising. Advertisements, however, are highly visible targets. When defending these commercials, broadcasters usually reply that they are hardly in a position to reject legitimate ads for legitimate products and that product claims are screened. Many advertisers try to keep a low profile in the controversy. They have a product to sell, know it appeals to children, and know how to market it to an audience of youngsters.

It is doubtful that any market is more competitive than that for cereals and snack foods. Much buying in these product categories is done impulsively, so the TV advertising invariably emphasizes that the edible is sweet, crunchy, and certainly "fun" to eat. (See 16.3.)

Proposed Trade Regulation Rules

In response to mounting pressures and concerns, the FTC in 1978 proposed the following three rules:

a. Ban all televised advertising for any product which is directed to, or seen by, audiences composed of a significant proportion of children who are too young to understand the selling purpose of or otherwise comprehend or evaluate the advertising.
b. Ban televised advertising for sugared food products directed to, or seen by, audiences composed of a significant proportion of older children, the consumption of which products poses the most serious dental health risks.
c. Require televised advertising for sugared food products not included in Paragraph b, which is directed to, or seen by, audiences composed of a significant proportion of older children, to be balanced by nutritional and/or health disclosures funded by advertisers.[16]

---

[16]43 *Federal Register* at 17969.

These proposed TRR would have had a severe impact on food marketers, the advertising industry, and broadcasters. In subsequent hearings and in the several years while these proposed rules were on the "front burner," the rhetoric, accusations, and histrionics surrounding the issue made fascinating reading. The FTC staff was characterized as "consumer crazies" and "national nannies" and was accused of "chasing rainbows." Advertisers and broadcasters were labeled "child molesters," "irresponsible bullies," and "unconscionable exploiters of gullible children."

16.3 / General Foods Corp —Super Sugar Crisp Photoboard

Sugar Bear triumphs again! His adversary is Sugar Fox, but the real winner is General Foods Corporation. Two clever animated characters are presented in continuing mini-stories about Super Sugar Crisp. The commercials are popular with children, and the repetitious nature of the messages builds high product identification.

B&B

BENTON & BOWLES
909 THIRD AVENUE
NEW YORK, N.Y.
(212) 758-6200

Client: **GENERAL FOODS CORP.**
Product: **SUPER SUGAR CRISP**
Length: **30 SECONDS · GFSC4013**
Title: **"ARMORED TRUCK"**

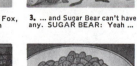

1. (MUSIC UNDER) SUGAR BEAR: My tummy wants somethin' yummy. (SFX) Better give it Super Sugar Crisp.

2. SUGAR FOX: I, Sugar Fox, will eat Super Sugar Crisp in here ...

3. ... and Sugar Bear can't have any. SUGAR BEAR: Yeah ...

4. a good breakfast, featuring Post Sugar Crisp cereal.

5. SUGAR FOX: Sugar Bear, I got Super Sugar Crisp, and you can't have any.

6. SUGAR BEAR: Bet it's yummy. SUGAR FOX: Yummy.

7. SUGAR BEAR: Yummy for my tummy?

8. SUGAR FOX: Yummy for your tummy.

9. Yummy? ... Tummy? ...

10. Sugar Bear! What're you doin' here?

11. SUGAR BEAR: Givin' my tummy somethin' yummy ...

12. yummy Super Sugar Crisp. (MUSIC OUT)

With the battle lines drawn, the opponents of the proposed rules won an initial victory in 1980 when Congress intervened and forbade the commision to issue any new TRR based on a standard of the "unfairness" of advertising practices. (Unfairness was the fundamental basis for the proposed children's rules.) A year later, the FTC threw in the towel, and the proposed rules were abandoned. To date, the FTC has not adopted any rules regulating children's advertising.

This was considered a victory by advertisers over the regulators, but it should be noted that the industry has instituted reforms to correct the most glaring abuses. The vehicles for these reforms were the NAB Television Code and the Children's Advertising Review Unit of the National Advertising Division at the Council of Better Business Bureaus. (Both are discussed in Chapter 18.) The reforms include a reduction of commercial time in children's programs, the banning of "host selling" on programs directed at children, the elimination of vitamin advertising on kids' shows, and an extensive list of dos and don'ts covering both product claims and production techniques in TV commercials.

The FTC has not been the only government agency concerned in the children's advertising issue. The FCC, which licenses broadcasters to serve the public interest, has also involved itself, because the public includes children. (The FCC's actions and proposed rule making are covered in the next chapter.)

The battle between buisiness and government regulators is not over. Struggles continue for years, heating up or subsiding. The players change, the balance of power shifts, issues focus here or there, and proposed "solutions" constantly evolve.

"...NO, HE CAN'T REALLY FLY...NO, THE BAD GUYS DON'T REALLY HAVE A RAY GUN... NO, THIS CEREAL REALLY ISN'T THE BEST FOOD IN THE WHOLE WORLD... NO, IT WON'T MAKE YOU AS STRONG AS A GIANT..."

Cartoon by Sidney Harris. Reprinted with permission.

Conclusions

This chapter outlines and attempts to provide insights into a complex and evolving relationship between the advertising industry and the FTC. With broad and largely undefined responsibilities, the commission can exercise a variety of options in dealing with what it considers unfair or deceptive advertising. Lawsuits can be initiated, or the commission can deal with continuing problems by issuing industry guides, advisory opinions, and trade regulation rules.

The FTC's expanding interest in broadcast advertising has made advertisers and broadcasters realize that the old days of regulators preoccupied with other matters are gone forever. The growing consumer movement and the tremendous changes in the organization and activities of the FTC partially account for this state of affairs.

Many advertisers begrudgingly agree to play the regulatory "game" if only the regulators will stop changing the rules. What they must remember is that regulatory agencies, like advertising agencies, are human institutions. Policies change with the times and with the people placed in high office. The five seats on the commission have sometimes changed dramatically in a matter of a few months. Newcomers invariably want to make their mark with a special proposal identifying them with the pursuit of some public good.

Rule making in the area of children's advertising is a classic example of such motives. With the enormous amount of time youngsters spend with television, it seems obvious that they are affected by advertising — but just how, and to what extent, is not clear. Child psychologists agree that what is really important is children's relationships and experiences with their family, in school, and with their peers. The hullabaloo over the Pink Panther or the Flintstones, and the ads that accompany them, is considered overblown by many people. Broadcasters and advertisers are not absolved, however, from the responsibility of presenting honest and worthwhile commercial programing.

Broadcasters and advertisers move when sufficiently prodded. If they are not prodded, they do not move. Nonetheless, they have eliminated many undesirable aspects of children's advertising. Consumer groups believe that the industry has a long way to go, however, and that only official government action will suffice. The proposed TRR governing children's TV advertising were primarily grounded in moral questions. The economic ramifications of the proposed rules mobilized the industry to respond in its own defense; moral questions often end up with political answers.

Regulation of the marketplace is necessary to protect both business and consumers. What is desirable is a regulatory system that strikes a balance between protecting the public (including children) and providing a free, competitive marketplace in which honest businesspeople can operate.

It is eminently clear that the philosophy of laissez-faire in the marketplace is dead and buried. Advertising is and will continue to be regulated. The responsibility of the advertising industry is to suggest needed legislation, discourage unnecessary regulation, maintain a program of educating the regulators in the day-to-day problems of the industry, and realize that it shares responsibility with the regulatory agencies to provide fair and honest service to the public.

16.4/FTC's Deceptive and Unsubstantiated Claims Policy Protocol

Advertising claims that come to the attention of the FTC staff are evaluated on the basis of the criteria contained in this protocol.

A. Consumer Interpretations of the Claim

1. List the main interpretations that consumers may place on the claim recommended for challenge, including those that might render the claim true/substantiated as well as those that might render the claim false/unsubstantiated.

2. Indicate which of these interpretations would be alleged to be implications of the claim for purposes of substantiation or litigation. For each interpretation so indicated, state the reasons, if any, for believing that the claim so interpreted would be false/unsubstantiated.

B. Scale of the Deception or Lack of Substantiation

3. What is known about the relative proportions of consumers adhering to each of the interpretations listed above in response to Question 1?

4. What was the approximate advertising budget for the claim during the past year or during any other period of time that would reflect the number of consumers actually exposed to the claim? Is there more direct information on the number of consumers exposed to the claim?

C. Materiality

5. If the consumers do interpret the claim in the ways that would be alleged to be implications, what reasons are there for supposing that these interpretations would influence purchase decisions?

6. During the past year, approximately how many consumers purchased the product* about which the claim was made?

7. Approximately what price did they pay?

8. Estimate, if possible, the proportion of consumers who would have purchased the product only at some price lower than they

*Throughout, "product" refers to the particular brand advertised.

did pay, if at all, were they informed that the interpretations identified in response to Question 2 were false.

9. Estimate, if possible, what the advertised product would be worth to the consumers identified by Question 8 if they knew that the product did not have the positive (or unique) attributes suggested by the claim. If the claim can cause consumers to disregard some negative attribute, such as a risk to health and safety, to their possible physical or economic injury, so specify. If so, estimate, if possible, the annual number of such injuries attributable to the claim.

D. Adequacy of Corrective Market Forces

10. If the product to which the claim relates is a low-ticket item, can consumers ordinarily determine prior to purchase whether the claim, as interpreted, is true; or invest a small amount in purchase and then by experience with the product determine whether or not the claim is true? Does the claim relate to a credence quality, that is, a quality of the product that consumers ordinarily cannot evaluate during normal use of the product without acquiring costly information from some source other than their own evaluative faculties?

11. Is the product to which the claim relates one that a consumer would typically purchase frequently? Have product sales increased or decreased substantially since the claim was made?

12. Are there sources of information about the subject matter of the claim in addition to the claim itself? If so, are they likely to be recalled by consumers when they purchase or use the product? Are they likely to be used by consumers who are not aggressive, effective shoppers? If not, why not?

E. Effect on the Flow of Truthful Information

13. Will the standard of truth/substantiation that would be applied to the claim under the recommendation to initiate proceedings make it extremely difficult as a practical matter to make the type of claim? Is this result reasonable?

14. What are the consequences to consumers of an erroneous determination by the

Commission that the claim is false/unsubstantiated? What are the consequences to consumers of an erroneous determination by the Commission that the claim is true/substantiated?

F. Deterrence

15. Is there a possibility of getting significant relief with broad product or claim coverage? What relief is possible? Why would it be significant?

16. Do the facts of the matter recommended present an opportunity to elaborate a rule of law that would be applicable to claims or advertisers other than those that would be directly challenged by the recommended action? If so, describe this rule of law as you would wish the advertising community to understand it. If this rule of law would be a significant precedent, explain why.

17. Does the claim violate [an industry] Guide or is it inconsistent with relevant principles embodied in a Guide?

18. Is the fact of a violation so evident to other industry members that, if we do not act, our credibility and deterrence might be adversely affected?

19. Is there any aspect of the advertisement — e.g., the nature of the advertiser, the product, the theme, the volume of the advertising, the memorableness of the ad, the blatancy of the violation — which indicates that an enforcement action would have substantial impact on the advertising community?

20. What, if anything, do we know about the role advertising plays (as against other promotional techniques and other sources of information) in the decision to purchase the product?

21. What is the aggregate dollar volume spent on advertising by the advertiser to be joined in the recommended action?

22. What is the aggregate volume of sales of the advertised product and of products of the same type?

G. Law Enforcement Efficiency

23. Has another agency taken action or does another agency have expertise with respect to the claim or its subject matter? Are there reasons why the Commission should defer? What is the position of this other agency? If coordination is planned, what form would it take?

24. How difficult would it be to litigate a case challenging the claim? Would the theory of the proceeding recommended place the Commission in a position of resolving issues that are better left to other modes of resolution, for instance, debate among scientists? If so, explain. Is there a substantial possibility of whole or partial summary judgment?

25. Can the problem seen in the ad be handled by way of a rule? Are the violations widespread? Should they be handled by way of a rule?

H. Additional Considerations

26. What is the ratio of the advertiser's advertising expense to sales revenues? How, if at all, is this ratio relevant to the public interest in proceeding as recommended?

27. Does the claim specially affect a vulnerable group?

28. Does the advertising use deception or unfairness to offend important values or to exploit legitimate concerns of a substantial segment of the population, whether or not there is direct injury to person or pocketbook, e.g., minority hiring or environmental protection?

29. Are there additional considerations not elicited by previous questions that would affect the public interest in proceeding?

chapter seventeen

Government Regulation—The Federal Communications Commission

Raised Eyebrows

The Federal Communications Commission, established by the Communications Act of 1934, is directly responsible to Congress for regulating interstate and foreign communications by television, radio, cable, and wire (see Chapter 1). Regulation of radio and TV stations constitutes only a portion of the FCC's work. Its responsibilities also include common carrier services (including telephone and telegraph), citizens' band communications, aviation and maritime radio, and a host of new technologies.

Like the Federal Trade Commission, the FCC is headed by five commissioners who are appointed by the President. Their seven-year terms must be confirmed by the Senate, and no more than three of the five may be members of the same political party. The workload at the FCC is spread among several bureaus. The Mass Media Bureau is of primary importance to broadcasters and the cable industry. Other bureaus are the Common Carrier Bureau, the Safety and Special Radio Services Bureau, and the Field Operations Bureau.

Radio and television stations are privately owned, but since they use the public airwaves, they are subject to regulation by the FCC through the Mass Media Bureau. Stations are not assigned their license in perpetuity. Radio stations must renew their license every seven years, and TV stations, every five years. Licensees are responsible for serving "the public interest, convenience, and necessity," and their performance must meet the scrutiny of the FCC. The Communications Act forbids the commission to act as a censor. Programing policies cannot be dictated, nor can advertising policies of licensees. At license renewal time, however, the commission may review both programing and commercial practices. The FCC does have an interest in broadcast advertising—not in the *content* of commercials (that falls within the purview of the

FTC), but in a number of categories, outlined in this chapter, that reflect on a licensee's responsibilities to the public.

Children's Programing and Advertising

In the 1960s, a neighborhood group of mothers in Newton, Massachusetts, concerned because a favorite kiddie show, *Captain Kangaroo* — (see 17.1), was being canceled by the CBS affiliate in the Boston area, organized Action for Children's Television (ACT). The interests and size of the group have grown remarkably, and today ACT is an influential and highly visible national citizens' organization. It emphatically made its presence known to the FCC, which in 1971 issued a *Notice of Inquiry and Notice of Proposed Rule Making* based on an ACT proposal. Three key recommendations were included: (1) that no sponsorship and no commercials be permitted in children's TV programs, (2) that program hosts and performers be banned from mentioning any product, service, stores, or brand names on these programs, and (3) that licensees be required to provide daily programing for children totaling not less than 14 hours each week. This programing would be oriented to different age groups, and none of it, of course, would carry commercials. The commission asked for comments from interested parties.

The response of the broadcast advertising industry to these recommendations was not unexpected. The broadcasters were alarmed at the prospect of losing all advertising revenues from their children's programing, especially in view of the proposal to increase both the quantity and quality of program service to children. The advertisers whose products are widely consumed by children decried the proposals as arbitrary,

17.1/Captain Kangaroo

A favorite network program host through the years has been Bob Keeshan, better known to the nation's small fry as *Captain Kangaroo*. His show ran as a weekday morning series on the CBS Television Network from 1955 to 1982, and then was moved to a morning slot on weekends. In this early photograph, the Captain poses with young admirers and a display of sponsors' products.

Photograph courtesy of General Mills, Inc.

discriminatory, and unsupportable — either legally or logically. Both the broadcasters and advertisers were particularly concerned about the importance the FCC had attached to the ACT recommendations. Proposed rule making by the commission was not to be lightly taken, and neither were the more than 100,000 signatures and letters from private individuals and citizens' groups filed in support of the ACT proposals.

Two years passed while the FCC mulled over the possible actions that could be taken in children's programing and advertising. A special Children's Television Unit was established at the commision, and it launched an extensive study into the entire issue of children's television. The report it submitted to the commissioners in 1973 contained a sizzling indictment against both children's advertising and programing.[1]

In the two years before this report came out, a number of reforms had been initiated within the industry in an effort to correct some wrongs and display good faith in attempting to resolve problems through self-regulation. Now it was the FCC's turn to act, and the industry waited expectantly to see what it would do. Two options were open to the commissioners — to adopt formal rules that would be binding on all stations or to adopt "recommendations" through a policy statement. Since so much time had passed while the FCC sat on the ACT proposals and considered rule making, some FCC watchers guessed that the commission would "chicken out" and go the policy statement route.

The *Children's Television Report and Policy Statement,*[2] released in 1974, dealt with the responsibilities of licensees in both programing and advertising to children. The commission commended and supported the industry's voluntary reduction of commercial time in children's programing. Licensees were urged to avoid "host selling" and other sales techniques that blur the distinctions between programing and advertising. A clear separation between program and advertising content was also called for by the commission. As for the proposed ban on commercials in children's programs, the policy statement declared:

The Commission believes that the question of abolishing advertising must be resolved by balancing the competing interests in light of the public interest. Banning the sponsorship of programs designed for children could have a very damaging effect on the amount and quality of such programing. Advertising is the basis for the commercial broadcasting system, and revenues from the sale of commercial time provide the financing for program production. Eliminating the economic base and incentive for children's programs would inevitably result in some curtailment of broadcasters' efforts in this area. Moreover, it seems unrealistic, on the one hand, to expect licensees to improve significantly their program service to children and, on the other hand, to withdraw a major source of funding for this task.[3]

It seemed that this controversial issue had been laid to rest, but like Lazarus, it rose again. In 1979, the record of broadcasters' service to the child viewer was resurrected in a long FCC staff report submitted to the commissioners. The purpose of the report, which was prepared by a Children's Television Task Force, was to assess broadcasters' performance in light of the 1974 *Children's Television Report and Policy*

---

[1]Jack Anderson, "Buried FCC Study Blasts Broadcasts," *Washington Post,* March 26, 1974.

[2]FCC, *Children's Television Report and Policy Statement,* FCC 74-1174, October 31, 1974.

[3]FCC, *Children's Television Report,* p. 15.

Statement. The report said that the television industry, through self-regulation, had generally complied with the advertising reforms called for in the 1974 statement, but it concluded that broadcasters had not fulfilled their obligations to provide enough educational programing for children. Thus, advertising issues were generally ignored, but it must be remembered that at this time the proposed FTC rule making regarding children's advertising was in full swing. The FCC elected to stay with programing issues, and in 1980 it issued a notice reopening the children's inquiry. The staff report had suggested a number of options—everything from repealing the 1974 policy statement to adopting rules that would require TV stations to present a certain amount of educational programing for children each week. The FCC's call for comments resulted in another debate over the worth of children's programing. Advertising aimed at children was not a central issue this time. When everyone had their say, the commissioners, taking no action, relegated the matter to the back burner. The installation of the new Reagan administration, dedicated to the general deregulation of American business, obviously discouraged new requirements for broadcasters in the area of children's television.

Sponsorship Identification

When Congress wrote the Communications Act of 1934, it recognized that a majority of licensees would support their operations through the sale of advertising time. Written into the act, in Section 317, is a requirement for the identification of sponsors. That section, in part, states:

All matter broadcast by any radio station for which any money, service or other valuable consideration is directly or indirectly paid, or promised to or charged or accepted by, the stations so broadcasting, from any person, shall, at the time the same is so broadcast, be announced as paid for or furnished, *as the case may be* [emphasis added].

The theory behind this requirement is that the public is entitled to know the identity of the sponsor of both programing and announcements. (The absence of such a requirement would present myriad opportunities for mischief in the form of propaganda sponsored by unidentified groups or persons.)

To help licensees meet the legal requirements, the FCC has issued guidelines and examples of potential problems.[4] A distinction is drawn between the phrases *furnished by* or *brought to you by* and *paid for* or *sponsored by.* The former two examples imply that the program or announcement was provided to the station at no charge. The latter two phrases make it clear that the sponsor *paid* to have the program or announcement broadcast.

In a particularly interesting case, two "sponsors" requested a waiver by the FCC of the requirements of Section 317. They were the U. S. Department of Defense and the U. S. Postal Service.[5] Both asked for permission to eliminate identification from the

---

[4]FCC, *Applicability of Sponsorship Identification Rules,* rev. of May 6, 1963, public notice, as modified by April 21, 1975, public notice.

[5]*Broadcasting,* September 19, 1977, p. 40.

spots they pay radio and TV stations to carry, believing that such an identification diminishes the effectiveness of the messages. It was also pointed out that some stations carry these messages at no charge and others are paid to do so. It was argued that money would be saved if separate versions were not necessary.

The commission flatly rejected the requests, stating, "Sponsorship identification is a critical aspect of broadcast operations, and licensees are cautioned that failure to adhere to the requirements will subject them to the full range of sanctions authorized by the Communications Act."[6] Perhaps because the U. S. government is often ranked in the top 30 national advertisers, primarily because of military recruiting campaigns, the FCC additionally stated, "We believe that the public is particularly entitled to know when the government is using tax dollars to persuade it."

Fraudulent Billing

The FCC is also concerned that licensees operate honest businesses, but dishonest people operate in all kinds of enterprises, and broadcasting is not an exception. Most fraudulent billing in radio and television is in connection with cooperative advertising. A dishonest station manager or employee acts in collusion with a local dealer or retailer. The victim is a national manufacturer who is sent an inflated bill by the retailer. (These problems were alluded to in Chapter 13.) Fraudulent billing can take many forms; in co-op advertising, the deceit usually comes in one of the following scams:

1. The station prepares an invoice billing the local retailer at a higher rate than the retailer actually paid. The bill is then submitted to the national manufacturer.

2. The station invoice fails to reflect discounts or bonus spots that would reduce the per-commercial cost.

3. The station bills for spots that did not run or for commercials that were not truly co-op. (For example, some commercials in a schedule may promote only the retailer and not mention the products of the national advertiser.)

4. The station invoice bills at the 60-second rate when, in fact, only 30-second commercials were aired.

5. Blank invoices or letterhead stationery mysteriously disappear from the station and find their way into the hands of a retailer.

"Clipping" is another form of fraudulent billing. The term refers to the practice of cutting away from a program in order to insert other material, usually a commercial. Networks and network advertisers are usually the victims. In affidavits to the network, the affiliate does not indicate that any part of network programing or commercials was clipped. Virtually all TV affiliates are compensated by their networks for the programing they carry, and thus, these affidavits really constitute an invoice.

Barter programing is also the target of clipping practices. An advertiser may have an agreement with a station to provide a program series that reserves half the

[6]*Ibid.*

commercial positions for the advertiser and allocates the remaining spots for sale by the station to other advertisers. If the station clips the commercials of the advertiser who barters the show, it constitutes fraudulent billing.

It is difficult to know how extensive the fraudulent billing problem may be. What is certain is that stations discovered by the FCC to engage in these practices are in deep trouble at license renewal time. A station in Las Vegas, Nevada, KORK-TV, lost its license primarily because of fraudulent billing and clipping practices. The owner of the station, the Donrey Media Group, appealed the commission's decision all the way to the U. S. Supreme Court, to no avail.[7]

Commercial Time Standards and "Program-Length Commercials"

Excessive numbers of commercials are clearly not in the interest of either the audience or the advertiser. A barrage of commercials that assaults the sensibilities of even the most tolerant audience seems inexcusable. Viewers sometimes think they're the only ones who complain, but advertisers have increasingly voiced their dissatisfaction as well. Time costs are such that advertisers do not want to see their messages buried in a cacophony of commercial noise.

On a number of occasions, the FCC has ventured into the area of commercial time standards, but it has always backed off. It has declined to establish rules that would distinguish overcommercialization from acceptable commercialism. The First Amendment and the no-censorship provisions of Section 326 of the Communications

[7]*Broadcasting,* May 7, 1979, p. 63.

"If you enjoy broadcasting, go into radio or television. If you don't, go to the FCC."

Drawn for *Broadcasting* by Jack Schmidt.
Copyright, *Broadcasting* magazine; reprinted by permission.

Act strongly deter the FCC from doing so, as do a number of precedents that leave programing and commercial policies to the discretion of licensees.

If, however, the commercial practices of licensees are such that the FCC questions "promise versus performance," stations could find themselves the object of an inquiry, a hearing, or even a short-term license renewal. The deregulation of radio by the FCC in 1981 eliminated the commission's commercial guidelines and its policy on so-called "program-length commercials." (Formerly, the FCC had generally endorsed the National Association of Broadcasters Radio Code's time standards, which permitted a maximum of 18 commercial minutes per broadcast hour. Radio stations that stayed within that limit were "safe.")

The television industry has not been deregulated, and, as a result, the FCC still scrutinizes the commercial time standards of TV licensees in terms of commission guidelines. If a station does not exceed 16 commercial minutes per hour, there should be no overcommercialization problems at license renewal time. (This is called "regulation by guidelines" by some and "regulation by raised eyebrow" by others.)

Stations are confused about what constitutes a program-length commercial. The FCC has attempted to clarify the matter and has cited examples: a half-hour program sponsored by a real estate developer in which the narration emphasizes the desirability of owning real estate generally and the desirability of buying real estate at the sponsor's development specifically, and a program sponsored by an association of lawn care and gardening supply dealers that contains both formal and informal plugs for products and prominently displays these products on camera. One major source of confusion is whether remote broadcasts from fairs and expositions, from the opening of a new store, or in conjunction with other such events constitute commercials.

In a get-tough policy dealing with these problems, the FCC targeted "programs that interweave program content so closely with the commercial message that the entire program must be considered commercial."[8] The expressed concern was over the subordination of the public interest by programing that was aired in the interest of salability.

It is important to note that there is nothing *illegal* about broadcasting a program-length commercial, even though the commission obviously frowns on this kind of programing. Violating the public interest standard established by the FCC would undoubtedly mean a hassle at license renewal time, and for most licensees it simply isn't worth it.

Most problems arise because logging program-length commercials as commercial material rather than program material invariably puts the station "over the top" in the commercial time standards it has pledged to the FCC. In TV, the commission is empowered to fine licensees that incorrectly log commercial matter as program material.

In a formal statement dealing with the applicability of commission policies on program-length commercials,[9] the FCC confined its concern to programs dealing with

---

[8] FCC, *Program Length Commercials*, 26 RR. 2d 1023 (1973).

[9] FCC, *Program-Length Commercials, Applicability of Commission Policies,* Public Notice 74-77.

the sale of goods and services. Thus, various religious and political programs and programs sponsored by nonprofit organizations do not fall under this commission policy.

Lotteries

Broadcasting a lottery on the public airwaves is a criminal offense.[10] The Justice Department may prosecute, and the punishment is a fine and imprisonment. Under FCC rules, penalties range from fines to revocation of a station's license. The three elements that constitute a lottery — prize, chance, and consideration — may seem rather simple, yet dozens of stations have been caught up in a snarl of problems with disgruntled contestants, sponsoring advertisers, or the FCC.

All three elements must be present, or a lottery does not exist. A *prize* is anything of value, such as cash, negotiable instruments, securities, merchandise, services, tickets, trips, and so forth. A chance must exist for participants to win a prize based in whole or in part on *chance* alone — not skill. (Competitions ranging from athletics to spelling bees would not qualify, because skill is required to win.) A *consideration* is the price one must pay to participate in the contest. The consideration is not limited to the payment of money. It may include an expenditure of substantial time and effort, or it may include the necessity for participants to have in their possession a certain product manufactured by a sponsoring advertiser, for example. If only product purchasers are eligible to participate in a contest in which there is a chance to win and a prize is awarded, the contest is a lottery.

Many stations conduct promotional contests and tie them in with one or more advertisers. When the FCC has found such contests to be lotteries, the station has usually declared that its misdeeds were inadvertent — that it didn't realize it was running a lottery. Some basic caveats may be helpful in avoiding such problems.

Prizes should be promoted as exactly what they are. Hotel accommodations in Hawaii do not constitute a "vacation trip" if the winner must meet all other expenses. The chance to win must also be clearly equal to every participant. It is a serious deception when legitimate entrants have no chance to win, as when a nonexistent winner is announced or when prizes are awarded to predetermined winners. Consideration — the price one pays to participate — is the most troublesome area, and the FCC has not always been consistent in determining what constitutes consideration. Some fine lines have been drawn in distinguishing legitimate contests from lotteries. For example, buying an admission ticket to a county fair, and thus being eligible to participate in a drawing in which a local auto dealer gives away a new car, does not constitute consideration. In this case, the auto dealer receives none of the revenues from the sale of admission tickets, and thus, the consideration does not flow directly or indirectly to the auto dealer.

Stations may find themselves in trouble for broadcasting information about a lottery, even when they have nothing whatever to do with conducting it. Even publiciz-

---

[10]18 United States Code 1304.

ing the weekly bingo game at a local church is a violation of the law. Local laws may permit bingo and its many variations, and the proceeds may go to charity, but these facts are immaterial, according to federal law. One station lost its license for broadcasting commercials that were actually disguised lottery information — disguised in the form of Biblical references that the station called "financial blessings."[11] The FCC was not amused.

State-operated lotteries are an exception to the ban on broadcasting lottery information. Congress amended the law in 1975 to allow the media to carry both advertising and information concerning lotteries that are authorized by law and conducted by one of the states.[12] More than a dozen states fall in this category, and millions of dollars are spent in the media to promote their lotteries. It should also be noted that the law permits stations in states *adjacent* to those with state-run lotteries to promote these lotteries over the air.

Broadcasters and advertisers may certainly sponsor contests that are publicized in the media, but caution should be exercised and legal advice sought to keep such contests within the legal limits.

Political Advertising

In a typical presidential election year, the FCC handles more than 20,000 inquiries and complaints arising from its political broadcasting rules.[13] Yet only two short sections in the Communications Act contain the FCC's authorization to regulate political broadcasting — Section 315 and Section 312. The following discussion covers only the basic problems that arise in political advertising campaigns — problems encountered by candidates, advertising agencies that develop their campaigns, and broadcasting stations and cable TV operators.

Section 315

No other section of the Communications Act has been the focus of so much confusion, debate, and litigation as Section 315. (See 17.2.) Its language serves as an umbrella to regulate political programing, political advertising, and matters involving the Fairness Doctrine (discussed later in this chapter).

In an effort to bring reform to the campaign process, Congress passed the Federal Election Campaign Act of 1971 and the Federal Election Campaign Act Amendments of 1974. Portions of both acts modified Section 315. The laws are designed to achieve four basic purposes:[14]

───────────────────────────────

[11]*Broadcasting,* January 30, 1978, p. 72.

[12] 18 U.S. Code 1307.

[13]*Report of the Staff of the FCC on the Operation and Application of the Political Broadcasting Laws during the 1980 Political Campaign.* Feb. 2, 1981, p. 1.

[14]*FCC, The Law of Political Broadcasting and Cablecasting: A Political Primer,* 1980, p. 5.

1.   Prevent discrimination between competing candidates by broadcasting and cable systems operators

2.   Make sure that candidates are allowed to speak freely on the air without censorship by broadcasters or cable operators

3.   Guarantee time rates to political candidates as favorable as those offered by broadcasters and cable operators to their most favored advertisers

4.   Make sure that candidates for federal elective office are given or sold reasonable amounts of time for their campaign.

17.2 / Section 315 of the Communications Act of 1934*

315. (a) If any licensee shall permit any person who is a legally qualified candidate for any public office to use a broadcasting station, he shall afford equal opportunities to all other such candidates for that office in the use of such broadcasting station: *Provided*, That such licensee shall have no power of censorship over the material broadcast under the provisions of this section. No obligation is imposed under this subsection upon any licensee to allow the use of its station by any such candidate. Appearance by a legally qualified candidate on any —

(1)   bona fide newscast,

(2)   bona fide news interview,

(3)   bona fide news documentary (if the appearance of the candidate is incidental to the presentation of the subject or subjects covered by the news documentary), or

(4)   on-the-spot coverage of bona fide news events (including but not limited to political conventions and activities incidental thereto),

shall not be deemed to be use of a broadcasting station within the meaning of this subsection. Nothing in the foregoing sentence shall be construed as relieving broadcasters, in connection with the presentation of newscasts, news interviews, news documentaries,

and on-the-spot coverage of news events, from the obligations imposed upon them under this chapter to operate in the public interest and to afford reasonable opportunity for the discussion of conflicting views on issues of public importance.

(b) The charges made for the use of any broadcasting station by any person who is a legally qualified candidate for any public office in connection with his campaign for nomination for election, or election, to such office shall not exceed —

(1)   during the forty-five days preceding the date of a primary or primary runoff election and during the sixty days preceding the date of a general or special election in which such person is a candidate, the lowest unit charge of the station for the same class and amount of time for the same period; and

(2)   at any other time, the charges made for comparable use of such station by other users thereof.

(c) For purposes of this section —

(1)   the term ``broadcasting station'' includes a community antenna television system; and

(2)   the terms ``licensee'' and ``station licensee'' when used with respect to a community antenna television system mean the operator of such system.

(d) The Commission shall prescribe appropriate rules and regulations to carry out the provisions of this section.

*47 U.S. Code Section 315, as amended by the Federal Election Campaign Act of 1971 and the Federal Election Campaign Act Amendments of 1974.

Although the effects of Section 315 are far reaching, this section is read very narrowly by both the commission and the courts. In order to understand the ramifications, its terminology must be carefully dissected.

Equal opportunities   Section 315 is often nicknamed the "equal-time" section, but that term does not appear in it. The law mandates equal opportunities for competing candidates, which may include equal time, but it also requires that a candidate have the right to reach an audience of approximately the same size as that of the opposing candidate. For example, if a TV station gave five minutes of free time to Candidate A at 8:00 P.M. and gave five minutes of free time to Candidate B at 8:00 A.M., that would certainly be providing an equal amount of time. Obviously this example does not constitute an equal opportunity.

Important in planning political advertising campaigns is an awareness of the FCC's "seven-day rule." This requires a candidate who wants an equal opportunity to make that request within one week of the opponent's broadcast or cablecast. If Candidate A's appearances were spread out over several weeks, Candidate B cannot demand that a station provide equal opportunities in the final week of the campaign. This rule allows broadcasters to make orderly plans and relieves them of the prospect of a multitude of candidates all demanding last-minute time that by then may not exist.

Although Section 315 refers only to equal opportunities for the candidates themselves, the FCC extended this legal concept in 1970. The *Zapple Rule* provides quasi-equal opportunities to supporters or spokespersons of a candidate who urge the candidate's election, discuss issues, criticize an opponent, and so forth. In this case, the FCC requires that a licensee must afford comparable time to the *spokesperson* for an opponent, not the opponent himself or herself. (In other words, candidates are entitled to the same opportunities that their opposing candidates enjoy; spokespersons for candidates are entitled to the same opportunities as their opponents' spokespersons enjoy.)

Legally qualified candidate   The FCC rules state that a legally qualified candidate is one who is eligible under the law to hold office if elected to it and that that person must announce his or her candidacy and meet any legal requirements that exist. For example, in many states, candidates must file by a certain date or publicly commit themselves to seeking election as write-in candidates. (Just because a candidate's name does not appear on a ballot doesn't necessarily mean that the person is not a legally qualified candidate.)

It is important to note that Section 315 refers only to legally qualified candidates — not their campaign managers, hired announcers, or other hangers-on. Political commercials that enjoy the protection of Section 315 must *use* the candidate in the message. In TV the viewer must see and/or hear the candidate; in radio the listener must hear the candidate. If only an announcer extols the virtues of a candidate for 30 or 60 seconds, Section 315 does not apply, but the Zapple Rule does apply.

Censorship   Section 315 says that a station "shall have no power of censorship over the material broadcast" by legally qualified candidates. In political advertising, this applies to the "use" of a station by candidates themselves—not commercials in which the candidate is neither seen nor heard.

What about the circumstance of the station manager who sells time to a candidate and then auditions the commercials and discovers that they are vicious, misleading, and smear the reputation of the opponent? A famous case heard by the Supreme Court in 1959 resulted in a judgment that broadcast licensees are immune from libel damages resulting from broadcasts by candidates.[15]

Exemptions   Because the hands of legitimate broadcast news operations were tied by the equal opportunity provisions, Congress granted relief in 1959 by exempting four categories of news coverage from these requirements. These categories are bona fide newscasts, news interviews, news documentaries, and on-the-spot coverage of bona fide news events. (See paragraph (a)(1), (2), (3), and (4) of Section 315.) Before that time, a news department covering a campaign by a major candidate could expect a competing but unknown candidate from an obscure splinter party to demand the same kind of coverage.

In 1975, in the so-called *Aspen Institute Rulings,* the FCC expanded the exemptions to two additional categories: candidates' news conferences and political debates. The theory was that these really qualified as on-the-spot coverage of bona fide news events. In covering debates, the commission requires that (a) the debate be arranged by a party not associated with the broadcaster, (b) it take place outside the broadcaster's studios, (c) it be broadcast live and in its entirety, and (d) the broadcaster cover the debate because of its legitimate news value—not for the purpose of giving a particular candidate a political advantage. Although these expanded exemptions have survived a court challenge,[16] they have been severely criticized as favoring well-known candidates from the major parties and short-changing unknown challengers.

Lowest unit charges   In the 1971 law, Congress added language to Section 315 that put candidates in a special category in buying commercial time to promote their cause. The law requires that broadcasters and cable operators charge *any* candidate running for *any* elective office the station's lowest unit rate "for the same class and amount of time for the same period." The lowest unit rate applies only to broadcast buys during a 45-day period preceding a primary election and a 60-day period preceding a general election. This provision was designed to decrease advertising costs to candidates. The rationale was that, since the airwaves belong to the public, it would clearly be in the public interest to provide candidates with as much access as possible in reaching voters. The print media, however, were *not* included in this requirement. Such an imposition on newspapers, magazines, and other print media, owned by private business, would risk a head-on collision with First Amendment protections.

---

[15]*Farmers Educational and Cooperative Union of America v. WDAY, Inc.* 360 U.S. 525 (1959).

[16]*Aspen Institute,* 55 FCC 2d 697 (1975); affirmed sub mon. Chisholm et al. v. FCC, 538 F.2d (D.C. Cir., 1976); cert. denied 97 S.Ct. 247 (1976).

In Section 315(b)(1), the term *class* refers to rate categories such as fixed-position, preemptible, run-of-station, and so forth. The term *amount of time* refers to the unit of time purchased—30 seconds, 1 minute, 5 minutes, or more. The term *same period* refers to the part of the broadcast day: prime time, drive time, Class A, AA, and so on.

Many of the questions directed to the FCC in an election year deal with the identification of the "lowest unit rate." Rate cards vary greatly, and discounts may be structured in a variety of ways—weekly volume discounts, total audience plans, annual volume discounts, grids, consecutive week discounts, and so on (see Chapter 12). For example, if a radio station charges $40 for a single 60-second commercial in morning drive time but only $35 to advertisers who buy 12 such announcements per week, the political candidate may buy a single morning drive-time commercial at $35.

Time-buyers for political candidates need to be familiar with the law so that they can put together the best possible schedule for their candidate at the discounted rates the law allows. Stations likewise need to be thoroughly conversant with the requirements to avoid possible complaints filed at the FCC by disgruntled candidates who think that they were denied the "lowest unit rate."

Section 312

The 1971 law added an important provision to Section 312 of the Communications Act of 1934: the FCC was empowered to revoke any station license "for willful or repeated failure to allow reasonable access to or to permit purchase of reasonable amounts of time for the use of a broadcasting station by a legally qualified candidate for federal elective office on behalf of his candidacy." Stations no longer had the option of refusing to sell time to candidates for president, vice president, or Congress.

Stations may, of course, refuse to sell any time to candidates running for state or local office or to organizations supporting particular ballot issues. Political advertising for successful stations is certainly not a major profit source, because of the lowest-unit-rate provisions. Most station sales managers have innumerable "war stories" to tell about their frustrations in dealing with candidates and their representatives. But the overriding and obvious public-interest concerns have made the broadcasting industry a crucial avenue of political communication. Most stations appreciate this important role and do their best to accommodate political candidates and organizations.

Applications of the Fairness Doctrine to Advertising

The Fairness Doctrine was incorporated into the Communications Act by Congress in a 1959 amendment of Section 315 that deals primarily with the appearance on a station of qualified candidates for public office. As noted earlier in this chapter, the amendment excluded from the equal opportunity provisions of this section the appearance of legally qualified candidates on bona fide newscasts, news interviews, and news documentaries or in on-the-spot coverage of bona fide news events. Additional language was then added: "Nothing in the foregoing sentence shall be construed as relieving broadcasters, in connection with the presentation of newscasts, news interviews, news documentaries, and on-the-spot coverage of news events, from the obligation imposed upon them under this Act to operate in the public interest, *and to afford reasonable opportunity for the discussion of conflicting views on issues of public importance* [emphasis added]." Most of the broadcasting industry assumed that this language was nothing more than a restatement of long-standing commission policy toward broadcast programing. When some broadcasters suggested that it might be applied to advertising, they were not taken seriously. But since the 1959 amendment, the Fairness Doctrine has raised some of the most controversial and confusing issues ever faced by broadcasters, the commission, and the courts.

Cigarette Commercials

On January 2, 1971, cigarette advertising vanished from the airwaves and became a fascinating chapter in broadcast history. The controversy surrounding cigarette smoking and health risks had raged for many years, and it triggered a sequence of events that eventually led to a congressional ban on cigarette advertising in the broadcast media.

In 1966, a young New York lawyer, John Banzhaf III, sent a request to WCBS-TV, CBS's flagship station in New York City, requesting free time to present views on the cigarette smoking controversy. He contended that the deluge of cigarette commercials urging the public to smoke was not being properly balanced by presentations on the dangers of smoking and that the station was thus not fulfilling its fairness obligations.

"$240 million . . . and he took it all with him!"

The station refused the request, stating that it had fulfilled its obligations through other types of programing. Banzhaf appealed to the FCC. In 1967, the commission upheld his complaint and stated that the Fairness Doctrine did apply, but it stressed that this application to cigarettes was unique and that it was based not only on fairness but on the public interest. The station was directed to use its own good judgment to see that adequate information on the dangers of smoking was allocated broadcast time.[17]

The industry was dismayed at the FCC decision and felt that the enormous revenues from cigarette advertising ($240 million annually) were in great jeopardy. The decision was appealed, of course, and in 1968 the U. S. Court of Appeals for the District of Columbia Circuit handed down a decision upholding the commission's action in requiring antismoking messages to be aired.[18] The decision was based on the broader "public interest" provisions of the Communications Act. The court ruled that the FCC's action had not violated either the Cigarette Labeling and Advertising Act of 1965 or the First Amendment. The court noted that advertising "barely qualifies" as constitutionally protected speech, but it stressed that the decision was not an invitation to the commission to scan the airwaves for other abuses. In the end, however, the court refused *equal* time for antismoking messages.

In a mad scramble to slow the progress of what appeared to be an inevitable cigarette advertising ban, the NAB Code Authority took action. A four-year phase-out program was adopted that would have eventually ended all cigarette advertising on

[17]*Applicability of the Fairness Doctrine to Cigarette Advertising,* 9 FCC 2d 921 (1967).
[18]*Banzhaf v. FCC,* 405 F.2d 1082 (1968).

"Until they settle the fairness-doctrine question, let's just tell them to buy it without telling them why."

radio and television by the end of 1973. Antismoking forces were not placated, and Congress finally passed legislation banning cigarette advertising from the airwaves effective January 2, 1971. President Richard M. Nixon signed the bill into law.

Many broadcasters and members of the advertising industry were irate, but to no avail. They protested that to ban the advertising of a legal product, especially in view of the government's massive tobacco farm subsidies, was the height of congressional hypocrisy. The broadcasting industry considered itself Congress's scapegoat, because lawmakers were under pressure to do something about the dangers of smoking. Since the print media were not prohibited from carrying cigarette advertising, broadcasters condemned the bill as discriminatory. The nation's newspapers, magazines, and outdoor billboard companies could now look forward to a windfall in new revenues, for three-fourths of the tobacco industry's advertising expenditures had been invested in the broadcast media.

Even though the scapegoat charge might have had some validity, much of the cigarette advertising had contained overt appeals to youth, had associated the product with glamour and virility, and had not conveyed the hazards of a cigarette habit. It was not in the public interest to use the public airwaves to promote the use of a dangerous product.

Extension of the Fairness Doctrine to Other Products

The broadcast advertising industry had been greatly unsettled by the commission's extension of the Fairness Doctrine to cigarette advertising. The continuous assurances that this decision was based on a unique set of circumstances were of little comfort. If cigarettes were subject to fairness, what other "controversial" commercials would be next? Nonbiodegradable detergents, beer and wine, over-the-counter drugs, gasoline, automobiles and air travel? The answer came in an important U. S. Court of Appeals decision handed down in 1971.[19] An environmental group, Friends of the Earth, attacked TV commercials for large automobiles and leaded premium gasoline because of growing air pollution problems. The court had no difficulty in finding that these commercials addressed a controversial issue of public importance and that airing them invoked Fairness Doctrine obligations on broadcasters.

The dam that the FCC and the broadcasters had sought to hold against further extensions of the Fairness Doctrine was collapsing. Now, even though a commercial itself was not explicitly controversial, the Fairness Doctrine would apparently apply if the product could be convincingly linked to a controversial subject.

Because the status of the Fairness Doctrine was becoming increasingly muddled, the FCC announced that it would hold hearings on the doctrine and that interested and qualified parties would be given an opportunity to present their views. A major task lay ahead for the commission.

---

[19]*Friends of the Earth v. FCC,* 449 F.2d 1164, 1165 (1971).

The FCC's Fairness Report

In 1974, the FCC released the long-awaited *Fairness Report.*[20] The document, the result of three years of investigation and study, was designed to serve as a reassessment and clarification of basic FCC policy. The advertising industry was particularly interested in Section III, "Application of the Fairness Doctrine to the Broadcast of Paid Announcements," which covered editorial advertising and advertisements for commercial products or services.

In regard to editorial advertising, the FCC stated:

Accordingly, we expect our licensees to do nothing more than to make a reasonable, common sense judgment as to whether the "advertisement" presents a meaningful statement which obviously addresses, and advocates a point of view on, a controversial issue of public importance. This determination cannot be made in a vacuum; in addition to his review of the text of the ad, the licensee must take into account his general knowledge of the issues and arguments in the ongoing public debate. Indeed, this relationship of the ad to the debate being carried on in the community is critical. If the ad bears only a tenuous relationship to that debate, or one drawn by unnecessary inference, the fairness doctrine would clearly not be applicable.

In regard to advertisements for commercial products and services, the FCC noted:

We do not believe that the underlying purposes of the fairness doctrine would be well served by permitting the cigarette case to stand as a fairness doctrine precedent. In the absence of some meaningful or substantive discussion, such as that found in the "editorial advertisements" referred to above, we do not believe that the usual product commercial can realistically be said to inform the public on any side of a controversial issue of public importance. It would be a great mistake to consider standard advertisements, such as those involved in the Banzhaf *and* Friends of the Earth, *as though they made a meaningful contribution to public debate. It is a mistake, furthermore, which tends only to divert the attention of broadcasters from their public trustee responsibilities in aiding the development of an informed public opinion. Accordingly, in the future, we will apply the fairness doctrine only to those "commercials" which are devoted in an obvious and meaningful way to the discussion of public issues.*

Both broadcasters and advertisers were satisfied with this policy. The day-to-day business of selling goods and services through the broadcast media would be insulated from Fairness Doctrine challenges. Only advertisers who wanted to address controversial public issues through advocacy or editorial advertising would have to concern themselves with the Fairness Doctrine.

Advocacy Advertising

Since the mid-1970s, consumers have been the target of an increasing barrage of advocacy advertising aimed at them by major corporations. Most of this advertising has appeared in print, rather than in the broadcast media. Advocacy advertising is directed to specific communication goals and is usually more provocative than the familiar institutional ads depicting a "good corporate citizen." Controversial public issues, however defined, are the focus of such ads. There is even controversy about the label

---

[20]FCC, *Fairness Report,* FCC 74-702, July 12, 1974.

for this advertising. *Issue advertising, editorial advertising, "advertorials," opinion advertising, controversy advertising,* and other similar terms are used.

Advocacy advertising evolved as top management in a number of companies decided to express a "corporate philosophy" in a total communications program. With an appreciation of the growing sophistication of advertising, these executives use advocacy ads to address various political, social, and economic issues.

Who are these advertisers, and what are their motives? They come primarily from the ranks of multinational corporations, oil companies, public utilities, heavy industry, financial institutions, and trade associations. Their motives obviously vary with circumstances. A special research project by the International Advertising Association has identified three "needs" for advocacy advertising.[21]

1. The corporation's constituencies will not tolerate silence. In the face of attack on company policies and practices, silence is interpreted as an admission of guilt.

2. The media are perceived by many companies to be failing in their responsibilities. Fair, accurate, or complete coverage in a controversy may not be obtained.

3. Advertisers taking part in public controversy want maximum control over the message delivered and the environment in which it is delivered. Ordinary press releases may be edited or not used at all by the media.

Other motives for advocacy advertising include the desire to build a constituency that has never before existed, to build public awareness of political issues affecting business, to respond to the public's distrust of business, to build support in resisting government regulation, and to win favorable support from employees, stockholders, and customers.

The decision to present advocacy advertising in response to particular needs has been further buttressed by a number of important Supreme Court decisions striking down the traditionally accepted limitations on the First Amendment rights of advertisers.[22] These decisions reflect the court's recognition that a commercial motive does not necessarily make an advertisement undeserving of First Amendment protection. Of particular note is the *First National Bank of Boston* v. *Bellotti* decision handed down in 1978, which held that corporations have a right to speak out on political issues and can spend corporate funds in doing so.[23] Writing for the majority, Justice Lewis F. Powell, Jr., declared, "The inherent worth of the speech in terms of its capacity for informing the public does not depend upon the identity of its source, whether corporation, association, union or individual."

Interpreting these decisions as a green light, corporate advertisers with particular communication concerns beyond routine commercial advertising instructed their advertising agencies to develop advocacy campaigns.

---

[21] International Advertising Association, *Controversy Advertising: How Advertisers Present Points of View in Public Affairs* (New York: Hastings House, 1977), p. 20.

[22] *Bigelow v. Virginia.* 421 U.S. 809 (1975).

  Virginia Pharmacy Board v. Virginia Consumer Council, Inc. 425 U.S. 748 (1976).

  Bates v. State Bar of Arizona. 433 U.S. 350 (1977).

[23] *First National Bank of Boston v. Bellotti,* 98 S.Ct. 1407 (1978).

Corporations do not enjoy any mandated right of access to any of the media for their advertising. Broadcasters have traditionally believed that they could refuse to sell time to companies or individuals (with the exception of candidates for federal elective office). That belief was challenged, leading to an extremely important Supreme Court decision that brought clarity to the "access issue" and a victory to the broadcasters. Writing for the majority, Chief Justice Warren Burger stated:

Since it is physically impossible to provide time for all viewpoints, however, the right to exercise editorial judgment was granted to the broadcaster. The broadcaster, therefore, is allowed significant journalistic discretion in deciding how best to fulfill its Fairness Doctrine obligations, although that discretion is bound by rules designed to assure that the public interest in fairness is furthered. . . . For better or worse, editing is what editors are for; and editing is selection and choice of material. That editors—newspaper or broadcast—can and do abuse this power is beyond doubt, but that is not reason to deny the discretion Congress provided. Calculated risks of abuse are taken in order to preserve higher values. The presence of these risks is nothing new; the authors of the Bill of Rights accepted the reality that these risks were evils for which there was no acceptable remedy other than a spirit of moderation and a sense of responsibility—and civility—on the part of those who exercise the guaranteed freedoms of expression.[24]

Thus, broadcasters are free to refuse to sell time for advocacy advertising—and also free to accept such advertising. That acceptance, however, is accompanied by Fairness Doctrine obligations spelled out in the FCC's 1974 *Fairness Report.* Second-guessing the motives of the advertiser presents a difficult problem for broadcasters concerned about these obligations. Some messages are so subtle that it would be impossible to find half a dozen people who agreed on a single interpretation of the advertiser's motives.

The reluctance of broadcasters to accept this advertising has been a frustration to corporations that feel print advertising may not communicate as effectively or may not reach the kind of audience or the mass of consumers available in television. Advocacy campaigns launched exclusively in newspapers and magazines obviously offer the corporation an opportunity to present lengthy, detailed arguments. Special interest publications reach select audiences. But for advertisers who want to reach a mass audience and build a national consensus for a particular viewpoint, television presents a more efficient media buy in terms of both cost and total audience reached.

Broadcasters who have declined to accept advocacy advertising center their reasons on two traditional arguments: (1) the public is best served by coverage of controversial issues through news and public affairs programing, and (2) those corporations with enormous sums to spend in advocacy advertising would control the agenda of public debate and exert excessive influence in the formation of public opinion (the "deep-pocket" theory).

The first argument is challenged by a number of corporations, notably oil companies, which assert that they have been "maligned, misquoted, misunderstood, misrepresented and generally sandbagged by TV news."[25] The second argument is rebutted

---

[24]*Columbia Broadcasting System v. Democratic National Committee,* 93 S.Ct. 2080, 2097 (1973).

[25] Frank Donegan, "Networks vs. Big Oil: Why TV News Is Coming Up Dry," *Panorama,* August, 1980, p. 54.

17.3/A Protest against "Censorship"

Frustrated at the refusal of the three major television networks to approve TV storyboards for corporate commercials, Kaiser Aluminum turned to print advertising. The script and visual for one of these commercials is shown here. Kaiser had the label "censored" added to the visual and incorporated it into ads that ran in a half-dozen major newspapers across the country. The ad complained that the rejection of the commercials was a restraint on corporate speech, noting further: "There is no doubt that television is one of the most powerful media in operation today. And we believe that access to this medium must be kept free and open."

Announcer

Is free enterprise an endangered species? How much government regulation is enough? Is business bad just because it's big? Or does a country like ours require a diversity of business—both big and small?

Will excessive control over big business lead to control over all our business?

The answers are up to you.

Whatever your views let your elected representatives know.

People, one by one, need to speak up now. You can help keep free enterprise free.

A message from Kaiser Aluminum.

One person can make a difference.

Courtesy of Kaiser Aluminum & Chemical Corporation.

by a number of corporate spokespersons. An executive at the Kaiser Aluminum & Chemical Corporation has addressed the "deep-pocket" theory (see also 17.3):

The salient fact here is that those who speak the loudest on ideas and opinions in this country are those who have the biggest soap boxes, not those with the biggest pocketbooks. Actors, athletes, politicians, activists and even bureaucrats . . . have access to television, which major corporations do not, and for all practical purposes they dominate the national debate. All we want to do is be able to participate.[26]

Stations will obviously be more receptive to those commercials that present views on subjects whose "other side" has already been covered in its programing. The problems multiply for issues raised in advocacy commercials that have not been fully covered on the station. Fairness Doctrine obligations will be fulfilled if the broadcaster can find another corporation, group, or individual to buy the response time to present the other view. This is usually unlikely, and then the station is obliged to present a contrasting view in its own programing or to seek out a spokesperson or group to respond free of charge to the original commercial. Thus, the revenues from advocacy advertising may be more than offset in expensive, time-consuming Fairness Doctrine obligations.

The networks, with some extremely limited exceptions by ABC, have steadfastly refused advocacy commercials. (See 17.4.) They cite the traditional reasons, but the economic ramifications of the Fairness Doctrine cannot be overlooked. Carrying such messages could, in effect, commit their hundreds of individual affiliates to possible Fairness Doctrine problems.

It is likely that American TV screens will present much more advocacy advertising in the 1980s and 1990s. Some of the messages will be useful and informative; in these cases, the public will clearly benefit. A proliferation of advocacy advertising, however, will inevitably include some messages that are misleading, incomplete, unfair, and designed to manipulate consumers. (Advertising for ordinary goods and services has always offered similar opportunities for mischief.) Consumers, individually and in groups, need to be aware of the increase in advocacy advertising, be able to recognize it, and understand the expanding First Amendment protection these ads enjoy.

Broadcasters, many of whom will be reluctantly cast in the role of "gatekeeper" for corporate speech, will have to struggle with their willingness to carry controversial messages and keep faith with the Fairness Doctrine. Broadcasters are required only to make a good-faith effort in determining whether a commercial invokes the Fairness Doctrine. As a legal requirement, it seems simple; as a moral issue, broadcasters must consider their objectivity or lack of it in evaluating these commercials, their dedication to profit goals, and their obligations to their audience.

Conclusions

This chapter outlines the primary responsibilities assigned to the FCC in regulating broadcast advertising. That regulation is confined to specific areas that are concerned

---

[26]*Broadcasting,* April 13, 1981, p. 144.

with the public-interest responsibilities of licensees. (Regulating the *content* of advertising falls within the jurisdiction of the FTC.)

The Communications Act of 1934 and various rules and regulations adopted by the FCC provide radio and TV stations with some strict guidelines for avoiding problems involving sponsorship identifications, fraudulent billing practices, lotteries, and acceptable commercial time standards. These matters are quite specific and generally not subject to the push and shove of regulatory politics. Other issues pertaining to licensees and broadcast advertising are not so simple.

Children's advertising and programing have been the subject of extensive investigation, lobbying, litigation, and general hand wringing, not only at the FTC but also at the FCC. Because the Communications Act forbids the FCC to censor programing or advertising and because of an intensive and effective industry lobby, the commission declined to adopt rules on children's advertising and programing that would be binding on licensees. Instead, the FCC adopted the 1974 *Children's Television Report and Policy Statement,* which outlined certain expectations for the nation's broadcasting industry. Most of the alleged abuses in advertising practices have been corrected through self-regulation. Programing insufficiencies for the nation's children appear to be the area of most obvious failure.

Political advertising, and the use of the broadcast media by candidates generally, constitutes a continuing headache for broadcasters. Section 315 of the Communications Act provides candidates with a special status in dealing with licensees. The provisions of the law are often confusing, and many broadcasters have discovered how easy it is to violate the law inadvertently. Seeking legal advice and carefully studying the FCC's rules can forestall problems for broadcasters in dealing with candidates. A spirit of accommodation doesn't hurt.

Section 315 also incorporates the famous — or infamous — Fairness Doctrine, which requires licensees to provide reasonable opportunity for the discussion of controversial public issues. In most instances, this doctrine has been applied to programing, but its application to cigarette commericials in 1967 triggered a sequence of events that alarmed both the broadcasters and the advertising industry. Would wholesale applications of the doctrine be applied to commercial messages? Following some interesting and very important court cases, the FCC adopted the 1974 *Fairness Report,* which applies the doctrine only to commercials that *explicitly* address controversial issues. Most advertisers breathed a sigh of relief, but those who were interested in presenting advocacy advertising messages were destined to face continuing frustrations. Many stations and networks refuse to carry these commercials, primarily because they wish to avoid a Fairness Doctrine hassle. This constitutes a classic confrontation between advertisers, who wish to exercise their First Amendment rights, and broadcasters, who are legally free to refuse to carry such messages.

Regulating broadcasting and advertising is hardly a cut-and-dried affair. Some specific problems have been effectively neutralized by intelligently developed regulation, and these remedies have been welcomed by the industry. Other problems evolve and change, and that is to be expected in an industry that is anything but static. It makes the examination and study of regulatory issues controversial and always interesting.

17.4/An Advocate of Advocacy

Why do two networks refuse to run this commercial?

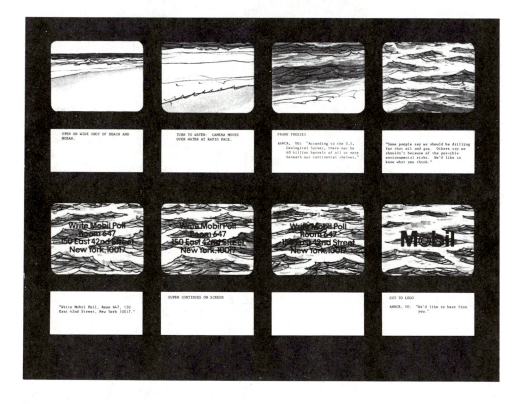

CBS:

"We regret that the subject matter of this commercial...deals with a controversial issue of public importance and does not fall within our 'goods and services' limitation for commercial acceptance."

ABC:

"This will advise that we have reviewed the above-captioned commercial and are unable to grant an approval for use over our facilities."

NBC:

"Approved as submitted."

As you can see from the storyboard reproduced above, we want to ask the public how it feels about offshore drilling.

But the policies of two national television networks prevent us from asking this question.

This is dangerous, it seems to us. Any restraint on free discussion is dangerous. Any policy that restricts the flow of information or ideas is potentially harmful.

The networks say that the public's need for information is best served in news programs prepared by broadcast journalists.

Behind the networks' rejection of idea advertising may be the fear that demands for equal time will be made. We have a reasonable answer to that. We offer to pay for equal time, when the request is legitimate.

©1974 Mobil Oil Corporation

We think *more* discussion, not less, is needed of vital issues such as the issue of America's energy needs. We're willing to buy the time to say what we should be saying. We're willing to buy time so you can hear opposing views.

But two big networks aren't willing to make time available, in this case.

You know the principle at stake here. You've seen it in writing, more than once:

*"Congress shall make no law...
abridging the freedom of speech."*

You've seen it in the First Amendment to the Constitution of the United States. So have we.

We'd like to know what you think about either of these issues. Write Room 647, 150 East 42nd Street, New York, N.Y. 10017.

chapter eighteen

Self-Regulation

Mirror, Mirror on the Wall

"The readiest and surest way to get rid of censure is to correct ourselves." This observation by Demosthenes, an orator and statesman of ancient Greece, is valid today, whether the subject be personal relationships, politics, or commerce. Criticism, censure, and even censorship are aspects of correction that can be employed either with sensitivity and restraint or with the heavy hand of formal regulation.

Public-interest obligations mandate the regulation of both broadcasting and advertising, and yet many professionals who work in the business find regulation by government an anathema. Their reasons are varied but are usually founded in a belief that government regulation is often uneven, unfair, or unduly burdensome to the honest businessperson. The concept of a self-regulatory body or bodies, administered by professionals who understand the industry, is far more attractive to them.

It is one thing to desire an effective mechanism for advertising self-regulation and quite another to create it. Self-regulation means that the industry must cooperate, provide financial support, and make some degree of individual and corporate sacrifice. Not everyone agrees to the price tag. In designing systems for self-regulation, a number of problems have been encountered. Decision makers at advertising agencies, client companies, and the media have varying degrees of respect and support for these systems. Some endorse self-regulation wholeheartedly, and others are skeptical and even hostile to the prospect of a self-regulatory organization "sticking its nose into our business."

A variety of requirements must be met in establishing workable self-regulation. The system has to provide a fair hearing to everyone concerned. Advertisers and their agencies may be called on to defend a single commercial or an entire campaign. Open and responsive communication is needed to make the system operate efficiently and effectively with a minimum of ruffled feathers. The Federal Trade Commission, the Federal Communications Commission, and various state and local consumer protection agencies should be apprised of the work of any self-regulatory entities.

The lack of sanctions is one obstacle to effective self-regulation. Voluntary cooperation is essential or the system won't work. By definition, a self-regulatory organization cannot impose fines, bring lawsuits, or throw anyone in jail. Reason, moral persuasion, and an appeal to the best motives of a company or individual are the primary weapons in the arsenal. For the most part, these weapons have been quite successful. Two other weapons are available in certain instances. In the case of self-regulation exercised by the media, a station, network, newspaper, or magazine may simply refuse to accept an advertisement. A final weapon is the threat of bad publicity. Most companies would rather change their ad campaign than have a "questionable" advertisement become the focus of news reports in the media.

A worldwide study of advertising self-regulation, sponsored by the International Advertising Association, identified common characteristics among well-developed systems of self-regulation:[1]

1.   involvement of or liaison with all possible interested parties to create a real exchange of ideas and a sense of participation

2.   the development of a positive identity for the self-regulatory effort rather than a defensive posture

3.   the firm, written commitment on the part of all participants—whether associations or individual firms—to join the self-regulatory effort and to reveal precisely the nature of their individual financial involvement

4.   the definition of precise areas of responsibility and clear-cut structures, whether these involve permanent staffs or volunteer committees

5.   the careful pilot testing of proposed self-regulatory procedures before they are publicly announced

6.   the need for procedures to launch publicly those self-regulatory codes that have been well tested and approved

7.   the need for a constant effort to establish and maintain a clear reputation for independence from special interests

8.   the establishment of clear-cut "time frames" and "activity cycles" through formalized plans and written schedules for administrative procedures and the accomplishment of agreed-upon objectives

9.   the formulation of policies and procedures to anticipate impending difficulties

10.   the establishment of a program of structured communications to reach audiences outside the advertising industry

---

[1]James P. Neelankavil and Albert B. Stridsberg, *Advertising Self-Regulation: A Global Perspective* (New York: Hastings House, 1980), p. 12.

In broadcasting and in advertising, codes of conduct and statements of ethical standards have been around for a long time. Although the principles (and the platitudes) in the early years of broadcast history were lofty, it soon became apparent that a code of self-regulation without enforcement or review mechanisms had little value on a day-to-day basis. Today, these mechanisms do exist. They have evolved over the years as a result of political pressures, criticism from many quarters, and the industry's own determination to fulfill its obligations to the public.

The broadcast advertising industry has been affected most dramatically by three self-regulatory entities: the broadcast standards departments of the various networks, first organized in the 1930s; the Code Authority of the National Association of Broadcasters, which began operations in the early 1950s; and the National Advertising Division of the Council of Better Business Bureaus, formed in the early 1970s.

Network Broadcast Standards Departments

Most of the day-to-day business of self-regulation in broadcasting falls to the three networks. Primarily in New York, but also in Los Angeles, the broadcast standards departments review thousands of commercials and programs each year. Public-interest considerations are paramount; in order to meet them, editors must be tough but reasonable. Network programing and advertising affect millions of viewers and listeners. Audiences must be treated with respect and not misled. At the same time, however, the network must permit advertisers to sell products fairly and forcefully. Balancing these objectives is not easy as the pressures continue to mount from advertisers, agencies, affiliates, consumer groups, the FTC, and other government entities.

Clearance Procedures

The broadcast standards departments of the three major networks function similarly. All operate independently of their respective programing and sales departments, and they report to top network management. The general procedures for processing commercials are also similar at each network.

Advertising agencies that annually produce many commercials designed for network use usually submit storyboards and scripts to all three networks at the same time. Many more commercials are submitted than are actually produced, for several reasons: some do not clear the networks; the agency and advertiser select just the best ideas; and the creative strategy may be changed.

Editors in the broadcast standards departments tend to specialize, reviewing commercials in one or two of many categories, such as personal products, over-the-counter medications, or automotive products. Commercials in storyboard or script form are carefully checked.

In a typical year, more than 50,000 commercials are reviewed by each of the networks. Thousands of them are "flagged." CBS, for example, states that it rejects two-thirds in various states of submission for reasons of taste, unsubstantiated claims, or network policy. Many of these ads are later revised to meet CBS standards.[2] If substantiation is needed for claims made in the commercial, the agency is asked to submit adequate documentation. Often, a network asks for a copy of the affidavit filed by the producer of a commercial. This document, which attests to the honesty and accuracy of the actual film or tape, is particularly important in demonstration commercials. In many problem areas, the agencies don't wait to be asked and automatically submit substantiation along with the initial script and storyboard. Because the clearance procedures can sometimes be lengthy, agencies and advertisers must plan well in advance. On a few occasions, it has taken up to a year for commercials for a new product to be cleared by the networks. Occasionally, if an advertiser is very familiar with networks' requirements, film or tape of the commercial may be submitted in addition to the script. Outside the problem areas, most commercials will clear the broadcast standards departments in a month or less.

The networks cannot totally rely on the expertise of their staff members, and for certain kinds of commercials, outside experts are consulted. For example, claims for nonprescription drugs are referred to physicians and pharmacists; mechanics and engineers are asked to render opinions on automotive advertising claims; and beauticians are consulted for claims made for hair care products.

[2] CBS Broadcast Group, *Program Practices,* n.d., p. 7.

"WE CAN'T SAY IT OUTRIGHT, FORBES, SO HERE'S WHERE YOU COME IN. WE WANT YOU TO IMPLY, WITH A LOOK, SHRUG, NUANCE OR WHATEVER, THAT OUR COMPETITOR'S PRODUCT STINKS."

Problem Areas

Commercials for certain products and services present special problems to the broadcast standards departments, and in reviewing them the editors must do their best to be both flexible and fair. They must respond to changes in audience sensibilities and in advertisers' creative and production techniques. And they must field criticisms and suggestions offered by interested government officials and affiliated stations. What was acceptable 15 years ago may not be acceptable today, and vice versa. Many personal products advertised on TV today, for example, were not permitted in the broadcast media a dozen years ago. On the other hand, efficacy claims made for many nonprescription medications years ago would never clear the networks today.

Exactly what are the problems? A laundry list of woes related by the editors

18.1/How One Network Handles Comparative Advertising Complaints

Comparative Advertising Guidelines

NBC will accept comparative advertising which identifies, directly or by implication, a competing product or service. As with all other advertising, each substantive claim, direct or implied, must be substantiated to NBC's satisfaction and the commercial must satisfy the following guidelines and standards for comparative advertising established by NBC:

1. Competitors shall be fairly and properly identified.

2. Advertisers shall refrain from disparaging or unfairly attacking competitors, competing products, services or other industries through the use of representations or claims, direct or implied, that are false, deceptive, misleading or have the tendency to mislead.

3. The identification must be for comparison purposes and not simply to upgrade by association.

4. The advertising should compare related or similar properties or ingredients of the product, dimension to dimension, feature to feature, or wherever possible by a side-by-side demonstration.

5. The property being compared must be significant in terms of value or usefulness of the product or service to the consumer.

6. The difference in the properties being compared must be measurable and significant.

7. Pricing comparisons may raise special problems that could mislead, rather than enlighten, viewers. For certain classifications of products, retail prices may be extremely volatile, may be fixed by the retailer rather than the product advertiser, and may not only differ from outlet to outlet but from week to week within the same outlet. Where these circumstances might apply, NBC will accept commercials containing price comparisons only on a clear showing that the comparative claims accurately, fairly and substantially reflect the actual price differentials at retail outlets throughout the broadcast area, and that these price differentials are not likely to change during the period the commercial is broadcast.

8. When a commercial claim involves market relationships, other than price, which are also subject to fluctuation (such as but not limited to sales position or exclusivity), the substantiation for the claim will be considered valid only as long as the market conditions on which the claim is based continue to prevail.

9. As with all other advertising, whenever necessary, NBC may require substantiation to be updated from time to time, and may reexamine substantiation, where the need to do

generally fall into three categories: problems with the commercial strategy, the product itself, or poor taste.

The commercial strategy involves not only *what* is said in an ad but also *how* it's presented. Thus, the following strategies may encounter clearance problems: dangling comparisons, the legitimacy of testimonials, the use of "puffery," the promise of guarantees, the substantiation of claims, product demonstrations and truthful production techniques, side-by-side competitive comparisons (see 18.1), and corporate-image commercials that may spill over into advocacy ads and thus invoke the Fairness Doctrine. (This final category is discussed in Chapter 17.)

Products that are troublesome include beer and wine, nonprescription medications (including analgesics, sleeping aids, stimulants, and assorted nostrums for sniffles and sneezes), children's products (primarily toys and assorted edibles), per-

---

so is indicated as the result of a challenge or other developments.

Challenge Procedure

Where appropriate, NBC will implement the following procedures in the event a commercial is challenged by another advertiser.

1. If an advertiser elects to challenge the advertising of another advertiser, he shall present his challenge and supporting data to NBC in a form available for transmittal to the challenged advertiser.

2. The challenged advertiser will then have an opportunity to respond directly to the challenger. NBC will maintain the confidentiality of the advertiser's original supporting data which was submitted for substantiation of the claims made in the commercial. However, NBC will ask the challenged advertiser to provide it with a copy of its response to the challenger and, where the response is submitted directly to NBC, the challenged advertiser will be requested to forward a copy of its response to the challenger.

3. Where NBC personnel do not have the expertise to make a judgment on technical issues raised by a challenge, NBC will take appropriate measures in its discretion to assist the advertiser and challenger to resolve their differences, including encouraging them to obtain a determination from an acceptable third party.

4. NBC will not withdraw a challenged advertisement from the broadcast schedule unless:

    a. it is directed to do so by the incumbent advertiser;

    b. the incumbent advertiser refuses to submit the controversy for review by some appropriate agency when deemed necessary by NBC;

    c. a decision is rendered by NBC against the incumbent advertiser;

    d. the challenged advertiser, when requested, refuses to cooperate in some other substantive area; or

    e. NBC, prior to final disposition of the challenge, determines that the substantiation for the advertising has been so seriously brought into question that the advertising can no longer be considered substantiated to NBC's satisfaction.

5. NBC may take additional measures in its discretion to resolve questions raised by advertising claims.

Reprinted from *NBC Broadcast Standards for Television*, October, 1982, p. 13. Courtesy of NBC.

sonal products (feminine hygiene products, hemorrhoid treatments, pregnancy test kits, "jock itch" medications, and the like), automobiles, and food products with nutritional claims.

Poor taste is considered a horrendous problem by the networks. Government regulators are unable to do anything in this area. Only the media can exert some controls by refusing to accept ads in questionable taste or by demanding revisions. Commercials with excessive threats are often rejected, particularly if they are directed at children. Many of the steamy perfume and cosmetic commercials are likewise rejected, and double entendres are often flagged. ("Nothing comes between me and my Calvins" caused quite a stir. An earlier campaign for National Airlines used the slogan "I'm going to fly you like you've never been flown before," and it precipitated a major industry debate over its acceptance on TV.) Commercials containing stereotypes of women, seniors, and various minorities are sometimes, but not always, rejected. No one agrees on exactly what constitutes stereotyping.

Other taste problems really center more on the product and its use than on its commercial presentation. The list includes toilet bowl cleaners, deodorants in a variety of categories, denture cleaners, mouthwashes, and a host of personal products for both men and women, some of which very few stations even allow on the air — contraceptives, for example. (See 18.2.) Both programs and advertising messages enter the privacy of the American household as invited guests, and most broadcasters and advertisers are concerned about offending viewers and listeners.

Appropriate scheduling is another concern. What is acceptable for adults is sometimes not acceptable for children. At least one network requires that commercials for feminine hygiene products be confined to periods when women make up a high percentage of the audience. Likewise, sexy commercials are often relegated to late-night time periods. Another network precludes commercials for toilet bowl cleaners in programs with a high proportion of children in the audience.

All these problems generate an abundance of disagreements between network editors and various advertising agencies and their clients. If an editor determines that a particular commercial does not meet the standards, the advertiser is asked to make specific changes. The advertiser may be required to modify the visual or aural portion of a commercial or both. Naturally, advertisers and agencies are less than pleased when such requests are made, because the changes may require that additional time and money be invested. Sometimes, in their opinion, the modifications dilute the ad's selling impact. Then the haggling and negotiating begin. One network vice president in charge of broadcast standards said, "If I were an advertiser, I think I'd go bananas trying to figure out why NBC rejects something, ABC accepts it, and CBS says to rewrite it."[3] Until a commercial meets network standards, however, it will not be aired on that network or its owned-and-operated stations.

Sometimes, the problems are so petty that the best way to cope with them is to develop a good sense of humor. One unamused agency president, however, expressed his exasperation with the networks, declaring that the problem with industry self-regulation is "not the fact that the regulation exists; the problem is the caliber and

---

[3]*Wall Street Journal,* March 27, 1974.

attitude of the people who administer the regulations. They tend to be people who are very narrow and literal-minded."[4]

There are two sides to every story, however, and the network editors complain that certain agencies and clients are excessively aggressive, slow to cooperate, unmindful of viewers' sensibilities, and quite willing to push to the very limits of legal standards and the networks' policies. These advertisers don't care about good taste and honest claims — they care only about the bottom line.

The responsibilities of the broadcast standards departments are destined to expand in the coming years, because an important partner in self-regulation, the National Association of Broadcasters Code Authority, was dismantled in 1982.

Codes of the National Association of Broadcasters

A court decision in 1982, the result of a lengthy antitrust suit brought by the U. S. Department of Justice, effectively brought a 30-year experiment in self-regulation to a close. The advertising provisions of the Radio and Television Codes, operating as the largest and most influential self-regulatory mechanism in broadcast advertising, were canceled by the Executive Committee of the National Association of Broadcasters as the result of a decision by U. S. District Judge Harold Greene.[5] He summarily enjoined one of several provisions in the Television Code that had been challenged by the Justice Department. That provision was the multiple-product announcement standard, or the so-called "piggyback" rule, which prohibited the advertising of two or more products or services in a single commercial of less than 60 seconds. (An example would be a 30-second commercial for the same corporate advertiser that contained a 15-second message for a dishwashing detergent followed by a 15-second pitch for a shampoo, with no integration to make it appear to be a single message.) The Code's provisions did permit 60-second piggybacks. The judge's decision declared that these restrictions constituted an unwarranted restraint on the rights of advertisers and represented a *per se* violation of the Sherman Antitrust Act.

The judge scheduled three other challenged provisions for trial: (1) the restrictions on the amount of commercial material that could be broadcast each hour ($9\frac{1}{2}$ minutes in prime time and 16 minutes at other times for network affiliates, and more for independent stations), (2) limits on the number of commercial interruptions in each program, and (3) limits on the number of consecutive announcements. Soon after Judge Greene's decision, the National Association of Broadcasters threw in the towel and agreed to a proposed consent decree. The NAB would eliminate the provisions challenged in the suit. The effect would be to end the government's antitrust suit and ultimately completely shut down the Code Authority. Motivating factors were the bleak prospect of winning and the sobering reality that, if such a court battle were lost, the NAB and subscribing Code stations might be sued for treble damages by any party that thought it had been hurt by the Code's restrictions.

---

[4]"Specter: Legal Expenses Are Inflating Ad Costs," *Broadcasting,* October 17, 1977, p. 44.

[5]*United States of America v. National Association of Broadcasters,* 536, F.Supp. 149 (D.D.C. 1982).

In arguments before Judge Greene, the NAB had defended the challenged provisions by pointing out that subscription to the Codes was voluntary; stations certainly did not have to belong, and many of them did not. The NAB also said that the government would be unable to show that the Codes were designed for an anticompetitive purpose—their true purpose was to serve the public interest. A final argument was that the Codes had been endorsed by various governmental bodies, including the FCC. (In fact, until the deregulation of radio in 1981, the FCC had used the Radio Code's commercial time limits as its own in evaluating station performance at license renewal time. In TV, the FCC continued to measure stations' performance in accordance with the commercial time limits incorporated in the Television Code.)

The president of the NAB, in commenting on the decision, said: "Broadcasting as a guest in the home is unlike any other business. Thus television broadcasters feel a unique responsibility to maintain a balance of programing and advertising. We are dismayed at a decision which undermines attempts at meaningful self-regulation."[6]

Brief History of the Codes

What was this "meaningful self-regulation"? Standards for broadcasting conduct and performance date back to the first decade of radio's existence as a commercial service. The first Radio Code was adopted by broadcasters in 1929. The document was general in nature, high-minded in its proclamations, and either given lip service or quickly forgotten. Revised codes were written by the broadcasters in 1935, 1939, and again in 1945.[7] The codes were primarily statements of ethical standards and were intended to serve as guides to individual broadcasters in meeting day-to-day responsibilities. When the FCC issued its famous "Blue Book" *(Public Service Responsibility of Broadcast Licensees)* in 1946, pressure mounted to organize a viable and enforceable mechanism for a self-regulatory code.

A code for television was first written in 1952, based primarily on the Radio Code and the Motion Picture Code. At the same time, a Code Authority Director was named and provided with a small staff. The Radio Code was revised again in 1960, and a year later, an administrative staff was assigned for both the radio and television codes. The impetus for this broadened formal organization—called the Code Authority of the NAB—was provided by a critical FCC, by outspoken members of the public and of Congress who were outraged by the "payola" and quiz show scandals, and by broadcaster's fears that extensive new government regulation would be on their necks. By 1961, the activities of both codes were combined in one office of the Code Authority director, who, with a staff and budget from subscriber fees, tackled the job of developing an effective self-regulatory mechanism.

Until Judge Greene's decision, the Code Authority operated with a staff of 33 people who, supported by an annual budget of approximately $1 million, worked in the New York headquarters on Madison Avenue, at the NAB in Washington, and in a

---

[6]*Broadcasting,* March 8, 1982, p. 37.

[7]Bruce A. Linton, *Self-Regulation in Broadcasting* (Lawrence, Kans.: Bruce A. Linton. 1967), p. 13. This three-part college-level study guide contains an excellent and comprehensive analysis of the Code Authority.

smaller Hollywood office. The radio and TV Codes were governed by separate boards of directors, whose membership included representatives from subscribing stations across the country, plus representatives from the various networks. The boards reviewed and recommended policy and provided consultation to the Code Authority staff. Changes in the codes were approved by these boards and then presented to the parent boards of the NAB: the Television Board of Directors, with 15 members, and the Radio Board, with 30 members. Only these parent boards were empowered to accept recommended Code changes, reject them, or modify them.

Content of the Codes

The radio and TV Codes, along with the lengthy guidelines and interpretations that accompanied them, contained provisions in three areas: programing standards, commercial time standards, and advertising standards.

Programing standards tended to be general endorsements of service to audiences and community responsibility. But even general programing provisions could initiate legal woes. In 1975, as the result of intense political pressure from the FCC, notably Chairman Richard Wiley, and the networks, notably CBS, the Television Code was changed to adopt what was called "family viewing time." New language in the Code stated:

Entertainment programing inappropriate for viewing by a general family audience should not be broadcast during the first hour of network entertainment programing in prime time and in the immediately preceding hour. In the occasional case when an entertainment program in this time period is deemed to be inappropriate for such an audience, advisories should be used to alert viewers.

The purpose was to defuse the mounting and vociferous concerns over violence in prime-time television programs by calling for family entertainment in the early evening hours. Adult program fare was banished to the later evening periods. Lawsuits, primarily instigated by a number of Hollywood writers and producers, started a chain of events that eventually led to a court decision declaring such restrictions a violation of the First Amendment.[8] As a result, in 1976, the programing standards of the Television Code were suspended pending resolution of a very complex appeals process and a private antitrust case against the Code and the networks. With the programing standards in a state of suspension, the Television Code was left with commercial time standards and advertising standards.

The commercial time standards were the target of the fatal antitrust suit by the Justice Department. The precarious status of these standards was recognized by the NAB's general counsel, who noted that broadcasting is "very vulnerable to antitrust charges," being an industry where "the name of the game" is increasing prices in a field of static inventory, where personnel readily move among companies, and where there's "a lot of talking between people" and "a lot of comparing of notes."[9]

---

[8]*Writers Guild of America v. American Broadcasting Company, et al.,* 423 F.Supp. 1064 (1976), *vacated,* 609 F.2d 355 (9th Cir. 1979), *cert. denied,* 449 U.S. 824, 101 S.Ct. 85 (1980).

[9]*Broadcasting,* May 25, 1981, p. 42.

Judge Greene's decision and the Code Authority's agreement to the consent decree meant that individual stations and networks were freed from the Code's rules on commercial time standards, yet there was no wholesale desertion of the guidelines. Neither broadcasters, advertisers, nor audiences seemed interesed in having the public airwaves become a babel of commercials. Limits on "clutter" had always been supported by the FCC, Congress, the public, and certainly by both broadcasters and advertisers. Excessive commercialization meant declining effectiveness for advertising messages and the possibility of viewer revolts, in the form of audiences that absented themselves during a long string of commercials or simply turned off the set.

The advertising standards were the most extensive portions of the Codes. The philosophy behind all the guidelines was essentially *preventive*, stopping abuses before they were aired and providing standards for advertisers to follow in preparing commercials that broadcasters would accept. Pages of dos and don'ts were developed in particular problem areas. Sensitive products included children's toys, nonprescription medications, personal products, beer and wine, weight reduction products and services, and foundation garments. And the techniques covered included testimonials, safety portrayals, comparison advertising, product demonstrations, and the like. The two major concerns were maintaining standards for good taste and substantiating the truthfulness of advertising claims. These advertising provisions were widely accepted. The networks were Code subscribers; so were the vast majority of television stations and more than half the nation's radio stations.

Additionally, the Code Authority served as "central clearance" for commercials in a number of product categories that by their very nature, or by the nature of the marketplace, were controversial: children's toys, premium offers directed at children, feminine hygiene products, and food products with cholesterol claims. Thus the Code Authority helped expedite the review of potentially controversial commercials and helped to avoid the endless wrangling that would occur if these commercials were individually reviewed by networks and stations.

When the Code Authority was dismantled, many questions were asked. Solid answers were elusive. Each individual network and station would have to assume responsibility for reviewing and accepting or rejecting commercial messages. Broadcasters, particularly those without a large staff and little expertise in self-regulation, could no longer count on the Code Authority to provide guidance and serve as central clearance.

Many advertisers, particularly those whose products fell into some of the problem areas, felt that they were up a creek without a paddle. They had become accustomed to (if not altogether happy with) the requirements of the radio and television Codes, and the obvious advantage was that all the competitors had to play by the same rules. Advertisers and agencies were concerned about mounting expenses in producing commercials for an industry in which everyone had a different set of rules. Some advertisers could be expected to take advantage of the absence of the Codes and produce commercials that would gain them a competitive edge. The Codes had an outright ban on accepting advertising for contraceptives (see 18.2), hard liquor (see 18.3), fortune telling, occultism, phrenology, palm reading, and the like, plus a prohibition on the advertising of "tip sheets" and other publications used for giving odds or promoting betting. Only time would tell if this kind of advertising would make inroads into commercial broadcasting.

One thing seemed very likely—the networks would have to assume even greater diligence in reviewing advertising material, and so would individual broadcasters. Their success in continuing the spirit of the Codes would undoubtedly vary. It would depend on the commitment of broadcast management to self-regulation, the financial resources allocated to such a goal, the cooperation (or lack of it) from advertisers and agencies, the role of Congress, the FCC, and the FTC, and the response of millions of listeners and viewers who depend on broadcasting for news, information, and entertainment.

18.2 / Contraceptive Advertising

Toys are undoubtedly the most controversial products advertised to children. For adults, personal products must head the list. Over the years, NAB Code Authority bans on the advertising of various product categories have been lifted: feminine hygiene sprays and powders, 1969; tampons, cosmetic douches, and sanitary napkins, 1972; body-lice remedies, 1974; enemas, 1976; pregnancy test kits and "jock-itch" remedies, 1979; incontinence products, 1980; and medicated douche products, 1981.

Bans on advertising of contraceptives were never lifted while the Codes were in existence, and very few stations have ever accepted commercials for these products. The debate over the acceptability of this advertising still continues. The major issues surrounding the controversy are summarized below:*

• the right of parents to determine the sexual education of their children

• the right of sexually active adolescents and others to get the contraceptive information they need

• the right of manufacturers to advertise their lawful wares

• the right of viewers of the public airwaves to be free from messages they find deeply offensive

*Rick Horowitz, "Should Contraceptives Be Advertised on Television?" *Channels*, October–November, 1981, p. 65.

• the duty of broadcasters to balance the current fare of sexual innuendo with "responsible sexuality"

• the need to establish national standards of taste in a nation of diverse sensibilities

A television storyboard for Trojans and a storyboard for Semicid® show two different approaches in advertising contraceptive products. Neither could be called heavy-handed. Thus, much of the debate centers not so much on the commercial but on the category itself. Proponents of this advertising include the Planned Parenthood Federation of America and the Population Institute, which point to the high incidence of teenage pregnancies and venereal disease. Their attitude is that sexually active youngsters are going to learn *something* about contraceptives and may as well get the right information.

Opponents express concern about such advertising entering the home, via the TV screen, unannounced. Their objections are often based on moral and religious beliefs about the use of contraceptives. In addition, they worry that such advertising may foster promiscuity, with or without contraceptives.

With the demise of the NAB Codes, individual stations and networks that formerly subscribed to them will have to make their own decisions regarding the acceptability of contraceptive advertising. Some stations will accept these ads; others never will. No matter how widespread or limited the acceptance, the debate over contraceptive advertising will not go away.

1.   To every thing there is a season.
And a time to every purpose under the heaven.

2.   ...a time to weep.
...a time to laugh.

3.   ...a time to mourn.
...and a time to dance.

4.   The makers of Trojan Condoms
believe there is a time for children.

5.   The right time. When they are wanted.

6.   And Trojans have helped people
for over half a century safely practice
responsible parenthood.

ADVERTISING · TELEVISION

client — WHITEHALL LABORATORIES
product — Semicid
title — Woman To Woman
job no.
date

video

audio

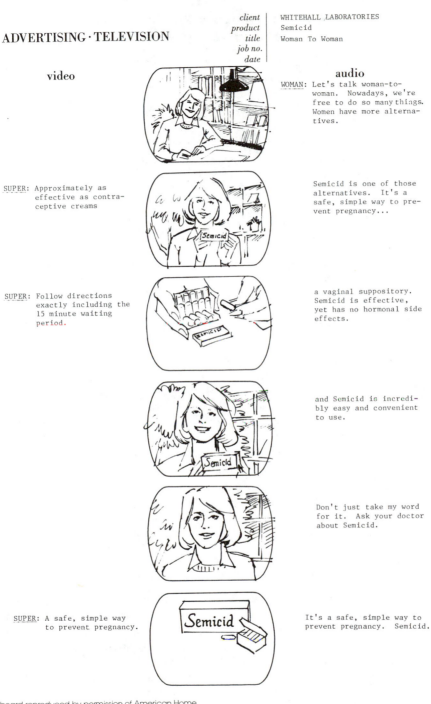

WOMAN: Let's talk woman-to-woman. Nowadays, we're free to do so many things. Women have more alternatives.

SUPER: Approximately as effective as contraceptive creams

Semicid is one of those alternatives. It's a safe, simple way to prevent pregnancy...

SUPER: Follow directions exactly including the 15 minute waiting period.

a vaginal suppository. Semicid is effective, yet has no hormonal side effects.

and Semicid is incredibly easy and convenient to use.

Don't just take my word for it. Ask your doctor about Semicid.

SUPER: A safe, simple way to prevent pregnancy.

It's a safe, simple way to prevent pregnancy. Semicid.

National Advertising Division and
National Advertising Review Board

If a list of all the people or groups that might have a hand in altering or censoring a radio or TV commercial before it is aired were compiled, it would look something like this:

- the client's advertising manager or other corporate officers
- the legal counsel for either the client or the advertising agency
- the agency's copywriter, art director, and account executives
- the production team
- the talent
- the networks' broadcast standards departments
- personnel at individual radio or TV stations or networks

Still, after all these layers of scrutiny, a commercial may be alleged to be dishonest, misleading, unfair, or exploitive in relation to its viewers or listeners. If all the *preventive* measures are still inadequate, then perhaps what is needed is a *corrective* self-regulatory mechanism. Such a "realization" was part of the philosophy behind the formation of the National Advertising Division of the Council of Better Business Bureaus and the National Advertising Review Board.

In the early 1970s, the shortcomings and outright failures of many self-regulatory efforts were obvious to everyone in the broadcast advertising industry and to many in government. Consumer groups were flexing new muscles and demanding reforms. A number of important members of Congress were turning their attention to advertising and marketing practices, and the possibilities of extensive new legislation loomed before an apprehensive advertising industry. What was needed was an effective and visible mechanism for processing complaints about advertising from the public and other sectors. It was, once again, an attempt to head government regulators off at the pass. The long-term goal was to upgrade the quality of advertising and the conscience of the industry. The short-term goal, however, was to present a workable plan for processing complaints and resolving problems through a voluntary, self-regulatory process.

National Advertising Review Board

The National Advertising Review Board was organized in 1971 by top industry leaders in four sponsoring organizations—the American Advertising Federation (AAF), the American Association of Advertising Agencies (AAAA), the Association of National Advertisers (ANA), and the Council of Better Business Bureaus (CBBB). Interested groups—including the media, a number of major consumer groups, and government officials—watched from the sidelines. Various organizational proposals for the NARB were developed and then modified before a draft was finally agreed on. During this time, advice and admonitions were plentiful from those who favored the plans, as well as from those who predicted failure.

In 1971, the final plan for a National Advertising Review Board was ready. Putting it into effect, through staffing and funding, followed soon afterwards. The new self-regulatory body was set up as follows: a chairperson and the presidents of the four sponsoring organizations sit on the board of the National Advertising Review Council (NARC), which is the parent organization of the NARB. The NARC appoints a part-time chairperson and 50 members to serve two-year terms on the NARB. Of these members, 30 represent national advertisers, 10 represent advertising agencies, and 10 are "public," or nonindustry, representatives. In addition, 10 agency alternates are appointed. All the industry members appointed to the NARB are top executives, and many of the public members are academicians or lawyers who have previously served in government. (Media representatives are not included on the NARB. Evaluating and acting on complaints would put such representatives in an untenable position because of possible conflicts of interest.) The 50 NARB members volunteer their services and are available to serve on five-person panels, appointed by the chairperson, to consider complaints about specific national advertising. These panels have the same makeup as the total NARB membership — 60 percent advertisers, 20 percent agencies, and 20 percent public members.

When this new self-regulatory system was inaugurated, it was envisioned that the NARB would have its hands full with a wide variety of cases. That did not happen. (In fact, in the first eight years of the NARB's existence, only 35 panels were convened.)[10] In recent years, only one or two cases have reached an NARB panel annually.

[10]Eric J. Zanot, "A Review of Eight Years of NARB Casework: Guidelines and Parameters of Deceptive Advertising," *Journal of Advertising,* Vol. 9, no. 4 (1980): 20.

18.3 / Liquor Advertising

Commercials for hard liquor have never been permitted on most stations and networks because of self-regulatory bans. The distilling industry itself has never pressed the matter. In fact, such commercials are prohibited by the Distilled Spirits Council of the United States. M. S. Walker, Inc., producer of Cossack Vodka, does not belong to that council. The company developed these radio commercials for use in broadcasts of Red Sox baseball games on WITS(AM) in Boston. The wife of baseball star Dennis Eckersley served as spokesperson. Soon after the commercials aired, complaints poured in. A variety of groups, ranging from the Center for Science in the Public Interest to Mothers Against Drunk Drivers, voiced their protest and threatened to challenge the station's license at renewal time. They cited the high interest in the baseball broadcasts, especially among young people. They charged that the station was flagrantly violating the public interest.

In response, the president of M. S. Walker said, "My position is that advertisers of products containing alcohol should be all on or all off the air."* He expressed the opinion that beer and wine are greater contributors to alcohol abuse among young drinkers than hard liquor. Beer and wine advertising is widely accepted in the broadcast media.

Because of the brouhaha, the commercials were changed, and the new one sounded more like a public service announcement than a commercial.

*"Invading Cossack Vows to Stay on Air," *Advertising Age,* May 10, 1982, p. 1.

M.S. WALKER, Inc., D/B/A ALLEN'S Ltd. • 20 Third Avenue, Somerville, MA 02143 • Telephone (617) 776 • 6700

BEFORE

HI! THIS IS NANCY ECKERSLEY, DENNIS' WIFE. MY HUSBAND THROWS A GREAT PITCH,

AND I THROW A GREAT PARTY. WHEN I THROW MY PARTIES I ALWAYS USE COSSACK VODKA.

WE'RE MAKING IT IN MASSACHUSETTS, AND COSSACK IS MADE IN MASSACHUSETTS. IN FACT

THE M. S. WALKER COMPANY MADE COSSACK SO GOOD IT IS NOW THE #1 SELLING VODKA IN

THE STATE.

TRY COSSACK ON THE ROCKS WITH LIME OR MIX IT WITH ORANGE JUICE, TOMATOE JUICE

OR QUININE WATER FOR THAT CONSISTENTLY FINE TASTE YOU'RE LOOKING FOR.

COSSACK VODKA HAS BEEN PRODUCED AND DISTRIBUTED BY THE M. S. WALKER OF MASS-

ACHUSETTS FOR OVER 50 YEARS. THE RETAILERS CARRYING COSSACK BELIEVE IN IT, AND

THE CONSUMER CONFIDENCE HAS MADE IT NUMBER ONE IN MASSACHUSETTS. I'M LIKE YOU---

I LOOK FOR QUALITY AND VALUE. COSSACK IS REASONABLY PRICED AND IS 80 PROOF.

THE NEXT TIME YOU HAVE A PARTY REMEMBER WHAT NANCY ECKERSLEY SAID---USE COSSACK

---THE MIXABLE VODKA. IT WILL BE A SURE HIT WITH YOUR GUESTS. SORRY ABOUT

THAT WORD "HIT" DENNIS-----.

COSSACK VODKA IS PREPARED BY ALLEN'S LIMITED, SOMERVILLE, MASS.

50TH Anniversary 1931 ☆ 1981

DON COSSACK VODKA • ALLEN'S CORDIALS, COCKTAILS, LIQUEURS, WHISKIES & IMPORTS • KENNEDY'S FINE PRODUCTS

M. S. WALKER, Inc., D/B/A ALLEN'S Ltd. • 20 Third Avenue, Somerville, MA 02143 • Telephone (617) 776 • 6700

AFTER

HI, THIS IS NANCY ECKERSLEY, DENNIS' WIFE AND THE SPOKESPERSON FOR COSSACK
VODKA. THE M.S. WALKER CO., BOTTLER OF COSSACK VODKA, WANTS TO COMMIT THIS
TIME TO INCREASING THE AWARENESS OF THE AREAS OF RESPONSIBILITY IN THE
DRINKING OF ANY KIND OF ALCOHOLIC BEVERAGE, ESPECIALLY TOWARD YOUNG PEOPLE.
AS ADULTS AND PARENTS, WE HAVE THE RESPONSIBILITY TO MAKE YOUNG PEOPLE
UNDERSTAND THE DANGERS OF DRINKING AT A YOUNG AGE--AT AN AGE WHERE THEY
HAVE NOT FULLY MATURED AND PEER PRESSURES ARE TREMENDOUS, OFTENTIMES
PREVENTING A YOUNG PERSON FROM REFUSING A DRINK.

AS PARENTS AND ADULTS, WE PLAY A ROLE IN SHAPING CHILDREN'S VALUES AND
LIVES, AND WE MUST MAKE THEM UNDERSTAND THAT GETTING DRUNK IS NOT FUN AND
THAT GETTING DRUNK CAN KILL. THE M.S. WALKER CO. ALSO BELIEVES THAT ALL
PRODUCERS OF ALCOHOLIC BEVERAGES THAT ADVERTISE HAVE A RESPONSIBILITY TO
EDUCATE THE PUBLIC ABOUT ALCOHOLIC ABUSE. IF WE ALL RECOGNIZE OUR
RESPONSIBILITY--PARENTS, PRODUCERS, AND ADVERTISERS ALIKE, OUR CHANCES ARE
MUCH GREATER OF SAVING A LIFE.

AND FINALLY, FOR ANY YOUNG PEOPLE LISTENING, HELP YOUR FRIENDS TO SAY "NO."
IT MAY BE YOUR CHANCE TO KEEP A FRIEND. THIS MESSAGE IS BROUGHT TO YOU
BY THE M.S. WALKER, CO., PRODUCERS OF COSSACK VODKA--AND THEY SHOULD KNOW.

DON COSSACK VODKA • ALLEN'S CORDIALS, COCKTAILS, LIQUEURS, WHISKIES & IMPORTS • KENNEDY'S FINE PRODUCTS

Courtesy of M. S. Walker, Inc.

Before a complaint ever reaches the NARB, it goes through a screening and negotiating process at the National Advertising Division of the CBBB. Usually, the problems are resolved at that level.

National Advertising Division

Operating as a separate investigative unit, the NAD has emerged as the "hidden backbone" of the NARB. With a staff of approximately a dozen people, the NAD monitors advertisements in a variety of national media, evaluates complaints, and conducts negotiations with those advertisers who are the object of complaints.

The complaints that pour into the NAD come from the following sources: an individual consumer or consumer group; a business competitor; local Better Business Bureaus (which refer matters involving national advertising to the NAD); the NAD's own monitoring program; and, in a few instances, some other miscellaneous source. All these complaints must be evaluated to identify legitimate grievances. The criteria used in evaluations include the following:

• Only national advertising complaints are investigated. Local ads are referred to a local BBB for investigation and action.

• If there is evidence of fraud, the NAD promptly refers it to the appropriate law enforcement agency.

• Truth and accuracy are the primary yardsticks. The NAD staff analyzes ads from the consumer's point of view in searching for deception. The test is what the consumer takes out of the ad, not what the admaker puts into it. Thus, deception by omission, obscure language, puffery, and unsubstantiated competitive comparisons may violate the NAD's standards of truth and accuracy.

• It is not necessary to prove that a portion of the audience has been deceived for the NAD to initiate action.

• Complaints about taste, morality, and social responsibility that do not involve consumer deception are not pursued by the NAD. (In cases where there has been sufficient concern, special NARB "consultive" panels have been convened to study and report on special problems.)

The flow chart in 18.4 shows that the NAD conducts an initial review of ads that have been questioned. Many complaints are dismissed. When an ad appears to have the capacity to deceive or when substantiation of its claims is desired, the NAD writes to the chief executive officer of the company—with a copy to its advertising agency—asking for substantiation.

In the vast majority of cases, the advertiser complies. Those companies that refuse to cooperate may find that the NAD refers the matter to an appropriate government agency. Substantiation that is submitted is evaluated and, possibly, provided to a challenger for review. The latter might happen in the case of a complaint from a competitor if the parties have agreed to the sharing of data. The NAD then conducts dialogues with all the concerned parties to resolve the matter. In some cases, the substantiation satisfies the NAD; in other cases, the advertiser may be asked to modify

18.4/Steps in NAD/NARB Process

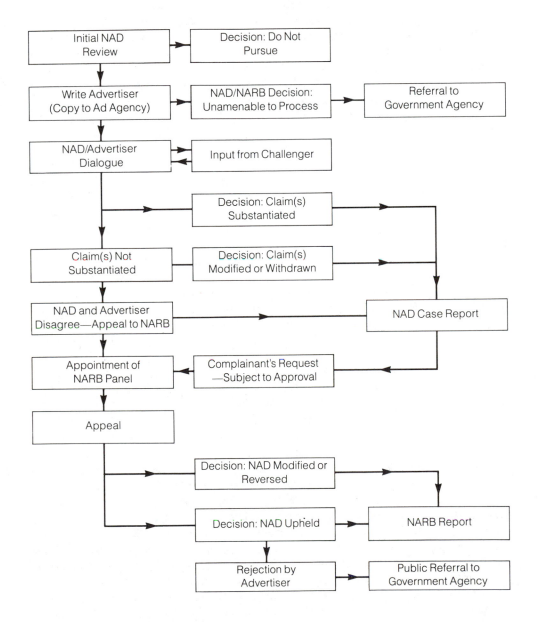

the claims or completely withdraw the advertising. Throughout these procedures, which typically run six months or less, the goal is achieving cooperation and fairness. The sole objective is to serve the public interest.

Virtually all of the problems are solved at the NAD level. Over the years, there has been an increasing willingness by advertisers to negotiate with the NAD and abide by its rulings. A monthly *NAD Case Report* is published and made available to the press, the advertising industry, and the public. (See 18.5.) It summarizes cases reviewed by the NAD in two categories: advertising claims that have been adequately substantiated and advertising that has been modified or discontinued. The purpose of this report is to avoid any kind of secrecy, maintain the excellent level of support for the work of the NAD, and make the information available to interested members of the public. The reports additionally serve as a notice to advertisers and agencies of the kinds of problem that result in an NAD action.

In a few cases, resolution of a matter between an advertiser and the NAD is not possible. An advertiser who concludes that the NAD's decision is not acceptable may appeal to the chairperson of the NARB and request a panel hearing. The chairperson appoints a five-person panel from the total board and carefully avoids any conceivable conflict of interest in making appointments. The NARB panel reviews briefs provided by both the NAD and the advertiser, and the advertiser and complainant each has an opportunity to present its side of the story in a full evidentiary hearing.

The final decision of the NARB is promptly related to the advertiser, who is given an opportunity to submit a statement to the press along with the findings of the NARB panel. If the decision goes against the ads in question, the advertiser is encouraged to promptly modify or withdraw them. If the advertiser refuses to cooperate or does not agree with the findings of the panel, the NARB chairperson is directed to inform the appropriate government agency.

Most national advertisers whose claims are found misleading or deceptive by the NAD or the NARB are willing to cooperate. They don't want bad publicity, and they are certainly not enthusiastic about the matter's being referred to the FTC or any other government agency. It should be noted that from the beginning, the FTC has made it clear that although self-regulatory efforts are commendable, it cannot and will not abrogate its legitimate role in the regulation of advertising.

The five NARB members who serve on a given panel act for the entire 50-person board. The panel itself is the "appellate court" for cases arising from the NAD. No additional appeal process exists, because the NARB hopes to expedite complaints, evaluate the validity of allegations, and reach a fair and speedy determination without duplicating the kind of endless maneuvering that typifies proceedings in the federal agencies and courts. NAD and NARB decisions *do not* carry the weight of law. They are part of a voluntary and self-regulatory mechanism, and advertisers who are the objects of complaints are not compelled to cooperate in the investigation. Although an advertiser could simply ignore the entire business, no thinking businessperson would do such a thing. The adverse publicity would be a public relations disaster.

One criticism that has been directed to the procedures of the NAD and NARB is the absence of well-developed rules or guidelines against which complaints are measured. (It's difficult for advertisers to abide by the "rules" if they don't know what they are!) In response to this criticism, the NAD and NARB have expressed the philosophy that trying to write and publish guidelines governing every conceivable advertising situation would be impractical, needlessly restrictive, and self-defeating.[11] The preference is for reaching judgments based on the merits of each situation, feeling that, as the organization grows in experience, precedents will emerge that can be used in further reviews.

[11]*A Review and Perspective on Advertising Industry Self-Regulation, 1971–1977* (New York: National Advertising Review Board, 1978), p. 5.

18.5/NAD Case Reports

Cases resolved by the NAD are summarized in a monthly *NAD Case Report*, which is released to the press. The three sample reports shown below illustrate the diversity of problems handled in connection with broadcast commercials.

GENERAL FOODS CORPORATION
Country Time Lemonade Flavor Frozen Concentrate
Ogilvy & Mather, Inc.

Basis of Inquiry—Newspaper advertising for Country Time Frozen Drink Concentrate made the following claims: "COLD FACT: Country Time Frozen Drink Concentrate tastes better than Minute Maid." "There aren't many things Americans agree on, but in a recent taste test people agreed that Country Time Lemonade Flavor Frozen Drink Concentrate tastes better than Minute Maid Frozen Concentrate for Lemonade . . . Country Time Frozen tastes better than Minute Maid. That's a cold fact."

The ad was challenged by the Coca-Cola Company/Foods Division, makers of Minute Maid Lemonade Frozen Concentrate, on the basis that the claim "people agreed that" would indicate all the people included in the taste test reached the same conclusion.

NAD requested details of the design of the taste test and the degree of preference for the advertiser's brand.

The advertiser provided results of blind-paired comparison taste tests in five cities between its product and Minute Maid Lemonade Frozen Concentrate. The data indicated that 55% of lemonade drinkers tested preferred Country Time. In addition, the advertiser informed NAD that the claim was limited to a coupon advertisement for Lemonade Flavor Frozen Drink Concentrate which had run its course and that it would not be run again. (#1883)

LJN TOYS LTD.
255 Computer Command (electronic toy)
In-House

Basis of Inquiry: A child-directed television commercial for the 255 Computer Command, an electronically controlled toy car, was questioned by the Children's Advertising Review Unit (CARU). The commercial showed a young boy holding the toy car up close to the camera lens. This technique distorted the size of the toy, making it appear larger than it actually is. CARU was concerned that children seeing this commercial presentation would not have a clear understanding of the car's actual size.

Advertiser's Response: The advertiser advised CARU that the commercial is no longer running and the Computer Command Toy has been discontinued. In addition, it stated its intention to take note of Children's Advertising Guidelines in the preparation of future advertising. (#1939)

MEMOREX CORPORATION
Video Tape
Leo Burnett Company, Inc.

Basis of Inquiry: A television commercial opened with a close-up of a spokeswoman stating: "Look at me. Do you like what you see? Good! Because it's not me." In the next frame, a live shot shows the same narrator standing alongside her image on a television set saying: "It's a recording of me. On new Memorex videotape. This remarkable tape has been recorded and re-recorded one hundred times. But I bet you still couldn't tell if it was Memorex or me." NAD asked for details of execution.

Advertiser's Response: Extensive technical data were presented confirming the claims using 20 Memorex video cassettes drawn from regular production. The VCR's used were also production items and a computer program was set up so that cassettes could record and re-record for 100 cycles. All cassettes were subjected to objective testing of six performance characteristics. Statistical analysis of the results confirmed the tapes performed as well after 101 re-recordings as in the first pass.

The commercial was produced over a period of two days. On the first day, the spokeswoman's image was recorded on a test cassette that had been recorded and re-recorded 100 times. On the second day, the commercial was taped on professional equipment while the test cassette was being played on the TV set.

NAD concluded the claims were substantiated. (#1956)

NARB Consultive Panels

To address continuing areas of complaint and to launch special investigations, the 50 volunteer NARB members may be called on to do more than sit in judgment on specific cases. Consultive panels have been organized to develop "white papers" on broader and more difficult matters dealing with taste and social responsibility. One panel was assigned to research advertising addressed to women or portraying women, and another studied advertising related to the area of energy and the environment. Comparative advertising, and the problems of identifying competitors in advertising, was the subject of another panel.

One particularly interesting report links product advertising with unsafe consumer practices. This document provides advertising guidelines for a number of "high-risk" products for the benefit of advertisers. Such products include appliances, automotive products, firearms, a variety of household products, power tools, health care products, various types of recreational equipment, and yard and garden equipment. The report cites a number of actual examples of safety violatons portrayed in advertising—for example, an "automobile commercial that shows the advertised car passing a long line of competitive models on a narrow two-lane mountain road while approaching a curve." Another example was "a commercial showing a woman placing a fly killer product on a kitchen table when the label clearly states the product is dangerous and must be hung out of the reach of children." The possible effects of advertising situations on children were also evaluated. Since youngsters are pretty suggestible and unpredictable, the panel raised questions about a "commercial showing an announcer hiding himself in the trunk of a car with the lid closed," and about "a chewing gum commercial showing a child in a park accepting gum from an outstretched hand, presumably of an adult." Probably most or all of these violations of safety and good sense were inadvertent. The advertisers certainly did not intend to encourage a disregard for safety. The NARB panel declared that "the number one problem is the 'inadvertent safety error,' the unsafe situation in which the product is presented rather than the claims made for the product iself."[12] The report concluded that advertisers can and should do more to "think safety" during the planning, creation, and review of their advertising and that they have a responsibility to educate consumers on how to prudently use a product.

Children's Advertising Review Unit

The controversies over advertising directed toward children did not escape the attention of the NAD. In response to the heightened activity at the FTC and FCC, as well as at other self-regulatory organizations, a special Children's Advertising Review Unit was established in 1974. Serving as a specialist group within the NAD, the CARU focuses its attention on advertising aimed at children under the age of 12. Its responsibilities include monitoring children's advertising in TV, radio and print; reviewing

─────────

[12]*Product Advertising and Consumer Safety, A Report on Product Advertising as a Factor in Unsafe Consumer Practices and Behavior.* Prepared by a Consultive Panel of the National Advertising Review Board, June, 1974, p. 2.

proposed advertising, on request, before its production; and responding to specific complaints. In handling these complaints, the CARU follows the same general procedures as the NAD. A complaint may be dismissed, or the CARU may ask a company to voluntarily modify or discontinue advertising that is untruthful, inaccurate or insensitive to children's special needs.

With the discontinuation of the NAB Code Authority's central clearance function in reviewing children's TV commercials for toys and premium offers, the CARU is likely to have an increased workload and responsibilities in the future.

Conclusions

Ethical codes are not uncommon in American business. Although frequently developed by well-meaning industry leaders, such codes are often not worth the paper they're printed on in the day-to-day business of commerce. The broadcast advertising industry has codes too, but it stands apart in making sure that its standards are applied and followed. To serve the interests of both the public and the industry, broadcasters and advertisers have designed self-regulatory mechanisms that are backed up with staffs and funds. Their efforts have created a complex self-regulatory system — and also a controversial one.

Philosophies vary on how to meet the industry's obligations to the public. The networks represent the oldest and one of the most successful means of self-regulation designed to prevent the broadcast of unacceptable commercials. Previously, the NAB Code Authority operated under a similar philosophy, designed to stop abuses before they could be perpetrated on the public. With the demise of the Code Authority's role in developing and administering specific proscriptions on commercials, individual stations and networks must assume greater responsibility in screening commercials before they are put on the air.

Other self-regulatory philosophies, like those of the NAD, are predicated on a belief that there must be a mechanism for correcting past wrongs in order to make things "right" now and in the future. In some respects, the corrective mechanisms pick up where preventive ones leave off, and as a result, the two philosophies of self-regulation complement each other admirably. The corrective philosophy functions most importantly in establishing precedents. An industry that is able to correct one of its members, and then widely publicizes that correction, wins favor with both the government regulators and with the public. The precedents established then serve to deter other advertisers who might either intentionally or inadvertently abuse their use of the nation's media.

Improvements are always needed, and advice is bountiful, yet solid solutions to genuine problems are still elusive. One continuing problem in the self-regulation of broadcast advertising is the need for standards to be adopted and adhered to at the local level. Lip service is worthless. Unfortunately, that is too often the response of local advertisers and local broadcasters who run to stay in place in a very hectic business. Time is money, especially in broadcast advertising.

Liaison with government entities at the federal, state, and local level should certainly be improved. A continuing and open dialogue between the regulators and the regulated would do much to mitigate problems and prevent what has in the past developed into confrontation politics. In addition, it would be in the best interests of the broadcast advertising industry to develop a strong public relations program explaining the extent of its self-regulation to the nation's audiences. Most consumers are totally ignorant of self-regulatory efforts.

The self-regulatory mechanisms described in this chapter serve as a collective conscience for broadcasters and advertisers. They are imperfect devices, because they are human institutions and are implemented through human judgments. Self-regulatory groups in broadcast advertising, however, have remained remarkably flexible over the years in response to changing public tastes and tolerances and changing pressures from within the industry and the political arena. If they remain flexible, they will undoubtedly grow in strength and influence in the future.

Aaker, David A., and Myers, John G. *Advertising Management,* 2nd ed. Englewood Cliffs, N.J.: Prentice-Hall, Inc., 1982.

Adler, Richard P., *et al. The Effects of Television Advertising on Children.* Lexington, Mass.: Lexington Books, 1980.

Anderson, Robert L., and Barry, Thomas E. *Advertising Management: Text and Cases.* Columbus, Ohio: Charles E. Merrill Publishing Co., 1979.

Arlen, Michael J. *Thirty Seconds.* New York: Penguin Books, 1979.

Baldwin, Huntley. *Creating Effective TV Commercials.* Chicago: Crain Books, 1982.

Baldwin, Thomas F. *Cable Communication.* Englewood Cliffs, N.J.: Prentice-Hall, 1983.

Barnouw, Erik. *The Sponsor: Notes on a Modern Potentate.* New York: Oxford University Press, 1978.

Bartos, Rena. *The Moving Target, What Every Marketer Should Know About Women.* New York: The Free Press, 1982.

Bellaire, Arthur. *The Bellaire Guide to TV Commercial Cost Control.* Chicago: Crain Books, 1982.

Bittner, John R. *Broadcast Laws and Regulation.* Englewood Cliffs, N.J.: Prentice-Hall, 1982.

Boddewyn, J. J., and Marton, Katherin. *Comparison Advertising, a Worldwide Study.* New York: Hastings House, 1978.

Book, Albert C., and Cary, Norman D. *The Radio and Television Commercial.* Chicago: Crain Books, 1978.

Bovee, Courtland, and Arens, William F. *Contemporary Advertising.* Homewood, Ill.: Richard D. Irwin, Inc., 1982.

Burton, Philip Ward. *Advertising Copywriting.* Columbus, Ohio: Grid Publishing Co., 1978.

Burton, Philip Ward, and Sandhusen, Richard. *Cases in Advertising.* Columbus, Ohio: Grid Publishing Co., 1981.

Busch, H. Ted, and Landeck, Terry. *The Making of a Television Commercial.* New York: Macmillan, 1981.

Clarkson, Kenneth W., and Muris, Timothy J., eds. *The Federal Trade Commission Since 1970: Economic Regulation and Bureaucratic Behavior.* Cambridge, N.Y.: Cambridge University Press, 1981.

Crompton, Alastair. *The Craft of Copywriting.* Rev. ed. Englewood Cliffs, N.J.: Prentice-Hall, Inc., 1982.

Cundiff, Edward W., Still, Richard R., and Govoni, Norman A. P. *Fundamentals of Modern Marketing.* 3rd ed. Englewood Cliffs, N.J.: Prentice-Hall, Inc., 1980.

Dizard, Wilson P., Jr. *The Coming Information Age: An Overview of Technology, Economics, and Politics.* New York: Longman, 1982.

Dunn, W. Watson, and Barban, Arnold M. *Advertising: Its Role in Modern Marketing.* 4th ed. Hinsdale, Ill.: Dryden Press, 1978.

Eastman, Susan Tyler, and Klein, Robert S., eds. *Strategies in Broadcast and Cable Promotion.* Belmont, Calif.: Wadsworth Publishing Co., 1982.

Fletcher, James E., ed. *Handbook of Radio and TV Broadcasting: Research Procedures in Audience, Program, and Revenues.* New York: Van Nostrand Reinhold, 1981.

Francois, William E. *Mass Media Law and Regulation.* 2nd ed. Columbus, Ohio: Grid Publishing Co., 1978.

Fridell, Squire. *Acting in Television Commercials for Fun and Profit.* New York: Harmony Books, 1980.

Garbett, Thomas F. *Corporate Advertising, the What, the Why and the How.* New York: McGraw-Hill Book Co., 1981.

Gardner, Herbert S., Jr. *The Advertising Agency Business.* Chicago: Crain Books, 1976.

Geis, Michael L. *The Language of Television Advertising.* New York: Academic Press, 1982.

Gilson, Christopher, and Berkman, Harold W. *Advertising Concepts & Strategies.* New York: Random House, Inc., 1980.

Hafer, W. Keith, and White, Gordon E. *Advertising Writing: Putting Creative Strategy to Work.* 2nd ed. St. Paul, Minn.: West Publishing Co., 1982.

Hanan, Mack. *Life-Styled Marketing: How to Position Products for Premium Profits.* Rev. ed. New York: American Management Association, 1980.

Hise, Richard T., Gillett, Peter L., and Ryans, John K., Jr. *Basic Marketing: Concepts and Decisions.* Cambridge, Mass.: Winthrop Publishers, Inc., 1979.

International Advertising Association. *Controversy Advertising: How Advertisers Present Points of View in Public Affairs.* New York: Hastings House, 1977.

Jamieson, Kathleen Hall, and Campbell, Karlyn Kohrs. *The Interplay of Influence: Mass Media & Their Publics in News, Advertising, Politics.* Belmont, Calif.: Wadsworth, 1983.

Jewler, A. Jerome. *Creative Strategy in Advertising.* Belmont, Calif.: Wadsworth Publishing Co., 1981.

Johnson, J. Douglas. *Advertising Today.* Chicago: Science Research Associates, Inc., 1978.

Jugenheimer, Donald W., and Turk, Peter B. *Advertising Media.* Columbus, Ohio: Grid Publishing Co., 1980.

Kaatz, Ronald B. *Cable: An Advertiser's Guide to the New Electronic Media.* Chicago: Crain Books, 1982.

Kintner, Earl W. *A Primer on the Law of Deceptive Practices.* 2nd ed. New York: Macmillan Co., 1978.

Kleppner, Otto. *Advertising Procedure.* 7th ed. Englewood Cliffs, N.J.: Prentice-Hall, Inc., 1979.

Kobs, Jim. *Profitable Direct Marketing.* Chicago: Crain Books, 1979.

Kotler, Philip. *Principles of Marketing.* Englewood Cliffs, N.J.: Prentice-Hall, Inc., 1980.

Malickson, David L., and Nason, John W. *Advertising —How to Write the Kind That Works.* New York: Charles Scribner's Sons, 1977.

Mandel, Maurice I. *Advertising.* 3rd ed. Englewood Cliffs, N.J.: Prentice-Hall, Inc., 1980.

Markin, Rom J. *Marketing.* New York: John Wiley & Sons, 1979.

McGee, William L. *Broadcast Co-op, the Untapped Goldmine.* San Francisco: Broadcast Marketing Co., 1975.

—————. *Building Store Traffic with Broadcast Advertising.* San Francisco: Broadcast Marketing Co., 1978.

McMahan, Harry Wayne. *Communication and Persuasion.* Spokane, Wash.: Stephens Press, 1981.

Murphy, Jonne. *Handbook of Radio Advertising.* Radnor, Penn.: Chilton Book Company, 1980.

Orlik, Peter B. *Broadcast Copywriting.* Boston: Allyn & Bacon, Inc., 1978.

Owen, Bruce M., Beebe, Jack H., and Manning, Willard G., Jr. *Television Economics.* Lexington, Mass.: Lexington Books, 1974.

Neelankavil, James P., and Stridsberg, Albert B. *Advertising Self-Regulation: A Global Perspective.* New York: Hastings House, 1980.

Nelson, Roy Paul. *The Design of Advertising.* 3rd ed. Dubuque, Iowa: Wm. C. Brown Co., 1977.

Nickels, William G. *Marketing Principles.* Englewood Cliffs, N.J.: Prentice-Hall, Inc., 1978.

Pember, Don R. *Mass Media Law.* 2nd ed. Dubuque, Iowa: William C. Brown, 1981.

Profitable Retail Television Advertising. New York: National Retail Merchants Association, 1977.

Ramond, Charles. *Advertising Research: The State of the Art.* New York: Association of National Advertisers, 1976.

Ray, Michael L. *Advertising and Communication Management.* Englewood Cliffs, N.J.: Prentice-Hall, Inc., 1982.

Ries, Al, and Trout, Jack. *Positioning: The Battle for Your Mind.* New York: McGraw-Hill Book Co., 1981.

Rohrer, Daniel Morgan, ed. *Mass Media, Freedom of Speech, and Advertising.* Dubuque, Iowa: Kendall/Hunt Publishing Co., 1979.

Rubin, Bernard. *Big Business and the Mass Media.* Lexington, Mass.: Lexington Books, 1977.

Runyon, Kenneth E. *Advertising and the Practice of Marketing.* Columbus, Ohio: Charles E. Merrill Publishing Co., 1979.

Sandage, Charles H., Fryburger, Vernon, and Rotzoll, Kim. *Advertising Theory and Practice.* Homewood, Ill.: Richard D. Irwin, Inc., 1981.

Schmidt, Benno C., Jr. *Freedom of the Press vs. Public Access.* New York: Praeger Publishers, 1976.

Schultz, Don E. *Essentials of Advertising Strategy.* Chicago: Crain Books, 1981.

Schwartz, Tony. *The Responsive Chord.* Garden City, N.Y.: Anchor Books, 1974.

Sigel, Efrem, ed. *Videotext: The Coming Revolution in Home/Office Information Retrieval.* New York: Harmony Books, 1980.

Simmons, Steven J. *The Fairness Doctrine and the Media.* Berkeley, Calif.: University of California Press, 1978.

Sissors, Jack Z., and Surmanek, Jim. *Advertising Media Planning.* 2d ed. Chicago: Crain Books, 1982.

Spero, Robert. *The Duping of the American Voter: Dishonesty and Deception in Presidential Television Advertising.* New York: Lippincott & Crowell, 1980.

Stone, Bob. *Successful Direct Marketing Methods.* 2d ed. Chicago: Crain Books, 1979.

Tolley, B. Stuart. *Advertising and Marketing Research.* Chicago: Nelson-Hall, 1977.

Videotex: Key to the Information Revolution. Middlesex, United Kingdom: Online Publications Ltd., 1982.

White, Hooper. *How to Produce an Effective TV Commercial.* Chicago: Crain Books, 1981.

Witek, John. *Response Television: Combat Advertising of the 1980s.* Chicago: Crain Books, 1981.

Wright, John W. *The Commercial Connection: Advertising and the American Mass Media.* New York: Dell Publishing Co., 1979.

Wrighter, Carl P. *I Can Sell You Anything.* New York: Ballantine Books, 1972.

index